Corporations

STEP · BY · STEP

Second Edition

David Minars, M.B.A., J.D., CPA

BARRON'S

This book is dedicated to my wife, Iris Elaine Minars, for her *joie de vivre*. My thanks to Anna Damaskos for her inspiration, support, and wise counsel.

Copyright © 2003, 1996 by Barron's Educational Series, Inc.

This publication is designed to provide accurate and authoritative information in regard to the subject matter covered. It is sold with the understanding that the publisher is not engaged in rendering legal, accounting, or other professional services. If legal advice or other expert assistance is required, the services of a competent professional person should be sought.

All inquiries should be addressed to:
Barron's Educational Series, Inc.
250 Wireless Boulevard
Hauppauge, New York 11788
http://www.barronseduc.com

International Standard Book No. 0-7641-2187-1

Library of Congress Catalog Card No. 2003044336

Library of Congress Cataloging-in-Publication Data
Minars, David.
    Corporations step-by-step / David Minars.—2nd ed.
       p. cm.— (Barron's legal-ease)
    Includes index.
    ISBN 0-7641-2187-1
    1. Corporation law—United States—Popular works. I. Title.
II. Series.
KF1414.6.M56   2003
346.73'066—dc21
                             2003044336

PRINTED IN THE UNITED STATES OF AMERICA

987654321

Contents

9 CORPORATE MANAGEMENT STRUCTURE: THE ROLE OF DIRECTORS

10 CORPORATE MANAGEMENT STRUCTURE: THE ROLE OF THE OFFICERS

11 THE CORPORATE OWNERSHIP: THE ROLE OF THE SHAREHOLDERS

16 HOW TO BUY AND/OR SELL AN ONGOING BUSINESS

CHAPTER 1

Introduction

WHAT THIS BOOK IS ALL ABOUT

The objective of this book is not to make you into a CPA or an attorney. It was, however, written for those individuals who wish to start out in their own business, with minimum capital and risk, and with the knowledge that in case their efforts are not successful, there are legal escape hatches for ending the enterprise at minimum personal cost (see Chap. 13). This book will also help you avoid fundamental and costly tax pitfalls.

There are many reasons why people go into business today. Many individuals feel that they have the expertise and ability to "make a go of it," or they want the personal freedom to achieve certain economic and personal goals, or they simply want their name on the door. This book will assist you in forming your own business, with minimal capital and legal requirements, and with the best legal protection available to any new business—the corporation. Note that there are a variety of legal forms through which you can conduct a business. The corporation is but one of these vehicles, the others being sole proprietorships, partnerships, joint ventures, and some other useful organizations. The corporate form of doing business may be in the mode of a small enterprise owned by a single person, as well as in the form of a multinational enterprise owned by thousands of individuals dispersed throughout the world. While the advantages of and the reasons for forming the corporate form will be explained throughout this book, it is important to note that the corporation is treated as a separate legal body with its own rights, privileges, duties, and liabilities. In addition, the corporation is subject to greater governmental regulation, taxation, and report filing than any other type of business enterprise. Regardless of these handicaps, the corporation remains the most viable and safest form of doing business. One of the greatest advantages of doing business as a corporation is that it permits individuals who are stockholders to carry on business for profit without subjecting their personal fortunes to unlimited personal liability due to the hazards of business failure.

STARTING OUT: LAWS AND REGULATIONS AFFECTING YOUR CORPORATION

Corporations are usually formed under state law, but federal laws also impose a heavy financial and regulatory burden on the emerging enterprise. For example, the corporate statutes of the state in which the corporation is formed are binding on the corporation no matter where it conducts its actual business. This means that the corporation is subject to regulation and taxation both in the home state of its incorporation, as well as in all other states where the corporation does business. Secondly, not only is the corporation itself subject to intense regulation, but also those individuals who are an integral part of the corporation's operations, such as its officers, directors and shareholders. Thirdly, the Internal Revenue Code permits the federal government to share in the corporation's profits.

Besides the federal and state laws that regulate corporations, there are laws and administrative regulations that govern the corporation's day-to-day operations, its bylaws, board of director resolutions, shareholder agreements, loan agreements, employment contracts, and payroll tax requirements. However, despite these difficulties, corporate opportunities can be maximized with minimum governmental interference.

Note that the corporation is a fictitious being or artificial entity independent of its owners or investors. However, despite this legal fiction, operating in the corporate mode has many advantages. A corporation is permitted to conduct business, acquire assets, and incur liabilities as if it was a "real person."

This volume will serve as your legal and financial handbook by explaining the expanding body of federal and state corporate regulations and how they apply to your growing corporation. We will show you how to avert potential financial and operating problems, and how to avoid costly tax traps thereby allowing you to harvest your hard earned corporate profits at minimum tax cost. With the knowledge and ideas learned from this book, your corporation will grow and prosper to the point where you may eventually decide "to go public" by selling stock in your successful venture. In short, this book will familiarize you with the complex maze of rules, regulations, and financial and tax procedures that must be followed when creating what is today probably the best way to start and operate a new and profitable business.

SEARCHING FOR CAPITAL IN YOUR GROWING BUSINESS

Most small corporations start up with capital of less than $100,000. However, as the successful corporation grows, it will need additional capital. Capital sources might include friends, relatives, banks, venture capital companies, and public offerings.

Venture capitalists are profit-oriented corporations who seek to purchase shares in young and growing corporations. They generally look for a potential return on their investment of 300 to 500 percent within five to seven years followed by a quick profit from the sale of the shares. Typically, they might invest $2 million to $5 million in a business. Because of the high risk involved, venture capitalists will look very closely at the business, including product line, services to be performed, and market potential. When investing, they may demand more than 50 percent ownership in the outstanding shares. Although they may have a controlling interest, they will usually allow the directors and officers to continue in control of the corporation's daily activities. Basically, the shareholders must weigh the benefits of receiving additional capital against a smaller share of the business. Most venture capitalists prefer to purchase equity (meaning ownership) interests in computer, communications, and biotechnology companies.

Assistance in finding venture capital private investors may be obtained from Venture Capital Networks, P.O. Box 882, Durham, New Hampshire 03824. A list of venture capital companies may be found in *The Guide to Venture Capital Sources* (Illinois: Capital Publishing Corporation, 10 South LaSalle Street, Chicago, Illinois 60603).

A corporation may also seek to go public by selling their shares to other investors in the marketplace. "Going public" is not for every corporation and should only be considered by high-growth companies with proven track records. A successful public offering results in an infusion of capital, imposed corporate image, the retention of key employees, and the possibility of listing on an organized stock exchange or traded in the over-the-counter (OTC) market. Both Apple Computer and MCI are traded OTC. The downside is dilution (meaning reduction) of the shareholder's interest, loss of privacy, and the costly legal and accounting expenses associated with a public offering. Such offering requires an initial filing with the Securities and Exchange Commission (SEC) followed by continuous periodic and annual reports. Most corporate owners never seriously consider selling to the public to finance growth and expansion because it is both time-consuming and very expensive. Instead they may seek a loan from a bank or involve themselves in a Small Company Offering Registration (SCOR). SCOR, also known as the Uniform Limited Offering Registration (ULOR), is now available in a majority of states. The SEC created SCOR to cut the cost of a regular SEC registration and make the process simpler and less costly. SCOR involves the services of a lawyer, an accountant, and a brokerage firm. The capital ceiling on a SCOR issue is $1 million, and the price of each share must be at least $5. Under SCOR regulations, corporations can sell common, preferred, and convertible shares, as well as other types of shares.

Blue sky laws are state statutes that regulate the sale of securities to the public. Most blue sky laws require the registration of new issues of securities with a state agency that reviews selling documents for accuracy and completeness. Where a corporation is required to register with the SEC, such filing usually serves as a substitution for a state filing.

The Small Business Administration (SBA) should also be contacted to determine if the corporation qualifies for a loan. The SBA regulates both Small Business Investment Companies (SBICs) and Minority Enterprise Small Business Investment Companies (MESBECs) who provide long-term capital to small businesses. The major difference between SBICs and MESBECs is that a MESBEC can only invest in small businesses that are at least 51 percent owned by minorities and socially and economically disadvantaged people.

ACTING AS YOUR OWN LAWYER

It is an old maxim of law that a man who acts as his own attorney has a fool for a client. Although the process of corporate formation is essentially very simple, most basic business situations can become complicated and require the guidance of an attorney. Remember that your trusted counsel is aware of both your personal idiosyncracies, business acumen, and most likely, your current financial status. Thus, your lawyer is in an excellent position to do the following: advise you in choosing whether to operate as a sole proprietorship, partnership, or corporation; help

you to establish the corporation; deal with any possible stock and securities laws; register trademarks, patents, and copyrights; file for licenses; purchase real estate for the business; negotiate a lease; deal with customer disputes and potential litigation; assist in estate planning; and handle possible liquidation or bankruptcy proceedings should the need arise.

For a fee, incorporation services are also available to help form your corporation. However, many of these costs, and in some cases virtually all of your start-up costs, can be reduced or eliminated by careful study and application of all the money-saving techniques discussed in this book.

Thus, the individual, before starting a business, should understand all basic issues, determine what legal aspects, if any, can be handled without legal help, and to then decide whether it is worthwhile in terms of time and money to proceed independently.

SELECTING A LAWYER

While wealthy individuals and corporations retain lawyers to handle their legal problems and to monitor unusual or complex transactions, the small business individual generally cannot afford this luxury. Upon analyzing the specific needs of the business, it might be prudent to enlist the services of an attorney whose skills and experience can help solve both common and unforeseen legal problems. The attorney can assist you in setting up the type of enterprise that you need, such as a partnership or corporation, and can negotiate any loans, leases and contracts applicable to your business. She will also advise your accountant as to what transactions must be recorded on your books and records for tax, environmental, health and safety regulations, and minimum wage requirements. If possible, avoid hiring an attorney on a costly monthly retainer basis. Find an attorney who bills by the hour and what services comprise billable hours. Thus, you will only be paying for services that you actually use rather than burdening your business with fixed monthly costs. Determine the attorney's rates in advance. Like any other professional, shop around for any attorney in whom you have trust and whose fees your new business can afford.

Selection is no easy task, but here are some suggestions for finding the right legal professional.

1. Talk to people in your community and ask who they use;
2. Talk to your accountant or banker;
3. Ask friends and relatives;
4. Look in the "yellow pages" for a listing of lawyers who specialize in business matters; and
5. In many states, the bar association will provide a lawyer referral and information service. This service can provide you with the name of a local practitioner in your area who can be contacted. An initial consultation may be obtained at a minimal fee or possibly free of charge if the attorney is seeking new clientele.

In selecting a lawyer, just don't settle on the first lawyer on your list. Set up an interview, ask about her education, area of expertise, and prior experience in business matters. Also determine whether you are comfortable with this person. Are her fees reasonable? Does she return calls quickly? Also determine whether she is practical minded and can fine tune your business, if necessary, without getting involved in complex legal issues that might prove costly.

CHAPTER 2 — Why the Corporation Is Best for You

FORMS AND FACTORS IN SELECTION

The selection of the best form of doing business is based on both tax and nontax factors. From a nontax viewpoint, there are at least eight principal forms of doing business. They include the sole proprietorship, general partnership, limited partnership, joint-stock company, business trust, corporation, limited liability company, and professional corporation. Each of these forms can be molded to take into account the particular situation of one or more individuals. For example, if a person wishes to start out with minimum legal restraints and capital, it is best to start off as a sole proprietorship. Later on, as the business grows, the individual can take in a partner and operate as a partnership. If the enterprise continues to grow even further, the partners can choose to incorporate to take advantage of fringe benefits, pension plans, and, perhaps, to raise additional capital. In addition, should later events occur that make it unprofitable to continue operations in the corporate form, a corporate liquidation, with minimal tax consequences, is always available to the unhappy corporate shareholders.

Furthermore, the Internal Revenue Code distinguishes between individuals, partnerships, and corporations (including associations). The sole proprietorship pays taxes at individual rates. A partnership pays no taxes while the partners do. Finally, a corporation is subject to tax rates as high as 35 percent although these rates can be avoided by making an "S corporation election" (see Chap. 15).

Other factors that enter into the selection of the form of doing business include formality of organization, capital and credit requirements, management and control, number of participants, the determination of salaries, how profits and losses are to be shared, the transferability of an ownership interest, and whether there is continuity of existence should an owner die or sell his interest.

Whether a single form of doing business, or a multiple of business organizations should be used requires careful consideration of additional tax and other aspects. For example, the use of multiple organizations might be used to achieve the following:

1. Separation of corporate functions, such as sales from product development to simplify operations and to increase efficiency;
2. Creating a separate enterprise to handle a new untried or competitive product;
3. Limiting the liabilities of each entity;
4. The protection of corporate assets in case of bankruptcy;
5. The protection of owners from lawsuits;
6. Minimizing the exposure of corporate assets to outside claims and lawsuits;

5

7. Simplify estate tax planning;
8. Eventually selling the entities so as to obtain lower capital gains rates; and
9. Flexibility in changing the form in response to business and legal developments.

On the other hand, multiple entities might result in increased legal and accounting costs, duplication of operations, problems when operating in different states and municipalities due to a multiplicity of state and municipal tax laws, and possible antitrust violations. Thus, considerable care should be taken when selecting the form or forms appropriate under the particular circumstances to achieve the best form of doing business in light of all possible contingencies.

EXAMPLE Henderson Tool Manufacturing Company is nationally known for the quality of its high-cost products. It now seeks to manufacture and sell a cheaper line of low-cost tools. However, Henderson's management believes that the image of quality long associated with its current products would be harmed by the introduction of a new and cheaper product line under Henderson's name. Therefore, Henderson sets up a separate corporation called Quality Hand Tools Inc. to manufacture and sell its new and cheaper line. The new company, in the eyes of the consuming public, would be a different company apart from Henderson. Thus, the manufacture and sale of a cheaper line of tools by a different company, separate and unassociated with Henderson, would not reflect negatively on the high quality products manufactured by Henderson.

THE INDIVIDUAL (OR SOLE) PROPRIETORSHIP
Definition
As the name suggests, this is a natural form of doing business at lowest initial cost. A major advantage to this form is that if the venture is successful, it may be converted into a partnership by the admittance of a new partner, or the venture may be converted into a corporation tax-free. The sole proprietor is the "boss." He may employ others, raise capital by borrowing, and enter into contracts that bind him personally. He is also liable for all negligent acts

committed by him personally, as well as those committed by his employees within the operation of the business. Credit can be obtained based on the extent of the business assets, as well as the proprietor's personal wealth. His personal liability is, therefore, unlimited. Of course, personal liability can always be reduced by either contractual limitation or insurance. There are no formalities involved in starting a business as a sole proprietor beyond any capital requirements. Thus, this form is very suitable for an individual who is seeking to start a one-person enterprise.

When operating as a sole proprietor, there is, generally, no continuity of existence, and, upon the death of the decedent (or owner), the business will generally terminate. However, the owner may, by will, permit the executor of the will to continue the business so that his heirs may receive a going concern. In effect, this technique permits a beneficiary, as a new owner, to continue what is perhaps a thriving business.

In a sole proprietorship, the owner pays individual taxes on net profits that may run from 15 to 35 percent. The sole proprietorship would also be subject to federal self-employment tax. Net losses generated by the business can be used to offset ordinary income. Thus, the choice is whether to incorporate with heavy governmental regulation, or to operate as a sole proprietor with minimal government scrutiny, a large degree of secrecy, and unlimited liability.

Advantages of a Sole Proprietorship
1. Requires minimal start-up capital.
2. Minimum legal and accounting fees upon start-up.
3. Lack of operating formalities, such as meetings of a board of directors. The individual is in complete control of the proprietorship.
4. Free access to trade in all state jurisdictions with minimum legal burdens.
5. A sole proprietor's protection as an individual by the Fifth Amendment's guarantee against self-incrimination.
6. Less governmental regulation than a corporation.

7. Possible availability of credit based not only on the business assets but also on the personal assets of the owner/proprietor.

8. Minimal legal and accounting problems upon termination.

9. Opportunity of a sole proprietorship to generate losses, which the owner can use to offset taxable income. This is particularly advantageous if large operating losses are expected in the initial years of operation.

10. Opportunity to operate under an "assumed" or "trade" name. If the sole proprietorship desires to conduct business under an assumed name, state statutes in many jurisdictions merely require that a certificate be filed in a public office.

11. Availability of certain types of pension plans to offset the effects of federal taxation.

Disadvantages of a Sole Proprietorship

1. Death of the principal automatically terminates the business.

2. The owner is subject to unlimited liability in case of breach of contract or liability due to some negligent action on the part of the owner or his employees. However, this disadvantage can be mitigated somewhat by the use of various forms of liability insurance.

3. The amount of capital available for use in the business is limited to the resources of the owner.

4. Income obtained by the owner from other sources will put the owner of a profitable business into a tax bracket as high as 35 percent.

5. The sole proprietorship form limits the number of retirement and profit-sharing plans that may be utilized.

   In some cases, the sole proprietorship option is virtually ruled out by circumstances. For example, a high exposure to legal risks may require operation in the corporate form in order to provide greater protection against personal liability, as in the case of a manufacturer of potentially hazardous consumer products.

THE GENERAL PARTNERSHIP
Definition

The Uniform Partnership Act (UPA), which is the law in virtually all states, defines a partnership as "an association of two or more persons to carry on as co-owners a business for profit." Partnerships are either general partnerships or limited partnerships. General partnerships consist of partners who are all general partners, while a limited partnership has both general and limited partners. The limited partnership is discussed in the next section.

Characteristics of a Partnership

A partnership is not a separate entity distinct from its owners, the partners. In a partnership, every partner is an agent of the partnership in dealing with third parties, and each partner is jointly (meaning that each copromisor is liable for the entire debt) and/or severally liable (meaning that each party is liable alone or individually) for the debts of the partnership. Thus, each partner may be sued individually for the entire amount of the alleged debt or for his proportionate share. No person can become a partner without the consent of all the other partners, and the death of a partner dissolves the partnership. A basic fiduciary relationship (meaning one of trust) among the partners imposes upon all of them the highest standards of good faith and loyalty.

Advantages of a Partnership

1. Partnerships are easy to create and generally require no approval from state or local authorities.

2. There are no formal annual meeting requirements, such as those mandated for corporations.

3. Partnerships are generally simple to operate.

4. The partnership is not subject to as many formal reporting requirements as imposed on corporations.

5. A partnership also has a tax advantage because it is not directly subject to federal income tax.

Profits and losses flow through to each individual partner on the personal level. Thus, the partnership acts as a "conduit" for partnership profits and losses.

6. Partnerships can also utilize various qualified pension and profit-sharing plans.

7. Partnerships may dissolve by mutual agreement while other types of entities, such as a corporation, requires statutory compliance when dissolving.

Disadvantages of a Partnership

1. Members are subject to unlimited personal liability for all the liabilities of the business.

2. Death of a partner terminates the partnership, which can cause difficulties in the continued operation of the business. Besides the death of a partner, a dissolution may occur when any partner indicates an intention to disassociate from the partnership. Dissolution can also occur when a change in the law prohibits further operation or by judicial decree, such as where the partnership can only be operated at a loss, or a partner perpetuates a fraud upon the other partners.

3. A partnership, because of its size and minimal assets, may find it difficult to raise any required capital.

4. A partner's interest in the partnership is not readily transferable.

5. Under the Internal Revenue Code, partner's profits are taxable to him whether or not there is an actual distribution of the profits to him. Thus, if the partnership decides to reinvest the partnership's profits, the partners must come up with the necessary cash with which to pay the applicable income taxes on the undistributed profits.

Important Partnership Agreement Provisions

Should individuals contemplating the appropriate form of doing business initially elect to operate as a partnership, they would have to draft an agreement containing the following elements in order to avoid potential disputes.

1. The identity of the partners.

2. The business of the partnership. Given the potential for unlimited personal liability, each partner should have the right to veto an attempt to expand the partnership's business purposes.

3. The nature and amount of each partner's capital contribution to the business, i.e., whether cash or property made available to the partnership is a loan or a capital contribution.

4. The duration of the partnership, including both its start-up date and termination date.

5. The ratio in which both profits and losses will be shared (the ratios need not be the same for both). If there is no provision in the partnership agreement relating to the distribution of profits and losses, profits and losses are shared equally by the partners regardless of differences in the amounts of their capital contributions.

6. The salaries and drawing accounts that will be paid or made available to partners.

7. The duties and responsibilities of each partner. If the partners are to serve in different capacities, then a clear delineation of each partner's job functions should be set out in the agreement.

8. The conditions upon which the partners will be admitted to the venture and the minimum qualifications a person must possess in order to become a partner.

9. The bases for dissolution prior to the agreed-to date of termination.

10. The rights of partners against a partner who wrongfully causes dissolution.

11. The identity of the winding-up partner or partners and whether the winding-up partners must provide a bond.

12. The terms upon which a partnership can be continued by the remaining partners upon the death, resignation, or bankruptcy of a partner (including a buy-out agreement that would be necessary if a continuation is to take place).

Experience among lawyers has shown that without a detailed written agreement governing its operations friction, lawsuits, and breakup will inevitably occur in a general partnership.

Once a partnership begins operations, a new partner cannot be admitted without the consent of all of the partners unless the agreement says otherwise. A partner can, however, assign his interest in the partnership, but the individual receiving the assigned interest, and who is called an assignee, cannot take part in partnership affairs. Finally, upon the death of a general partner, his estate does not become a partner in the firm. Upon the death of a partner, the surviving partners have a right to use of specific partnership property. However, they also have a duty to account to the decedent's estate for the value of the deceased partner's interest in the partnership. Because of these deficiencies, a partnership generally cannot raise large amounts of investment capital for its business through the broad distribution of ownership. It is because of these limitations individuals tend to view the corporation as the preferable mode of operation when contemplating any new business venture.

THE LIMITED PARTNERSHIP
Definition

The limited partnership form of doing business can only be created according to the formalities stated in the Uniform Limited Partnership Act (ULPA), which has been adopted in virtually all states. Furthermore, a majority of states have adopted the Revised Uniform Limited Partnership Act (RULPA).[1] These statutes form the basis for the limited partnership.

Under the ULPA, a limited partnership is defined as a "partnership formed by two or more persons having as members one or more general partners and one or more limited partners." The limited partners, as such, shall not be bound by the obligations of the partnership. In many respects, the principles applicable to a general partnership also apply to a limited partnership.

Operating the Limited Partnership

A limited partnership requires that there be at least one partner who will assume the risks of a general partner and be subject to unlimited liability. Contributions of a limited partner may consist of cash or other property, but not services. A limited partner has no control over the business nor may he participate in the management of partnership affairs.

Because of his lack of participation in management, the personal liability of a limited partner is limited to his capital contribution. Because of the restricted role of a limited partner the death or assignment of her interest in the partnership does not interrupt the continuity of the limited partnership. In effect, the limited partner's right to assign his interest is almost identical to that of a corporate shareholder. If a limited partnership wishes to do business in another state, it must first comply with the statutory provisions of that jurisdiction. Failure to comply with such provisions may result in the limited partner being subject to liability as a general partner.

Formation

Under ULPA, two or more persons desiring to form a limited partnership shall sign and swear to a certificate, which shall state:

1. The name of the partnership;
2. The character of the business;
3. The location of the principal place of business;
4. The name and place of residence of each member; general and limited partners being respectively designated;
5. The term for which the partnership is to exist;
6. The amount of cash and a description of and the agreed value of the other property contributed by each limited partner;

[1]States that have enacted RULPA include Alabama, Arizona, Arkansas, California, Colorado, Connecticut, Delaware, Florida, Georgia, Hawaii, Idaho, Illinois, Indiana, Iowa, Kansas, Kentucky, Maryland, Massachusetts, Michigan, Minnesota, Mississippi, Missouri, Montana, Nebraska, Nevada, New Hampshire, New Jersey, New Mexico, New York, North Carolina, North Dakota, Ohio, Oklahoma, Oregon, Pennsylvania, Rhode Island, South carolina, South Dakota, Tennessee, Texas, Virginia, Washington, West Virginia, Wisconsin, and Wyoming. Louisiana has not enacted either the ULPA or RULPA.

7. The additional contributions, if any, agreed to be made by each limited partner and the times at which or events on the happening of which they shall be made;

8. The time, if agreed upon, when the contribution of each limited partner is to be returned;

9. The share of the profits or the other compensation by way of income, which each limited partner shall receive by reason of his contribution;

10. The right, if given, of a limited partner to substitute an assignee as contributor in his place, and the terms and conditions of the substitution;

11. The right, if given, of the partners to admit additional limited partners;

12. The right, if given, of one or more of the limited partners to take priority over other limited partners, as to contributions or as to compensation by way of income, and the nature of such priority;

13. The right, if given, of the remaining general partner or partners to continue the business on the death, retirement, or illness of a general partner; and

14. The right, if given, of a limited partner to demand and receive property other than cash in return for his contribution.

The certificate must then be filed in the appropriate office as determined by state law.

THE LIMITED LIABILITY PARTNERSHIP (LLP)

The limited liability partnership (LLP) is a relatively new form of business entity that has grown rapidly in recent years. It combines the corporate characteristic of limited liability for the owners with the nontaxability applicable to a partnership. The LLP is formed under a separate state statute that generally applies to organizations offering services. Many large law and accounting firms have become LLPs in recent years.

THE CORPORATION
Definition

The corporation is the dominant form of doing business in the United States today. Corporations range in size from one shareholder to millions as in the case of General Motors. Although formed according to state statute, there are innumerable capitalization and operating structures that can be utilized by the corporation.

How A Corporation Differs From Other Types of Doing Business

State corporate statutes set forth requirements that must be met before the corporate entity is deemed to be validly formed. Upon compliance with certain state formalities, such as the preparation of articles of incorporation (sometimes called the certificate of incorporation or corporate charter), the payment of organization taxes and filing fees, the drafting of bylaws, and an initial meeting of incorporators and a board of directors, the corporation comes into existence.

Comparison With a Partnership

Each partner is personally liable for the debts of the partnership. In addition, the death, illness, or bankruptcy of any partner dissolves the partnership. Thus, the partnership is subject to limited duration. In a corporation, the shareholders are generally subject to limited liability, i.e., the amount of capital (cash or property) that they have invested in the corporation. In addition, the death, illness, or bankruptcy of any director, officer, or shareholder does not dissolve the corporation.

Comparison With a Limited Partnership

A limited partnership has one or more general partners and one or more limited partners. The liability of a general partner is unlimited while the liability of a limited partner to partnership creditors shall not exceed the amount of their investment. This liability is similar to that of a corporate shareholder.

Broadly speaking, corporations cannot come into existence until there has been strict compliance with a state's incorporation law. The failure to comply with all prescribed legal formalities can result in the entity being treated as either a partnership, a sole proprietorship, or a debtor-creditor relationship based on the fact that one or more parties are using the capital (i.e., cash and property) belonging to another group (i.e., the shareholders). The result would be unlimited liability for all parties concerned.

Advantages of a Corporation

1. Shareholders enjoy limited liability. For example, if they each invest $5,000 into the corporation and it eventually fails, they have lost no more than the amount invested. Furthermore, under the Internal Revenue Code, they can deduct up to $3,000 per year in stock losses on their personal tax return.

....

WARNING *This limitation is not absolute. In many states, corporate shareholders of a small business corporation are personally liable for unpaid corporate wages. For example, under Section 630 of the Business Corporation Law of New York State, the ten largest shareholders shall be jointly and severally liable for the unpaid wages and salaries of corporate employees. This rule does not apply to publicly listed corporations.*

....

2. It may be formed for a variety of purposes, both profit and nonprofit. Note that the thrust of this book is a detailed discussion of only profit-oriented corporations.

3. Ownership of corporate stock may be freely transferred by sale or gift, subject only to certain corporate restrictions.

4. The corporation has an unlimited life and is not affected by the death of a director, officer, or shareholder, no matter what the size of the shareholder's ownership in the corporation.

5. The corporation may purchase, hold, and sell property in the corporate name.

6. The corporation enjoys great flexibility in selecting the methods it will use in raising capital.

7. The corporation has numerous tax advantages available to it, such as pension and profit-sharing and the election of S corporation status (see Chap. 15).

8. A corporate employee, even if there is only one, can receive workers' compensation, an insurance benefit not available to a self-employed person operating as a sole proprietor. This feature provides a strong incentive for one shareholder to incorporate and operate as a single-shareholder corporation.

Disadvantages of a Corporation

The corporation is an expensive way of doing business. The cost varies based upon the amount and type of stock to be authorized and issued, the size of the planned corporation, the amount of business done, and the type of labor force needed. In addition, initial incorporation costs include filing fees, organization taxes, and attorney's and legal fees. Of course, these fees vary with the size of the corporation to be formed.

1. The corporation is subject to greater governmental regulation and control than any other form of doing business, and there are more formalities and restrictions that must be observed.

2. The corporation is subject to double taxation, once at the corporate level and again at the shareholder level when a distribution of profits, called dividends, is made. However, the Internal Revenue Code offers certain tax elections, such as the S corporation election, that can mitigate and even eliminate taxes at the corporate level.

3. Majority shareholders may be in a position to make business decisions that are not in the best interests of the minority shareholders. This danger is greater in close corporations that have three to five shareholders who may have different operating philosophies.

4. Voting rights enjoyed by shareholders may be diluted where there is a wide-spread or increased ownership of corporate stock.

5. Management and control of the corporation rests with the duly elected directors and officers and are, thus, separate from the shareholders who are the true owners of the corporation.

THE LIMITED LIABILITY COMPANY (LLC)

Currently, substantially all new pass-through entities (meaning that the business will not be taxed as a separate entity, but that the shareholder will be taxed at personal rates)—are formed as limited liability companies (LLCs) rather that as partnerships or S corporations. See Chapter 15 for a discussion of Federal taxation.

The LLC was originally created in 1977 as a hybrid entity with both partnership attributes and limited liability, and gained great popularity after the IRS took a favorable view toward these entities.

Once it is decided to limit an owner's personal liability, a decision must be made as to whether to form an LLC or a regular corporation. The document creating the LLC is called the Articles of Organization. As with a regular corporation, all of the owners of an LLC enjoy limited personal liability. This means that the member of an LLC is not personally liable for business debts. By comparison, partners of a partnership and sole proprietors are personally liable for all business debts.

While an LLC may resemble a partnership, it is actually a separate legal entity distinct from its members. LLC members own a membership interest rather than a share of stock or a partnership interest. All of its members operate the LLC unless they agree that it be run by a single member or a management group. The best way to manage the LLC is by an operating agreement signed by all the members stipulating all internal operating procedures and how the business is to be run.

Members of an LLC can agree to distribute LLC profits and losses in any way they so desire. While it is normal to distribute profits and losses according to the percentage of assets that each member contributes, there is no requirement that this rule be followed. By comparison, a regular corporation must distribute profits to shareholders, in the form of dividends, according to the number of shares they own.

Under "check-in-the-box" Federal regulations, the IRS automatically treats single-owner LLCs as sole proprietorships and multi-owner companies as partnerships unless they elect to be treated as corporations. The tax treatment by each state varies so that an incorporator should check the tax law for the state of incorporation.

While state statutes are not uniform, they are generally more accommodating to LLC owners and less restrictive than the laws governing other types of pass-through entities. Thus, the use of the partnerships and S corporations as a form of doing business has declined dramatically over the last few years. Note that more LLCs are being formed in Delaware by out-of-state operators because that state's laws, like its corporate laws, are said to be the most flexible.

OBSERVATION *Why should an LLC be used rather than an S corporation or partnership? S corporations cannot have more than 75 shareholders and one class of stock. LLCs have no such restrictions. In a general partnership, the partners are personally liable. Members of LLCs have limited liability.*

THE CLOSELY HELD (OR FAMILY) CORPORATION

A "closely held" corporation is one whose shares are owned by one stockholder or a closely knit group of shareholders. There is no definite maximum number, but it is a general thought that a corporation with less than fifteen shareholders is a closely held corporation. Delaware corporate law provides that a close corporation cannot have more than thirty shareholders. If the shareholders are related, the entity is sometimes referred to as a family corporation.

The main purpose of a closely held corporation is to assure the limited liability of all shareholders and to keep ownership and control within a group of shareholders who share the same profit-directed goals. If the business operated as a partnership, the lack of limited liability would be a major problem (although partially solvable by the use of liability insurance). Generally, the traditional corporate "hats" of director and officer, normally separate functions performed by different people (except for corporate presidents), are simultaneously worn by the shareholders at all times. Thus, the separate identities of directors, officers, and shareholders are missing with the result that a few individuals own and operate the corporation. Unlike publicly held corporations, a closely held corporation's securities are not generally traded on the open market.

Advantages of a Closely Held Corporation

1. Besides limited liability, internal operations of the enterprise can be controlled as if it were a partnership.
2. Admission of new shareholders can also be restricted.
3. Unless agreed to otherwise, all shareholders, acting as directors, may participate equally in the management of the business.

4. Shareholders can settle disagreements with relative ease.

5. The shareholders can always convert the corporation into an S corporation that will enjoy tax-free treatment similar to that of a partnership.

Disadvantages of a Closely Held Corporation

1. Shareholders of a closely held corporation tend to impose strict limitations on the authority of the directors to manage the affairs of the corporation.

2. A closely held corporation must still adhere to the formalities of a larger corporation, such as the filing of a certificate of incorporation, and rules requiring board of directors and mandated annual shareholder meetings.

3. Shareholders might have difficulty selling their stock since outsiders might be reluctant to purchase closely held corporate stock of unknown value, and that may also be subject to certain restrictions.

PROFESSIONAL SERVICE CORPORATIONS (PSCs)

Members of the professions (i.e., those entities engaged in the practice of law, medicine, or accountancy etc.) have found themselves confronted with a substantial tax liability because of their status as either sole proprietorships or partnerships. By forming a professional service corporation (also called a professional association or PA in some states) and incorporating their practice, professionals and their employees become eligible to participate in employee fringe benefit and pension and profit-sharing plans. The corporate contributions to these plans are tax deductible, and the income generated by these retirement plans accumulates tax-free until later distribution to its employee/participants. All states have enacted corporate legislation with similar characteristics allowing professionals to incorporate their practices. For example, statutes generally require that only people who are individually eligible to provide the professional service may do any of the following:

1. Own stock in the corporation;
2. Serve as an officer or director;
3. Perform professional services on behalf of the corporation.

Formation of the professional corporation does not shield the professional shareholder from personal liability to third parties caused by his own negligence. However, the express language of most professional corporate statutes creates liability solely against the doctor who rendered or supervised the negligent service. This prevents other practitioners who are shareholders from being held jointly liable for the negligence of other employees unless the practitioners supervised the wrongful professional acts or participated in the wrongdoing.

EXAMPLE A patient sued a doctor for malpractice. The doctor was a shareholder, along with other doctor/shareholders, in a professional corporation. The patient also sued all of the other doctor/shareholders. The express language of most professional corporate statutes creates liability solely against the doctor who rendered or supervised the negligent service and not against nonparticipating doctors.

Due to the enormous liability exposure of professional practitioners, such as doctors, lawyers, and accountants, it is still essential that all professional shareholders carry liability (malpractice) insurance.

Occasionally, the outlook and demeanor of a particular professional or group of professionals prevents the use of the professional corporation. That is, do they have their own personalized approach or are they too casual in their practices to be burdened with the requirements of corporate life. Each professional's situation must be carefully reviewed so that the decision to incorporate can be prudently made.

WHICH TYPE OF ENTITY IS BEST FOR YOU?

Before starting a new business venture, the prudent individual must determine which form of doing business is best. The three basic forms are the sole proprietorship, the partnership, and the corporation. There are also hybrid operating forms, such as the limited partnership, the professional service corporation (PC or PA), and limited liability company (LLC). If there is a special tax benefit to be gained from a particular form of doing business, then that form should be studied carefully. After the selection of the best-suited type of organization has been made and operation has begun, the business must be reviewed periodically for any potential problems. This process should be undertaken in consultation with the owner's attorneys, accountants, and bankers. For the present, business owners with substantial personal assets to protect will undoubtedly use the corporate form. Partnerships are risky due to the unlimited liability applicable to its owner/partners. At the same time, LLCs are relatively new; and business advisors are much more comfortable with established forms, such as corporations. With the commencement of any new business, entrepreneurs may eventually find that another form of doing may be more suitable than the one they are now using based on the entity's current operating problems. If so, adoption of another form of doing business is usually readily available.

CHAPTER 3

Operating As a Corporation

INTRODUCTION

When properly formed, the corporation is a separate legal (or artificial) entity that has the power to hold property in the corporate name, sue and be sued, enjoys unlimited life, and can be held criminally liable for crimes that it commits. Control of the corporation is centralized in its board of directors who are elected by the shareholders. The actions, purposes, and goals of the corporation, as a distinct and separate entity, are wholly separate from the demands of the shareholders, even if there is only one shareholder. Thus a shareholder has no interest in the corporate property itself, but merely those rights conferred by state law and/or the corporation's articles of incorporation based on ownership of corporate shares.

EXAMPLE The board of directors of Growth Hormone Products Inc. purchased 1,000 shares of Lewmark Ironworks Corporation stock at a bargain price. Lon Thaddeus, the sole shareholder of Growth, sees an opportunity to "make a quick killing in the stock market" by having the shares transferred to him at the original purchase price for eventual sale at an opportune moment. Growth's directors have a valid objection asserting that the shares are the property of the corporation.

In effect, Thaddeus, although the sole shareholder, has no valid claim to the Lewmark shares.

Note that in a closely held corporation the majority shareholders generally elect qualified associates and friends as directors to assure their continued loyalty. The power to remove a director at the next annual shareholders meeting goes a long way in assuring the directors' allegiance to the shareholders.

On occasion, courts will ignore the corporate enterprise in cases where the corporation is used to perpetuate a fraud. For example, the corporate form has in the past been used to defraud creditors, circumvent certain laws, and/or to promote certain fraudulent or criminal acts. In such situations, the courts have disregarded the corporation in order to criminally charge the shareholders who are participants in the illegal schemes.

THE CORPORATION AS A "PERSON"

A corporation is an "artificial being" existing only in accordance with state or federal statutes. It has many of the rights, duties, powers, and liabilities given to natural persons. Thus, the corporation is usually regarded as a person with certain constitutional protections.

The corporation enjoys the right against unreasonable searches and seizures granted by the

United States Constitution.[2] The corporation does not have the privilege afforded individuals against self-incrimination, but it is entitled to due process and equal protection under the law.[3]

Although state statutes give the corporation the right to sue and be sued, it cannot appear in a court of law unless represented by a duly licensed attorney.

THE CORPORATION AS "CITIZEN AND RESIDENT OF A STATE"

A corporation is usually a resident of its state of incorporation. Corporate residence is relevant for various purposes, such as whether it can sue and be sued in a particular state, the type and amount of taxes payable, and the statute of limitations applicable to certain lawsuits. A statute of limitations requires the party (called the plaintiff) to file a lawsuit within a specified period of time after the legal claim arises. The plaintiff who fails to file suit within the period of limitation loses the right to recover on the claim.

Besides the state of incorporation, the corporation can also be treated as a resident of any place where it is qualified to do business or is actually doing business.

A corporation can only act through its corporate officers (i.e., the president, vice-president, and so on) who are the agents of the corporation. An agent is one who acts on behalf of another, in this case the corporation.

---

[2]Fourth Amendment.
[3]Fifth and Fourteenth Amendments of the U.S. Constitution.

CHAPTER 4

Selecting a State in Which to Set Up Your Corporation

INTRODUCTION

If you decide to incorporate, the next step is to select a state in which to do business. If the intended corporate operation is primarily localized, or the entity intends to hold property exclusively in one state, then it is usually best to incorporate in that state. However, if the business plans to operate in more than one state, it might be wise to form two or more corporations, or one in each state, to promote flexibility in operation. Judicious selection requires a comparison of whether it is advantageous to have one or more corporations, or just one corporation engaged in multi-state activities. Of course, should the incorporators elect to do business as a single corporation, they can later dissolve, liquidate, and incorporate in another state or several states as the situation dictates. What follows is a discussion for determining which state or jurisdiction has the most favorable business climate for corporate activities.

WHAT FACTORS TO CONSIDER WHEN INCORPORATING

The consequences of incorporating and doing business in one or more states is based on many factors. Before incorporation, the following critical factors should be considered.

1. What are the fees for incorporation?
2. What are the applicable corporate tax rates?
3. Is there a state stamp tax on the issuance of shares?
4. What are the restrictions on the use of a corporate name?
5. Must the books and records be kept within the state?
6. For what purposes can a corporation be incorporated?
7. Can there be only one shareholder?
8. What is the minimum amount of capital required in order to begin operations?
9. Are there any restrictions on what the corporation may own?
10. How broad are the powers given to the corporation (i.e., Can they make loans to third parties or employees, borrow money, issue certain classes of stock, make charitable contributions)?
11. Can different classes of shares be issued, (i.e., preferred and common shares, voting and nonvoting)?
12. How may shares be acquired (i.e., besides cash, can they be issued for goods and services)?
13. What are the rules with regard to the payment of cash, stock, and property dividends?

14. Are there limitations on the voting rights of shareholders?

15. Can the stock carry preemptive rights?

16. To what extent do incorporators enjoy limited liability?[4]

17. What are the minimum number of shareholders that must be present in order to hold a valid shareholder meeting?

18. Must shareholder meetings be held in the state of incorporation?

19. What are the rules applicable to proxies?

20. Can shareholders create voting agreements?

21. Can the corporation issue convertible shares?

22. Can the board of directors hold meetings outside the state of incorporation?

23. What are the procedures for removing a director?

24. What are the rules for corporate dissolution?

25. Are court decisions and administrative regulations supportive of corporations?

DELAWARE: THE BEST STATE FOR INCORPORATING

Delaware remains the most popular state for incorporation. The advantages offered by Delaware far outweigh the benefits available in other states, and no other jurisdiction offers the accommodations available to a corporation's formation and management. At least forty percent of the corporations listed on the New York Stock Exchange are incorporated in Delaware.

Incorporating in Delaware offers the following advantages.

1. Perpetual or limited existence;

2. Lenient rules for reserving a corporate name;

3. Broad operating powers, including the incorporation for any lawful business purpose;

4. Reasonable filing and incorporation fees;

5. The issuance of a broad class of stocks, such as common and preferred;

6. Minimal restrictions on the payment of dividends;

7. Vote by a majority of the shareholders on such matters as corporate merger and dissolution;

8. The election of only one or more directors.

9. Liberal provision for the indemnification of officers and directors for litigation expenses; and

10. Simple annual reports that permit the corporation a high degree of privacy.

Note that the freedom to operate a corporation with minimal legal and regulatory standards is of little value for those individuals wishing to operate as a closely held corporation. Unless a corporation plans to have a large number of directors, officers, and/or shareholders, and/or seeks to operate in more than one state, there is little advantage in incorporating in Delaware. In fact, the advantages of Delaware as the state of incorporation have been mitigated as other states have modernized their corporate statutes.

THE MODEL BUSINESS CORPORATION ACT (MBCA) AND THE LATER REVISED MODEL BUSINESS CORPORATION ACT (RMBCA)

Although Delaware has distinct advantages for incorporating large publicly held and private corporations, many businesses, including those closely held, choose to incorporate where their principal place of business is to be located. This is due to the fact that in many states, corporation law is influenced by the Model Business Corporation Act (MBCA) and the later Revised Model Business Corporation Act (RMBCA).[5] This act is designed to

---

[4]For example, under Section 630 of the Business Corporation Law (BCL) of New York State, the ten largest shareholders are jointly and severally liable personally for all wages and salaries due to its employees and laborers for services that were performed for the corporation. This rule is applicable to nonpublic corporations only.

[5]States that have statutes based in whole or in part upon the MBCA and its later revisions include Alabama, Alaska, Arizona, Arkansas, Colorado, Connecticut, Florida, Georgia, Hawaii, Idaho, Illinois, Indiana, Iowa, Kentucky, Louisiana, Maine, Maryland, Massachusetts, Michigan, Mississippi, Montana, Nebraska, New Jersey, New Mexico, New York, North Carolina, North Dakota, Oregon, Pennsylvania, Rhode Island, South Carolina, South Dakota, Tennessee, Texas, Utah, Vermont, Virginia, Washington, West Virginia, Wisconsin, and Wyoming.

balance the interests of management, shareholders, and the public. Although competition for business and the adoption of the MBCA and RMBCA has tended to promote uniformity in most states' corporate law, there are still major differences remaining among the various states that have adopted either the MBCA or RMBCA. Some states do not follow either act. For example, New York State uses the Business Corporation Law (BCL).

The RMBCA, which is discussed throughout this book, has been adopted at least in whole or in part by a majority of the states in the nation. Thus, the rules and regulations creating and governing the corporation vary from state to state and the specific statutes must be consulted for details. For incorporators planning only single purpose local operations with minimal capital and a small number of directors and stockholders, incorporation in the state where they plan to principally do business is probably preferable.

CHAPTER 5

Promoters and Preincorporation Transactions

WHAT IS A PROMOTER?

A promoter is an individual who provides the organizational initiative for forming the corporation for a specific purpose or purposes. Promoters are often called "insiders," as opposed to the "outsiders" or ultimate investors because their initial efforts and resources help establish the corporation. Prior to incorporation, promoters usually have the status of joint venturers subject to unlimited liability. Once the corporation is formed, promoters sometimes continue in control. Promoters can be but need not be shareholders.

If there is more than one promoter, the law imposes fiduciaries duties (meaning a trust relationship) towards one another and towards the future corporation. Note that since the corporation is not yet in existence, any self-dealing is not improper. However, once the corporation is formed, promoters must make full disclosure to the board of directors and/or to any shareholders regarding any transactions involving secret and regular profits so that the newly formed corporation has an opportunity to consent or reject the transactions. Failure to make disclosure may make the promoter personally liable for any profits earned from these transactions.

Technically, the promoter lacks any power to bind a corporation not yet formed. In addition, the corporation, upon its formation, does not become automatically bound by the promoter's contracts. Instead, the corporation's board of directors weighs the advantages of the contract prior to its approval. Therefore, contracts made by the promoter usually bind the promoter personally unless the agreement stipulates that only the corporation shall be held liable. If such a provision exists, there is usually also a clause stating that if the corporation is never formed, or the board of directors do not accept the promoter's contracts, the promoter will not be held liable.

A promoter's compensation may take the form of cash, stock, stock options, or a salaried position.

CORPORATE LIABILITY FOR A PROMOTER'S CONTRACTS

As a general rule, promoters are personally liable for the contracts they make, even though made on behalf of a corporation to be formed. The imposition of personal liability is based on the principle that one who acts as an agent for a nonexistent principal (the corporation) is himself liable on the contract in the absence of an agreement to the contrary. Note that a contract signed by a promoter before the corporation is formed is not binding on the corporation. Not until the board of directors' approval of the contract does the corporation become liable.

DRAFTING THE PREINCORPORATION AGREEMENT TO AVOID PROBLEMS

Promotional activities made in anticipation of the formation of a corporation consist of developing a business opportunity, investigating whether the proposed business can be economically viable, hiring an attorney to draw up articles of incorporation, assembling the necessary corporate personnel, and acquiring property to set the corporation in motion. Agreements also include those made among the promoters themselves, agreements among prospective shareholders, stock subscriptions agreements whereby individuals agree to take and pay for unissued shares of the future corporation, and in the case of a large corporation, underwriting agreements (the act of investigating the marketplace prior to selling corporate shares).

OBSERVATION *To avoid litigation, all preincorporation agreements must explicitly clarify the rights, duties, and intentions of all parties. The* written *contracts should stipulate the rights and duties of all parties, whether the promoter is initially bound, whether her liability is to continue upon the formation of the corporation, and the legal consequences to all parties if the corporation refuses to ratify or adopt any or all parts of a contract. These agreements must be also be written in conformity with the statutory requirements of the state of incorporation.*

CHAPTER 6

Incorporation

STEPS IN THE FORMATION OF THE CORPORATE ENTITY

T
he power to grant a certificate or articles of incorporation is vested in the individual states. The federal government has no power to grant corporate charters except as to territories under its jurisdiction, such as the District of Columbia, and except as incident to the conduct of its own business. Incorporation procedures vary from state to state, and corporate existence may begin at different times, depending on the statutes and court decisions applicable to corporations in the state of incorporation. A private corporation, which is the focus of this book, is one organized by private individuals with a profit motive, with governmental consent.

DOMESTIC VERSUS FOREIGN CORPORATIONS

A corporation doing business in the state where it is incorporated is known as a domestic corporation. All other corporations doing business in that state are foreign corporations. For example, a Delaware corporation incorporated in Delaware and doing business in both New York State and Delaware is a domestic corporation for Delaware purposes but a foreign corporation while doing business in New York State.

A corporation wishing to do business in a state other than its state of incorporation must meet the licensing requirements of the state where it intends to do business. The usual procedure is to file an application with the secretary of state in the state where it intends to operate certifying to the corporation's name, date and state of incorporation, the nature of its business, the location of its principal place of business, and enclosing a copy of its certificate of incorporation and other significant data. This information is usually accompanied by a registration fee payable to the intended state. Once operation commences, the corporation is then also subject to all rules applicable to domestic corporations within the state, such as use of a corporate name and the payment of corporate income and franchise taxes.

A DE JURE CORPORATION VERSUS A DE FACTO CORPORATION

As stated in Chap. 2, a corporation cannot come into existence except upon compliance with the statutory laws of the state of incorporation. Once the details regarding the new corporation are settled, the promoters, now known as the "incorporators," must draw up and sign the articles of incorporation, or as it is sometimes called, the corporate charter, and file it with the secretary of state. The signatures of the incorporators are generally notarized and must be accompanied by the proper fees. A properly filed corporation is referred to as a *de jure* corporation. A *de facto* corporation arises when there has been a good faith attempt to comply fully with the state's statutory corporate laws and an exercise of corporate powers. A de facto corporation's existence cannot be attacked by anyone except the state of incorporation. Thus a de facto corporation enjoys the benefits of a properly formed corporation which means that the shareholders have the same limited liability as those enjoyed by a properly formed corporation.

What the applicable RMBCA section says *Section 2.03 of the RMBCA states that unless a delayed effective date is specified, the corporate existence begins when the articles of incorporation are filed. The secretary of state's filing of the articles of incorporation is conclusive proof that the incorporators satisfied all conditions precedent to incorporation except in a proceeding by the state to cancel or revoke the incorporation or involuntarily dissolve the corporation.*

THE ROLE OF THE INCORPORATOR

The person or persons who execute the articles of incorporation, or certificate, are known as the incorporators. In most states, they must be at least eighteen years of age. The steps taken by one or more incorporators for incorporation purposes, in varying combinations or in different chronological order, usually begin as follows:

1. Select a state of incorporation;
2. Select and obtain clearance for use of a corporate name, reserve name if deemed advisable;
3. Have the first meeting of incorporators to adopt bylaws. Minutes of this first meeting, and all subsequent meetings, must be kept;
4. Draw up any required preincorporation agreements;
5. Publish the notice of intention to incorporate, if required by state law;
6. Draft and have signed (and in most states have signatures notarized) the articles of incorporation;
7. File the properly signed articles of incorporation with the proper state authorities, usually the secretary of state;
8. Secure the necessary governmental approval, whether it be federal or state, to issue the appropriate number of shares;

9. Obtain subscriptions from investors for a given number of shares;
10. Secure payment by subscribers of minimum capital;
11. Order the corporate stationery, such as the corporate seal, share ledger, minute book, and shares of stock, usually from a law stationer;
12. Adopt a system of accounting and select either a calendar or fiscal year end pursuant to the Internal Revenue Code;
13. Apply for an employer identification number;
14. Establish one or more corporate bank accounts;
15. Make all advantageous tax elections, if deemed beneficial, such as S corporation status and Section 1244 small business stock election;
16. Obtain payments for additional shares of stock;
17. Issue shares after payment of appropriate transfer taxes;
18. Subsequently file with the state listing the shareholders, directors, number of officers, location of main office, and designation of agent to receive any legal notices or claims;
19. Investigate and if deemed beneficial, establish employee benefit and stock option plans;
20. If the corporation is to take over a going business, a target date should be set at some time in the future, so that all steps can be taken, such as the acquisition of assets and the assumption of liabilities, without unnecessary haste.

What the applicable RMBCA section says *Section 2.01 states that one or more persons may act as the incorporator or incorporators of a corporation by delivering articles of incorporation to the secretary of state for filing.*

THE ARTICLES OR CERTIFICATE OF INCORPORATION

Except for minor variations, the required contents of an articles of incorporation, or certificate, are fairly uniform among the states. Generally, the articles must set forth the following standard information.

The Name of the Corporation

The name of the corporation must include the word "corporation," "incorporated," "company," or "limited." Abbreviations such as "Corp.," "Inc.," "Co.," and "Ltd." are also permitted. The secretary of each state usually maintains a list of pre-existing corporate names that cannot be used for the new corporation. The proposed name should not be allowed to deceive the public as to the corporation's purposes, nor may it be the same as that of another existing domestic or foreign corporation authorized to do business in the state. The thrust of this rule is to make sure that each corporation has a unique name, that is not deceptively misleading, and to prevent fraud. As a practical matter, to avoid costly and time-consuming litigation, the incorporators should select at least two other corporate names, in order of preference, should the first name selected be unobtainable. If the intended corporation plans to do business in other states, check with those states to see that the name is also available. In determining the actual corporate name, the correct spelling, punctuation, and inclusion of the word "The," if desired, should be precisely set forth.

Words that are generally prohibited in a corporate name include "bank," "bank and trust," and "insurance," since these words imply corporate powers that the newly formed entity may not have. When selecting a name, keep in mind the cost of reproducing the name on corporate stationery and other property. A name should also be chosen that is easily recognizable so that any future goodwill generated will be quickly identified with the name.

Because corporate names are granted to corporations on a first-come, first-served basis, many states permit the reservation of a corporate name. This technique permits the still-to-be-formed corporation, for a nominal fee, to hold the corporate name for a limited period of time, usually sixty days, with the power to request an additional sixty-day extension until the corporate papers can be prepared and filed.

What the applicable RMBCA section says *Section 4.02 (a) allows the reservation of a corporate name for a non-renewable 120-day period.*

If the name is similar to that of another affiliated company doing business within the state, the incorporators must obtain written permission (sometimes called a letter of consent) from the existing corporation to use the name.

What the applicable RMBCA section says *Section 4.01, governing the use of a corporate name, states that a corporate name must contain the word "corporation," "incorporated," "company," or "limited," or the abbreviation "corp." "inc.," "co.," or "ltd.," or words or abbreviations of like import in another language. In addition, the name may not contain language stating or implying that the corporation is organized for a purpose other than that permitted by the RMBCA and its articles of incorporation.*

A corporation may use the name (including the fictitious name) of another domestic or foreign corporation that is used in this state if the other corporation is incorporated or authorized to transact business in this state and the proposed user corporation has merged with the other corporation.

The Purposes of the Corporation

The usual practice is to define the principal business actually contemplated by the corporation. In most jurisdictions, the purposes clause states that the corporation may engage in "any lawful purpose." The purposes clause should be drafted so as to prevent ventures into unauthorized areas that may be deemed risky. On the other hand, the purposes clause should be general enough to permit current operations and to allow for expansion and growth without having to amend the articles of incorporation should new corporate opportunities arise. Thus, the drafting of the purposes clause should be done in the most general of terms without going into specific terminology or circumstances.

The Powers of the Corporation

Corporate purposes should not be confused with corporate powers although there is a tendency in many jurisdictions to define the principal purpose of the business without differentiating between its purposes and powers. The articles of incorporation must include the scope and powers of the operation. The extent of the authority of a corporation to conduct its business is limited by the laws of the state under which it is incorporated. Every state corporation act contains a list of corporate powers that every corporation organized within its jurisdiction automatically possesses. Thus, the express powers of the corporation need not be specifically enumerated, but except for those powers restricted by law, a corporation may engage in any act in furtherance of its lawful purposes, i.e., dealing in real estate. Implied powers are those that are inferred from the express powers and are incident to the furtherance of the corporation's business.

An *ultra vires* act is one which is beyond the powers of the corporation. As will be discussed in Chap. 9, *ultra vires* acts result in certain legal consequences.

Thus, the safest procedure when forming a corporation is to express its purposes in the most general terms pursuant to the prevailing philosophy of the catchall "lawful purpose" clause and to avoid enumerating any express powers that may be implied under law.

Duration of Life

A corporation generally enjoys perpetual or unlimited life. Some state statutes mandate that if the life is not "perpetual," it must be so stated in the articles of incorporation. Virtually all corporations elect perpetual life since termination of corporate existence after a stated period will result in a legally questionable status.

Authorized Shares That May Be Issued and Their Description

All jurisdictions require that the articles of incorporation set forth the kinds and amounts of capital stock (or shares) the corporation is authorized to issue. This requirement defines the number of shares (or certificates) in each class, such as common and preferred, and whether they are par value or no par value shares. In every corporation, one class of stock must represent the basic ownership interest. Where a corporation issues only one class of stock, the shares are generally referred to as "common shares." Common shares generally vote for directors. They are also entitled to profits in the form of dividends declared by the directors, and the right to receive corporate assets in case of liquidation after all creditors have been paid.

In an effort to appeal to all types of investors, corporations may issue two or more classes of stock with different rights or privileges or in a series at specific dates. Thus, special classes, called preferred stock, with certain rights and/or privileges may be created. A common type of preference is to give the preferred shareholders a prior claim to earnings. Because they are to receive certain special preferences, preferred shareholders are usually called upon to sacrifice certain inherent rights of capital stock, such as the right to vote for directors.

Par Value Stock

Shares that are given a fixed, arbitrary, and not necessarily, realistic market value are called par value shares. At present, the par value associated with most capital stock issuances is very low (i.e., $1, $5, $10). As will be discussed later in this book, the purpose of these low amounts per share is to encourage the sale of stock and to avoid the contingent liability associated with stock sold below its par value. Stock with a low par value is rarely, if ever, sold below its par.

In some states, organization and transfer taxes are based on either authorized number of shares, the total par value of all of the shares authorized, on the issuance of the shares, or on the transfer of shares. In states that charge a transfer tax based on par value, a low par value may result in lower taxes.

No Par Value Stock

Stock that has no fixed value is called no par value stock. The rights and privileges of the no par value holders are the same as those who hold par value. The issuance of no par value stock avoids the issue of contingent liability for stock that was issued for less than par value (called a discount). It also avoids the question of determining the true value of the stock because presumably, the stock will be issued at its fair market value. Thus, the distinction between the two is not a distinction of rights and privileges, but of the form of issuance and the shareholder's liability in connection with the price paid for the stock.

OBSERVATION *Many states have statutes that require that before a corporation commences to do business, it must receive for its stock a minimum amount of compensation. In many states the minimum amount specified is $1,000.*

What the applicable RMBCA section says *Section 2.02(a)(3), governing the articles of incorporation, states that:*

a. The articles of incorporation must set forth:

1. a corporate name for the corporation that satisfies the requirements as to a proper designation, such as "Corporation" or "corp.";

2. the number of shares the corporation is authorized to issue;

3. the street address of the corporation's initial registered office and the name of its initial registered agent at the office; and

4. the name and address of each incorporator.

b. The articles of incorporation may set forth:

1. the names and addresses of the individuals who are to serve as the initial directors;

2. the purpose or purposes for which the corporation is organized;

3. any provision that under the RMBCA is required or permitted to be set forth in the bylaws; and

4. a provision eliminating or limiting the liability of a director to the corporation or its shareholders for money damages for any action taken, or any failure to take any action, as a director, except liability for (A) the amount of a financial benefit received by a director to which he is not entitled; (B) an intentional infliction of harm on the corporation or the shareholders; (C) unlawful distributions; or (D) an intentional violation of criminal law.

Designation of Secretary of State or Registered Agent

In most jurisdictions, the secretary of state and/or a registered office with a registered agent must be designated for service of process. In some states, the corporation must have designated *both* the secretary of state and registered agent, while in other states it is optional. Even without designating the secretary of state as an agent, most jurisdictions have statutory provisions that automatically make the secretary of state the agent for service of process, other notices and demands, and official communications with the state. Later changes in the registered office and/or agent must be filed with the secretary of state. The purpose of having a registered office and an agent is that a third party may have difficulty finding a corporation and therefore, should have, at all times, a place or person on which to serve notice of process.

Limitations on Directors

The certificate of incorporation designates the number of directors, their terms of service and duties, and their liability to the shareholders. When the membership of the first board of directors has been decided upon prior to the filing of the articles of incorporation, the articles may list their names. Naming the directors in advance may assist in the completion of the incorporation process. However, there is no requirement that they be selected in advance because they can be subsequently chosen at the first meeting of the incorporators or at the first shareholders meeting. To a limited extent, a corporation may indemnify its directors and officers for the reasonable expenses of a lawsuit by or on behalf of a corporation. The corporation may also indemnify directors and officers for judgments, settlements, and fines levied against them for actions committed by them, which they deemed to be in the best interests of the corporation. The corporation may also indemnify a director or officer in criminal cases where it is shown that the individuals believed that they acted in good faith, without knowing that they were in violation of the law, and that they did not personally profit from the transactions that they are charged with. Many states require that the directors be shareholders unless the articles or bylaws state otherwise.

The maximum and minimum number of directors is purely discretionary and may be increased or decreased from time to time as circumstances dictate.

Other Provisions

Incorporators may insert other provisions, mainly for the regulation of the internal affairs of the corporation. These directives cannot contravene existing corporate statutes and/or existing public policy. Examples of these provisions include the following:

1. the requirement, if not stated in the jurisdiction's statutory law, that the directors and officers be shareholders;
2. that certain procedures involving a vote of shareholders be higher than the percentage required by state law;
3. limitations on the power of corporate officers to enter into contracts (i.e., contracts for more than $100,000 require approval of the board of directors);
4. that certain matters, while solely within the discretion of the board of directors to act upon, also be submitted to the shareholders for their approval, (i.e., that the corporation purchase the stock of another corporation);
5. the time and place of shareholders meetings;
6. corporate transactions involving directors;
7. the procedure for terminating directors with and without cause;
8. filling director vacancies;
9. management's compensation;
10. restrictions on the transfer of shares.

The articles of incorporation in all jurisdictions must be signed by the incorporator or incorporators. Some states also require acknowledgement. The purpose of requiring acknowledgment by the incorporators is to prevent the employment of fictitious signatures. Approval of other state agencies, such as for example the state education department in case the new corporation intends to operate as a school, is sometimes required. Publication in a newspaper may also be mandated. Upon filing, the state issues a certificate of incorporation, which is either conclusive or presumptive evidence that the new corporation is in full compliance with the law and can commence operations. The articles of incorporation can always be amended at a future date, usually with shareholder consent.

COMPLETING THE ORGANIZATION OF THE NEW CORPORATION

Once the formalities discussed above have been completed, certain procedures must be undertaken to insure the smooth transition from an intangible concept into an actual operating entity. Steps that must be taken to complete the incorporation process include the calling of an initial meeting by the incorporators. At this meeting the incorporators will, among other things, appoint the requisite individuals who will prepare and adopt the corporate bylaws, set up the requisite books and records, obtain a corporate seal, and open a company bank account.

Accounting systems, payroll records, and other employee fringe benefits must also be established. These vital record keeping procedures will be discussed in detail in Chap. 12. All corporate books and records are normally kept at the corporation's principal place of business.

FUNCTIONS AND PURPOSES OF THE INITIAL CORPORATE MEETING

The launching of the new corporation is usually initiated at the first meeting of the new corporation. The first meeting, assuming the presence of a quorum (a simple majority), is generally called by the incorporators who take the following actions.

1. The election of permanent directors if the incorporators have elected to act as "dummy" or "temporary" directors.
2. The adoption of stock subscription agreements by the new board of directors. An individual may become a shareholder in a new corporation by subscribing to shares either before or after incorporation. This subscription contract is then adopted by the newly appointed board of directors.
2. The election of corporate officers.
3. The approval of business related matters, such as any employment agreements, leases, and the transfer of property to the corporation.
4. The adoption and approval of the bylaws and corporate seal.
5. The approval of legal and other expenses incurred in the formation of the corporation.
6. An application may be submitted for approval allowing the corporation to request authorization to operate in jurisdictions other than the state of incorporation.

7. The election of S corporation status pursuant to the provisions of the Internal Revenue Code allowing the corporation tax treatment similar to that accorded a partnership.
8. The election of Section 1244 of the Internal Revenue Code applicable to the corporate stock so that ordinary losses of up to $50,000 on a single tax return or $100,000 on a joint tax return can be taken in case the business fails.
9. The selection of the corporation's general counsel and independent accountant.
10. The approval of the setting up of the corporate records and the accounting system.

DRAFTING AND ADOPTING BYLAWS

Bylaws govern the internal conduct of the corporation. The initial bylaws may be formulated by the incorporators, shareholders, or board of directors. They must be reasonable and not arbitrary, and must be consistent with both the state statutory laws and the articles of incorporation. For example, they must apply equally to all persons within the same class (i.e., the common or preferred shareholders). Bylaws cannot restrict the fundamental rights of shareholders. For example, they cannot obstruct the right of a shareholder to examine the corporation's books and records for legitimate purposes such as possible mismanagement of the corporation. They are usually adopted by the directors at their first corporate meeting and are binding on the corporation, its officers, and its directors. Standard bylaws include the following:

1. The qualifications for being a corporate officer;
2. The duties and powers of the corporate officers;
3. The date of the annual stockholders meeting;
4. Quorum requirements for shareholders meetings;
5. The qualifications for serving as a director;
6. Compensation to be paid to officers and directors;
7. The rules for conducting shareholders and directors meetings;
8. Creating committees of directors;
9. Fixing the method of declaring dividends;
10. The rules regulating voting and proxies;
11. Indemnification of officers, directors, and other corporate employees;
12. The year-end accounting period to be used by the corporation;
13. The method of accounting to be adopted, i.e., cash or accrual, and other accounting practices;
14. Who is responsible for certain records, reports, and audits;
15. How important documents must be executed; and
16. Establishing a method for amending the bylaws.

Generally, the power to alter or repeal any bylaws are vested in the board of directors unless the power to do so is reserved to the shareholders in the articles of incorporation. In addition, the shareholders usually have the power to amend or repeal any board-adopted bylaw. Generally, the procedures for amending bylaws are easier than those applicable to the amending of the articles of incorporation, because unlike the articles of incorporation, the bylaws are not required to be filed with the secretary of state.

What the applicable RMBCA section says *Section 10.20, governing the amending of bylaws, states that a corporation's board of directors may amend or repeal the corporation's bylaws unless either the articles of incorporation reserve this act exclusively to the shareholders; or the shareholders, in amending or repealing a particular bylaw provide expressly that the board of directors may not amend or repeal that bylaw. In addition, a corporation's shareholders may amend or repeal the corporation's bylaws even though the bylaws may also be amended or repealed by the board of directors.*

THE MECHANICS OF ISSUING STOCK CERTIFICATES

Generally, corporate books and records are sold in complete packages through legal stationers or corporate service companies, such as Julius Blumberg, Inc. located in New York City. These records come in the form of a three-ring looseleaf binder consisting of a copy of the articles of incorporation, the corporate seal, a section for keeping the corporate minutes of each directors and shareholders meeting, a stock ledger containing the authorized number of shares upon which the corporation's name is printed, and all other documents required by law pertaining to the operation of the corporation. Although in most jurisdictions a corporate seal is no longer necessary, it is sometimes used to affix the corporation's mark on stock certificates, bonds, and other important documents to indicate that this is a corporate transaction rather than that of an individual director or shareholder.

A stock certificate represents ownership in a corporation. Statutes permit the issuance of stock certificates only after they have been fully paid for. The usual stock certificate is hand-engraved, is generally eight inches by eleven inches in size, and is usually purchased from a legal stationer. If there is more than one class of stock, each class is printed in a different color. The certificates are bound in a stock transfer ledger that is part of the corporate package, but they are easily separated from a ledger stub by tearing along a perforated line. Each certificate is prenumbered and contains an empty box, usually in the upper right hand corner of the certificate, permitting the appropriate corporate officer to designate the number of shares purchased so long as the amount does not exceed the number of shares authorized in the articles of incorporation. The certificate usually states that the corporation is organized under the laws of a specific state, the name of the stockholder purchasing the certificates, whether they are common or preferred, and whether the shares are par or no par value. An example of a typical share of stock appears on page 189. When issued, the stockholder's name and address is entered in the corporation's stock ledger account and on a stub in the stock book, with the number of shares issued, the amount paid for the shares, and the amount of stock transfer taxes paid. The certificates are usually signed by two or more corporate officers, such as the corporate secretary and president and may be imprinted with the corporate seal. If the shares were bought from another shareholder, the seller's name will also appear in the records. If there is more than

one class of stock issued (i.e., common and preferred), then another stock ledger account containing the same information must be maintained for this other class. The corporation relies upon the stock register to ascertain who is to receive corporate notices and dividends, and who is entitled to vote in corporate matters. Thus, it is important that the purchasing stockholder make sure that his name is entered in the corporate stock records. Shares that are previously owned and that are sold to a new shareholder are indorsed on the back of the certificate by the seller. The stock purchaser then has the right to have the shares registered in his name merely by displaying the properly indorsed stock certificate to the appropriate corporate officer.

OBSERVATION *The prudent shareholder who purchases shares should keep them in his own personal possession (a vault is suggested) rather than leave them with the corporation. Allowing the corporation to retain the shares is unadvisable and may lead to accounting errors and possible fraud.*

Unless there is notice of a possible forgery of the indorser's name, or fraud, the corporation is legally required to enter the new stockholder's name in the corporate records.

OBSERVATION *Prior to commencing operations, it would be wise to have the independent CPA who is hired by the corporation to audit the books and records also audit the stock transfer book to determine that all stock certificates, whether issued to stockholders or unissued, tie into the number of certificates printed by the printer. Missing or unaccounted for certificates may result in potential lawsuits by rightful shareholders who may claim that they were not apprised of certain corporate actions that required shareholder approval.*

Appropriate printed declarations on the certificates may also indicate the relative rights and restrictions governing a particular class of stock, such as a prior shareholder voting agreement to vote the shares a certain way.

CHAPTER 7

Recognition or Disregard of the Corporate Entity

INTRODUCTION

One of the principal purposes of forming a corporation is that shareholders escape unlimited liability by recognizing that the corporation is an entity separate, distinct, and apart from its shareholders. However, under certain circumstances, courts will sweep aside this dual personality concept by concluding that the corporation and its shareholders are really one entity thereby making the shareholders personally liable for all corporate debts. Lawyers call this concept "piercing the corporate veil." Remember that while the corporate form will shield its shareholders against liability for breach of contracts and corporate negligence (called torts), a corporation cannot be formed to defeat existing creditors.

EXAMPLE George owed his creditors $100,000. He, therefore, incorporates the X Corporation and has the board of directors call a meeting authorizing the corporation to assume all of George's debts. Thus, the sole purpose of this entire arrangement is to defeat the claims of George's creditors for pre-existing personal debts. Nevertheless, the newly formed corporation cannot be used as a shield to defeat the rights of the creditors, and George remains personally liable. Had the corporation initially incurred the debts, George, as its sole shareholder, would enjoy complete protection from the claims of the corporate creditors.

Even if a corporation is a de jure corporation (see Chap. 6) or one that is validly formed, a shareholder may still be liable for a corporation's debts and illegal acts if the corporation is being used as a vehicle to perpetrate a fraud or for criminal activities. Thus, in cases involving such activities, courts will pierce the corporate veil and hold the shareholders personally liable under the rule that the corporation is a sham, "alter ego" or "instrumentality" of the shareholders. On the other hand, where corporate formalities are substantially observed, and the corporation was not formed to cheat or defraud third parties or to engage in unlawful activities, even a sole controlling shareholder will enjoy limited liability.

What the applicable RMBCA section says *Section 2.04, governing liability for preincorporation transactions, states that all persons purporting to act as or on behalf of a corporation, knowing there was no incorporation under the RMBCA, are jointly and severally liable for all liabilities created while so acting.*

PERSONAL LIABILITY DUE TO DEFECTIVE INCORPORATION

In Chap. 6, it was stated that a de facto corporation arises when there has been a good faith attempt to comply fully with the state's statutory corporate laws and an exercise of corporate powers.

Furthermore, a de facto corporation enjoys the same benefits that a properly formed corporation possesses, such as perpetual existence, the right to operate as a corporation, and the power to elect S corporation status. At the same time, the shareholders have limited liability.

However, this rule does not mean that the shareholders can completely ignore the legal requirements of forming a corporation and still avoid personal liability.

To avoid problems after incorporation you should observe these steps:

1. Follow all corporate formalities listed in this book;
2. Issue stock only after it is fully paid for;
3. Make sure you call director(s) and shareholder(s) meetings;
4. Keep accurate books and records;
5. Open up a corporate checking account;
6. Do not use the corporate funds to pay your own personal expenses; and
7. Hire an independent accountant to review the corporate books and records.

EXAMPLE Three shareholders attempted to form a corporation. However, they did not have a final meeting with their attorney so they could sign the articles of incorporation, there was no issuance of corporate stock, and no directors or shareholders meetings were ever held. In addition, the shareholders failed to distinguish between the property owned by them personally and the property to be owned by the corporation. These facts indicate a defective incorporation, thereby preventing the shareholders from enjoying the protection against personal liability afforded by a properly formed corporation.

There are several other factors that will also cause the courts to ignore the legitimate existence of the corporation thereby making the shareholders personally liable. They include domination of the corporation by one shareholder, thus permitting operation as a "dummy" corporation, incorporation to evade legal restrictions, lack of minimal initial capital, and shareholder-employees of a professional corporation who are involved in negligent or wrongful conduct.

OPERATING AS A PROFESSIONAL SERVICE CORPORATION

The use of the professional corporation does not significantly alter the personal relationship that exists between the individual practitioner and his client. The professional corporation must, however, still maintain the formalities of a regular corporation. For example, most state laws provide that each shareholder-employee of a professional corporation shall be personally and fully liable for any negligent or wrongful act or misconduct committed by her or by any person under her direct supervision and control while rendering professional services on behalf of such corporation.

Note, however, that the shareholders of a professional corporation do enjoy freedom from personal liability when it involves the contractual debts and obligations of the corporation. Thus, all business contracts executed by the corporation will not subject the shareholder of the professional service corporation to personal liability.

EXAMPLE Shareholder-employees of a professional corporation will not be held liable for a rental lease executed on behalf of the corporation and naming the corporation as tenant.

....
WARNING *This chapter was devoted to the principle that so long as the legal corporate fiction is properly maintained and that all corporate formalities are observed, shareholder liability will be avoided in virtually all instances. However, if a shareholder, seeking to help the corporation, makes a personal guarantee of payment to a creditor, should the corporation fail to pay, then the advantage of unlimited liability vanishes. The ultimate result is the personal liability of the shareholder for this particular transaction should the corporation eventually default.*
....

CHAPTER 8

Financing the Corporation

INTRODUCTION

A corporation raises or obtains capital, i.e., cash, land, buildings, and operating equipment, through the issuance of shares of stock, sometimes called equity securities or capital stock. These shares represent the collective ownership in the corporation and may consist of one class of stock, called common shares, or several classes of stock, called common, common class A, common class B, etc., or preferred shares.

What the applicable RMBCA sections says *Section 1.40(21) states that "shares" mean the unit into which the proprietary interests in a corporation are divided.*

Because the capital stock is supposed to reflect the total value of the corporation's assets, the law insists that the shares be issued for equivalent value. The consideration paid by the shareholder or shareholders is recorded or credited to the corporation's capital stock or stated capital account. Thus, if $100,000 has been paid into the corporate treasury in return for stock issued, the capital of the corporation is $100,000. The corporation's balance sheet, which is a listing of a corporation's assets, liabilities, and capital (also called owners' or shareholders' equity) at a particular date (let's assume January 1, 20XX), after receipt of $100,000 in return for its common stock, would appear as follows:

THE THROCKMORTON CORPORATION
Corporate Balance Sheet
January 1, 20XX

Assets	
Cash	$100,000
Capital	
Common Stock (or Stated Capital)	$100,000

Note that while the total value of the stock issued is fixed, a corporation's net assets (assets less liabilities) will grow or shrink once business commences. If net assets grow and exceed the corporation's capital there will be a *surplus* or earned surplus. CPAs call it retained earnings. If the net assets fall below capital, the corporation is said to have a *deficit* in retained earnings.

Using the above balance sheet data, assume that Throckmorton made $50,000 in profits for the month of January, 20XX. This $50,000 resulted in additional cash of $25,000 and accounts receivable (monies owed to the corporation from sales) of $25,000. The balance sheet at the end of January would appear as follows:

THE THROCKMORTON CORPORATION
Corporate Balance Sheet
January 1, 20XX

Assets		
Cash	$125,000	
Accounts Receivable	25,000	$150,000
Capital		
Common Stock (or Stated Capital)	$100,000	
Retained Earnings (or Surplus)	50,000	$150,000

Note that corporate profits don't always automatically translate into immediate cash.

The authorized number, classes of shares that may be issued, and their rights and limitations, is found in the articles of incorporation.

What the applicable RMBCA section says *Section 6.03 states that a corporation may issue the number of shares of each class or series authorized by the articles of incorporation. Shares that are issued are outstanding shares until they are reacquired, redeemed, converted, or cancelled. Secondly, the reacquisition, redemption, or conversion of outstanding shares is subject to the limitations set forth in the RMBCA. Third, at all times that shares of the corporation are outstanding, one or more shares that together have unlimited voting rights and one or more shares that together are entitled to receive the net assets of the corporation upon dissolution must be outstanding.*

Sufficient shares should be authorized to meet both the corporation's present and future operating requirements. If the corporation issues more shares than are legally permissible, the excess number of shares issued are void.

What the applicable RMBCA section says *Section 6.01 (a) states that the articles of incorporation must prescribe the classes of shares and the number of shares of each class that the corporation is authorized to issue. If more than one class of shares is authorized, the articles of incorporation must prescribe a distinguishing designation for each class, and prior to the issuance of shares of a class, the preferences, limitations, and relative rights of that class must be described in the articles of incorpora-tion. All shares of a class must have preferences, limitations, and relative rights identical with those of other shares of the same class except to the extent otherwise designated in the articles of incorporation.*

Secondly, the articles of incorporation must authorize (1) one or more classes of shares that together have unlimited voting rights, and (2) one or more classes of shares (which may be the same class or classes as those with voting rights) that together are entitled to receive the net assets of the corporation upon dissolution.

Shares sold by a corporation are called *issued and outstanding*. Shares authorized but not yet issued are called *unissued* shares. Ownership of the shares does not mean that the shareholders or stockholders directly owns the assets of the corporation. For example, assume that a corporation owns a delivery truck. Corporate records will list the corporation as the true owner of the truck and not the name of any particular shareholder. On the other hand, the ownership of shares entitles the shareholders to share proportionally in profits and losses, to corporate assets if there is a partial or complete liquidation, indirect control over the affairs and operations of the corporation by allowing shareholders to vote for directors, and perhaps, the right to purchase new issues of stock of the same class (called the preemptive right). As we shall see, there may also be restrictions and limitations. Thus, a share of stock is viewed as a collection of rights and restrictions in the hands of the shareholder.

Debt securities represent legal obligations that must be repaid and create a debtor (the corporation) - creditor relationship. Debt securities consist of notes and bonds issued by the corporation that must be repaid ahead of all of the common and, if there are any, the preferred shareholders in the event of liquidation of the corporation. The chief distinction between debt and stock is that the corporation is under no obligation to repay its shareholders the amounts that they have invested in the corporation, whereas, the corporation is obligated to repay all debts by various specified due dates.

If the articles of incorporation so state, the board of directors may be obligated to set up a sinking fund (a redemption fund in the hands of a trustee) to retire (or redeem) large amounts of debt, such as bonds, and to retire certain types of outstanding common and preferred stock at specified future dates.

PAID-IN CAPITAL

When a corporation receives payment for its shares in excess of its par or stated value, the excess is allocated to a capital account called paid-in capital. No such account exists where the corporation issues only no par value stock.

The board of directors can, however, elect to give no par value a definite or stated value. If this is the case, then any proceeds received in excess of the designated stated value is treated as paid-in capital.

EXAMPLE 1 $110,000 has been paid into the treasury of Zen Transit Corporation as compensation for 10,000 shares with a $10 par value stock. The corporation's balance sheet would appear as follows:

Assets		
Cash		$110,000
Capital		
Common Stock	$100,000	
Paid-In Capital	10,000	$110,000

EXAMPLE 2 Using the facts illustrated in **EXAMPLE 1**, suppose that instead the corporation issued 10,000 shares of no par value stock for the same $110,000. The corporation's balance sheet, would appear as follows:

Assets	
Cash	$110,000
Capital	
Common Stock (or Stated Capital)	$110,000

EXAMPLE 3 Using the facts illustrated in **EXAMPLE 1**, suppose that the corporation issued 10,000 shares of no par value stock, but with a stated value of $11 for the same $110,000. The corporation's balance sheet, would appear as follows:

Assets		
Cash		$110,000
Capital		
Common Stock	$100,000	
Paid-In Capital (or Stated Capital)	10,000	$110,000

The result would be the same as if the corporation issued $10 par value stock for $11 per share.

COMMON STOCK

The articles of incorporation authorize a corporation to issue several kinds of stock having varying rights, preferences, privileges, and limitations. Thus, the capital stock of a corporation usually consists of both *common stock* and *preferred stock*. Common stock represents the residual interest of the corporation, which means the common shareholders bear the risk of loss and enjoy the benefits of any profits. If a corporation issues only one class of stock, that issue is by definition common stock.

Each share of common stock represents a right to participate proportionately in the control of the corporation by exercising the right to vote on corporate matters submitted to them, the right to any dividends declared by the board of directors, and the right to distributions of corporate assets upon liquidation. Note that the common shareholder's participation in distributions due to a partial or complete corporate dissolution occurs only after payment of all claims having priority, such as to holders of debt securities (notes and bonds) and/or to preferred shareholders. Thus, all other claims against the corporation must be paid ahead of those of the common shareholders. These types of distributions are sometimes referred to as liquidating dividends, which could, under certain circumstances, be fully or partially taxable under the Internal Revenue Code.

OBSERVATION *If a corporation's common stock is owned by one shareholder, the number of shares authorized but unissued is immaterial for ownership purposes.*

In an effort to appeal to various groups of investors, a corporation can issue more than one class of stock. While classes of stock having preferential rights are called preferred stock, a corporation can accomplish the same thing by issuing two classes of common stock, Class A and Class B. In this type of situation, Class A usually has the right to vote while Class B does not. In turn, Class B stockholders have priority over the Class A shareholders when it comes to dividend payouts and distributions due to a partial or complete corporate dissolution. There are other novel strategies involving Class A and Class B common stock.

EXAMPLE 1 The Georgetown Oil Corporation was incorporated by five individuals. The articles of incorporation stipulate that the corporation is authorized to issue 10,000 shares of Class A common with the right to vote which will be issued equally to all five shareholders. The corporation is also authorized to issue 1,000,000 shares of Class B nonvoting common stock to be sold to the public in the event that the corporation is successful and wishes "to go public."

EXAMPLE 2 The articles of incorporation of Maximum Manufacturing Inc. stipulates that the corporation is authorized to issue 10,000 shares of Class A common with the exclusive right to vote for directors and will pay $1 in dividends per share annually. The corporation also plans to issue Class B shares that shall have the exclusive right to vote on all other corporate matters and will pay $2.50 annually in dividends.

In a smaller corporation, the issuance of more than one class of common stock can also be done to assure control to a minority shareholder.

EXAMPLE The Polemus Watch Corporation has three shareholders, Allen, Bates, and Charles. The corporation can issue one share of Class A Common Stock to Allen who contributes $100, two shares of Class B Common to Bates for $200, and two shares of Class C Common to Charles for $200. The shares of all three classes can have identical rights, such as the right to receive dividends if declared and the right to assets upon dissolution; the shares will only

be different in that each class will have the right to elect one director and to vote as a class on any matter requiring shareholder approval.

Both common and other classes of shareholders may be given the option to exchange their shares into common stock and vice versa. This is known as the *convertibility* feature applicable to a particular class of shares. For example, the Class A shares could be convertible into Class B shares at the option of the shareholders.

Using the technique whereby there are two classes of common stock, voting and nonvoting, is also an effective shield against takeover by another company should another group of investors attempt to acquire the corporation by purchasing a large block of the Class B common shares.

....

What the applicable RMBCA section says *Section 6.01 (c) states that the articles of incorporation may authorize one or more classes of shares that have special, conditional, or limited voting rights, or no right to vote, except to the extent prohibited by the RMBCA. The shares may also be redeemable or convertible as specified in the articles of incorporation at the option of the corporation or the shareholder, or another person or upon the occurrence of a designated event; for cash, indebtedness, securities, or other property; and in designated amounts or by formula. Thirdly, the articles of incorporation may also state that the shares may entitle the holders to distributions calculated in any manner, including dividends that may be cumulative, noncumulative, or partially cumulative. Finally, articles can declare that the shares may have preference over any other class of shares with respect to distributions, including dividends and distributions upon the dissolution of the corporation.*
....

PREFERRED STOCK

In order to permit the corporation to create unique ownership schemes when raising capital, corporate statutory laws permit the issuance of other types of stock, called preferred stock. Holders of this class of stock sacrifice certain rights, such as the right to vote in return for other special rights, such as a high dividend payment, the right to guaranteed annual dividends, and the right to convert into common stock (called convertible preferred). Preferred dividends can be cumulative, cumulative-to-the-extent-there-are-earnings, noncumulative, participating and nonparticipating, issued in a series at different dates, and convertible into common stock at the option of the holder. A corporation may also have other preferred stock classifications, such as Class A and Class B with certain rights.

EXAMPLE The incorporators of Lumen Corporation wish to raise $200,000 in capital. The articles of incorporation stipulate that 10,000 shares of $10 par value common shares are to be authorized and issued while 1,000 shares of $100 par value nonvoting preferred shares will also be issued. While $200,000 ($100,000 in common + $100,000 in preferred) in capital may ultimately be raised by the corporation, only the common shareholders, with the authority to vote, will have control over the corporation.

The rights enjoyed by each class of preferred stock must be spelled out in the articles of incorporation. For example, the annual dividend to be paid on each share of stock can be expressed in terms of specific dollar amounts ($4 per share preferred) or as a percentage of par value (4 percent preferred). Most preferred stock has a par value.

EXAMPLE The Bohemia Pottery Corporation plans to issue 10,000 shares of $100 par value preferred stock paying $5 per share annually. Alternatively, the articles of incorporation could state that each share will pay 5 percent annually meaning $5 per share ($100 × 5 percent).

Dividends on preferred stock are usually paid quarterly. A dividend, in full or in part, can only be paid if declared by the board of directors.

Other types of preferred stock can be issued by a corporation. They are as follows:

Noncumulative Preferred Stock

If a dividend is not declared on this type of stock for any given year, the obligation ceases for that particular year. The board of directors, in their discretion, can pass up the opportunity to declare a dividend for the year for various reasons, such as the reinvest-

ment of corporate funds for growth or a poor earnings record for the year.

EXAMPLE The Peterson Extrusion Corporation earned $1,000,000 in net income after taxes but decided to plow back all of the profits in a program of plant modernization. Thus, it is a reasonable and legitimate business purpose and the board of directors is under no obligation to declare a dividend to the preferred shareholders for that particular year.

Cumulative Preferred Stock

Cumulative preferred stock gives the shareholder the right to receive a dividend, usually each quarter before the payment of any common dividends. If the dividends are not paid for a particular period, they accumulate and are called dividends in arrears. The articles of incorporation can be written to provide that "the holders of preferred stock shall be entitled to cumulative dividends of 6 percent per year to be paid out of net income after federal taxes or out of retained earnings (surplus)."

EXAMPLE 1 In 20X4, the Simpson Quarry Corporation has issued 10,000 shares 5 percent cumulative $100 par value preferred stock for a total of $1,000,000. If in 20X4 no dividends were paid, at the end of the year there would be preferred dividends of $50,000 (10,000 shares × $100 × 5 percent) in arrears. If the board seeks to declare dividends in 20X5, they would have to pay the arrears of $50,000 plus the 20X5 dividend before any dividends can be paid in 20X5 to the common shareholders.

EXAMPLE 2 Using the facts given in **EXAMPLE 1**, assume that in 20X5, the board of directors declare a cash dividend of $125,000. $100,000 ($50,000 + $50,000) would be paid for 20X4 and 20X5 to the preferred shareholders and the balance of $25,000 would be paid to the common stockholders.

Dividends in arrears do not become an actual corporate liability until declared so by the board of directors. Of course, a corporation cannot guarantee that a dividend will be paid every year, so that the arrearages accumulate every year until paid. Since the

	Preferred Stock	Common Stock	Total
Regular dividend, preferred (5,000 shares × $8)	$40,000		$40,000
Dividend to common shareholders (25,000 shares × 4):		$100,000	100,000
Remaining $60,000 ($200,000 − $140,000):			
Preferred $\dfrac{5,000 \text{ shs.}}{30,000 \text{ shs.}} \times \$60,000$	10,000		10,000
Common $\dfrac{25,000 \text{ shs.}}{30,000 \text{ shs.}} \times \$60,000$		50,000	50,000
Total dividends	$50,000	$150,000	$200,000
Number of shares outstanding	5,000	25,000	
Dividend per share	$10.00	$6.00	

amount of arrears may influence potential investors, they should be reported in the financial statements as a footnote.

Participating Preferred Stock

Participating preferred stock allows preferred shareholders to receive additional amounts of dividends after the dividends stipulated in the articles of incorporation are paid to both the preferred and common shareholders on a ratable basis. The formula for payment can be based on either the total outstanding par value for each class of stock or on the number of shares of each class outstanding.

EXAMPLE Zinc Metals Corporation has outstanding stock composed of 5,000 shares of 8 percent, $100 par value participating preferred stock and 25,000 shares of no par common stock. The preferred stock is entitled to participate equally with the common, share for share, in any dividend distributions, which exceed the regular preferred dividend of 8 percent and a $4 per share common dividend. In 20XX, the board of directors declare dividends of $200,000 for the current year. The dividends for both the preferred and common stock will be $10 and $6, respectively, computed as shown above.

Nonparticipating Preferred Stock

Nonparticipating preferred stock is preferred stock that is entitled to its current annual dividend only, regardless of the dividends paid to the common shareholders. There is no unanimous agreement among the states as to whether nonparticipating preferred stock is cumulative or not. If the incorporators want to issue noncumulative preferred stock, it should state so in the articles of incorporation with such wording as "preferred shares issued and outstanding shall be non-participating."

Preferred Shares With a Liquidating Preference

The articles of incorporation may provide that in the event that the corporation is liquidated, the preferred shareholders are to receive assets up to a specified amount, for example, up to their par value. This preference makes the preferred shares more attractive to investors.

"Callable" or Redeemable Preferred Stock

This type of stock is subject to involuntary redemption at the option of the board of directors at a fixed price at specific future dates. The call or redemption price is usually a fixed price containing a premium above the price originally paid for the stock or its par value. The premium sometimes consists of a stated percentage of the price paid or a year's worth of dividends. When preferred stock is cumulative, all dividends in arrears must be paid in addition to any other premiums. A corporation will usually exercise its redemption privilege when it no longer needs the capital generated by the preferred stock and/or when the required dividends attributable to the preferred stock are high in relation to market conditions. The articles of incorporation can be written to include a statement, such as "the holders of any preferred stock shall be subject to a redemption of $110 per share plus any unpaid dividends in arrears."

Preferred stock cannot be redeemed when it will create a situation whereby creditors might not be paid.

EXAMPLE Major Paint Supply Inc. wishes to call in (or redeem) $500,000 of its callable preferred stock because of its high annual dividend requirement. The corporation has $500,000 in its treasury, but also owes its creditors an equal amount. The preferred stock cannot be redeemed because there is the risk that there will not be sufficient funds with which to pay the creditors.

Both the issued and outstanding common and preferred stock are presented on a corporation's balance sheet in the capital stock section.

EXAMPLE At its inception, the Tennessee Line and Tackle Corporation sold 10,000 shares of $10 par value common stock for $115,000. It also sold 1,000 shares of its noncumulative 6 percent $100 par value preferred stock for $100,000. The corporation's balance sheet would appear as follows:

Assets		
Cash		$215,000
Capital		
Preferred Stock		$100,000
Common Stock	$100,000	
Paid-In Capital	15,000	$115,000
		$215,000

Preferred Stock Issued in a Series

This technique permits a corporation to authorize a class of preferred shares that will be issued in installments over a period of time as fixed by the board of directors. This permits the corporation to sell blocks of shares in the marketplace when economic circumstances deem it most advantageous.

TAX ASPECTS REGARDING THE ISSUANCE AND SALE OF CORPORATE STOCK
Capital Gains and Losses

Eventually, a shareholder may want to dispose of his stock in the corporation. Under the Internal Revenue Code, stock held for longer than one year that is sold results in either a long-term gain or loss. This means that if the stock is sold at a gain, it cannot be taxed at a rate of more than 15 percent. Short-term capital gain (stock held for less than a year) is taxed at ordinary rates (i.e., up to a maximum rate of 35 percent). If the stock is sold at a loss, both long-term and short-term capital losses offset ordinary income up to $3,000 per year. Under the Internal Revenue Code, a net capital loss in excess of $3,000 can be carried over to offset future capital gains or, subject to the $3,000 annual limitation, offset against other income on a dollar-for-dollar basis until used up.

EXAMPLE For 20X4, John Varney earned $50,000 in ordinary income and sustained a long-term capital loss of $5,000. He may offset $3,000 against his current year's salary and carry forward the remaining $2,000 to be deducted in 20X5 against capital gains and ordinary income.

Section 1244 Stock

Section 1244 permits a special tax treatment for losses due to the sale of certain stock. The stock must be the common stock, voting or nonvoting, of a domestic corporation. This means that other types of stock convertible into common stock cannot qualify as Section 1244 stock. Ordinarily, stock losses are characterized as either long-term or short-term and thus, will have limited use in offsetting ordinary income. However, if the stock is "Section 1244 stock," a large part of the stock loss (up to $100,000 on a joint tax return) can be taken as an ordinary deduction if the owner of the stock is an individual or a partnership. The technique for electing the tax benefits of Section 1244 are discussed in Chap. 15.

Partial 50% Capital Gain Exclusion for Small Business Stock

A noncorporate taxpayer who holds for more than five years qualified small business stock issued after August 10, 1993, can exclude 50 percent of any gain on the investor's sale or exchange of the stock. This tax benefit is discussed in Chap. 15.

TREASURY SHARES

Sometimes the corporation reacquires outstanding shares. Outstanding shares that are reacquired by the corporation are called treasury shares. The corporation may reacquire shares for several reasons; to fund a company pension plan, to reduce the number of shareholders who have an interest in the corporation, to eliminate dissident or unhappy shareholders, to keep outsiders from gaining control of the corporation, to use the stock to acquire other companies, and for later reissuance as circumstances dictate. Treasury shares are essentially the same as unissued capital stock.

The reacquired treasury shares do not have any voting rights, nor do the shares participate in the distribution of dividends or net assets upon dissolution. Under the Internal Revenue Code, as a general rule, the sale of treasury shares by the corporation does not result in a taxable gain or deductible loss to the corporation.

STOCK SUBSCRIPTIONS AND STOCK OPTION PLANS

Corporations may have difficulty finding an individual who is willing to pay for all of the stock at once. Rather than lose a potential purchaser, the corporation may draw up a contract allowing a specified number of shares to be purchased and paid for in full or in installments as determined by the corporation's board of directors. Thus, a subscription contract provides a future corporation of assurance of capital.

Many state incorporation statutes contain provisions authorizing the board of directors to establish stock option plans as a performance incentive. A

stock option plan is an agreement to issue stock at terms that are beneficial to either a certain group of employees or to all employees. Stock option plans are used by corporate employers to attract, retain, and motivate key management. A stock option plan is usually based on a company's expected favorable performance, which will usually cause the price of the stock to rise. When this occurs, the employees have the right to purchase the stock at its lower option price and then sell at the higher market price. The price at which the stock may be purchased may be its fair market value at the time of its purchase. In other cases, the stock option plan may give the employee the right to purchase stock at a future date at a fixed price. Shares that are part of an option plan cannot be voted until the option is exercised, and the stock is paid for and issued. Share options are usually evidenced by certificates known as "warrants."

What the applicable RMBCA section says *Section 6.24, governing share options, states that a corporation may issue rights, options, or warrants for the purchase of shares of the corporation. The board of directors shall determine the terms upon which the rights, options, or warrants are issued, the form and content, and the consideration for which the shares are to be issued.*

The taxation of stock option plans are largely governed by the Internal Revenue Code. If the employee exercises his option, the purchase price becomes the cost basis of the stock. If the stock is later sold at a profit, and certain other conditions mandated by the Internal Revenue Code are met, the profits are taxed as long-term capital gain at rates no greater than 15 percent.

PREEMPTIVE RIGHTS

Frequently, the board of directors of an existing corporation will issue additional shares to finance corporate expansion and operations. These new shares might be the result of a new authorization or due to an amendment to the articles of incorporation. In this particular situation, existing shareholders may enjoy "preemptive rights." Preemptive rights allow an existing shareholder to purchase a new issue of shares in proportion to the amount of shares that he currently owns before it is offered to others. Thus, if the shareholder owns 1,000 common shares out of 10,000 common shares outstanding, he is permitted to purchase 10 percent of the new issue.

As a general rule, holders of one class of stock do not have a preemptive right to acquire the shares of another class of stock to be issued. The certificate of incorporation may also specifically deny or limit preemptive rights. Thus, the board of directors may have to amend the articles of incorporation to specifically authorize this type of shareholder option.

What the applicable RMBCA section says *Section 6.30, governing preemptive rights, states that the shareholders of a corporation do not have the preemptive right to acquire the corporation's new issues except to the extent that the articles of incorporation so provide. However, a statement in the articles that "the corporation elects to have preemptive rights" (or words of similar import) means that the shareholders have a preemptive right.*

EXAMPLE 1 During 20XX, the Mason Brick and Mortar Corporation, with an authorization of 10,000 $1 par value common stock, has issued 9,000 of its $1 par value Class A Common shares. Roland Hook, a shareholder owning 15 percent of the outstanding common shares, demands the right to subscribe to the rest of the shares in proportion to his present holdings. Since the remaining 1,000 common shares do not represent a new issue, Roland cannot exercise any preemptive right.

EXAMPLE 2 Using the facts in **EXAMPLE 1**, assume that in December 20XX, the corporation authorizes the issuance of 10,000 shares of Class B Common shares. Since this is a newly authorized issue, Roland may exercise his preemptive rights in proportion to his current percentage of ownership. Thus, Roland has a preemptive right to purchase 15 percent of the newly authorized stock.

Preemptive rights do not apply to treasury stock nor to shares covered by option plans offering stock to directors, officers, and key employees.

OBSERVATION *A closely held corporation owned by a small group of shareholders might find the utilization of preemptive rights useful in maintaining control of the corporation. By exercising their rights to participate in the issuance of any newly authorized shares, they are in a position to maintain their proportional ownership in the existing corporation.*

If shares of the corporation are expected to be widely held or of different classes, it might be wise to prohibit the use of preemptive rights to avoid unforseen problems regarding the exercise of any rights.

CONSIDERATION FOR WHICH CAPITAL STOCK CAN BE ISSUED

Section 6.21(b) of the RMBCA states that the board of directors may authorize shares to be issued for consideration consisting of any tangible or intangible property for the benefit of the corporation, including cash, promissory notes, services performed, contracts for service to be performed, or other securities of the corporation. In the absence of fraud, the judgment of the board of directors or shareholders as to the value of consideration received is deemed to be conclusive.

EXAMPLE An attorney forms a corporation. Her basic legal fee for forming a corporation is $1,500 but she accepts 150 shares of $10 par value common stock in return for her services. The value of her services paid for by the issuance of the corporation's $10 par value common stock is based on the honest judgment of the board of directors. In the absence of fraud or capriciousness on the part of the board, the value of the consideration received for the stock cannot be challenged by any creditor or other stockholder.

Once par value stock has been issued, the purchasing stockholder can eventually resell it for any price the selling shareholder is able to obtain. On the other hand, if the issuing corporation were to repurchase the stock, it can do so and the stock, in the hands of the purchasing corporation, becomes treasury stock. The corporation can then resell the stock again for any discretionary value without regard to any par of stated value.

No par value stock can be issued for any consideration representing the fair market value of the stock as determined by the board of directors or if the articles of incorporation so provided, by the shareholders.

....

What the applicable RMBCA section says *Section 6.21 (b) states that the board of directors may authorize shares to be issued for consideration consisting of any tangible or intangible property for the benefit of the corporation, including cash, promissory notes, services performed, contracts for service to be performed, or other securities of the corporation.*

....

THE SALE OF DEBT INSTRUMENTS TO FINANCE THE NEW CORPORATION

As previously stated, the sale of stock represents ownership and entitles the shareholder to a share of earnings, control of the business, and a proportionate share of assets in case of liquidation. However, in some situations, a corporation may want to resort to debt financing (the issuance of bonds and notes payable) for such matters as financing operations on a short-term basis or as a source of funds for large financial commitments, such as the purchase of land and buildings. The use of debt is also a useful technique for a small corporation in a situation where the shareholders do not wish to dilute their control over the corporation by issuing additional shares of stock. When used by a corporation, debt financing creates a debtor (corporation) and creditor (lender) relationship. Bonds issued by a corporation are generally governed by an indenture or trust agreement. The indenture generally contains the basic terms of the issuance, the face or par value of the bonds (i.e., $1,000, $5,000, $10,000), the rate of interest to be paid (i.e., a "coupon" rate of 6 percent annually or 3 percent every six months), the maturity date of the issuance, whether the bonds are secured, any conversion features, and whether the corporation is required to set up a bond sinking fund to redeem the bonds at their maturity date. Most bond issues also have a call feature. This feature gives the corporation a chance to buy back and retire the bonds at a given

price, usually above their face value, before maturity. These callable bonds give the corporation a great deal of financial flexibility. If the market rate of interest on loans drops below the rate being paid on the bonds, the corporation can exercise their call option and buy back the costly bonds. They can later issue new bonds at a lower price.

....

OBSERVATION *Convertible bonds, like all other bonds, carry the benefit of having priority of repayment before all preferred and common shareholders. There is also the additional opportunity to convert to preferred or common stock should the possibility of potential stock appreciation occur thereby causing a conversion from bond to stock ownership. In view of the speculative nature of the bonds, the articles of incorporation must contain an authorized amount sufficient to cover the possible conversion of all bonds in stock.*

....

Notes can also be issued on either a short-term or long-term basis. When issuing notes, the lending contract names the parties involved, a description of the debt, the rate of interest to be paid, and whether the loan is secured by company assets (called a secured loan), by a shareholder's personal guarantee, or both.

One basic distinction between debt and stock, or equity ownership, is that there is no obligation to repay the shareholder at any time in the future, whereas the corporation is legally bound to ultimately repay the debt. Secondly, debt instruments are required to pay interest annually, which is tax deductible by the corporation. Dividend payments are not tax deductible because they represent a distribution of profits and not a cost of financing.

The authority to borrow money is generally not stated in the articles of incorporation but falls within the general authority of the board of directors who manage the affairs of the corporation. However, the articles of incorporation might contain provisions that restrict the power of the board to incur debt. These restrictions might include what percentage of corporate assets may be pledged as security for the loans and the requirement that all borrowings by the corporation above a certain amount, i.e., $500,000, be approved by a majority or all of the shareholders. These restrictions are generally upheld by courts if they are deemed reasonable.

Note that in case of a corporation liquidation, the creditors who own notes and bonds issued by the corporation have priority over all shareholders.

CONVERTIBLE SHARES AND DEBT INSTRUMENTS

A convertible security is a security that can, by its terms, be exchanged for other securities, i.e., bonds convertible into preferred stock or common stock (i.e., $1,000 shares of $1 par value common received by shareholder in exchange for one $1,000 bond), or preferred stock convertible into common stock according to some predetermined ratio. The conversion is generally at the option of the owner of the security. Conversion privileges for holders of both shares of stock and bonds are found in the articles of incorporation. Some states permit bondholders to convert their bonds into either common or preferred shares upon the happening of some specific event, such as the failure to make an interest payment to the bondholders at the specified due date. If an individual converts bonds into additional shares or one class of shares is converted into another class (i.e., preferred shares into common), the securities received by the corporation generally revert to the status of authorized but unissued.

EXECUTING AND ISSUING THE SHARES

Generally, shares are not issued until fully paid for. They may bear the corporate seal but are usually signed by two or more corporate officers, such as the president and vice president or corporate secretary and treasurer. State statutes usually require corporations to maintain records of their shareholders in their stockholder ledger accounts showing names and addresses and the number and classes of stock held. The record book is normally open to reasonable inspection by directors, officers, and shareholders. For legal purposes, the name in the corporate records is conclusive evidence of stock ownership.

THE DUTY OF THE ISSUING CORPORATION TO REGISTER STOCK CERTIFICATES

The Uniform Commercial Code, or UCC, which is the law in virtually all states, contains the rules that govern the registration of stock certificates. The UCC sets forth the conditions that must be satisfied before the issuer is required to register the securities. The conditions that must be met in order to register the securities are as follows:

1. The securities must be properly indorsed,
2. There must be reasonable assurance that the indorsements are genuine,
3. The issuer has no duty to inquire into adverse claims,
4. The applicable tax laws have been complied with and
5. The transfer, pledge, or release is in fact rightful.

Where the above preconditions are satisfied, the issuing corporation must register the transfer of stock or risk being held liable for damages for the wrongful refusal to do so. Conversely, an issuer may refuse to register the securities where any precondition is not met.

CHAPTER 9 — Corporate Management Structure: The Role of Directors

INTRODUCTION

Since the corporation is a legal fiction, it can only operate through its agents who are composed of its board of directors, officers, and designated employees. An agent is one who is given the authority to act on behalf of another. While ultimate control of the corporation rests with the shareholders, actual conduct of the corporation's affairs is delegated by the shareholders to duly elected corporate directors.

What the applicable RMBCA sections say *Section 8.01 states that except as provided by a shareholder agreement (discussed in Chap. 11), each corporation must have a board of directors. In addition, all corporate powers shall be exercised by or under the authority of, and the business and affairs of the corporation managed under the direction of, its board of directors, subject to any limitation set forth in the articles of incorporation or in a previously executed shareholder agreement.*

Section 8.03 of the RMBCA states that a board of directors must consist of one or more individuals, with the number specified in or fixed in accordance with the articles of incorporation or bylaws.

If a board of directors has power to fix or change the number of directors, the board may increase or decrease by 30 percent or less the number of directors last approved by the shareholders, but only the shareholders may increase or decrease by more than 30 percent the number of directors last approved by the shareholders.

The articles of incorporation or bylaws may establish a variable range for the size of the board of directors by fixing a minimum and maximum number of directors. If a variable range is established, the number of directors may be fixed or changed from time to time, within the minimum and maximum, by the shareholders or the board of directors. After shares are issued, only the shareholders may change the range for the size of the board or change from a fixed to a variable-range size board or vice versa.

Finally, directors are to be elected at the first annual shareholders meeting and at each annual meeting thereafter unless their terms are staggered.

The directors, operating *as a board and not as individuals,* have the supreme power of control and broad operating authority over the corporation. Their authority is exercised at a properly convened meeting of the board. As a general rule, the articles of incorporation cannot limit the authority or qualifications of directors to manage the business if it is a publicly listed corporation. However, some state statutes permit the "sterilization" or restriction of the authority of the board of directors of a nonpublic, or closely held corporation. This limitation must be set forth in the articles of incorporation. This provision relieves the directors of liability due to their negligence while in office and instead makes shareholders totally liable. This limitation, in effect nullifying the authority of the directors, must also be noted conspicuously on the face or back of every voting and nonvoting stock certificate issued by the corporation.

EXAMPLE A provision in the certificate of incorporation of Salvo Sales Corporation, a closely held corporation, transfers the board of directors' authority to manage the corporation to all of the shareholders. All of the incorporators and all of the existing shareholders are aware of this provision and have approved. The issued shares also contain notification of the transfer of the directors' authority to the shareholders on the front of every certificate. This arrangement is valid and nullifies the shareholders' benefit of limited liability with respect to any negligent acts or illegal acts authorized by them. Their liability arises from the fact that it is now the shareholders of the closely held corporation, and not the directors, who are initiating and approving corporate actions.

Both the articles of incorporation and/or the bylaws can prescribe qualifications for serving as a board member.

EXAMPLE The articles of incorporation of Freemont Financial Corporation Ltd., a closely held nonpublic corporation, requires that there be at least five directors, that each board member own at least 10 percent of the outstanding shares, and that two board members be officers of the corporation. The remaining three members must not be employees of the corporation. The articles of incorporation also requires that no nonemployee director be an attorney connected with or associated with a banking institution doing business with the corporation.

The basic structure of the corporation appears as follows:

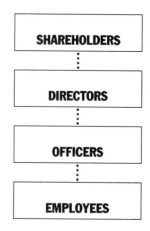

It should be noted that by selecting directors whose views and business philosophy mirror that of the shareholders, the shareholders indirectly control the corporation's affairs. Thus, certain groups of shareholders, who own large blocks of stock, can influence the management of the corporation by electing directors sympathetic to certain stockholder interests, thereby shaping and controlling the composition of the board.

RELATIONSHIP OF DIRECTORS TO CORPORATION

Although the directors are selected by the shareholders, once elected, they serve the corporation, and not the stockholders. The directors guide the general policies of the corporation. The directors' position is one of a fiduciary (or trustee on behalf of the corporation) and owe a duty of loyalty only to the corporation. This means that their business decisions must take into account the best interests of the corporation and must not reflect personal motivation or self-interest.

EXAMPLE The directors of Formica Tops Inc. are seeking land on which to construct their new manufacturing facility. Marsha Collins, a director of Formica, is aware that her brother Norville owns land that would make a suitable plant site. The fair market value of the property is $10,000. Marsha, as director, and without notifying the remaining board members that the seller is her brother, induces the remaining directors to purchase the land for $50,000, thereby benefiting her brother. Marsha has breached her fiduciary duty to Formica. Upon discovering the facts, Formica, through its other directors, may sue Marsha to recover any excess purchase price, in this case, $40,000.

Note that in the above example, the corporate director will most likely be removed from her place on the board due to breach of her fiduciary duty.

Since the directors' responsibilities are fiduciary in nature, they cannot permit another party to attend directors' meetings in their place. Thus, directors cannot vote by proxy. A proxy is a grant of authority given by one individual to another to vote in his place (see Chap. 11).

EXAMPLE Arthur Daniel is elected a director of the Macro Tube Corporation. He cannot attend the first meeting of the directors so he sends his attorney in his place. This act is in violation of his fiduciary responsibilities because he has no authority to delegate his functions as a director to third parties, even though the individual appointed may be equal to or even better qualified than the director to serve in such capacity.

What the applicable RMBCA sections says *Section 8.60, governing conflicting interests, states that a conflicting interest means the interest a director of the corporation has with respect to the proposed transaction involving the corporation. Sections 8.61, 8.62, and 8.63 state any transaction in which a director (and even an officer) has an interest are voidable by the corporation unless the transaction is either fair to the corporation or is approved, ratified, or authorized by a vote of the disinterested directors or shareholders after full disclosure of all the relevant facts.*

NUMBER AND QUALIFICATION OF DIRECTORS

Traditionally, shareholders select board members from their own ranks. Usually, a director must be at least 18 years old. While state statutes do not place a maximum on the number of directors that a corporation may have, most state statutes prescribe a minimum of three. Some state statutes now permit one or two directors where there are only one or two shareholders. In other states, a single incorporator can designate herself as the sole director. A shareholder is sometimes also a director but this is not a necessary

requirement to be a director unless the articles of incorporation or bylaws require such ownership.

OBSERVATION *To lessen the chance of a deadlock in matters brought before the board, it is preferable to have an odd number of directors.*

As previously stated, the authority of the directors to act is vested in the entire board. In most states, the "entire board" means the number of directors in office if there are no vacancies. The number of directors permitted to serve may be fixed by the articles of incorporation, the bylaws, or by action of the shareholders and may be changed by a vote of the "entire board."

What the applicable RMBCA section says *Section 8.02 states that the articles of incorporation or bylaws may prescribe qualifications for directors. A director need not be a resident of this state or a shareholder of the corporation unless the articles of incorporation or bylaws so prescribe.*

OBSERVATION *Many professional ethics pronouncements prevent outside professionals doing business with the corporation from serving on the board. For example, the independent certified public accountant who renders an opinion regarding the financial condition of the corporation cannot serve on the board since her membership would impugn her creditability as an independent evaluator of the financial condition of the corporation.*

DIRECTORS: HOW CHOSEN

While the original directors are named in the articles of incorporation, they usually serve as "dummies" who then resign when the shareholders select their successors at the first meeting of the shareholders. A director whose term has expired generally continues to serve until a successor is chosen at a special meeting called for this purpose or at the next annual meeting of the stockholders. A valid annual shareholder meeting to elect a director requires a *quorum* of shares present. A quorum means the majority of shares entitled to vote. Once the quorum is present, the meeting will not be terminated if one of the shareholders leaves. Usually, each share of voting stock is entitled to one vote.

EXAMPLE 1 The Thompson Asphalt Co. Ltd. has 100 common stock shareholders. Seventy-five shareholders show up at the annual shareholders meeting. One hour later, thirty shareholders leave. This is a valid shareholder meeting since a quorum (majority entitled to vote) was initially present.

EXAMPLE 2 The board of directors of Hancock Fruit Inc. is composed of nine members. Six members show up at the first directors meeting and ratify an important contract. The corporation's articles of incorporation and bylaws contain no provision relating to quorum requirements. A quorum is present and the ratification is valid.

In some states, all directors can be chosen by a plurality (meaning the largest number of votes cast) of the shareholder votes cast providing that there is a quorum present.

EXAMPLE The Ludwig Supply Ltd. has 100 common stock shareholders. Seventy-five shareholders show up at the annual shareholders meeting. Three directors must be chosen out of a list of ten candidates. Candidate A gets 30 votes, Candidate B gets 20 votes, and Candidate C gets 15 votes. The remaining shareholders vote for the other available candidates. Since Candidates A, B, and C have received the largest amount of votes, they have been elected directors at the valid shareholder meeting.

The term "plurality" is not to be confused with majority, which means receiving more than half of the votes cast. Some states require a majority of the votes cast in order to elect a director.

The selection of directors may also be staggered. For example, the articles of incorporation may have one third of the directors elected to three-year terms. This allows for greater continuity and less disruption regarding the functioning of the corporation.

In a closely held corporation, it is sometimes mandated in the articles of incorporation that all shareholders be present at a shareholder meeting in order to constitute a quorum so that directors can be elected. The danger here is deadlock, in that the mere absence of a single shareholder can stymie the corporation's ability to elect a viable and functioning board of directors. Thus this technique is dangerous and should be avoided.

Once elected, a director always has the power to resign by tendering his resignation. The resignation will not however, relieve her from liability for any gross negligence or other fraudulent acts committed while serving on the board.

PRINCIPAL DUTIES AND POWERS OF DIRECTORS

A director has one vote, and generally, the majority rules. Corporate directors, acting as a collective board and not as individuals, hire and fire corporate officers, i.e., the president and vice president establish director and officer compensation, set corporate policy regarding product and service pricing, oversee major contract negotiations, make decisions regarding the declaration and payment of dividends, obtain corporate financing, enter into borrowing arrangements, execute the issuance of notes and bonds, authorize the purchase and sale of major corporate assets, and commence lawsuits against third parties.

The board may hire outside consultants to assist in the management of the corporation so long as the board retains ultimate supervisory authority.

A director has an absolute right to inspect the corporate books and records that can be enforced in a court of law. Should a director abuse this right, she is subject to damages for breach of her fiduciary duty. She may also be removed from the board.

EXAMPLE Selena Troy owns 15 percent of the voting common shares of the Down Corporation. She heads up a group of shareholders who are dissatisfied with the performance of the current board and opposes their reelection in 20XX. Selena has asked for a list of the shareholders so she can procure their proxies. Down's board of directors refuses her request. Selena can go to court to force the board to give her the list. The acquisition of the list for the solicitation of proxies is a legitimate business reason.

Directors generally have the authority to designate executive committees composed of at least two directors, to exercise board authority in such matters as executive compensation, employee pension and retirement benefits, and accounting principles to be adopted by the corporation. Executive committees generally do not have the power to approve basic fundamental changes in the operation of the corporation, such as a merger or consolidation with another corporation. Delegation of authority to the executive committee does not, however, relieve the entire board of directors of any liability with respect to any decisions made by the committee.

While directors generally have the authority to designate executive committees, they do not have the power to delegate policy-making and discretionary powers to corporate officers.

What the applicable RMBCA section says *Section 8.25 states that unless the articles of incorporation or bylaws provide otherwise, a board of directors may create one or more committees and appoint members of the board of directors to serve on them. Each committee must have two or more members who serve at the pleasure of the board of directors. The committees may function pursuant to powers granted by the board, but do not have the power to authorize distributions, approve a plan of merger, adopt, amend, or repeal bylaws, or fill vacancies on the board of directors or on any committee.*

TIME AND PLACE OF DIRECTORS MEETINGS

Meetings of the board, whether regular, special, or annual, may be held at any designated place either within or outside the state of incorporation unless otherwise provided for in the articles of incorporation or bylaws.

What the applicable RMBCA section says *Section 8.01, governing directors meetings, states that the board of directors may hold irregular or special meetings in or out of this state. Second, unless the articles of incorporation or bylaws provide otherwise, the board of directors may permit any or all directors to participate in a regular or special meeting by, or conduct the meeting through the use of, any means of communication by which all directors participating may simultaneously hear each other during the meeting. A director participating in a meeting by this means is deemed to be present in person at the meeting.*

OBSERVATION Directors at many companies hit by the recent accounting scandals such as Enron, Tyco, and WorldCom followed most of the accepted standards for boards, such as showing up regularly for meetings and establishing codes of ethics. They failed, however, to question enough and to think of dissent as an obligation—qualities that directors at the highest-performing companies routinely exhibit.

HOW A BOARD OF DIRECTORS MEETING FUNCTIONS

In general, the vote of the majority of the directors present if a quorum (the minimum number of directors that must be present before business can be transacted) is present, constitutes an act of the board.

What the applicable RMBCA section says *Section 8.24, governing directors' quorum and voting, states that unless the articles of incorporation or bylaws require a greater number, a quorum of a board of directors shall consist of a majority of the fixed number of directors if the corporation has a fixed board size; or majority of a defined number of directors are present. The articles of incorporation or bylaws may authorize a quorum of directors to consist of no fewer than one third of a fixed or defined number of directors.*

Note that some very small corporations think that these meetings are unnecessary. They are wrong.

The board of directors generally meet once a month. Smaller corporations may find that a meeting every three to six months, or even annually is legally sufficient to take care of any old, current, or new business. Special meetings can be called if demanded by unusual circumstances. Directors may also participate in meetings by means of a conference call or other similar procedure so long as they can hear one another. A corporation may also be bound for the actions taken by the board even if there has been no actual meeting.

EXAMPLE Lawrence Behr, a member of the board of directors of the Premier Fuel Corporation negotiated with the Star Real Estate Ltd. for newer and larger office quarters. No formal board meeting was held regarding the authorization and signing of the contract, but a majority of Premier's other board members were aware of the transaction and knew that larger office space was needed but never voiced their objections to the deal. The facts indicate that there was ratification or acquiescence of the contract by the board.

The date of any regular directors meetings are found in the articles of incorporation or bylaws. Minutes are kept of the meeting by an officer of the corporation, usually the corporate secretary.

OBSERVATION *Some articles of incorporation require a unanimous vote of all of the directors in order to validate any action taken by the board of directors. This type of provision is dangerous in that it can lead to "the tyranny of one" whereby one director will refuse to validate the actions approved by the remaining members of the board unless his demands are met.*

DIRECTORS' COMPENSATION

Directors have the authority to fix their own compensation. With the increased risk of possible shareholders' lawsuits for mismanagement, directors' compensation has shown a noticeable increase. Directors fees are fully taxable for federal tax purposes.

What the applicable RMBCA section says *Section 8.11 states that unless the articles of incorporation or bylaws provide otherwise, the board of directors may fix the compensation of directors.*

LIABILITY OF DIRECTORS FOR INDIVIDUAL AND BOARD ACTIONS

Corporate directors have traditionally been held personally liable for gross negligence only and not for normal errors of business judgment.

What the applicable RMBCA section says *Section 8.30, governing the general standards of conduct applicable to directors, states that a director shall discharge his duties as a director, including his duties as a member of a committee, in good faith, with the care of an ordinarily prudent person in a similar position, and in a manner that he believes to be in the best interests of the corporation. In discharging his duties, the director is entitled to rely on the information, opinions, reports, and statements presented by other corporate officers, other employees,*

legal counsel, public accountants, and other experts. A director shall not be liable for any action taken as a director, or for any failure to take action if he performs his duties in compliance with this section.

Thus, under the so-called business judgment rule, a corporate director or officer can usually avoid liability for poor business judgments. Directors can also be held liable if they knowingly, or even unknowingly, authorize the corporation to engage in ultra vires acts (acts beyond the scope of the corporation), and for the corporation's failure to comply with federal and/or state laws and regulations. They may also be subject to criminal penalties. Liability has also been found when the directors declare improper dividends.

EXAMPLE Martin Bonner, a certified public accountant and director of the Worthington Pump Co. Ltd., voted with the corporation's board to declare a dividend that was in fact illegal. The shareholders can remove him for negligence in office and hold him liable for damages. As a CPA, he should have known that the dividend was illegal.

Directors are also held accountable after being put on notice of possible wrongdoing or negligent acts by corporate employees if they fail to investigate.

EXAMPLE The board of directors of Purifoy Carton Corporation authorized Max Samson, its president, to sell one of the corporation's buildings, a major asset. It appeared that the president subsequently entered into a contract whereby the building was sold at half its alleged true value to his father. Several shareholders complained to the board, which, in turn, failed to investigate the allegations. Finally, one of the complaining shareholders hired an independent real estate firm, which verified the fact that the building was sold at a price far below its true market value. The directors will be held liable for failing to investigate the questionable acts of one of its key corporate employees after being put on notice.

Directors who *personally* guarantee the faithful contracts and other obligations in their own capacity as private individuals are personally liable.

EXAMPLE Vera Tow was a director of the India Spice Corp. Ltd. The corporation was in financial difficulties and the corporate treasurer asked Vera to personally guarantee all contracts for the purchase of goods. Fearing that the corporation would go bankrupt if it was unable to purchase its inventory, Vera personally signed all subsequent corporate contracts as guarantor. Unfortunately, the corporation was unable to pay for the goods, and Vera was forced to pay out of her own pocket. Of course, Vera can always seek reimbursement from the corporation, which under the circumstances appears highly unlikely.

Directors may, however, engage in independent business so long as these activities do not compete with the corporation's business.

While corporate directors may be held accountable for gross negligence and other acts of noncompliance with various laws, courts rarely interfere with a decision of the board unless fraud or intentional wrong can be shown. Courts cannot force directors to act wisely, but they can compel them to act honestly.

Thus, as more and more corporations find themselves in financial difficulties due to poor management performance, there is an increasing tendency by shareholders to sue the directors for their mistakes. Many directors are now finding themselves at greater risk if they choose to serve on a corporate board. As a result of their increased legal exposure, most corporations maintain insurance polices that indemnify the directors for damages that may result from adverse judgments. In effect, by paying the insurance premiums, the corporation is indirectly agreeing to reimburse the directors for any liabilities associated with their performance as directors.

Corporate policy regarding indemnification for the costs of defending a lawsuit, as well as repayment for any adverse judgments rendered against a director, is found in the corporation's articles of incorporation and its bylaws.

···

What the applicable RMBCA section says *Section 8.51, which governs corporation indemnification for a director's legal costs, fees, and judgments, states that a corporation may indemnify an individual made a party to a proceeding because he is a director if the director conducted himself in good faith and reasonably believed that he was acting in the best interests of the corporation. He may also be reimbursed in the case of any criminal proceeding if he had no reasonable cause to believe that his conduct was unlawful.*

···

HOW TO AVOID DIRECTORS' DEADLOCK

Dissension and directors' deadlock is very common in a closely held corporation. In a typical closely held corporation, the shareholders elect themselves both directors and officers, and friction and distrust is commonplace. A deadlock usually occurs when there are an equal number of directors who have split their votes equally on a corporate matter thereby preventing the corporation from functioning. The result is potential chaos and possible bankruptcy to a profitable corporation. There are, however, mechanisms that can be utilized to prevent directors' deadlock from permanently harming the corporation.

One such technique is the buy-sell agreement whereby all the parties agree either in advance or at the time the deadlock occurs that one faction should buy out the other at a fair price. Often it is the senior directors who will buy out the junior members. A second possibility is to have one of the shareholders set a price at which he is willing to repurchase the stock of the other shareholders. Buy-sell agreements are discussed in Chaps. 15 and 16.

A third possibility is to simply dissolve the corporation. For dissolution to occur, there must be a directors' deadlock that the shareholders are unable to break that will eventually cause the corporation irreparable damage and possibly force it into bankruptcy. Corporate dissolution is discussed in detail in Chap. 13.

A fourth possibility is to submit the issue causing the deadlock to an arbitrator. The advantages of arbitration are that it is quick, inexpensive, and informal as opposed to a court proceeding.

Finally, the parties can agree in advance that where there is an even number of directors and the split is 50/50, the parties shall petition a court of proper jurisdiction to appoint a provisional director who will determine the facts and render a decision, thereby breaking the deadlock.

UNAUTHORIZED ACTS: THE ULTRA VIRES DOCTRINE

Operating as a director carries not only a duty of loyalty to the corporation, but the concurrent duty to act within the legal confines of the articles of incorporation. Most corporate articles give the corporation broad operating powers that also carry the implied power to undertake any transaction that is incident to the normal operation of the corporation. Unfortunately, a corporation may enter into a transaction that is beyond the legal authority of the corporation. Such acts are termed *ultra vires* acts, meaning beyond the authority of the corporation to act. Ultra vires acts are not necessarily illegal, but an illegal act would automatically be ultra vires.

EXAMPLE Klondike Soda Distributors Inc., purchased 10,000 cases of vodka for resale. State statutes require that a corporation engaged in the wholesale purchase and resale of beer, wine, and spirits have a liquor license. In addition, all corporate officers must be licensed by the state liquor authority to sell such products. Officers receive their licenses after an extensive personal background check. Since the corporation has not met state legal standards, the purchase of the vodka is unauthorized, illegal, and ultra vires.

OBSERVATION *A corporation is prohibited from making political contributions in federal elections by the Federal Elections Campaign Act of 1974 (18 United States Code Section 321). Such contributions are unlawful and carry severe civil penalties for both the board of directors and the corporation.*

What the applicable RMBCA section says *Section 3.04, which governs ultra vires acts, states that:*

a. *Except as provided in section (b) below, the validity of corporate action may not be challenged on the ground that the corporation lacks or lacked power to act.*

b. *A corporation's power to act may be challenged:*

1. *in a proceeding by a shareholder against the corporation to prevent the ultra vires act;*

2. *in a proceeding by the corporation, directly, derivatively, or through a receiver, trustee, or other legal representative, against an incumbent or former director, officer, employee, or agent of the corporation; or*

3. *in a proceeding by the Attorney General for fraudulent or illegal acts.*

c. *In a shareholder's proceeding to prevent an unauthorized corporate act, the court may prevent or set aside the act, if equitable to all the parties to the proceeding, and may award damages for loss (other than anticipated profits) suffered by the corporation or another party because of the prevention of the unauthorized act.*

CHAPTER 10

Corporate Management Structure: The Role of the Officers

INTRODUCTION

Corporate officers are hired by the board of directors. In certain instances, the articles of incorporation may provide that the shareholders and not the directors have the authority to hire corporate officers. (See Chap. 9.) Although in the general sense the board of directors are the definitive administrators of corporation policy, the corporate officers are the true agents of the corporation. Each officer has the authority to bind the corporation for the day-to-day acts within the officer's actual or apparent authority.

EXAMPLE 1 Martha Fray is a major shareholder and director of the Wisconsin Sales Corporation. She hires Johanna Norton as vice president of sales and signs her to a two-year contract. Norton is aware that Fray is not a corporate officer but accepts the employment anyway. Xavier Hollis, president of the corporation, repudiates the agreement, and Norton sues. The corporation will prevail because an individual who is a director has no actual or apparent authority to bind the corporation.

EXAMPLE 2 Suppose that in **EXAMPLE 1**, Norton was unaware that Fray was not a corporate officer and acted in good faith in accepting employment. Since it appeared that Fray acted within her apparent authority as a corporate "officer," Norton will pre-

vail in a subsequent lawsuit for breach of her employment contract.

ELECTION OF OFFICERS: PERIOD OF SERVICE

Officers serve for a period as fixed by the articles of incorporation or bylaws. Unless the articles of incorporation or bylaws state otherwise, corporate officers generally serve for one year. They may also be removed during this period with or without cause by the board of directors.

EXAMPLE Felton Smith is hired as president of Kimble Threads Inc. for a period of one year. After six months, Kimble's board meets and determines that Smith's performance as president is unsatisfactory and removes him. The board has exercised their legal prerogative of removal. Of course, there is always the likelihood that Smith will sue for unlawful breach of his employment contract claiming that he was terminated without just cause.

An officer elected by the shareholders cannot be removed by the board, although the board does have the authority to suspend the officer's powers for cause. On the other hand, an officer elected by the shareholders may be removed with or without cause by a vote of the shareholders.

EXAMPLE William Hyams was president of the Radcliffe Laser Disc Corporation. He held his position by a vote of the shareholders. The corporation was having financial difficulties selling its products due to tough competition from other forms of entertainment. Therefore, Hyams formed the Cleveland Sound Corporation making himself the sole shareholder. Cleveland then used a "front man," and acting as its president negotiated a contract whereby Radcliffe sold laser discs to Cleveland at a 50 percent discount, well below their regular wholesale price. He also kept Radcliffe's board of directors in complete ignorance about the financial terms of the contract. Upon discovery, the board had the authority to suspend him from office for cause and to seek his eventual removal.

If no successor has been appointed, a corporate officer holds over and continues to serve in office until re-election or appointment of a new officer.

QUALIFICATIONS OF A CORPORATE OFFICER

There are no statutory qualifications for being a corporate officer. However, the articles of incorporation or bylaws may require that an officer be either a director or own a stated number of the corporation's shares. Some states permit an officer to hold more than one office but other states may have limitations. For example, New York State statutes permit two or more offices to be held by the same person except for the offices of president and secretary.

DESIGNATION OF CORPORATE OFFICERS

The usual corporate officers appointed by the board are the president, vice president, secretary, treasurer, and general manager. In addition, the nature of the corporation's business may require additional corporate officers, such as assistant treasurers, and auditors. Subordinate officers, pursuant to the corporate bylaws, are usually appointed by senior officers.

The President

The president usually has the authority to manage the business of the corporation. These dealings include the signing of contracts, stock certificates, checks, notes, hiring key personnel, institute corporate litigation, and making all other commitments on behalf of the corporation. However, absent specific authority from the board of directors, the president does not have the authority to make unusual or extraordinary contracts. Some corporations refer to the president as the "CEO" or "chief executive officer" but use of this imprecise title varies from corporation to corporation.

EXAMPLE Francine Whitman, president of the Alluvia Paper and Timber Co. Inc. entered into a contract with Sturdevant Real Estate Corporation to sell all of its timberlands to Sturdevant. Without these valuable lands, Alluvia cannot continue to operate. This extraordinary contract, absent authority from the board of directors, is beyond the authority of the president to execute.

The Vice President

Although the vice president has no authority in his individual capacity, he is empowered to act in place of the president in case of the latter's death, illness, or incapacity. The vice president may also be authorized to perform additional duties and may also be subject to certain restrictions as stated in the corporation's bylaws.

EXAMPLE Calvin Cooler is vice president of Seaforth Towel Co. Ltd. Calvin, although an officer, was not a director. The bylaws of the corporation required that any person holding the office of president must also be a director. Upon the death of the president of the corporation, Calvin would be unable to become president due to the restriction in the bylaws.

OBSERVATION *Where the bylaws require that the president also be a director, removal from the board would automatically disqualify the president from continuing in such capacity.*

The Corporate Secretary

The corporate secretary exercises authority equal to that of a general manager. In her limited role, she usually attends all corporate meetings, keeps minutes, distributes corporate notices, certifies corporate records, and has possession of the corporate seal when the circumstances dictate. Unless specifically given such authority, the corporate secretary has no right to enter into contracts on behalf of the corporation.

The Corporate Treasurer

The corporate treasurer is the chief financial officer of the corporation. As chief custodian of the corporate funds, she is frequently designated to countersign notes, checks, miscellaneous corporate instruments, and stock certificates. She also has the duty to see the corporate records are accurately kept to insure the faithful reporting of the corporation's financial condition. The corporate treasurer, like the corporate secretary, cannot enter into contracts on behalf of the corporation.

The General Manager

The role of the general manager is to administer the ordinary business of the corporation. Her general functions include hiring and firing employees, setting their compensation, purchasing materials and supplies, and paying corporate debts. If the corporation is a small corporation, the directors or shareholders may have narrowed these functions. The office of general manager requires no formal appointment board of directors and is usually appointed by the president of the corporation.

Unauthorized acts committed by corporate officers, unless illegal, may be ratified by the express authority of the board of directors. The board may also impliedly ratify the unofficial acts of the officer by accepting the benefits of the transaction.

EXAMPLE The vice president of a corporation, although authorized to enter into contracts not exceeding $100,000, entered into a $1 million contract. Shortly thereafter, the president of the corporation, who was also a director, authorized payment. The board was duly apprised of the payment but no formal action was taken by them to approve the payment. The board was deemed to have impliedly accepted the benefits of the unauthorized act.

What the applicable RMBCA section says *Under Section 8.41, each officer has the authority to perform the duties set forth in the bylaws or those prescribed by the board of directors.*

RESIGNATION OR REMOVAL OF OFFICERS

An officer can resign at any time by delivering notice to the corporation. The resignation is usually effective when the notice is delivered to the corporation. The board of directors may also remove a director either with or without cause at any time. The resignation or removal of an officer does not absolve him of any liability for negligent, fraudulent, or criminal acts committed while in office.

What the applicable RMBCA section says *Under Section 8.43, an officer can resign at any time by delivering notice to the corporation. The resignation is effective when the notice is delivered to the corporation unless the notice specifies a later effective date. The board of directors may also remove a director either with or without cause at any time.*

COMPENSATION OF THE OFFICERS

Officers' compensation is fixed by the board of directors. In view of the litigious nature of most shareholders, officers who are also board members should avoid voting on a resolution fixing their compensation. Officers' compensation must be reasonable in amount based upon the size and complexity of the corporation's activities. Excessive compensation is considered a waste of corporate assets. Directors who approve excessive compensation to officers can be held liable for negligence in failing to determine the appropriate amount of compensation due an officer.

EXAMPLE Frank Donald is hired as vice president in charge of marketing for the Rya Manufacturing Corporation. Although various amounts of compensation have been discussed between the board and Donald, no specific amount has been agreed upon. Donald starts work and begins receiving a small draw on which to live until his salary is determined. After working three months, the board has still not come to a decision regarding his salary. In disgust, Donald quits the corporation and sues for his unpaid salary. He may recover the reasonable value of his services.

OBSERVATION *Never hire a corporate officer without first determining her rate of compensation, and other* *employee benefits, i.e., group insurance, stock options, medical benefits, etc. in advance.*

TRANSACTIONS WITH THE CORPORATION

Officers, like directors, are fiduciaries who owe complete loyalty to the corporation.

What the applicable RMBCA section says *Section 8.42, which governs the standards of conduct of a corporate officer, states that an officer shall discharge his duties in good faith, with the care of an ordinarily prudent person in a similar position, and in a manner that he believes to be in the best interests of the corporation. In discharging his duties, the officer is entitled to rely on the information, opinions, reports, and statements presented by other corporate officers or employees, legal counsel, public accountants, and other experts. An officer shall not be liable if he performs his duties in compliance with this section.*

Officers may, however, make contracts with the corporation so long as they deal openly and in good faith. If they secretly benefit in their dealings with the corporation, they may be required to disgorge their profits to the corporation because they have breached their fiduciary duty. The corporation may also be entitled to damages. Officers must also refrain from taking personal advantage of corporate opportunities that are presented to the corporation.

EXAMPLE Margaret Johnson was the president of Acme Investments Ltd. The corporation specialized in buying and selling stocks, bonds, and other types of securities. Margaret was personally given the right to purchase 100 acres of valuable shorefront property and exercised this option. Margaret need not account to Acme since the opportunity came to her personally and the corporation was not in the business of acquiring real estate. Of course, if she later negotiates the sale of the land to Acme, and realizes a secret profit, she could be compelled to account to the corporation.

Officers may, however, engage in independent businesses so long as their activities do not compete with the corporation's business.

EXAMPLE Preston Phillips is president of the Jacoby Medical Supply Corporation. The corporation manufactures and sells medical equipment, office furniture for medical offices, personalized stationery, office computers, and medical software. Preston sets up another corporation, making himself the sole shareholder, that will sell furniture to the general public. Preston's new corporation is in direct competition with that of his current employer, and Preston is in breach of his fiduciary duties.

LIABILITY FOR NEGLIGENCE

Officers, like directors, are liable for gross negligence while in office. The corporate officer is also held liable for the negligent acts of subordinates that she could have detected through the exercise of reasonable care and business judgment. Note that as a senior officer of the corporation, she must review the conduct and activities of subordinates. Officers are not, however, liable for ordinary judgmental errors made in the course of exercising their corporate responsibilities.

EXAMPLE Wallace Ford, treasurer of the Totem Woodworking Corporation, was required to obtain the countersignature of either the president or, in his absence, vice president of the corporation where the amount exceeded $10,000. Through a series of ingenious stratagems, he was able to forge the signatures of either corporate officer when required to do so. The corporation usually issued at least ten checks weekly in amounts exceeding $10,000. Such amounts were needed to meet the weekly payroll, as well as inventory purchases. All of the officers met weekly to discuss corporate business. At no time was the absence of the issuance of large check amounts ever discussed. Upon discovery, the corporate treasurer was held criminally liable for fraud and immediately dismissed. The shareholders and directors may also hold the president and vice president for negligence. It appears that they were derelict in failing to question how the corporation could issue checks for large amounts over an extended period of time without being asked to countersign.

OBSERVATION *In the above situation, the outside auditors could also be held liable for failing to detect the fraud perpetrated by the treasurer.*

While corporate officers may be held liable for the acts of subordinates that they could have detected through the exercise of reasonable care and business judgment, directors are only liable *after being put on notice* of possible wrongdoing by corporate employees and fail to investigate.

LIABILITY BASED UPON PERSONAL GUARANTEE OF A CORPORATE OFFICER

Officers who *personally* guarantee the faithful contracts and other obligations in their own capacity as private individuals and not as corporate officers are personally liable.

EXAMPLE Paul Morton was president of Cutie Pie Clothing Co. Inc. The Bell Corporation wished to enter into a contract to sell Cutie Pie $1 million of raw materials for the manufacturing of clothing. Fearing that Cutie Pie would be unable to pay for the goods, Bell asked Morton to personally sign the contract in his own individual capacity, as well as in his capacity as corporate president. Should Cutie Pie prove unable to pay for the goods, Morton will have to pay for the goods out of his own pocket. Of course, Morton can always seek reimbursement from Cutie Pie.

DETERMINING REASONABLE COMPENSATION UNDER THE IRC: PAYMENTS TO SHAREHOLDER-EMPLOYEES

With corporate tax rates as high as 35 percent, the denial of part of an officer's compensation as a deduction can result in a hefty tax bite.

Compensation paid to a shareholder-officer, such as a president or vice president in the form of salary, bonus, or fringe benefits is tax deductible. Compensation payments are deductible by the corporation as long as they are reasonable and necessary in amount. They are also taxable to the officer-employee. If however, the salary is deemed unreasonable, excess compensation may be treated as a nondeductible dividend thereby resulting in an additional tax liability to the corporation.

EXAMPLE The South Gas Corporation is 100% owned by Philip Merritt, who also serves as the corporation's president. For the year 20XX, the income statement of the corporation appeared as follows:

Sales		$900,000
Cost of goods sold		500,000
Gross Profit		400,000
Operating expenses	$150,000	
Merritt's salary as president of South Gas	250,000	400,000
Net income		$ -0-

After the tax return was filed in 20X1 for 20XX, the Internal Revenue Service, on audit, challenged Merritt's salary payment claiming that his salary was not reasonable in amount. After a lengthy battle, the corporation settled for a salary deduction of $200,000, as opposed to $250,000. Assuming a corporate tax rate of 15 percent on the first $50,000 of corporate taxable income, the corporation will owe an additional $7,500 ($50,000 × 15 percent) in taxes. However, Merritt's total income from the corporation remains unchanged since the disallowed $50,000 is now treated as dividend income in Merritt's hands.

Reasonableness of compensation is determined on a case-by-case basis. Such factors as the officer-employee's qualifications, nature and extent of his work, the complexities and size of the business, salary amounts paid to officers in similar positions in other corporations within the same industry, and whether nondeductible dividends were declared and paid are some of the elements that determine reasonableness.

The board of directors and the corporation can avoid the question of unreasonable compensation by setting the officer's salary at the beginning of the year in a written contract so as to be independent of the corporation's final net income for the year. The directors' resolution fixing the officer's salary should also state the reasons for the high salary, such as increased sales and responsibilities and outstanding past performance.

Closely held corporations should also consider payments of tax-free benefits to shareholder employees, such as medical plans and group-term life insurance.

Some owners of closely held corporations elect to be taxed under the rules of Subchapter S in order to avoid double taxation. Other owners of closely held corporations retain regular corporation, or Subchapter C status, to utilize the 15 to 35 percent marginal corporate tax rates and to benefit from tax-free fringe benefits, such as health and accident insurance.

NEGOTIATING A COMPREHENSIVE EMPLOYMENT AGREEMENT

The following is a checklist of points that must be covered in any employment contract.

1. The names of the parties.
2. The title and duties associated with the position.
3. That the officer shall engage in no other outside activities without permission from the board of directors.
4. The period of employment.
5. Compensation and other benefits.
6. Conditions under which employment will be terminated.
7. What the estate of the officer is to receive in case of death.
8. The rights of the parties in case of the officer's sickness or disability.
9. Retirement benefits.
10. The officer cannot disclose any trade secrets or confidential information learned by reason of her association either during or after ceasing to be associated with the corporation.
11. For a certain period of time after the officer ceases to be associated with the corporation, she will not manage, operate, or join any business entity such as a partnership or corporation that competes with her current employer.
12. Any inventions, designs, etc. conceived during the employment of the officer shall belong to the corporation.
13. Should a breach of contract occur, all parties shall agree to submit to personal jurisdiction before a proper court in the state where the principal office of the corporation is located.
14. That the agreement shall be governed by the laws of a particular state.
15. That this agreement supersedes all previous employment agreements (if any) entered into between the parties.
16. The agreement must be signed by both parties.

A comprehensive employment agreement is an excellent method of avoiding potential conflicts and lawsuits.

CHAPTER 11

The Corporate Ownership: The Role of the Shareholders

INTRODUCTION

The stockholder is the true owner of the corporation, whether at law, where the stock is held in the name of the shareholder, or in equity where the stock is held by one person for the benefit of another. Examples would be shares held by guardians for minors or by executors or administrators of an estate.

....

What the applicable RMBCA section says *Section 1.40(22) states that a "Shareholder" means the person in whose name shares are registered in the records of the corporation or the beneficial owner of shares to the extent of the rights granted by a nominee certificate on file with the corporation.*

....

Shares, which are treated as transferable personal property (meaning that it is movable as opposed to real estate, which cannot be moved) can also be the subject of co-ownership, such as a joint tenancy (with rights of survivorship) or a tenancy in common.

EXAMPLE 1 Barnes and Nobel own 100 shares of the Pennsalt Corporation as joint tenants with the right of survivorship. If Barnes dies, Barnes's ownership in the shares passes automatically to Nobel and not to Barnes's heirs.

EXAMPLE 2 Barnes and Nobel own 100 shares of the Pennsalt Corporation as tenants in common. Barnes stipulates in his will that when he dies, Endicott is to receive his interest in the shares. When Barnes dies, Endicott receives 50 shares. If Barnes sold his interest to Zemoli before he dies, then Zemoli and Nobel would be co-owners as tenants in common.

When a corporation issues shares, the name and address of the purchasing shareholder is recorded in the corporation's stockholders' ledger account together with the number of shares owned. This person is called the "record owner." If a shareholder pays for the share but fails to subsequently receive them, she is still the "equitable or beneficial owner" who may compel the corporation to issue the shares to her together with any applicable dividends.

A QUICK OVERVIEW OF THE RIGHTS AND PRIVILEGES OF A SHAREHOLDER

The more common rights of a shareholder is the right to a stock certificate, the right to transfer the stock, the right to vote, the right to dividends if and when declared, the right to inspect the corporate books, a possible "pre-emptive right" to purchase a percentage of any new issuances, and the right to a proportional share of corporate assets upon a corporate dissolution.

OBSERVATION *As discussed in Chap. 8, where a shareholder claims that the security has been lost, destroyed, or wrongfully taken, the issuing corporation must issue a new security in place of the original security if certain requirements imposed by the issuer are met.*

BASIC RECORDS RELATING TO STOCK: THE STOCK CERTIFICATE AND STOCK TRANSFER BOOK

Stock certificate and stock transfer books are part of the special corporate records involved in accounting for stock. A stock certificate book contains stock certificates that are issued when bought by the shareholder. They are removed from the stock book when issued leaving a stub on which is written the name of the stockholder, the number of shares issued, the serial number applicable to each share (i.e., certificate number 777) and the date the shares were issued. The stock certificate ledger contains the names of the stockholders, their addresses, the number on the certificates, and the number of shares issued. A sample of the stock transfer ledger appears on pages 218 and 219.

OBSERVATION *In many states, the board of directors may provide for uncertificated stock under Article 8 of the UCC. This means that the actual stock need not be issued. Instead, the corporation sends the holder of stock a letter or some other form of notice containing the same information found on the face of the stock certificates.*

What the applicable RMBCA section says *Section 6.26, governing shares without certificates, states that unless the articles of incorporation or bylaws provide otherwise, the corporation may authorize the issue of some or all of the shares of any or all classes without certificates. Within a reasonable period of time after the issue, the corporation must send the shareholder a letter or some other form of notice containing the same information found on the face of the stock certificates.*

The corporation must maintain a current list of shareholders so that dividend payments, notices of annual stockholder meetings, and voting proxies may be sent to the proper persons.

THE EXERCISE OF DIRECT AND INDIRECT CONTROL OF THE CORPORATION BY SHAREHOLDERS

Generally, unless they sit on the board of directors, shareholders have no authority to control the day-to-day operations of the corporation. Indirectly, shareholders can exert their influence by electing directors and amending the certificate of incorporation, which requires a vote of the majority of the outstanding shares entitled to vote.

Shareholders may also, by a two-thirds vote of all outstanding shares, approve such organizational changes, such as a merger or sale of all corporate assets.

As discussed in Chap. 9, some state statutes permit the "sterilization" or restriction of the authority of the board of directors of a nonpublic or closely held corporation. This limitation must be set forth in the articles of incorporation. Thus, all management authority is transferred to the shareholders. This arrangement also nullifies the shareholders' benefit of limited liability with respect to any negligent acts or illegal acts authorized by them acting in place of a duly constituted board of directors.

EXAMPLE A provision in the certificate of incorporation of Standard Horse Farms Inc., a closely held corporation, transfers to all of the shareholders the board of directors' authority to manage the corporation. The shareholders' management powers also subject them to personal liability arising from the fact that they, acting in place of the directors, are initiating and approving corporate actions.

What the applicable RMBCA section says *Section 7.32, regarding shareholder agreements, states that an agreement among the shareholders of a corporation that complies with this section is effective among the shareholders and the corporation even though it is inconsistent with one or more other provisions of the RMBCA in that it eliminates the board of directors or restricts the discretion or powers of the board of directors. The existence of an agreement authorized by this section shall be noted conspicuously on the front or back of each certificate for outstanding shares or on the information statement required within a reasonable time after the issuance of the certificates.*

An agreement authorized by this section shall cease to be effective when shares of the corporation are listed on a national securities exchange or regularly traded market.

OBSERVATION *Shareholders' agreements cannot be used to deny the right of shareholders to inspect the corporation's books and records, to bring stockholders' derivative actions, or to seek dissolution alleging corporate waste of assets.*

CONVENING SHAREHOLDERS MEETINGS

Shareholders may convene either "regular" or "special" meetings at a time and place fixed in the bylaws. "Regular" meetings are held at least once a year for the election of directors and to conduct any other required corporate business. "Special" meetings are called when circumstances dictate.

To control the number of special meetings that may be called by troublesome shareholders, the corporate bylaws may state that a minimum percentage of shares, i.e., 10 percent to 50 percent, be owned by the shareholder demanding that a special meeting of shareholders be convened. In addition, many corporate statutes state that a shareholder may only call a special meeting with regard to matters that are the proper subject of shareholder review. Matters regarding the normal activities of the corporation, such as the hiring and firing of officers, setting product prices, and borrowing money, are not subject to shareholder action. However, shareholder action is permitted where the directors contemplate fundamental changes in the corporate structure or the election or removal of a corporate director.

EXAMPLE Brenda Carton, a major shareholder of Solis Paper Goods Corp. Ltd., was unhappy with the performance of the board of directors. She felt that the directors had taken a series of steps that were detrimental to the future growth of the corporation and wanted to have their actions reviewed at a duly called special meeting of the shareholders. The certificate of incorporation stated that any person holding more than five percent of the outstanding common shares of the corporation may request that board of directors (or designated corporate officer) call a special meeting within 30 days after a written request for such meeting. Pursuant to the corporation's bylaws, the meeting must be held at corporate headquarters. Following such guidelines, Brenda sought to have a special meeting of the shareholders convened. Such action cannot be taken by Brenda since her request pertains to the board's activities involving the normal operations of the corporation.

PLACE AND TIME OF MEETINGS

The place designated for shareholders meetings may be within or outside the state of incorporation. If no place is designated, most state laws fix the place of the meeting at the corporate headquarters. All notices must state the place, time, and hour of the meeting. Notice of the meeting must be given to every shareholder entitled to vote, either personally or by mail. Notice of any meetings need not be given to any shareholder who gives the corporation a signed waiver of notice prior to a called meeting of the shareholders.

What the applicable RMBCA section says *Section 7.20, governing shareholders' list of meetings, states that after fixing a record date for a meeting, a corporation shall prepare an alphabetical list of the names of all its shareholders who are entitled to notice of a shareholders meeting. The shareholders' list must be available for inspection by any shareholder, beginning two business days after notice of the meeting is given or which the list was prepared. Refusal or failure to prepare or make available the shareholders' list does not affect the validity of action taken at the meeting.*

WHO IS ELIGIBLE TO VOTE?

Every shareholder who is registered on the books as owning shares is entitled to vote. If the shares are pledged and transferred to a pledgee or nominee, the pledgor, who is still the true owner, is entitled to vote. Shares held by a domestic or foreign corporation can be voted by an officer of the owner shareholder corporation as the owner corporation's bylaws permit. Eligibility of a shareholder to vote is determined by the record date, which is fixed in advance by the board of directors. The record date is generally ten to fifty days before the date of the shareholders' scheduled meeting. Trustees of a voting trust may vote shares only if the shares have been transferred into the trustee's name. Treasury shares owned by the corporation are *not* entitled to vote.

WHAT IS A PROXY?

A proxy is a power of attorney given by a stockholder authorizing a designated person to vote the shareholder's stock. A proxy must be in writing and signed by the shareholder granting the proxy. The person exercising the proxy need not be a shareholder in the corporation although this is usually the case. Proxies are generally valid for a period not exceeding eleven months but can be extended.

Proxies are generally revocable. Proxies can also be revoked due to the death or incompetency of the shareholder. Proxies can be made *irrevocable* by a shareholder, who in a signed authorization (or appointment) granting the proxy, states that it is irrevocable, and the person granted the proxy has either agreed to buy the shares or has loaned the shareholder money and is holding the shares as security against repayment. Irrevocable proxies are also created pursuant to a voting trust agreement (see the next section).

What the applicable RMBCA section says *Section 7.22, governing proxies, states that a shareholder may vote his shares in person or by proxy. An appointment of a proxy is valid for eleven months unless a longer period is expressly provided in the appointment form. A proxy is revocable unless the appointment form states that it is irrevocable and is coupled with an interest (meaning that the proxy holder has an interest in the stock).*

VOTING TRUST AGREEMENTS

The voting trust agreement is a device to concentrate shareholder control in one or more trustees who seek to control corporate affairs by electing specific directors. Voting trustees can also exercise any other ordinary shareholder rights associated with the ownership of the shares. A voting trust arrangement requires that the shareholders transfer their shares to a voting trustee who will in return issue voting trust certificates to the beneficial owners (the shareholders who are the real owners of the shares). The voting trustee is the legal owner of the shares who can vote the shares as she sees fit. Thus, the voting trustee occupies a fiduciary position in relation to the shareholder members and can be removed by them for violating this trust. Most voting trust agreements are good for ten years and can be renewed for an additional ten year period.

Voting trust agreements are generally irrevocable unless all of the members mutually agree to terminate the arrangement.

What the applicable RMBCA section says *Section 7.30, governing voting trusts, states that one or more shareholders may create a voting trust, conferring on the trustee the right to vote or otherwise act for them. They must sign an agreement setting out the provisions of the trust (which may include anything consistent with its purpose) and transferring their shares to the trustee. A voting trust is valid for not more than ten years after its effective date and may be extended for an additional ten year period.*

VOTING AGREEMENTS

Two or more shareholders may enter into an agreement to vote their shares in a certain way. This "pooling agreement," which must be in writing, requires that the members cast their votes in a certain way, such as which directors to elect. The advantage of a voting agreement over a voting trust agreement is that it is easier to form and that unlike a voting trust agreement, legal title remains with the shareholders. To avoid potential conflicts among the parties, most voting agreements contain an arbitration clause stating that all disputes arising among the parties be settled by binding arbitration. Some agreements contain a provision giving the arbitrator an irrevocable proxy allowing her to vote the shares as she sees fit should the shareholders fail to agree on the way to vote certain matters.

As stated on page 59 in convening shareholders meetings, matters regarding the normal activities of the corporation are not subject to approval by a voting agreement. However, a shareholder agreement to dissolve the corporation is generally held to be valid.

What the applicable RMBCA section says *Section 7.31, governing voting agreements, states that two or more shareholders may provide for the manner in which they will vote their shares by signing an agreement for that purpose. This agreement is specifically enforceable.*

RESTRICTING THE TRANSFERABILITY OF SHARES: THE RIGHT OF FIRST REFUSAL

A corporation, by its articles of incorporation, bylaws, or by shareholder agreement, typically has the power to reasonably restrict the free transferability of its outstanding shares. This can be done by conspicuously noting the restriction on the front or back of the certificate. For example, the corporation or the other shareholders can be given the *right of first refusal*, meaning the opportunity to purchase the shares at the best price obtained by the shareholder from outside third parties. A variation of this arrangement may require that the selling shareholder first offer the shares to the other shareholders.

What the applicable RMBCA section says *Section 6.27, governing the restriction of shares, states that the articles of incorporation, the bylaws, an agreement among shareholders, or an agreement between the shareholders and the corporation may impose restrictions on the transfer or registration of transfer of shares of the corporation. A restriction does not affect shares issued before the restriction was adopted unless the holders of such shares are parties to the restriction agreement. The restriction must be conspicuously noted on the front or back of the certificate.*

HOW MANY SHARES DOES IT TAKE TO HOLD A VALID SHAREHOLDERS MEETING?

A quorum is the number of votes necessary to validate a meeting. The certificate of incorporation or bylaws usually fixes the number of shares necessary to constitute a valid meeting of the shareholders. Once a valid shareholders meeting is commenced, no quorum is necessary to adjourn the meeting.

The normal quorum is the majority of shares entitled to vote.

EXAMPLE Label Sticker and Tag Co. Inc. has 1,000 common shares outstanding. The certificate of incorporation provides for a majority of the shares to be present to constitute a valid meeting. At a duly called stockholders meeting, 5 out of 20 shareholders, owning 515 common shares attend the meeting. The normal quorum requirement has been met because the shareholders present own the majority of the outstanding shares and the meeting can proceed.

The certificate of incorporation can provide for a lesser quorum, that is a lesser amount of shares to be present, but in no case, less than one third of the amount of shares entitled to vote.

EXAMPLE Hedon Hydrogen Producers Inc. has 300 common shares outstanding. The certificate of incorporation provides for a lesser quorum of one third of the shares to be present to constitute a valid meeting. At a duly called stockholders meeting, 2 out of 10 shareholders, owning 105 common shares attend the meeting. The lesser quorum requirement has been met because the shareholders present own over one-third (105/300) of the outstanding shares and the meeting can proceed.

In many states, a greater quorum, i.e., more than a majority, can be required for a valid shareholders meeting but only if provided for in the certificate of incorporation and not in the bylaws.

Shareholders present at a meeting where the number of shares necessary to constitute a quorum has not been met have the authority to adjourn the meeting.

EXAMPLE Roxberry Apple Farms Ltd. has 100 common shares outstanding. At a duly called stockholders meeting, 2 out of 10 shareholders, owning 105 common shares attend the meeting. The lesser quorum requirement has been met because the shareholders present own over one-third (105/300) of the outstanding shares and the meeting can proceed.

Shareholders meetings are called annually to elect directors. Directors are elected by a plurality (meaning the largest number of votes cast). All other actions require a majority of the votes cast. One major exception to these voting requirements is that any proposed merger, sale of corporate assets, or dissolution requires a positive vote of two-thirds of the shares entitled to vote.

EXAMPLE Kramer Public Relations, Inc. had 75 common shares outstanding. Since the corporation was not doing well, the directors, at the corporation's annual meeting, proposed that the corporation be dissolved. Thus, all the assets were to be sold, all corporate liabilities paid, and the balance of the proceeds distributed to the shareholders. At least 50 shares (or two-thirds) would have to vote yes to approve the proposed dissolution.

HOW CUMULATIVE VOTING WORKS

Usually, the articles of incorporation provide that shareholders vote for an entire slate in a "straight" vote. Thus, the shareholders with the most shares (called the majority shareholders) will always be able to outvote minority shareholders (those shareholders with minimal votes) relating to either the election of directors or other ordinary corporate matters. Cumulative voting is a technique whereby minority shareholders concentrate all of their voting strength on one or more individual directors with the hope that they are elected. It is an excellent way of helping to preserve minority shareholder representation on the board of directors. The formula is the number of shares held times the number of individual directors to be elected.

EXAMPLE 1 Barton Cain owns 105 shares of Soloway Sugar Refining Corp. Soloway's articles of incorporation stipulate cumulative voting for the election of directors. Barton may cast 420 votes (number of shares held [105] times directors to be elected [4]) for one or more directors of his choice.

EXAMPLE 2 Mary Benis owns 105 shares and Todd Tryon owns the other 300 shares of the Rochester Travel Agency Ltd. Rochester's articles of incorporation stipulate cumulative voting for the election of directors. Mary wants to elect A, B, and C as directors while Todd wants X, Y, and Z. In straight voting, Todd would be able to elect X, Y, and Z, thereby, denying Mary representation on the board. However, under cumulative voting, Mary would have 315 votes (105 shares × 3 directors). If Mary concentrates *all* of her votes on either A, B, or C, she will be able to elect at least one director. Todd has 900 votes (300 shares × 3 directors).

If Todd spreads all of his votes among X, Y, and Z, each will receive 300 votes (900/3). Since Mary's 315 votes will always exceed the votes needed to elect at least one director, she is always assured at least some representation on the board.

Thus, cumulative voting is an excellent device for use in a closely held corporation where minority shareholders always fear that they will be shut out from representation on the board. Note that cumulative voting only applies to the election of directors. All other corporate matters are usually decided by straight voting.

THE RIGHT TO INSPECT THE CORPORATION'S BOOKS AND RECORDS

Shareholders have an unqualified right to inspect the corporation's books and records, including the minutes of shareholders meetings, by making a demand on a corporate officer or director. Such inspection is permitted if done in good faith and its purpose is to protect either the corporation's or shareholders' interests. For example, an inspection of the list of shareholder's names for purposes of instituting a challenge to the current board by soliciting proxies is a proper demand for seeking an inspection. Even a competitor who owns shares can seek inspection although information relating to clients and other business secrets may be withheld.

Generally, inspection is limited to individuals of record for at least six months or to shareholders who own at least 5 percent of any stock or 5 percent in aggregate of all shares outstanding.

EXAMPLE 1 Susan Beckwith, a 20 percent shareholder in the Express Bus Service Corporation, seeks to obtain a list of the shareholders' names so that she can solicit enough proxies to challenge the current board of directors. Her action is deemed to have as its purpose the protection of shareholder rights, and indirectly the corporation, and is, therefore, a proper request.

EXAMPLE 2 Ronald Walters, is a 15 percent shareholder in the Planet Restaurant Inc., a closely held corporation. Ronald seeks to obtain information regarding the value of certain investments held by the corporation. This information will enable him to value his shares in the corporation. His action is deemed to have a valid business purpose and is a proper request.

Generally, prior to inspection, a shareholder is required to furnish an affidavit to the corporation stating that her sole purpose is not contrary to the interests of the corporation, and that for the next five years, she will not sell the shareholders list to an outside third party. Upon written request to inspect the corporation's books and records, most state statutes require that the corporation mail to the shareholder the latest annual balance sheet, income statement, and any applicable interim financial report.

. . . .

What the applicable RMBCA section says *Section 16.01, governing corporate records, states that a corporation shall keep as permanent records minutes of all meetings of its shareholders and board of directors, a record of all actions taken by shareholders or board of directors without a meeting, and all actions taken by committee. The corporation shall maintain a record of its shareholders in a form that permits a list of the names and addresses of all shareholders in alphabetical order by class of shares showing the number and class of shares held by each.*

. . . .

THE RIGHTS OF A MINORITY SHAREHOLDER

Although minority shareholders must abide by the decisions of the majority shareholders, they can object to certain majority actions under one or more conditions. These conditions include when the minority shareholders feel that the vote of the majority is contrary to the best interests of the corporation, when a vote is solely for the benefit of the majority, or when the action of the majority is in contravention of the corporation's articles of incorporation or bylaws. It is said that the majority have a fiduciary duty to the minority shareholders and must do their utmost to act in good faith.

EXAMPLE 1 At a duly called annual meeting of the Doughboy Musical Corporation, the majority shareholders vote to transfer rights to valuable musical compositions to a competitor, thereby crippling the corporation. The actions of the majority may be restrained by the legal action of the minority.

EXAMPLE 2 Exeter, Fredrico, and Grainger, who constitute all of the shareholders of the Amalfi Pizza Cheese Corporation, unanimously adopt a bylaw stating that no shareholder may dispose of his shares without first offering them to the corporation for purchase at their fair market value. The purpose of the bylaw was to prevent the sale of the shareholders' stock to a stranger who may prove hostile to the best interests of the corporation. Exeter and Fredrico later sought to repeal the bylaw. Such action may be prevented by Grainger, the minority shareholder.

Note that in that last example, the shareholders adopted a bylaw to give the corporation the first opportunity to purchase stock that a shareholder wishes to sell. Frequently, shareholders eventually want to sell, or sometimes die leaving their shares to a next of kin. This of course creates a potential risk to the corporation that an individual may inherit the stock who is less than compatible with the other shareholders or stated goals of the corporation. The problem in case of a proposed sale or death of a shareholder is that the corporation may not have the cash funds required to purchase the shares at their fair market value.

To avoid this potential problem, small closely held corporations usually take out an insurance policy on the life of each shareholder covering the current and potential value of the shares that they own. Should a shareholder die, the proceeds are paid to the corporation who uses them to repurchase the shareholder's outstanding stock. These policies must be reviewed annually to make sure that the insurance coverage is sufficient to repurchase the stock.

MINORITY SHAREHOLDERS' SUITS

Any wrongs committed against the corporation are supposed to be redressed by the board of directors. Sometimes, however, the board acts for the benefit of the majority shareholders to the detriment of the minority owners. In such cases, the obligation of the minority shareholder is to first make a demand upon the directors to correct the alleged wrong. If the directors fail to heed the request of the minority shareholders, or if they investigate and find wrong-doing but fail to take corrective action, the aggrieved minority shareholder may bring a *derivative action* on behalf of the corporation. Although the corporation is named as a defendant, the corporation is the real party in interest, i.e., the party entitled to recover if the plaintiff wins. The lawsuit is brought in the name of and in behalf of the corporation. The relief sought is in the form of compelling abusive directors and officers to account to the corporation for losses caused by their negligence, breach of fiduciary duty, or any other misconduct.

To maintain a derivative suit, the plaintiff must be the actual owner in the shares or have a beneficial interest in the shares of the corporation against whom the derivative action is sought.

EXAMPLE In 20XX, five shareholders of Dalton Dance Schools Inc. entered into a voting trust agreement. The shareholders transferred their shares to the trustee and received in return voting trust certificates. Any one of the shareholders may maintain a derivative action on behalf of Dalton.

Note that any damages recovered usually go to the corporation because it is said that the shareholders who bring such lawsuits are acting as guardians of the corporate entity.

PERSONAL LIABILITIES APPLICABLE TO THE SHAREHOLDERS

While a stockholder's liability is ordinarily limited to the amount of his investment, under certain conditions they may become liable to the corporation, to judgment creditors, and to wage earners.

Liability to the Corporation

The unpaid balance of a stock subscription is an asset of the corporation. A shareholder will, therefore, be liable to the corporation for the unpaid balance of his stock subscription (see Chap. 8). For example, when stock is bought on the installment basis, payment must be made on the due date of the installment. If payment is not made, the corporation may exercise its option to sue for the balance of the price of the shares or declare a forfeiture of the stock.

Second, if par value stock is issued for less than its full value (i.e., discounted stock), the stockholder is liable to the corporation for the difference between the price paid and the par value of the stock. In legal terms, the corporation is said to have issued *watered stock*.

EXAMPLE Lido Photography Studios, Inc. issued $5,000 of common stock to their attorney for legal services involving the formation of the corporation. In fact, the services were worth only $1,000. The attorney has been issued watered stock and is liable to the corporation for the $4,000 ($5,000 – $1,000) difference.

Because the RMBCA 6.21 provides that the director's good faith valuation of property is conclusive as to the adequacy of consideration, the concept of "watered stock" has diminished in legal importance.

Finally, a shareholder may be liable to the corporation when the corporation is insolvent and, in contravention of state statutes, pays an illegal dividend. If the corporation fails to seek repayment, another stockholder, in the form of a shareholders' derivative suit or as stated below, a judgment creditor, may do so.

Liability to Corporate Creditors

In cases of corporate insolvency, an unpaid creditor, having unsuccessfully sued the corporation, may sue the shareholder for the unpaid balance of the subscription price.

Second, par value stock may have been issued for less than its full value (discounted stock or watered stock). Thus, besides being personally liable to the corporation, the shareholder will also be held liable to an unpaid creditor in case of corporate insolvency for the difference between the price paid and the par value of the stock.

Finally, a shareholder may be liable for unlawful dividends received by her. A corporation may not declare and pay dividends if it causes its liabilities to exceed its assets. Thus, state corporate statutes generally declare illegal any dividends that would cause corporate liabilities to exceed corporate assets.

EXAMPLE The Sunset Steamship Corporation was virtually insolvent. The board of directors declared and paid a cash dividend thereby rendering the corporation insolvent and unable to pay its creditors. To the extent that the dividend payments rendered the corporation insolvent, they were illegal since their payment denied recovery to the creditors. Thus the stockholders are generally liable for any dividends received by them.

Note that in the above case, the recovery of any dividends from the shareholders does not exonerate the directors for their negligence or wrongful intent in declaring and paying the illegal dividend. Directors who vote in favor of an illegal dividend are jointly and severally liable to the corporation for the amount declared. On the other hand, directors who, in good faith, rely on the corporate financial statements prepared by others to declare a dividend will not be held liable.

EXAMPLE The certified public accountants for Budget Tool and Equipment Rental Corporation prepared the company's financial statements without listing a $500,000 judgment levied against the corporation. Thus, the statements showed the corporation to be solvent when in fact it was insolvent due to the judgment. The board of directors, believing the corporation to be in sound financial condition, declared and paid a $100,000 cash dividend, thereby rendering the corporation insolvent. The directors will not be held liable because they relied on the financial statements prepared by their outside independent accountants.

In some states, shareholders are not liable if they received their dividends in good faith and were unaware that the declaration and payment of dividends were illegal.

What the applicable RMBCA section says *Section 6.22 states that a purchaser from a corporation of its own shares is not liable to the corporation or its creditors with respect to the shares except to pay the consideration for which the shares were authorized to be issued.*

Thus, the RMBCA makes the shareholder liable for the difference, or discount, between the price actually paid for the stock and the consideration, i.e., the par or stated value, fixed by the board of directors.

Liability of Shareholders for Unpaid Wages

In some states, the ten largest shareholders of a non-public closely held corporation are personally liable for all unpaid wages owed by the corporation to its employees. This liability does not extend to independent contractors. An independent contractor is one who does not work for the corporation in an employee capacity and has complete charge and supervision over the work she does for another. Examples of independent contractors include outside legal counsel or the corporation's independent certified public accountant.

EXAMPLE Haddon Art Galleries Inc. declared itself bankrupt in Federal Bankruptcy Court. At the time of its bankruptcy, it owed its employees back wages. Haddon was owned by fifteen shareholders. The ten largest shareholders will be held personally liable, if after the bankruptcy proceeding is terminated, the wages remain unpaid.

DIVIDEND DISTRIBUTIONS

Shareholders seek income in the form of stock appreciation and the payment of dividends. Dividends may take the form of cash, stock, or other corporate property and may be paid either out of profits or in liquidation. This complex topic will be discussed in Chaps. 13 and 15.

CHAPTER 12

Dividends, Distributions, Stock Splits, and Stock Repurchases

INTRODUCTION

D ividends represent payments by a corporation of an equal amount to each shareholder of both preferred and common stock outstanding. Each dividend, in the form of either cash, the corporation's stock, or property, is based on the number of shares held by each shareholder. Cash and property dividends are usually taxable to the shareholder. Stock dividends are generally nontaxable. A corporation does not have a legal obligation to pay dividends. While creditors can force a corporation into involuntary bankruptcy if it does not meet its required interest payments on debt, shareholders, even as owners, do not have a similar right if the corporation is unable to pay dividends.

While the most common type of dividend is in the form of cash, a corporation may, at its option, pay dividends in the form of its own stock, called a stock dividend, or in property. Stock and property dividends are usually paid by a corporation that is short of cash.

EXAMPLE The Speedy Fleet Taxi Service, Inc. is owned by 40 shareholders. Since it was in the process of upgrading its fleet of taxis, it sought to conserve its cash. At the same time, the shareholders were demanding a dividend. The board of directors therefore declared and paid a stock dividend of one share of common stock for every ten common shares outstanding. This means that a shareholder owning ten shares would receive one share.

OBSERVATION *In all states, dividend payments are prohibited if the corporation is insolvent or would be rendered insolvent by the distribution. Insolvency in this sense means that if the corporation made the payments, it would be unable to pay any debts as they become due in the ordinary course of the debtor's business. Insolvency can also occur when a corporation's liabilities exceed its assets.*

EXAMPLE Calhoun Leather Crafts Ltd. has a deficit of $1,000 in its retained earnings account at the end of the year. It seeks to pay a $1,000 cash dividend to its shareholders. Calhoun, because of its deficit, cannot pay the dividend. This rule would also be applicable if the corporation sought to save cash by paying either a stock dividend or distributing property other than cash to the shareholders.

UNDERSTANDING ACCOUNTING PRINCIPLES GOVERNING THE PAYMENT OF DIVIDENDS

The basic accounting equation for any business entity, including a corporation, is as follows:

Assets = Liabilities + Capital (or Shareholder's Equity)

Assets consist of cash, accounts receivable, inventory, equipment, land and buildings, and other miscellaneous holdings. Liabilities consist of accounts payable, wages payable, long-term notes and mortgages payable, and other miscellaneous payables.

Shareholders' equity consists of common stock and preferred stock (if any) issued and out-standing, and earned surplus (simply called surplus). Certified public accountants preparing financial statements refer to surplus as *retained earnings*.

EXAMPLE Ramirez Movie Theaters Corporation issued 1,000 shares of $10 par value preferred stock for $10,000 and 15,000 no par value shares of common stock for $15,000. Assume that the company also had retained earnings of $5,000 at November 1, 20XX. If the corporation earned $13,400 for the month and paid $2,000 in dividends, the ending stockholders' equity section of the balance sheet would show the following:

RAMIREZ MOVIE THEATERS CORPORATION
Stockholders' Equity
For the Period Ended November 30, 20XX

Preferred Shares (Par Value $10: 1,000 Shares Issued and Outstanding)	$10,000
Common Stock	15,000
Total Value of Shares Outstanding	$25,000
Retained Earnings	16,400
Total Shareholders' Equity	$41,400

Any dividends paid to stockholders would come out of retained earnings. The payment of dividends is a distribution of corporate profits and *not* an expense of doing business. That is why dividends paid are not tax deductible by the corporation.

A statement of retained earnings for the period would show the following activities for the period.

RAMIREZ MOVIE THEATERS CORPORATION
Statement of Retained Earnings
For the Period Ended November 30, 20XX

Retained Earnings November 1, 20XX	$5,000
Net Income for the Period	13,400
Subtotal	$18,400
Less: Dividends	2,000
Retained Earnings, November 30, 20XX	$16,400

A corporation that does not have any retained earnings, which is usually the result of continuous operating losses, generally cannot pay dividends. A corporation lacking retained earnings is said to have a *deficit*.

Note that there is no corollary between the balance sheet figures based on costs and estimates and the true value of the business. The reason is that accountants use the cost principle rather than valuing assets at their true fair market value at the date the financial statements are presented. Thus, land bought by the corporation in 1980 for $10,000 might be worth $100,000 in today's market, but is still shown on the books of the corporation at its original cost of $10,000. Therefore, the term "book value" is a misnomer and does not reflect the true value of the stock.

EXAMPLE At year end, Climate Tree Nurseries Ltd. had assets consisting of land with a cost basis of $100,000, total liabilities of $50,000, and 10,000 shares of authorized $5 par value common stock of which 1,000 shares were issued and outstanding. The book value of the common shares outstanding is $50 per share calculated as follows:

Total Assets	$100,000	
Less: Total Liabilities	50,000	
Shareholders' Equity	$ 50,000	
		= $50
Divided by Outstanding Common Shares	1,000	

Now assume that the land, which had a cost basis of $100,000, had a fair market or liquidation value of $300,000. The value of the common shares outstanding based on fair market value would be $250 per share calculated as follows:

Total Assets	$300,000	
Less: Total Liabilities	50,000	
Shareholders' Equity	$250,000	
		= $250
Divided by Outstanding		
Common Shares	1,000	

Note that the par value of the shares is $5, the book value is $50, and the fair market value of the shares is $250. Thus, the book value of a share of stock does not represent its par value or fair market value.

If at a later date, the corporation pays a 5 percent dividend on its $100 par value common stock, a shareholder will receive $5 per share even though the stock's book or fair market value may be much higher (or lower).

STOCK SPLITS AND REVERSE STOCK SPLITS

When a corporation divides up its authorized and issued shares into a greater number of shares, i.e., two shares for every old one, it is termed a stock split.

From a legal viewpoint, a stock split results in an increase in the number of shares outstanding and a corresponding *decrease* in the par or stated value (in the case of no par value stock given a stated value) per share. A stock decrease, although it results in an increase in the number of shares outstanding, does not decrease the par or stated value of the shares. Thus, when the board of directors votes to split its stock, it does not change total shareholders' equity but merely increases the number of shares owned by the shareholders.

EXAMPLE The Gin Rummy Playing Card Corporation had 1,000 shares of $10 par value common stock outstanding when its board voted to split the stock in half. This action reduces the par value of the stock to $5 and increases the shares to 2,000 shares outstanding. The corporation's shareholders' equity section both before and after the stock split, assuming retained earnings of $5,000, would appear as follows:

STOCKHOLDERS' EQUITY BEFORE STOCK SPLIT

Common Stock:	
1,000 shares at $10 par	$10,000
Retained Earnings	5,000
	$15,000

STOCKHOLDERS' EQUITY AFTER STOCK SPLIT

Common Stock:	
2,000 shares at $5 par	$10,000
Retained Earnings	5,000
	$15,000

A corporation can also declare a reverse stock split where outstanding shares are combined into a lesser number of the same class, i.e., one new share for every three outstanding.

A stock split and a reverse stock split require board action. In some states, it may also require advance shareholder approval. The articles of incorporation must also be amended to change the par value or stated value of the shares.

TAX CONSEQUENCES *There are no tax consequences to a stock split except to divide the cost basis of each share in case of a split, or to multiply the basis of the stock in case of a reverse stock split.*

EXAMPLE 1 Roy Hamilton bought 100 shares of the Zebra Maintenance Corp. for $1,000. One year later, the corporation votes to split the stock, i.e., two shares for every old one. The old cost basis of $10 per share ($1,000/100 shares) is reduced after the split to $5 per share ($1,000/200 shares). Should Roy later sell 100 shares for $2,000, his capital gain, for tax purposes, would be $1,500 ($2,000 sales price − $500 [100 shares sold × $5]).

EXAMPLE 2 Same facts as in **EXAMPLE 1**, except that Zebra votes a reverse stock split, i.e., one new share for every five shares outstanding. The old cost basis of $10 per share ($1,000/100 shares) is increased to $50 per share ($1,000/20 shares). Should Roy later sell ten shares for $2,000, his capital gain, for tax purposes, would be $1,500 ($2,000 sales price − $500 [10 shares sold × $50]).

Note that both a stock dividend and stock split do not involve an expenditure of corporate assets.

FRACTIONAL SHARES (OR SCRIP)

A corporation may issue fractional shares or scrip, such as a 1/10 fractional share for every share held. These fractional shares entitle the shareholder to dividends, and the right to receive a full share in return for enough scrip to equal one share (e.g., ten 1/10 fractional shares equals one full share). A corporation may also issue money equal to the value of a fractional share.

What the applicable RMBCA section says *Section 6.04, governing fractional shares, states that a corporation may issue fractions of shares or pay in money the value of fractions of a share. Each certificate representing scrip must be labeled "scrip." The holder of a fractional share is entitled to exercise the rights of a shareholder, including the rights to vote, receive dividends, and to participate in the assets of the corporation upon liquidation.*

DISCRETION OF THE DIRECTORS TO DECLARE A DIVIDEND

The determination of whether or not to declare a dividend is left to the discretion of the board of directors. Even if the corporation has sufficient funds with which to pay dividends, the law does not require that they do so. In addition, courts will not interfere with the decision of the board not to declare dividends unless there is evidence of bad faith or dishonest motives.

EXAMPLE The board of directors of The Ace Safe Company, Inc. is in the process of expanding their operations in certain foreign countries. Pursuant to this corporate expansion process, Ace Safe has accumulated surplus funds, or as accountants call it, retained earnings, far in excess of the amount needed to support its program. Wallace Brown, a major shareholder, brought a court action demanding that the board declare and pay a cash dividend charging that the corporation has ample funds for both expansion and the payment of dividends. In reply, the corporate board feels that unknown contingencies arising from the expansion program may arise requiring additional financing. Wallace cannot win. Absent a showing of bad faith or dishonest purpose on the part of the board, courts will not compel a board of directors to declare a dividend.

WHO IS ENTITLED TO A DIVIDEND?

Once a dividend is lawfully declared, the shareholder becomes a creditor of the corporation. Holders of preferred shares have rights that take precedence over the rights of common stock. The dividend preferences may be classified as being current, cumulative, and/or participating.

The Current Preference

A current dividend preference requires that a current preferred dividend must be declared and paid before any dividends can be paid on common stock.

Cumulative Preferred Preference

This rule states that if all or part of the specified current dividend is not paid in full, the unpaid balance becomes a dividend in arrears. Cumulative dividends in arrears must be paid before any common dividends can be paid. If preferred stock is noncumulative, it can never be in arrears. Thus, if dividends are not declared on noncumulative preferred stock, they are lost forever.

Participating Preferred Preference

Participating preferred stock allows preferred shareholders to receive additional amounts of dividends after the dividends stipulated in the articles of incorporation are paid to both the preferred and common shareholders on a ratable basis.

The actual computations showing the distribution of dividends based upon the number and classes of shares outstanding was illustrated in Chap. 8.

WHEN SHAREHOLDERS ARE ENTITLED TO PAYMENT OF A DIVIDEND

The board of directors may declare a dividend payable in cash, stock, or corporate property.

A typical cash dividend declaration found in the board minutes might be as follows:

On November 30, 20X4, the Board of Directors of the Acme Refrigerator Corp. hereby declares a $1.00 per share cash dividend on the 10,000 shares of no par common stock outstanding. The dividend will be paid to stockholders on January 5, 20X5 to those listed on the corporate records at December 5, 20X4.

Note that the above declaration involves three important dates:

1. **The Declaration Date.** This is the date that the board officially declares a dividend. Upon declaration of the dividend by the board, a dividend liability is created. In the above example, the declaration date is November 30, 20X4.
2. **The Record Date.** In order to determine which shareholders are entitled to receive a dividend, the board must fix a record date in advance. The record date is generally no more than fifty days before the date of payment. In the above example, the record date is December 5, 20X4.
3. **The Date of Payment.** This is the date on which the checks are disbursed by the corporation. In the above example, the payment date is January 5, 20X5.

What Does Ex-dividend Mean?

In order to receive a dividend, an individual must have bought or owned the stock before the ex-dividend date, which is four business days before the holder of record date. Thus, if the holder of record date is May 5, the stock will go ex-dividend on May 1. Therefore, an individual must have bought the stock on the last day of April in order to get the dividend.

WHO IS ENTITLED TO THE DIVIDEND IF NO DATE OF RECORD IS SPECIFIED?

If the directors do not specify a date of record, the dividend belongs to the owner of the shares on the date that the dividend was declared.

EXAMPLE Stafford Uniforms Inc. declared a $1.00 per share cash dividend on June 1, 20X1 payable on July 1, 20X1. On June 5, Mary Hume sold her shares to Clark Baylor. Mary is entitled to the dividend since she was the owner of record on the date that the dividend was declared.

THE RIGHT OF A CORPORATION TO REPURCHASE ITS OWN OUTSTANDING SHARES

A corporation has the power to repurchase its own outstanding shares. A corporation might do this to consolidate its ownership into the hands of a small group of investors or to prevent the shares from falling into the hands of individuals who might be hostile to the best interests of the corporation, such as a competitor.

To protect creditors, reacquisitions and redemptions are subject to legal restrictions similar to those applicable to dividends. A corporation can only repurchase its own shares if it has sufficient retained earnings or if the repurchase will not render the corporation insolvent.

EXAMPLE The Bayou Water Supply Company Ltd. has 10,000 common shares outstanding. It also has only $500 in retained earnings. The corporation seeks to repurchase 1,000 shares with a fair market value of $10,000 owned by Digby Mantle, a shareholder. Bayou cannot repurchase the shares since it would render the corporation insolvent.

Insolvency can also occur when a corporation's liabilities exceed its assets.

What the applicable RMBCA section says *Section 6.40 (a), governing distributions to shareholders, states that a board of directors may authorize and the corporation may make distributions to its shareholders subject to restrictions set forth in the articles of incorporation. Section 6.40 (c) states that no distribution may be made if, after giving it effect, the corporation would not be able to pay its debts as they become due in the usual course of business or the corporation's total assets would be less than the sum of its total liabilities plus the amount that would be needed to satisfy the preferential rights of a designated class of shareholders.*

CHAPTER 13

Terminating the Corporation: Dissolution, Mergers and Consolidations, and Bankruptcy

THE SALE OF CORPORATE ASSETS

A mere sale of some or even all of corporate assets, may not amount to a dissolution. Such sale might be part of a redeployment of the corporation's operations into new and more potentially lucrative areas of operations. On the other hand, if irreconcilable differences arise among persons who are active in the management of a corporation, particularly a close corporation, a dissolution might be the only solution.

What the applicable RMBCA section says *Section 12.01, governing the sale of corporate assets in the regular course of business, states that a corporation may sell, lease, or dispose of all, or substantially all, of its property in the usual or regular course of business. Unless required by the articles of incorporation, shareholder approval is not required.*

Section 12.02, governing the sale of corporate assets not in the regular course of business, states that a corporation may sell, lease, or dispose of all or substantially all, of its property otherwise than in the regular course of business on terms stipulated by its board of directors. Shareholder approval is required.

DISSOLUTION

The dissolution of a corporation requires that the entity file a certificate of dissolution. As a result, its operations are terminated, its assets distributed first to its creditors and then to its shareholders, and the corporation then ceases to exist.

OBSERVATION *If all the corporate assets are sold prior to launching new activities, the directors are permitted to declare dividends provided legal standards are met. This includes having adequate retained earnings and enough capital with which to pay off all creditors.*

Voluntary Dissolution

In virtually all states, there are two methods of dissolution: voluntary and involuntary proceedings. A voluntary proceeding can be initiated by either the corporation's board of directors or by its shareholders. A few states require that a majority of the directors approve while other states set lower requirements. Upon approval by directors' vote for voluntary dissolution and subsequent ratification by the shareholders, a certificate of dissolution is filed. Although the corporation is technically dissolved, the directors are given the power to wind up the corporation's affairs. This process involves selling the corporation's assets, paying off all corporate obligations, and making liquidating distributions to the shareholders.

EXAMPLE The Candor Fragrance Corporation, a close corporation, is composed of four shareholders who also serve as directors. Although they specialize in producing and distributing womens' toiletries, two of the shareholders wish to expand into men's fragrances while the other two owners refuse to do so. This impasse continues for several months with the result that there has been a substantial falloff of business and bankruptcy is now possible. Absent a provision in the articles permitting the use of an arbitrator (see Chap. 9) to settle director deadlock, a voluntary dissolution might be the best solution. A certificate of dissolution would be filed, the corporate assets would be sold, and the creditors and shareholders given liquidating payments.

Although the above example is extreme, it does offer the shareholders capital in the form of corporate distributions, with which to pursue their own opportunities. For example, some owners might start their own corporation specializing in both mens' and womens' toiletries. Of course, a corporate buy-sell agreement might allow one group of shareholders to sell their shares either back to the corporation or to the remaining shareholders.

Involuntary Dissolution

In an involuntary dissolution, a group of shareholders owning a specific percentage of the corporation's outstanding stock, usually less than 50 percent, petition a court of proper jurisdiction to dissolve the corporation. After review of all the facts, the court may grant dissolution and appoint a receiver to wind up the corporation's affairs.

This method, called a *judicial liquidation*, is based on one or more grounds. They include the following:

1. The corporate directors are so deadlocked that the corporation cannot continue to function in a profitable manner and is in danger of insolvency; or

2. The directors have acted in an oppressive or illegal manner, such as selling off valuable corporate assets to family and friends at a fraction of their true market value; or

3. The corporation has been abandoned by its officers and directors and has ceased to function as a viable entity; or

4. The shareholders are hopelessly deadlocked and, after several meetings, are unable to elect directors as successors to the old directors; or

5. The articles of incorporation, when the corporation was formed, specified a limited life for the corporation, and the duration of life provided for has expired. This last situation is extremely rare in today's corporate environment because virtually all new articles of incorporation designate a perpetual life for the corporation.

Note that dissolution is a potent weapon for the minority shareholder. Thus, many articles of incorporation provide that in order to avoid possible involuntary dissolution, the corporation must purchase the minority shareholder's shares at their fair value. Part of this provision also requires that an independent qualified arbitrator be employed to ascertain the fair value of the dissident's shares.

When winding up corporate affairs pursuant to either a voluntary or involuntary dissolution, directors may continue the corporation for the purposes of winding up corporate affairs.

EXAMPLE The Cedric Wine Corporation correctly continued in its operations for three years after filing its certificate of dissolution for the purposes of suing other parties and for settling lawsuits brought against the corporation as defendant.

What the applicable RMBCA section says *Section 14.30 states that a court may dissolve a corporation for any of the following reasons: it is established that the corporation obtained its articles of incorporation through fraud; the corporation has continued to exceed or abused its authority; the directors are deadlocked in the management of the corporation; the shareholders are deadlocked in voting power and have failed for a period of at least* *two consecutive meetings; a proceeding has been brought by a creditor that has been reduced to judgment and remains unpaid.*

Directors who are engaged in winding up the corporation's affairs run the risk of personal liability for any debts incurred or illegal acts performed during the process.

EXAMPLE The Klein Handbag Corporation was in the process of dissolution. Part of the procedure required that the inventory be auctioned off to pay the creditors. The auction proceeds were used to pay off only part of the corporation's obligations to its creditors. Without paying the balance due the creditors, the directors declared an illegal dividend to the shareholders. The directors can be held personally liable for payment of the dividend. Their duties as trustees required that they pay off the creditors ahead of the shareholders.

What the applicable RMBCA sections says *Section 14.01 permits dissolution by a vote of a majority of the incorporators or initial directors. Section 14.02 permits dissolution by means of a vote of the directors followed by vote of the majority shareholders entitled to vote. Section 14.03 states that once a decision to dissolve is reached, the corporation must file articles of dissolution with the secretary of state. The articles must set forth the name of the corporation, the date that dissolution was authorized, and how it was authorized. Section 14.06 requires that the dissolving corporation notify known creditors of the dissolution within 120 days following the date of dissolution. Section 14.07 requires that the dissolved corporation must publish a notice of dissolution so that unknown creditors can receive notice.*

Finally, a corporation can be dissolved by the state of incorporation for failing to pay its annual corporate and franchise taxes, for failing to file any required annual reports, for continuous ultra vires acts, for criminal activities, and for procuring articles of incorporation based on fraud.

What the applicable RMBCA section says *Section 15.30 states that the secretary of state may commence a*

proceeding to administratively dissolve the corporation when it does not pay its taxes, does not file its annual report, fails to employ a registered agent for service of process, fails to notify the secretary of state that it has changed its registered agent, or that the stated period of life applicable to the corporation has expired.

MERGERS AND CONSOLIDATIONS

A merger is the absorption of one corporation (called the acquired or target corporation) by another corporation (called the acquiring corporation). A consolidation is the union of two existing corporations to form a new corporation.

In a merger, the acquired corporation ceases to exist and the acquiring corporation survives. In a consolidation, both corporations disappear and a new corporation is created.

EXAMPLE 1 Allison Gear Corporation is acquired by Blue Chip Office Machines Inc. in a merger. Allison ceases to exist after the merger is completed.

EXAMPLE 2 The Brandy Wine Corporation and Spirit Waters Inc. combine into a new corporation to be called Brandy Wine and Spirits Ltd. Both Brandy Wine and Spirit Waters cease to exist after the transaction is completed. This transaction is best described as a consolidation.

Neither a merger or consolidation can wipe out the rights of the creditors without their consent, and the continuing corporation, in case of a merger, or the new corporation, in case of a consolidation, become liable for the debts of the merged or consolidated corporations.

Whether the transaction is cast as either a merger or as a consolidation, the same corporate rules apply. This means that the board of each constituent corporation must approve the merger or consolidation by a majority vote. The proposal is then submitted, usually in abbreviated form, to the shareholders for their approval. A shareholder who disapproves of the proposed transaction is often accorded the right to receive cash for his stock based upon its appraised value.

What the applicable RMBCA sections says *Sections 13.01 through 13.31 give shareholders the right to dissent corporate actions involving shareholder approval, including mergers and consolations, sales of corporate assets, and amendments of the articles of incorporation. Section 13.01 states that a dissenter means a shareholder who is entitled to dissent from a corporate action. Section 13.21 requires that the shareholder deliver a written notice to the corporation of his intent to demand payment for his shares. Section 13.25 states that the corporation shall pay the dissenter what it estimates to be the fair value of the shares. Section 13.28 gives the dissenting shareholder the right to reject the corporation's offer. Section 13.30 states that if the demand for payment is unsettled, it may petition the court to determine the fair value of the shares plus any applicable accrued interest.*

After the plan of merger or consolidation is approved by both the directors and shareholders, it is filed with the secretary of state. When state formalities are satisfied, articles of incorporation are issued to either the surviving or newly formed consolidated corporation.

TAX IMPLICATIONS *Under the Internal Revenue Code, mergers and consolidations fall under a set of rules called "Type A" mergers and consolidations. Two classes of Type A mergers have been accepted by the IRS. The first involves the acquiring corporation transferring its shares to the acquired or "target" corporation in exchange for the acquired corporation's assets and liabilities. The stock received by the target corporation is then distributed to the shareholders of the acquired corporation in return for their stock.*

Another variation of the merger technique is to have the acquiring corporation exchange its shares for the shares held by the target corporation's shareholders. Simply stated, the Internal Revenue Code recognized either a merger of stock for assets or stock for stock.

In a Type A consolidation, the acquired corporations have their assets acquired by the *new* corporation. The stock of the new (or acquiring corporation) is then distributed to the shareholders of the acquired corporations pursuant to a plan of complete liquidation. As with a merger, an alternative plan of consolidation permits an exchange of stock for stock followed by a complete liquidation of the acquired corporations.

Provided that the parties follow a specific set of rules set down by the Internal Revenue Code, both the mergers and consolidations discussed will be tax-free.

What the applicable RMBCA sections says *Section 11.01, governing mergers, states that one or more corporations may merge into another corporation if the board of directors of each corporation adopts and its shareholders approve a plan of merger.*

Section 11.02 states that a corporation may acquire all of the outstanding shares of one or more classes or series of another corporation if the board of directors of each corporation adopts and its shareholders approve the exchange.

Note that in both mergers and consolidations, the legal obligations of the old corporations must be assumed by the successor corporation.

OBSERVATION *In today's competitive marketplace, many small corporations are finding it advantageous to seek a merger or consolidation with another corporation that is engaged in the same or similar line of business. From the perspective of management, a merger or consolidation is usually superior to a dissolution. The merger or consolidation produces a synergistic effect (i.e., the total is greater than the sum of the parts, or 2 + 2 = 5) because excess assets are sold off, overhead is reduced, superfluous employees are either retired or terminated, there is an exchange of new ideas between the combined or new corporations, and new markets are opened.*

BANKRUPTCY

There are two types of bankruptcy actions applicable to businesses. Bankruptcies filed under Chapter 7 of the federal Bankruptcy Code involve the liquidation of a business's or an individual's assets to pay outstanding debts. Typically, creditors receive only a portion of the amount that they are owed.

Chapter 11 bankruptcies allow for a restructuring of the debts of a corporation and a continuance of corporate business. Unless a trustee is appointed by the court, the debtor corporation will retain possession of the business and may continue to operate with its own management. The court may appoint a trustee for cause, such as a showing of dishonesty, incompetence, or gross mismanagement, which would work to the detriment of the creditors.

....

OBSERVATION *In December, 1995, Phar-Mor Inc., a discount-drugstore chain, emerged from nearly three years of bankruptcy and is now operating under new ownership as a publicly traded company. Its founder was sentenced to prison for fraud and embezzlement resulting in the corporation filing for bankruptcy protection in 1992.*[6]

....

Under Chapter 11, a committee is created to represent creditors during the reorganization. A plan of repayment of existing debt, or to reduce current debts, is developed and then submitted to the creditors for their approval and to the Bankruptcy Court for its confirmation. The thrust of the plan is that it be fair to all of the parties involved and that it comply with all bankruptcy laws. Once the plan is confirmed by the Bankruptcy Court, it is binding on all creditors. A bankruptcy under this chapter may also permit courts to terminate lawsuits that have not yet been filed against the corporation.

A Chapter 11 bankruptcy can, under certain circumstances, be converted to a Chapter 7 liquidation by parties other than the debtor.

A corporation that has had debts discharged in bankruptcy is barred from instituting another bankruptcy action subsequent to the current one for six years.

A more complete discussion of Bankruptcy is found in *Barron's Bankruptcy Step-by-Step*.

....

[6]*The Wall Street Journal*, December 4, 1995, pg. B5

CHAPTER 14

Establishing the Accounting Records

SETTING UP THE CORPORATE RECORDS

When starting up a new corporation, the Internal Revenue Code requires that a system of recordkeeping suitable for the business must be set up. Note that failure to keep proper business records can lead to tax audits, additional taxes, and in extreme cases, even criminal charges.

CHOOSING THE RIGHT TAX YEAR

A corporation must calculate its net income on the basis of a tax year. The "tax year" is the annual accounting period the corporation uses for maintaining its records and reporting income and expenses. The corporation can use either a calendar year or a fiscal year.

Calendar Year

A corporation adopts a tax year when it files its first income tax return. The corporation must adopt its first tax year by the due date, not including extensions, for filing a return for that year.

The due date for filing returns for regular corporations and S corporations is the 15th day of the 3rd month after the end of the tax year. If the 15th day of the month falls on a Saturday, Sunday, or legal holiday, the due date is the next day that is not a Saturday, Sunday, or legal holiday.

EXAMPLE The Solar Roofing Repair Corp.'s year end is December 31, 20X3. March 15 of the following year falls out on Saturday. The corporate tax return (Form 1120) is due Monday, March 17. If March 15 is a Friday, the return is due on that Friday.

The Fiscal Tax Year

A regular fiscal year is 12 consecutive months ending on the last day of any month except December. A 52–53 week year is a fiscal tax year that varies from 52 to 53 weeks. If a corporation adopts a fiscal year tax year, it must maintain its books and records and report income and expenses using the same tax year.

Generally, S corporations and personal service corporations (PSC's) or professional associations (PA's) must use a regular tax year unless the corporation has a business purpose for electing a fiscal year.

52–53 Week Tax Year

A corporation can elect to use a 52–53 week tax year if it keeps its books and records and reports its income and expenses on that basis. If the corporation makes this election, the tax year will always be 52 or 53 weeks long, and will always end on the same day of the week. The corporation may choose to have the tax year always end on either:

1. The date a specified day of the week last occurs in a particular month, or
2. The date that day of the week occurs nearest the last day of a particular calendar month.

For example, a corporation may elect a tax year that always ends on the last Monday in March.

To make the election, the corporation must file the tax return for the 52–53 week year and attach a statement showing:

1. The day of the week on which the tax year will always end,
2. Whether it will end on the last such day of the week in the calendar month or on the date such day of the week occurs nearest the end of the month, and
3. The month in which or with reference to which the tax year will end.

BUSINESS PURPOSE TAX YEAR

A business purpose for a tax year is an accounting period that has a substantial business purpose for its existence. Both tax and nontax factors must be considered in determining if there is a substantial business purpose for a requested tax year.

One nontax factor that may be sufficient to establish a business purpose for a tax year is the annual cycle of business activity, called a "natural business year." The accounting period of a natural business year includes all related income and expenses. A natural business year exists when a business has a peak period and a nonpeak period. The natural business year is considered to end at or soon after the end of the peak period. In the absence of substantial distortion of income, or other factors showing that the change is requested for purposes of tax advantage, the showing of a natural business year will ordinarily be accepted as a substantial business purpose for approval of a change in accounting period. A business whose income is steady from month to month, year-round, would not have a natural business year as such. In considering whether there is a business purpose for a tax year, significant weight is given to tax factors. A prime consideration is whether the change would create a substantial distortion of income, such

as the shifting of a substantial portion of deductions, from one year to another so as to reduce tax liability.

Other nontax factors, based on the convenience of the taxpayer, usually will not be sufficient to establish that a business purpose exists for a particular tax year. These factors include the use of a particular year for regulatory or financial accounting purposes and the hiring patterns of a particular business, such as the fact that a firm typically hires staff during certain times of the year.

CHOOSING THE RIGHT ACCOUNTING METHOD

Upon incorporation, the enterprise should set up books using an accounting method that clearly shows income for the accounting period that is the corporation's tax year. The corporation must also decide whether to use a single or a double entry bookkeeping system. The single entry system is simple and easy to maintain, but may not be suitable for every corporation. Corporations may find the double entry system better because it has built-in procedures to assure accuracy and control.

Single entry

The single entry bookkeeping system is based on the profit or loss statement and includes only the corporation's business income and expense accounts. It can be a simple and very practical system for a small corporation just starting out. For tax purposes, this system records all income and expenses through the use of a daily summary of cash receipts and a monthly summary of cash receipts and cash payments.

Double entry

The double entry bookkeeping system uses books, called journals, and is based on both the income statement and the balance sheet. Transactions are first entered in a journal and then monthly totals of the journal transactions are entered in ledger accounts. Ledger accounts include income, expense, asset, liability, and net worth (the difference between what your business owns and what it owes). These accounts are used to prepare a company's financial statements.

Many computer software packages are available to enable the new corporation to install and operate a complete set of accounting books and records.

ACCRUAL VERSUS THE CASH BASIS OF ACCOUNTING
Accrual Accounting

Accrual accounting is based on the fundamental principle that all income earned for a period must be matched with the expenses assignable to that period. This process "matches" the revenue earned for the period with the expenses incurred for the same period irrespective of when the income has been received or the expenses paid. All companies listed on the various exchanges (i.e., New York, American, etc.) use the accrual basis of accounting. Small businesses, particularly professional and service type organizations, tend to use the "cash basis" of accounting.

Cash Basis

Under the cash basis, income is recorded when received, and expenses are recorded when paid. This method is simple but does not match income and costs for a given period.

EXAMPLE Polar Contractors Inc. performed work billed at $7,300 during the month of September, 20X3. The company received payments of $4,000 on September 16 and $3,300 on October 12. Wages of $2,600, the only expense, was paid on September 30. The difference in net income for the months of September and October, would be as follows:

	Cash Basis		Accrual Basis	
	September	October	September	October
Revenue	$4,000	$3,300	$7,300	None
Expense	2,600	None	2,600	None
Net Income	$1,400	$3,300	$4,700	None

It is evident from the illustration that the accrual basis gives more accurate results because it reflects the correct net income earned in each period.

Accrual accounting is the method preferred by accountants, but many small businesses prefer the simplicity of the cash basis of accounting.

OBSERVATION *The cash receipts and disbursements method of accounting is used by most individual taxpayers and most noncorporate businesses that do not have inventories. The accrual method must be used where inventories are a material income producing factor. The hybrid method, which is really a combination of the cash and accrual methods, can be used only with approval from the IRS.*[7]

HOW TO SUPPORT ALL THE ENTRIES MADE IN THE CORPORATE BOOKS

Sales slips, invoices, canceled checks, paid bills, duplicate deposit slips, and any other documents that explain and support entries made in your books should be filed in an orderly manner and stored in a safe place. Memorandums or sketchy records that approximate income, deductions, or other items may not be allowed by the Internal Revenue Service (IRS) and may result in additional taxes and other charges.

HOW TO GET AN EMPLOYER IDENTIFICATION NUMBER (EIN)

A corporation must obtain an employer's identification number (EIN) for tax purposes by obtaining and filing Form SS–4 with its local IRS office. This form is available from IRS and Social Security Administration offices. The EIN is used on filed tax returns and correspondence with the IRS.

A sole proprietorship or partnership converting into a corporation needs a new EIN. A corporation converting to an S corporation does not need a new EIN.

PAYROLL RECORDS

An employer, regardless of the number of employees, must maintain all records pertaining to payroll taxes (income tax withholding, social security, and unemployment tax) for at least four years after the tax becomes due or is paid, whichever is later.

Employers must withhold taxes from all employees, including corporate officers. In order to do so, a new employee must fill out Form W–4

[7]IRC Reg. §1.446-1(c)(2)(ii).

(Employee's Withholding Allowance Certificate) listing her appropriate exemptions and then sign it. The corporation will then withhold income tax based on the IRS's withholding tables. If the employee for some reason does not prepare a W–4, the corporation must treat her as a single person with no withholding exemptions. The corporation must advise its employees to prepare a new certificate if their status changes (e.g., there is a decrease in the number of their dependents). This new certificate must be filed prior to December 1 of the next year.

On or before January 31, the corporation must provide employees, the IRS, and state and local tax agencies with copies of Form W–2 (Wage and Tax Statement) listing salary earned and taxes withheld for the last calendar year.

....

OBSERVATION *Employees who expect to have no tax liability can be exempt from income tax withholding by certifying on form W–4 to his employer that he had no federal income tax liability in the preceding year, and expects to have no tax liability for the current year as well.*

....

If an employee receives tips of $20 or more in a month, the corporation must report these tips for tax purposes on or before the tenth of the following month.

The corporation must deduct social security taxes from the employee's salary, and must also match the employee's contribution. Form 941 is used to remit withholding taxes and social security deductions to the IRS. A completed Form 941 is found in back of this book. Form 941 must filed by the last day of the month following the end of the quarter, i.e., April 30, June 30, September 30, and January 31 of the following year. For example, Form 941 for the first quarter of the year (January 1 to March 1) must be filed by April 30. The corporation must also deposit the withholding and social security deductions in a separate account. This is accomplished with Form 501 (Federal Tax Deposits, Withheld Income, and FICA taxes). This form, along with the remittances, is sent to a bank authorized to accept tax deposits. An employer is either a monthly or semiweekly depositor. An employer is a monthly depositor if the aggregate amount of employment taxes for the lookback period, (i.e., the twelve month period ending the preceding June 30) is $50,000 or less. An employer will be a semimonthly depositor for the entire calendar year if the amount of employment taxes reported for the lookback period (i.e., the twelve month period ending the preceding June 30) exceeds $50,000.

Unemployment tax is paid to both the state and the federal government. The IRS gives a partial credit for unemployment taxes paid to the state. The corporation must first register with the state Bureau of Labor; it will then receive an identification number so that its deposits will be credited to its corporate account. The corporation's employment experience rate will partly determine how much unemployment tax it must pay; the rate will change depending on how many employees are hired and fired. For example, if the corporation terminates a large number of employees, its unemployment tax rate will increase because of the higher demand placed on the state's unemployment fund.

The federal unemployment tax (FUTA) is less than the state rate. Because wages are calculated on a December 31 basis rather than the corporation's fiscal year-end, Form 940 (and the simpler Form 940–EZ) is due no later than the following January 31. The corporation must then file Form 940 (or Form 940–EZ) with the IRS to show how the corporation computed the unemployment tax. If the amount exceeds $100, the corporation should use a Special Deposit Card 508 (Federal Unemployment Tax Deposit) and pay the tax to an authorized bank before January 31. If the tax is under $100, it may remit the amount directly with Form 940 (or Form 940–EZ). A completed Form 940–EZ is found in back of this book. Usually the corporation must have at least two full-time employees before the unemployment tax will exceed $100.

If the corporation hires individuals to perform services as independent contractors, it must file an annual information return (Form 1099) to report payments totaling $600 or more made to any individual in the course of trade or business during the calendar year. The records in support of Form 1099 must list the name, address, and social security number of every independent contractor employed, along with pertinent dates and the amounts paid each person. The reports do not have to be mailed with copies of Form 1099 but must be available for examination by the IRS if required. Each payment must be supported by an invoice submitted by the contractor.

PAYROLL TAXES

The most common types of payroll deductions are Social Security taxes, federal, state and city withholding taxes, and miscellaneous items, such as insurance premiums, employee savings, and union dues.

Social Security Taxes

All corporate employers covered are required to collect the employee's share of Social Security tax by deducting it from the employee's gross pay and to remit it to the government along with the employer's share. Both the employer and the employee are taxed at the same rate, currently 6.2 percent (2003) based on the employee's gross pay up to an $87,000 annual limit.

Medicare is a two-part program designed to alleviate the high cost of medical care for those over age 65. The Basic Plan, which provides hospital and other institutional services, is financed by a separate Hospital Insurance tax (also called the Medicare tax) paid by both the employee and the employer at the rate of 1.45 percent on the employee's total compensation. The Voluntary Plan takes care of the major part of doctors' bills and other medical and health services and is financed by monthly payments from all who enroll plus matching funds from the federal government.

The combination of the O.A.S.D.I. tax, often called Federal Insurance Contribution Act (F.I.C.A.) tax, and the federal Hospital Insurance Tax make up the Social Security tax. The combined rate for these taxes, 7.65 percent on an employee's wages to $87,000 and 1.45 percent in excess of $87,000, is changed annually by acts of Congress. The corporate employer is required to remit to the government its share of F.I.C.A. tax along with the amount of F.I.C.A. tax deducted from each employee's gross compensation.

Income Tax Withholding

Federal and some state income tax laws require employers to withhold from the pay of each employee the applicable income tax due on those wages. The amount of income tax withheld is computed by the employer according to a government-prescribed formula or withholding tax table. The amount to be withheld for the pay period depends on each employee's taxable wages, marital status, and claimed dependents.

If the income tax withheld plus the employee and the employer social security taxes exceeds specified amounts per month, the employer is required to make remittances to the government at given intervals during the month. Monthly deposits are not required if the employer's liability for the calendar quarter is less than $500. Instead, the tax liability is remitted with the employer's quarterly payroll tax return.

EXAMPLE Assume a weekly payroll of $10,000, entirely subject to F.I.C.A. and Medicare (7.65 percent), income tax withholding of $1,500, and a deduction of $100 in union dues.

The entry to record the wages and salaries paid and the employee payroll deductions would be:

Wages and Salaries		$10,000
Less:		
F.I.C.A. Taxes Payable	765	
Withholding Taxes Payable	$1,500	
Union Dues	100	2,365
Net Payroll Payable		$ 7,635

Unemployment Taxes

Another payroll tax levied by the federal government in cooperation with state governments provides a system of unemployment insurance. All employers who (1) paid wages of $1,500 or more during any calendar quarter in the year or preceding year or (2) employed at least one individual on at least one day in each of twenty weeks during the current or preceding calendar year are subject to the Federal Unemployment Tax Act (F.U.T.A.). This tax is levied *only on the employer* at a rate of 6.2 percent (2003) on the first $7,000 of compensation paid to each employee during the calendar year. However, a credit is granted for up to 5.4 percent of wages paid to the state government so that the amount paid to the federal government may be as low as 0.8 percent.

State unemployment compensation laws differ from the federal law and differ among various states. Therefore, employers must be familiar with the unemployment tax laws in each state in which they pay wages and salaries. Although the normal state tax may range from 3 percent to 7 percent or higher, all states provide for some form of merit rating under which a reduction in the state contribution rate is allowed.

In order not to penalize an employer who has earned a reduction in the state contribution rate, the federal law allows a credit of 5.4 percent even though the effective state contribution rate is less than 5.4 percent.

EXAMPLE The Cable Telephone Corporation, which has a taxable payroll of $100,000, is subject to a federal rate of 6.2 percent and a state contribution rate of 5.7 percent. But because of stable employment experience, the company's state rate is 1 percent. The computation of the federal and state unemployment taxes for Cable Telephone is as follows:

State unemployment tax	
payment (1%)($100,000)	$1,000
Federal unemployment	
tax (6.2% – 5.4%)($100,000)	800
Total federal and state	
unemployment tax	$1,800

The federal unemployment tax is paid annually on or before January 31 of the following taxable calendar year. State contributions generally are required to be paid quarterly.

The IRS has established an electronic funds transfer (EFT) system for federal tax deposits by which employer withheld taxes may be transferred to a financial institution authorized to collect such funds on behalf of the government.

MISCELLANEOUS FRINGE BENEFITS

While employee compensation is taxable, the tax law encourages certain types of fringe benefits by allowing the corporation to deduct the cost of the benefit while permitting the employee to exclude the value of the benefits from her income. Some of the suggested benefits are as follows:

Pension and Profit-Sharing Plans

A newly formed corporation can set up pension, profit-sharing, and stock bonus plans, which give rise to immediate tax deductions for the corporation while enabling the corporation to attract and keep qualified individuals. Earnings in these plans are not taxable to the employees until the payments are actually received at a later date. A *pension plan* can be either contributory or noncontributory. Under a noncontributory pension plan, contributions are made solely by the corporation. Under a contributory pension plan, the employee makes additional contributions to supplement those made by the corporation.

Under a *profit-sharing plan*, the employer allocates a share of corporate profits according to some predetermined formula. Incidental benefits such as disability, death, or medical insurance can also be provided as part of a profit-sharing arrangement. A profit-sharing plan can be established in addition to or in lieu of a pension plan.

A *stock bonus plan* is a special type of arrangement whereby the employer's stock is contributed to a trust. The stock is then allocated to each participant in the trust for eventual distribution to them.

Qualified pension, profit-sharing and stock plans must meet complex rules in order to achieve their favorable tax treatment of immediate deductibility.

Cash or Deferred Arrangement Plans

Corporate executives can sign agreements calling for compensation to be paid at future dates. Such agreements result in a tax savings because the income will be spread over several future periods, thereby resulting in the income being taxed at lower rates.

EXAMPLE Wade Flag, a retired baseball player, is hired by Syndicated Restaurant Chains Inc. to represent them at all public events sponsored by the chain. Syndicated initially proposed a salary agreement calling for annual payments of $300,000 per year for three years or a total of $900,000. Instead,

Flag demanded and eventually received a contract calling for specified payments of $90,000 per year to be paid over ten years thereby allowing the income to be taxed at a lower personal rate.

Life Insurance Arrangements

The corporation can make the following programs available to its employees.

1. *Group-term.* Under this arrangement, the corporation provides group insurance coverage for its employees. The corporation gets a deduction for the premium payment, and the premiums attributable to the first $50,000 of coverage are excluded from the employee's gross income.
2. *Split-dollar.* Split-dollar insurance is an arrangement in which the corporation purchases life insurance on certain key employees. The corporation pays that part of the premium equal to the annual increase in the cash value of the policy, and the employee pays the balance of the premium.
3. *Key-employee.* Key-employee insurance is a form designed almost exclusively to compensate the corporation for the loss of a vital employee whose services are important to the success of the enterprise. The insurance proceeds received by the corporation in the event of the employee's death are nontaxable. The premiums, however, are nondeductible by the corporation.

Health Insurance Arrangements

These plans may include the following:

1. *Accident and health insurance.* A corporation may provide accident and health insurance coverage for its employees. Under the Internal Revenue Code, the employer's premium payments are deductible by the corporation and are not included in the employee's income. Moreover, the actual payment of the insurance benefit is not included in the employee's income.
2. *Medical reimbursement plans.* This type of plan allows employees to exclude from income amounts received as reimbursement for medical expenses they incur for their medical care and those of their spouses and dependents.

Cafeteria Plans

These are plans that offer employees the option of choosing cash or certain nontaxable fringe benefits, such as group term life insurance, accident and health benefits, or child care. If the employee chooses cash, the cash is taxable. However, if the employee instead chooses a nontaxable fringe benefit, the value of the benefit is excluded from gross income. The fact that the employee could have chosen cash will not cause the fringe benefit to be taxed. The plan cannot discriminate in favor of highly compensated employees or their dependents or spouses. Employer plans may specify what benefits are offered and may limit the amount of benefits that individual employees may receive.

Dependent Care Assistance Programs

An employer can set up a dependent care assistance program that provides for care of an employee's children or other dependents. The purpose of the program is to allow the employee to work. Payments up to $5,000 annually are excluded from the employee's gross income.

"Flextime" programs

In order to allow employees to spend more time with their families, some corporations offer "flextime" where employees can arrange their work schedules in different ways, such as four ten-hour days with three days off, work from home part of the day, etc.

The Family and Medical Leave Act of 1993

Under the Family and Medical Leave Act (FMLA), covered employers must provide access to up to twelve weeks' leave per calendar or fiscal year for the employee's own illness, the illness of a close family member, or the birth or adoption of a child. This act applies to employers with fifty or more employees in each day of twenty or more workweeks in a year in which an employee seeks to take leave.

Other Miscellaneous Benefits

Corporations may also provide such nontaxable fringe benefits as qualified employee discounts, de minimis (meaning minimal cost) fringe benefits, such as free coffee, free parking subject to a monthly statutory limit, and the use of athletic facilities, such as employer owned tennis courts.

CHAPTER 15

Taxation of Corporations

ORGANIZATIONS TAXED AS CORPORATIONS

While the sole proprietorship and general and limited partnerships are subject to a single tax at the individual or personal level, the corporation is subject to double taxation. This tax burden is frequently cited as the major disadvantage of doing business in the corporate form. Corporations are required to pay an entity-level tax on their taxable income. They file tax returns (Form 1120 or Form 1120A if they meet certain requirements) and pay tax on corporate taxable income at specific rates. Shareholders pay additional tax (at their own individual rates) on dividends that are declared and paid from the corporations earnings and profits. This means that corporate stockholders are effectively taxed twice on income, once at the corporate level and again when profits are distributed by way of a dividend. Shareholders must also eventually pay a tax on capital gains (stock losses can offset a shareholder's ordinary income up to $3,000 per year) from the subsequent sale of their shares.

Current corporate tax rates are as follows:

Rate	Taxable Income	Tax
15%	Up to $50,000	$7,500
25%	$50,000–$75,000	6,250
34%	$75,000–$100,000	8,500
39%	$100,001–$335,000	91,650
34%	$335,001–$10,000,000	3,286,100
35%	$10,000,000–$15,000,000	1,750,000
38%	$15,000,000–$18,333,333	1,266,667
35%	Over $18,333,333	

For a corporation that has taxable income in excess of $100,000 for any taxable year, the amount of the tax is increased by the lesser of (1) 5 percent of the taxable amount over $100,000 or (2) $11,750. The extra 5 percent surtax is designed to phase out the benefits of the lower rates on the first $75,000 in taxes.

Secondly, the maximum tax rate on corporate taxable income increases from 34 percent to 35 percent for corporate taxable income in excess of $10 million. In addition, in order to recapture the benefits of being subject to a lower 34 percent tax rate, corporate taxable income in excess of $15 million is subject to an additional tax equal to the lesser of (1) 3 percent of the excess or (2) $100,000.

EXAMPLE 1 For 20X3, Derby Horse Farms, Inc. has taxable income of $335,000. The corporate tax liability will be $113,900 determined as follows:

Taxable Income	Tax Rate	Tax
$ 50,000	× 15%	$ 7,500
25,000	× 25%	6,250
260,000	× 34%	88,400
235,000 ($335,000 – $100,000) ×	5%	11,750
		$113,900

EXAMPLE 2 For 20X3, Zinnia Art Galleries, Inc. had taxable income of $400,000. The tax liability for the corporation would be $136,000 calculated as follows:

Rate	Taxable Income		Tax
15%	First	$50,000	$ 7,500
25%	Next	25,000	6,250
34%	Next	325,000	110,500
			124,250
Add: Surtax $335,000 – $100,000			
= $235,000 × 5%			11,750
	Total tax		$136,000

An alternate method for calculating the corporate tax liability of $136,000 would be to multiply $400,000 × 34 percent.

EXAMPLE 3 For 20X3, The China Paint Corporation had taxable income of $14 million. The tax liability for the corporation would be $4,800,000 calculated as follows:

15%	Up to $50,000	$	7,500
25%	$50,000–$75,000		6,250
34%	$75,000–$100,000		8,500
39%	$100,001–$335,000		91,650
34%	$335,001–$10,000,000		3,286,100
35%	$10,000,000–$14,000,000		1,400,000
			$4,800,000

An alternate method for calculating the corporate tax liability of $4,800,000 would be as follows:

$10,000,000 × 34%	$3,400,000
4,000,000 × 35%	1,400,000
$14,000,000	$4,800,000

A personal service corporation (PSC) or professional corporation (PA) does not enjoy the benefits of having the first $50,000 taxed at 15 percent and the next $25,000 at 25 percent. Instead, a PSC must pay a flat tax of 35 percent on all of its taxable income. Thus, assuming that a personal service corporation had taxable income of $80,000, its tax liability for the year would be $28,000 ($80,000 × 35 percent).

Filing Requirements

The corporate tax return filed is Form 1120 unless the corporation is a small business corporation entitled to file the shorter Form 1120-A. Form 1120-A may be filed if *all* of the following requirements are met:

1. Gross receipts or sales do not exceed $500,000.
2. Total assets do not exceed $500,000.
3. The corporation is not involved in a dissolution or liquidation.
4. The corporation is not a member of a controlled group (controlled by other corporations).
5. The corporation does not file a consolidated tax return.
6. The corporation does not have ownership in a foreign corporation.
7. The corporation does not have foreign shareholders who directly or indirectly own 50 percent or more of its stock.

AVOIDING DOUBLE TAXATION: THE S CORPORATION

S corporations can avoid paying corporate income taxes if all the shareholders consent to taxation of corporate income at the shareholder level. Although there are exceptions, most often the corporation itself is not a tax-paying entity. This is in sharp contrast to the separate taxpayer status held by regular corporations who are subject to double taxation. In effect, the election makes the S corporation a tax-reporting rather than a tax-paying entity. The income of the corporation flows through to the individuals as if the reporting entity was a partnership. Simplified, the S election treats the corporation as if it is a partnership. S corporations file Form 1120S annually.

EXAMPLE Roy Eric is the sole shareholder of the Office Design Corporation. For the year 20X3, Design earned taxable income of $400,000. Office Design's directors elected to distribute all after-tax earnings as a dividend to Roy. Assume that he is in the 35 percent tax bracket. The total federal taxes paid on the $400,000 of taxable earnings would be $228,400 calculated as follows:

		Taxes Paid
Taxable income	$400,000	
Less: Corporate tax at 34%	136,000	$136,000
Balance distributed as a		
dividend	$264,000	
Less: Individual tax at		
35%	92,400	92,400
After-tax dollars	$171,600	
Total taxes paid		$228,400

If Roy had elected S corporation status for 20X3, his total tax liability would have been $140,000 ($400,000 × 35 percent) resulting in a tax savings of $88,400 ($228,400 – $140,000).

In order to qualify under Subchapter S, a corporation must be a small business corporation. The following additional requirements must be met in order to be a small business corporation.

1. Must be a domestic corporation.
2. Must not have more than 75 shareholders
3. Must include only eligible shareholders.
4. Must have only one class of stock.

There are other limitations as well.

OBSERVATION *The corporation may not have more than 75 shareholders. Thus, if a husband and wife own shares as joint tenants, they are considered as one shareholder for this purpose. However, should the couple later divorce, then each would count as a separate shareholder even if the stock is still held jointly. If one spouse dies while the couple is married, there is only one shareholder as long as the stock remains in the deceased shareholder's estate.*

Individuals (other than nonresident aliens), estates, and certain trusts are eligible to hold stock in an S corporation. Among the trusts, which are not eligible shareholders of S corporation stock, are trusts adopted to administer tax-qualified retirement plans.

The IRS has also ruled that a corporation cannot qualify for an S election if it has a partner as a shareholder.

POINT TO REMEMBER *To elect S corporation status, the corporation must be a domestic corporation, owned by not more than 75 shareholders. Only one class of stock may be issued, although differences in common stock voting rights are permitted. Finally, none of the shareholders can be nonresident (an individual who is not a citizen or resident of the United States) shareholders.*

Election to be Classified As an S Corporation: Time for Election

Election to be an S corporation must be filed either at any time during the taxable year that immediately precedes the first taxable year for which the election is to be effective or at any time before the 16th day of the third month of the year to be so affected. A small business corporation must file Form 2553 (Appendix 7) (Election by a Small Business Corporation). See completed form in Basic Forms and Materials in back of text. All of the shareholders who own stock on the date the S corporation election is filed must consent to the election. If the stock is jointly owned, both joint owners must sign the consent form. Persons who are shareholders during any part of the year preceding the date of the election is made must also consent to the election even though they are not shareholders on the election date. An election made after the 15th day of the third month of the election year is treated as made for the next tax year.

EXAMPLE Sundial Wheat Growers, Inc. is incorporated on January 1, 20X3 and decides to be an S corporation beginning in 20X3. The election must be made no later than March 15, 20X3 to be effective for the year 20X3. If the election is made *after* March 15, 20X3, Drake will not have S corporation status until 20X4.

OBSERVATION *Generally, the IRS will give notification of acceptance of an S corporation election within 60 days after Form 2553 has been filed. Form 1120S is not to be filed until notification of acceptance is received.*

When Corporation Tax Return and Remaining Tax Due Must be Paid

Filing of the corporate tax return and payment of any balance of taxes owed are due in full by the 15th of the third calendar month following the close of the tax year. If the corporation uses a December 31 year end, it files its tax return by March 15. If it uses a fiscal year end and it ends, for example, on June 30, the tax return, and any payment, is due by September 15 (two and half months later).

A corporation can also get an automatic extension to the 15th day of the sixth month after the month of the due date of the corporate tax return by filing Form 7004 by the regular due date of the tax return. This form is an application for extension in place of filing the actual corporate tax return. Any remaining taxes due with the regular tax return must be filed with the extension.

A corporation may also have to pay estimated taxes by making four installments of estimated tax each year.

TRANSFERRING PROPERTY TO THE CORPORATE ENTITY: HOW TO CREATE A TAX-FREE TRANSFER

Section 351 of the Internal Revenue Code permits the shareholders of a corporation to defer recognition of a gain or loss on the transfer of assets to a corporation. The transfer of properties may either be made when a new corporation is formed or may reflect additional capital contributions to an existing corporation. A gain recognized by transferors of assets with a low basis to a corporation will not result in a taxable event if the following three requirements are met.

1. The person or persons making the transfer to the corporation must together control the corporation immediately after the exchange.
2. Each of the transferors must receive back stock.
3. The corporation does not assume any liabilities of a particular transferor or acquire property from a particular transferor subject to a liability if the purpose is to avoid a federal income tax on the exchange.

The utilization of Section 351 results in the following tax consequences.

1. No gain or loss is recognized by the transferor or transferors after the exchange is consummated.
2. The corporation succeeds to the transferor's adjusted basis for the property received by it.
3. The transferor's basis for the stock or securities received by him is the same as his adjusted basis for the property transferred.

EXAMPLE Alex Hayden owns a machine with a cost basis of $2,000 and a fair market value of $20,000. Hanna Baron owns land with a cost basis of $40,000 and a fair market value of $20,000. They both transfer their property to a newly organized corporation in exchange for equal shares of stock. Under Section 351, Alex's $18,000 gain and Hanna's $20,000 loss are not recognized.

How to Meet the "Control" Requirements of Section 351

All the transferors will be subject to a tax on the transfer of property to a corporation unless they meet the "control" test. "Control" means at least 80 percent of the combined voting power of all classes of voting stock and, in addition, at least 80 percent of all other classes of stock of the corporation. If two or more classes of voting stock are issued, the transferors must own at least 80 percent of the total voting power, irrespective of the number of shares issued in each class of stock. Furthermore, if two or more classes of nonvoting shares are issued, the transferors must also receive at least 80 percent of the number of shares in each class of nonvoting shares.

EXAMPLE Antony Neff and Baker Mackenzie, as individuals, form Barton Fixtures Corporation. Antony transfers property with an adjusted basis of $30,000, fair market value $60,000, for 50 percent of the stock. Baker transfers property with an adjusted basis of $40,000, fair market value $60,000, for the remaining 50 percent of the stock. Gain to either individual is not recognized because immediately after the transfer, Antony and Baker own at least

80 percent of the total combined voting power of all classes of stock.

Control Must Exist "Immediately After the Exchange"

The transferors of property to the corporation must be in control "immediately after the exchange." Control is defined as ownership of at least 80 percent of the total combined voting power of all classes entitled to vote and at least 80 percent of the total number of shares of all other classes of stock.

If a partnership distributes its assets to a new corporation in exchange for the corporation's stock and immediately thereafter transfers the stock to the partners, the control requirement is met. The control requirement would even be met if the partnership first dissolved and the former partners then transferred the property to the newly formed corporation.

If the transfer possesses the characteristics of a donative intent, the control requirements will be met.

EXAMPLE David Burke transfers land, which is an appreciated asset, to a new corporation in return for 100 shares. Immediately thereafter, David makes a gift of 30 shares to his grandchildren. The control requirement will still be satisfied.

Definition of Property

As discussed in the above paragraphs, the term "property" includes cash and intangibles, such as goodwill and patents, but excludes services that will be performed in the future.

LEASING PROPERTY TO THE CORPORATION INSTEAD OF TRANSFERRING IT

There may be a tax savings to the corporation if it leases rather than purchases corporate assets. The corporation receives an immediate tax deduction while preserving its working capital so it can be invested in more profitable ventures.

THE USE OF DEBT IN THE CAPITAL STRUCTURE: THIN INCORPORATION

Under a procedure called "thinning," assets are transferred to the corporation not only for stock but also for debt securities, such as notes payable to the shareholders. The advantage is that the interest

payable by the corporation to the shareholders is tax deductible by the corporation. By contrast, dividends paid on the stock are not a deductible item but represent a distribution of profits. Thinning of the capital structure also enables the shareholders to share with the general creditors of the corporation in case of insolvency. If the shareholder's entire interest in the corporation was in the form of a stock investment, the entire investment may be lost in case of an insolvency proceeding.

Thinning also allows the corporation an opportunity to distribute the cash of a prosperous corporation to its shareholders in the form of a loan repayment. This permits the shareholder to receive dollars at no tax cost.

•••

DANGER ZONE *If the debt-to-equity ratio of a closely held corporation is excessive, some of the alleged debt might be treated as stock by the IRS. That is, so-called interest and principal payments to the shareholders may be taxed as ordinary dividends, assuming adequate earnings and profits in the corporation. The point at which a debt-to-equity ratio becomes excessive is not clear. Court cases and the IRS have suggested that ratios exceeding three to one or four to one should be treated as excessive.*

•••

EXAMPLE 1 Robert Downs starts a new corporation and invests $100,000. He takes back $80,000 in 10 percent ten year notes and $20,000 in common stock. This situation, showing a ratio of four to one would most likely be viewed as one of thin incorporation and the notes would be treated as equity. Thus, any interest payments attributed to them would be treated as nondeductible dividends.

EXAMPLE 2 Same facts as in **EXAMPLE 1**, except that Downs takes back $50,000 in notes and $50,000 in stock. Thin incorporation would not be an issue in this case and any interest paid on the notes would be tax deductible.

Checklist for determining whether thin capitalization is a problem.

1. Is it in fact, a true debt instrument? Does it call for an unconditional promise by the corporation to repay the debt at a specified time?

2. Is there a conversion privilege (debt to equity)?

3. Is there a fixed interest rate?

4. Is there a relationship between the proportion of stock held by an investor and the proportion of debt held by that investor?

5. Has shareholder debt been subordinated to outside creditor debt?

6. The debt-to-equity ratio of the corporation's capital structure should be examined. Although no clear-cut rule of thumb can be given, if the debt-to-equity ratio of shareholders' holdings exceeds three to one, a careful evaluation is required.

ASSURING ORDINARY LOSS DEDUCTIONS UNDER SECTION 1244

Section 1244 rules permit an ordinary loss to be claimed for qualifying stock issued by small business corporations. Clearly, an ordinary loss is more advantageous to an investor than a capital loss deduction. Original stockholders that contribute up to $1,000,000 of corporate capital are permitted to deduct realized capital losses against their other income without regard to the usual annual limitation that applies to the sale of regular stock (currently $3,000). The annual Section 1244 deduction limit is $50,000 per taxpayer ($100,000 for a joint return). Losses in excess of the dollar ceiling in any given year are considered capital losses. To qualify, the corporation must be primarily an operating company rather than a company engaged in investing.

Section 1244 stock must be common stock issued by a small business corporation. This means that the amount of money and other property received by the corporation for its stock as a contribution to capital and as paid-in surplus (retained earnings) cannot initially exceed $1 million.

EXAMPLE Helen Allen, who is married filing a joint tax return, is one of the original stock purchasers of Halo Cosmetics Ltd. whose stock qualifies for Section 1244 treatment. Two years ago, in 20X1, she bought the stock for $200,000. During 20X3, she sold all of the stock for $50,000 thereby sustaining a $150,000 loss ($200,000 − $50,000). On her joint return for 20X3, she can deduct $100,000 as an ordinary loss. The remaining portion of the loss $50,000 ($150,000 − $100,000) is treated as a long-term capital loss. Assuming that Helen has no other capital gains, she can deduct $3,000 of the remaining $50,000 capital loss in 20X3 and $47,000 ($50,000 − $3,000) will be carried forward to future years.

An S corporation can elect Section 1244 treatment.

How to Make the Election

A board resolution must be passed prior to the original issuance of the shares. The resolution would appear as follows:

Section 1244 of the Internal Revenue Code permits ordinary loss treatment when the holder of Section 1244 sells or exchanges such stock at a loss or such stock becomes worthless. The stock to be issued by this domestic corporation shall be issued as "Section 1244" stock. It is the desire of this corporation to secure for its shareholders any benefits accorded them under Section 1244.

Thus, it is hereby resolved that all stock of this corporation initially issued shall be designated "Section 1244" at the time of issuance thereof. The officers are hereby authorized and empowered to perform all acts necessary to carry out the issuance of such stock in the manner prescribed by the Internal Revenue Code.

PARTIAL CAPITAL GAIN EXCLUSION FOR SMALL BUSINESS STOCK HELD FOR FIVE YEARS

A noncorporate taxpayer who holds for more than five years qualified small business stock issued after August 10, 1993, can exclude 50 percent of any gain on the sale or exchange of the stock. The amount of gain eligible for the exclusion is limited to the greater of (1) ten times the taxpayer's basis in the stock or (2) $10 million of gain from stock in that corporation. The exclusion is on a shareholder-by-shareholder basis.

EXAMPLE Archer Corless acquired all 100 shares of the Allentown Screw Corp. common stock in 20X2 (after August 10, 1993) by transferring property with a cost of $10,000 and a fair market value of $40,000.

Allentown is a qualified small business corporation. In June of the year 20X7, Archer sold all of the stock for $100,000. The excluded gain would be $45,000 calculated as follows:

Selling Price	$ 100,000
Less: Cost Basis	10,000
Realized Gain	$ 90,000
Exclusion Percentage	50%
Excluded Gain	$ 45,000

The limitation under the Internal Revenue Code is the greater of $10,000 or $400,000 ($40,000 × 10). Thus, none of the $90,000 is subject to the limitation.

The rules establishing what constitutes qualified small business stock for purposes of this rule are as follows:

1. The stock must be acquired by the taxpayer at original issuance after August 10, 1993. Thus, stock acquired by purchase from a prior stockholder is not eligible for the exclusion.
2. The corporation must be a C corporation that uses at least 80 percent of its gross assets in the active conduct of a qualified trade or business.
3. A qualified trade or business is any trade or business other than personal service type businesses, such as health, law, or engineering.
4. As of the date of issuance of the stock, the corporation's gross assets cannot exceed $50 million.

ELECTION TO AMORTIZE ORGANIZATION COSTS

Under the Internal Revenue Code, a corporation may elect to amortize its organizational expenses over a period of sixty months or more for tax purposes beginning with the first month of corporate operations. To qualify for the election, the expenditure must be incurred before the end of the taxable year in which the corporation begins doing business. These expenditures include fees paid for legal services in drafting the corporate charter, costs of merger or consolidation, bylaws, minutes of organization meetings, fees paid for accounting services, and fees paid to the state of incorporation. The costs do not include costs of issuing and selling the stock and costs incurred in the transfer of assets to a corporation.

EXAMPLE Vanko Cosmetics, Inc. a newly organized corporation, was formed on June 30, 20X3, and began doing business on July 1. The corporation will have a December 31 year end. Vanko incurred the following expenses in organizing the business:

Legal fees for drafting corporate charter	$ 600
Fees paid for accounting services	700
Fees paid to state of incorporation	500
Costs of selling shares of stock	2,000
	$ 3,800

Amortization for the six months (July 1 to December 31, 20X3) will be $180, calculated as follows:

Legal fees for corporate charter	$ 600
Accounting fees	700
Fees paid to state	500
Organization expenses	$ 1,800

$1,800 ÷ 60 months = $30 per month × 6 months = $180. The cost of selling the shares may not be amortized.

WARNING *Failure to elect amortization of expenses of the corporation's organization on the corporation's initial tax return will result in their permanent capitalization without the ability to deduct these expenditures. Therefore, it is imperative to properly categorize these costs as amortizable because any attempt to improperly deduct the entire cost in the first year will result in their permanent disallowance.*

The corporation's election is made by attaching to its initial tax return a statement indicating the amount and nature of the expenditures, the date the expenditures were incurred, the period over which it will be amortized, and date of incorporation.

ELECTION TO AMORTIZE BUSINESS START-UP EXPENSES

A distinction must be made between a corporation's organization expenses discussed in the preceeding section and its start-up expenses. Start-up expenses are qualifying expenditures made in connection with the creation or acquisition of a trade or business. They include market surveys, advertising, outside consulting services, training costs prior to starting a business, and travel and entertainment. A separate election may be made to amortize start-up expenses over a period of sixty months or more starting with the first month that corporate business begins.

The corporation's election is made by attaching to its initial tax return a statement indicating the amount and nature of the expenditures, the date the expenditures were incurred, the period over which they will be amortized, and the date of incorporation.

LIMITED DEDUCTIONS: CHARITABLE CONTRIBUTIONS AND CAPITAL GAINS AND LOSSES
Introduction

Corporations making contributions to recognized charitable organizations are allowed a maximum deduction of 10 percent of their taxable income. Any charitable contributions in excess of the allowed deduction can be carried forward five years.

Accrual of Charitable Contribution Allowed

A charitable contribution can be deducted by an accrual basis corporation, even if the contribution has not been paid by year-end, as long as:

1. The contribution has been accrued by year-end, as authorized by the board of directors, and
2. The contribution is paid by March 15 of the following year for a calendar-year company, or 2½ months after the close of the corporation's fiscal year.

EXAMPLE For 20X3, Sexton Batteries, Ltd. had total sales of $100,000 and operating expenses of $35,000 before deducting charitable contributions of $20,000. Sexton may deduct $6,500 in contributions for the year calculated as follows:

Taxable Income Before Deducting Contributions	$ 100,000
Less: Operating Expenses	35,000
	$ 65,000
Contribution limitation (10% × $65,000)	$ 6,500

The remaining contributions of $13,500 ($20,000 – $6,500) are carried over for five years.

A corporation may not deduct any charitable contribution if the corporation had a net operating loss for the year.

Capital Gains and Losses

A corporation determines its capital gains and losses in the same manner as other taxpayers.

Gains

Unlike the individual, the tax rate on net capital gain for a corporation is not limited to 15 percent.

Losses

The $3,000 deduction for capital losses in excess of capital gains available to individuals is not allowable to corporations. Thus, a corporation can only use capital losses to offset capital gains.

1. Excess capital losses may be carried back three years and then forward five years.
2. Carryback and carryforward losses are treated as short-term capital losses in the year to which they are carried.

PERSONAL HOLDING COMPANY TAX
Introduction

The personal holding company (PHC) penalty tax is imposed in order to discourage the use of the corporate form as an "incorporated pocketbook" to shelter the income of high tax bracket individuals from the individual tax rates. To be considered a personal holding company (PHC), the corporation must satisfy two tests—the "adjusted ordinary gross income" test and the stock ownership test.

The "Adjusted Ordinary Gross Income" Test

The personal holding company (PHC) income test is satisfied if the corporation's personal holding company equals or exceeds 60 percent of its total ordinary gross income. PHC income means unearned income such as interest, dividends, rents, and royalties in addition to amounts received under personal service contracts. There are exceptions to this complex rule.

The Stock Ownership Test

The stock ownership test is satisfied if at any time during the last half of the taxable year more than 50 percent of the outstanding stock of the corporation is owned, directly or indirectly, by or no more than five individuals. Individuals are regarded as constructively owning any stock owned by members of their families (called the attribution rule under the IRC). Almost all closely held corporations will meet the 50 percent ownership test.

EXAMPLE The Damon Holding Corp. which is owned by four shareholders, has adjusted ordinary gross income of $100,000 for the year. The $100,000 is composed of interest, dividends, rents, and royalties. Since the corporation is owned by less than five individuals for the entire year, and all of its income is unearned income, Damon is a personal holding company.

If a corporation is a personal holding company for a given year, it is subject to a flat rate of 39.6 percent on any undistributed PHC income *in addition* to whatever corporate income tax it already pays.

ACCUMULATED EARNINGS TAX

This tax is imposed on the accumulation of earnings beyond the reasonable business needs of the corporation. These reasonably anticipated needs include planned additions to plant facilities, planned retirement of debt, and a provision for working capital needs. Investments are generally not regarded as reasonable business needs. A corporation is allowed to accumulate $250,000 of earnings before it must prove that the accumulation is for its reasonable business needs. The accumulated earnings credit is reduced to $150,000 for corporations primarily engaged in the business of providing professional services, such as accounting, law, health, engineering, architecture, actuarial, sciences, performing arts, and consulting.

THE USE OF FOREIGN SUBSIDIARIES

A United States corporation can form a foreign subsidiary to operate in a country where the tax rates are lower than that of the United States. The foreign corporation would pay the foreign income taxes on the subsidiary's profits and accumulate the income until such time that the parent corporation deems it appropriate to make payment to the United States parent. Upon such payment, the parent would take a direct credit against its United States federal tax liability for any foreign taxes paid.

EXAMPLE In 20X1, Maryland Manufacturing Corporation, incorporated and operating in the United States, formed a subsidiary corporation in a foreign country with tax rates that were substantially lower than United States tax rates. Over the years, the subsidiary accumulated $300,000 in net income on which it paid $50,000 in foreign taxes. In 20X6, the parent corporation deemed it appropriate to have the subsidiary transfer the profits to the United States parent. The distribution was included in the combined taxable income of the parent and resulted in a final overall federal tax liability of $400,000. The parent is now permitted to take a foreign tax credit of $50,000 based on the foreign income thereby resulting in a net tax payable of $350,000 ($400,000 – $50,000).

THE USE OF MULTIPLE CORPORATIONS TO REDUCE TAXES AND TO PROTECT CORPORATE ASSETS

Some incorporators form more than one corporation to minimize their tax exposure and to protect assets. Unfortunately, minimizing taxes by forming multiple corporations does not lower taxes under current tax laws. If two or more corporations are members of a controlled group (e.g., two or more corporations that are owned directly or indirectly by the same shareholder or shareholders), all member corporations are limited to a total of $50,000 being taxed at 15 percent, $25,000 being taxed at 25 percent, and $10 million being taxed at 34 and 35 percent.

EXAMPLE Corporations A, B, C, and D are owned by Cedric Holmes, the sole shareholder. Their individual taxable income for the year 20X3 is $35,000 and their tax liabilities are calculated as follows:

Corporation	Taxable Income	Tax Liability
A	$15,000	$ 2,500*
B	$15,000	2,500
C	$15,000	2,500
D	$15,000	2,500
	$60,000	$10,000

*$12,500 × 15% = $1,875
2,500 × 25% =   625
$15,000 $2,500

Note that the same tax liability of $10,000 would result if Holmes, as the sole shareholder, owned one corporation that had net income of $60,000.

As stated in Chap. 2, the use of multiple corporations might be used to simplify operations, increase efficiency, and limit the exposure of corporate assets to outside claims and lawsuits. On the other hand, multiple entities might result in increased legal and accounting costs, duplication of operations, problems when operating in different states and municipalities due to a multiplicity of state and municipal tax laws, and possible antitrust violations.

DIVIDENDS AND THE REDEMPTION OF STOCK

When a corporation repurchases its own stock, two possibilities can result.

1. First, the redemption might be treated as a taxable dividend, or
2. The redemption might be considered an exchange of stock, thereby resulting in capital gain treatment. It depends on the particular circumstances.

A tax-free recovery of the shareholder's stock basis is not permitted if the distribution is equivalent to a dividend. A distribution might be considered equivalent to a dividend if the shareholder's percentage of ownership in the corporation remains the same.

EXAMPLE Edgar Wyler, who is unmarried and has no relatives, owns all of the 100 shares outstanding of the Keller Shipping Corp. Edgar redeems 50 shares costing $1,000 for $10,000, at a time when the corporation has retained earnings of $20,000.

Since Edgar still continues to own all of the outstanding shares, thereby retaining the same percentage of control over the corporation, the proceeds from the sale are treated as dividends subject to ordinary income tax rates.

Where the redemption completely terminates the shareholder's interest in the corporation, any profits can be treated as capital gains subject to a maximum rate capital gains rate of 15 percent.

EXAMPLE Chester Benny and Ruth Marlin each own 50 shares of the Rostand Book Co. Inc. Chester redeems his 50 shares costing $1,000 for $10,000, at a time when the corporation has retained earnings of $20,000. Since the redemption completely terminated his interest in the corporation, any long-term profits can be treated as capital gains subject to a maximum tax rate of 15 percent.

Thus, from the above discussion of this complex topic, not all stock redemptions can be given capital gains treatment.

"DEATH TAX" REDEMPTIONS: CORPORATE BUY-SELL AGREEMENTS

The Internal Revenue Code has a special provision that enables estates of deceased shareholders to more easily redeem their shares that make up a significant portion of the deceased shareholder's estate. Where the value of the stock redeemed is more than 35 percent of the decedent's gross estate with certain adjustments, the estate will *not recognize gain from the redemption* if the proceeds are used to pay all estate taxes, funeral expenses, and administration expenses imposed on the estate.

EXAMPLE Jade Phillips dies in 20X3 and her gross estate is valued at $1,000,000. Her death, funeral, and administration expenses totalled $300,000. At the time of her death, she owned $500,000 worth of stock of Georgia Foods, Inc., a small business corporation. She bought the stock five years ago for $100,000. Because the value of the decedent's stock exceeds 35 percent of her gross estate, in this case 50 percent ($500,000/$1,000,000), the executor of Jade's estate may redeem $300,000 of stock tax-free. This amount is necessary to pay all of the decedent's death, funeral, and administration expenses. If it were not for this provision in the Code, the estate would have to pay a tax based upon the gain due to the redemption.

Certain types of stock repurchase agreements expedite these redemptions. These arrangements, called either stock redemption or cross-purchase agreements, assure the further continuance of the corporation. These agreements may also give the corporation or shareholders the right of first refusal should the stock become available due to the death of a shareholder, or because a shareholder wishes to sell her stock.

Agreements involving the sale of stock may take the following forms.

1. **The Stock Redemption Agreement.** This type of arrangement binds both the shareholders and the corporation. On the death of the shareholder, when the shareholder wishes to sell his stock back to the corporation, or in the event of a director deadlock that cannot be broken the corporation is bound to repurchase the shares.

2. **The Cross-Purchase Agreement.** This type of agreement obligates each of the shareholders to buy each other's shares in case of the death of a shareholder or if one of the shareholders wishes to sell.

The advantages of these types of arrangements is that they guarantee a ready market for the stock in case of death or the need for immediate cash by one of the shareholders. It also enables the executor of an estate to fix the value of the stock for estate tax purposes.

The purchase price can be established by either a fixed-dollar amount subject to annual review, by book value at date of death, by an independent CPA or other qualified appraiser, or by a formula based on prior earnings of the corporation for a stated period of time.

A detailed discussion involving the contents of a buy/sell agreement for purchasing a business is in Chap. 16.

ESTATE TAXATION
Introduction

The Federal estate tax, which dates from 1916, is imposed on a decedent's entire taxable estate. It is essentially a transfer tax on the right to pass property at death. Generally, the federal estate tax will be imposed to the extent that the value of the decedent's estate exceeds a certain exempt amount.

During 2001, tax legislation was passed that will slowly phase out the federal estate tax as of January 1, 2010, when it will be repealed. However, the tax bill also includes a "sunset provision," meaning that the entire tax bill will no longer be in effect as of January 1, 2011. In other words, the old estate tax law (with a $1,000,000 exemption) will once again be in effect on January 1, 2011, unless Congress and the President take action to extend the repeal.

Under current tax law, the exemption amounts will increase until 2010 as shown in the table below:

Year of Decedent's Death	Exemption Amount
2002	$1,000,000
2003	$1,000,000
2004	$1,500,000
2005	$1,500,000
2006	$2,000,000
2007	$2,000,000
2008	$2,000,000
2009	$3,500,000
2010	$ Repealed
2011	$1,000,000

Gifts made by the decedent during his or her lifetime may reduce the exemption. Because of this exemption, a majority of Americans die without being subject to a federal estate tax liability. Currently, estate tax rates range from 40 percent to 55 percent and some estates pay an even higher percentage. The new tax law makes modest decreases in the rates, and in 2009, the highest rate will still be at least 45 percent. The new rates are as follows:

Year of Decedent's Death	Maximum Tax Rate
2002	50%
2003	49%
2004	48%
2005	46%
2006	47%
2007	46%
2008	45%
2009	45%
2010	0%
2011	55%

Determining the Gross Estate

The gross estate includes all property in which the decedent had an interest at the time of his or her death, with the exception of certain family owned businesses as previously described above. While this rule appears to be simple to apply, there are special Code provisions that make the determination of ownership complex and difficult.[8]

How to Determine the Value of Property at Death

Property values are determined at the date of death. The estate's executor may also select an alternate valuation date that can be as long as six months after the date of death if certain conditions are met.[9] This optional valuation date can be an important factor in minimizing the bite of estate taxes on the decedent's estate.

Stocks and Bonds

The typical investment portfolio presents few valuation problems for the executor. The value of securities can usually be ascertained by reference to accessible reports of actual market transactions. Corporate bonds that are actively traded are valued in the same manner.

OBSERVATION Interests in Close Corporations and Other Businesses. *The Internal Revenue Code Regulations indicate that the value of bonds in close corpora-*

tions is arrived at by giving consideration to "the soundness of the security, the interest yield, the date of maturity, and other relevant factors."[10] In the case of stock, "the company's net worth, prospective earning power and dividend paying capacity, and other relevant factors" must be taken into account.[11]

Alternate Valuation Rules

The value of the property on the date of its transfer generally determines the amount that will be subject to the gift tax or the estate tax. Under certain conditions, however, an executor can elect to value estate assets on an alternate valuation date.[12]

The alternate valuation date election was designed as a relief from economic hardship that could result if estate assets decline within the six month period immediately after the date of death. If the election is made, all assets of the estate are valued six months after death or on the date of disposition if this occurs earlier. The election covers all assets in the gross estate and individual assets cannot be selectively valued.

EXAMPLE 1 Daw's gross estate consists of the following property:

	Value on Date of Death	Value Six Months Later
Stock in G Corporation	$ 860,000	$ 600,000
Stock in Z Corporation	$ 440,000	$ 500,000
Total	$1,300,000	$1,100,000

If Daw's executor elects the alternate valuation date, the estate must be valued at $1,100,000. It is not permissible to value the Z stock at its cost of $440,000 and choose the alternate valuation date for the balance of the gross estate.

EXAMPLE 2 Use the same facts as in Example 1 except that the executor sells the stock in Z Corporation for $550,000 five months after Daw's death. If the alternate valuation date is elected, the estate must be valued at $1,150,000 ($600,000 +

---

[8]IRC §2031.
[9]IRC §2032. (Also see Chapter 2.)
[10]IRC Reg. §20.2031–2(f)(1).
[11]IRC Reg. §20.2031–2(f)(2), Rev. Rul. 59–60, 1959–1 CB 237.
[12]IRC §2032.

$550,000). As to the stock in Z Corporation, the value on its date of disposition controls because that date occurred prior to the six months' alternate valuation date.

The alternate valuation date election is not available unless the estate is required to file Form 706 (Estate Tax Return).

FINDING HELP ONLINE
www.irs.gov
The Internal Revenue Service is very helpful by providing information as to how to set up a new business. Look for the market-segment guides on the Web site; they go into tax issues for various businesses. Start exploring "Tax Info for Business" or go directly to the small-business pages at www.irs.gov/small-biz/index.htm and select

"New Business." The IRS may also be reached at 800-829-1040.

www.sba.gov
The Small Business Administration's website has pages on "Starting Your Business" with links to many other helpful sources. On the IRS and SBA sites, an individual may order a free CD-ROM, "Small Business Resource Guide," produced by the agencies. For more information, phone the SBA at 800-827-5722.

cch.com
CCH Inc., a tax-information publisher, offers an excellent free introduction to start a business. Select "CCH Business Owner's Toolkit."

CHAPTER 16

How to Buy and/or Sell an Ongoing Business

INTRODUCTION

There is no absolute value that can be put on a business, although value, when determined, must be translated into terms of money. A valuation is a means of justifying the premium in the asking price of a business. While net worth is a primary factor in valuing most privately owned businesses, one cannot rely entirely on balance sheet figures because they are based upon original cost and, therefore, do not purport to reflect the current replacement value of assets.

Another issue is goodwill. Goodwill may not be reflected on the balance sheet, but it may be material in amount, and the common practice of ignoring goodwill on the corporation's balance sheet might lead to a serious undervaluation of a company's assets.

CHECKLIST OF DIFFERENCES BETWEEN A LARGE AND SMALL BUSINESS AS A DETERMINANT FACTOR IN SELECTING A VALUATION TECHNIQUE

1. Small businesses are likely to be sole proprietorships, partnerships, or S corporations while a large enterprise is usually organized as a regular corporation. The inability of a large corporation to elect S corporation status may lower its resale value.

2. If a corporation is small, the owner-shareholder plays a greater role in the success of the company. This situation may call for the owner to continue her role as the manager after the purchase of the business.

3. Larger companies usually pay their managers the market rate in salaries while smaller businesses tend to pay their managers only what they can afford.

4. Larger companies tend to have a more accurate picture of their financial condition, which might increase their tax burden, while small companies tend to use the accounting policy which produces the lowest possible tax liability.

5. Large businesses tend to be sold for cash and stock while small enterprises are usually sold for a cash down payment plus monthly payments for a fixed number of years.

6. Larger businesses have usually been in business longer than smaller entities, thus making it easier to study and evaluate their financial history and potential future value.

7. Most larger companies use the accrual basis of accounting while smaller businesses tend to use the cash basis. Under the Internal Revenue Code, the cash method of accounting may not be used by any regular corporation, except by qualified personal service corporations, and entities with average annual gross receipts of $5 million or less for all prior taxable years.

8. Larger companies usually have audited financial statements while smaller companies tend to have compiled statements (financial statements where the CPA compiles the accounting data according to generally accepted accounting principles but does not express an opinion as to the accuracy of the financial statements).
9. Larger companies generally have better accounting records than smaller entities.
10. Larger companies tend to have highly paid executives whose compensation package includes a "golden parachute" (a costly severance package) given upon termination.
11. Larger companies tend to have more union problems than smaller companies.

Some of the more important and useful methods of valuation are discussed below.

HOW TO VALUE AN ONGOING BUSINESS

Suppose that you decide to purchase an ongoing business. It does have its advantages. First, there is a recognized product with established sales outlets. Second, you have experienced employees working for you. Third, there is no start-up or break-in period where costly mistakes are made in order to "learn the ropes." Of course, purchasing an ongoing business can be costly, and there is always the ongoing risk that you, as a buyer, may overpay. The other side of the coin is that you, as a seller, may risk undervaluation of, perhaps, your most valuable asset, your business. What follows is a basic discussion regarding the use of certain methods for accurately valuing an ongoing corporation.

Tangible Book Value

This value is determined by the company's last balance sheet. Basically the computation involves subtracting the entity's total liabilities from its total assets.

DANGER *Since balance sheet assets are reflected at cost, which ignores fair market value, and since goodwill may not be recorded on the balance sheet, a business with high resale value assets or unrecorded goodwill should avoid this method.*

Adjusted Tangible Book Value

This method takes the book value of all assets and liabilities and adjusts them to fair market value.

EXAMPLE Bantam Sales Company Inc. presents the following financial data:

	Reported Net Book Value	Fair Market Value
Inventory	$ 20,000	$ 25,000
Land and plant	45,000	60,000
Equipment	50,000	100,000
	$115,000	$ 185,000
Liabilities	20,000	

Assuming that there is unrecorded goodwill of $40,000, the fair market value of the company would be $205,000 ($185,000 + $40,000 − $20,000).

Liquidation Value

This method assumes that the business ceases operations, sells its assets, pays off all of its liabilities, and distributes the remaining cash to its shareholders in proportion to their stock ownership.

EXAMPLE Sundial Paper Corporation, which has 10,000 shares of common stock outstanding, plans to liquidate by selling all of its assets, paying its liabilities, and making a liquidating distribution to its shareholders. Assuming assets with a net realizable value of $200,000, and liabilities of $50,000, each shareholder would be expected to get $15 per share calculated as follows:

Estimated fair market value of assets	$ 200,000
Less: Liabilities	50,000
Net liquidation value	$ 150,000
Outstanding number of shares	10,000
Liquidation value per share	$ 15

Replacement Value

Where there is a strong possibility that many assets are undervalued, an independent appraiser or a panel of appraisers may be called in by the buyers or sellers of the stock.

Price-Earnings Multiple

This method utilizes the company's price-earnings ratio. The price-earnings (P/E) is simply the market value of the share divided by the earnings per share.

EXAMPLE Norris Road Repair Inc. has a net income of $50,000 annually and 50,000 common shares outstanding or earnings per share (EPS) of $1 per share ($50,000/50,000 shares). The market value of the shares is estimated at $20 per share. Thus, the P/E or multiple will be $20 ÷ $1 or 20. Since the company has 50,000 shares outstanding, the value of the entire company would be 50,000 shares times $20 per share or $1,000,000. Stated another way, the entire business may be valued by multiplying the total net income of $50,000 by the price earnings multiple of 20 to arrive at $1,000,000.

How to Get the Best Tax Break

Once the buyer and the seller have decided to structure the transaction as a taxable purchase of assets, they must then decide whether to allocate the total sales price among the individual assets sold or whether to merely agree on and set forth in a single lump-sum price.

OBSERVATION *Note that in allocating the purchase price of a business to the newly acquired assets, the capitalized cost of goodwill and most other intangibles, such as licenses, patents and covenants not to compete acquired after August 10, 1993, and used in a trade or business, are ratably amortized over a 15-year period beginning in the month of acquisition.*

EXAMPLE On January 2, 20X3, Lion Supermarkets Ltd. acquired all of the net assets of Iris Flower Corporation for $200,000. Among the acquired assets were the following intangible assets:

Goodwill	$ 20,000
Patents	10,000
Licenses	5,000
A covenant not to compete for five years	30,000
	$ 65,000

All of the above assets are amortizable ratably over a period of 15 years beginning with the first month of the acquisition.

SALES OF CORPORATE SHARES AND ASSETS

In disposing of a corporate business, the deal can be constructed as either a taxable or nontaxable event. In a taxable deal, the seller might be seeking the following:

1. Avoiding double taxation, once at the corporate level, and a second at the stockholder level.
2. Establishing an ordinary loss so as to offset ordinary income.
3. Controlling the timing of the loss so as to obtain the best tax advantages.
4. The spreading out of the seller's tax liability for as long as possible so as to avoid an immediate tax liability.
5. Converting ordinary gain into capital gain so as to take advantage of the lower 15 percent personal capital gains rate.

Generally, the provisions of the Internal Revenue Code governing the sale, disposition, and liquidation of regular (or C) corporation shares and assets also apply to S corporations. Several methods are available to both types of corporations for disposing of corporate assets. Some of the more common ways for either a C or S corporation are

1. Sale of the corporation's stock. This gives the seller capital gain. The buyer may then liquidate or continue to operate the business as a subsidiary.
2. Sale of the corporation's assets and either liquidates or continues as an investment company or in a new business.
3. Liquidation of the corporation followed by the sale of corporate assets. This technique requires that the corporation recognize gain on any appreciated assets distributed.
4. The shareholder or shareholders can sell part of their stock and have the corporation redeem the remainder. In effect corporation funds are used as part of the purchase price. The seller

gets capital gains treatment and the buyer or buyers get control of the corporation.

There are significant tax differences that result to both the corporation and its shareholders depending on the method selected. Our discussion will focus on the legal and tax implications resulting from disposing of and liquidating corporate shares and assets that are unique to C and S corporations and their shareholders.

OBSERVATION *A seller might want to think about making some estate tax planning steps prior to the sale. For example, the seller might consider making gifts of stock to younger family members who may be subject to lower tax rates. Thus, if notes are received by the seller, any interest income would be taxed at a lower rate. This technique should be planned with great care since the IRS may contend that the proceeds should be taxed to the original seller who is responsible for the corporate sale rather than to the owner of the stock at the time of the execution of the sales contract.*

SALE OF STOCK OF A REGULAR C CORPORATION

When a shareholder of a C corporation sells her shares, determining gain or loss is the simplest of the acquisition transactions. The shareholder's stock basis will be his original cost adjusted, if at all, only by stock dividends and splits. Stock basis is then subtracted from the proceeds of the sale to determine gain or loss.

Whether the gain or loss is treated as long-term or short-term capital gain or loss depends merely on the shareholder's holding period, i.e., more than one year is treated as long-term capital gain or loss and one year or less is treated as short-term capital gain or loss. If part or all of the consideration is deferred into a later tax year, the seller's gain can be reported using the installment method of accounting. If part of the total consideration received by the seller of the stock represents an agreement with the purchaser not to compete for a specific period of time, the consideration received for the agreement is taxed as ordinary income.

Stock sales are popular with sellers because they are less complex and costly to the seller and

there is only one level of taxation, i.e., capital gains. No adjustments are made to the basis of the assets even if the purchase price of the stock is higher than the basis of the assets reported for tax purposes. This can be a disadvantage to the purchaser since the increased costs of the assets, and the resultant higher depreciation, is not available to the purchaser.

EXAMPLE Cheryl Cain has been the sole shareholder since 20X3, of the Sharp Wire and Conduit Corp., a regular C corporation. She owns 5,000 common shares having a $10 par value. The net assets of Sharp Wire were $50,000 ($65,000 – $15,000). Cheryl sold the stock for $60,000 to Walter Bigelow. She will have a long-term capital gain of $10,000 ($60,000 – $50,000). Bigelow, the purchaser, will not adjust the basis of the assets to reflect their stepped-up basis.

SALE OF ASSETS OF A REGULAR C CORPORATION

When a corporate seller sells assets, the transaction is reported by determining the gain or loss recognized on the sale of each individual asset. The buyer simply records the assets at their acquisition cost. The corporation may be liquidated after the sale has been completed. The corporation recognizes gain or loss with respect to the assets sold. Any properties that were not sold by the corporation can be distributed to the shareholder or shareholders as part of the liquidation. The selling corporation must recognize gain at the time the distribution occurs as if the properties had been sold. The shareholders of the selling corporation report their gain on the liquidation as capital gain or loss.

SELLING S CORPORATION STOCK

An S corporation shareholder poses greater problems than those associated with a C corporation when selling stock. While the holding period rules for S corporation stock are the same as those for C corporation shareholders, an S corporation shareholder faces the tax rule that a corporation's S election will terminate if the shares are sold to an ineligible shareholder. For example, partnerships, corporations, and nonresident aliens cannot be shareholders in an S corporation.

HOW TO HANDLE THE INSTALLMENT SALE OF A BUSINESS

The installment method of reporting involves the seller's treatment of each payment received from the sale as part gain and part nontaxable recovery of her basis in the property sold. Under the Internal Revenue Code, sales of publicly traded property, including stocks and bonds, and inventory do not qualify for the installment method. However, the sale of privately held stock, *not listed on a national exchange*, would qualify. The installment method must be used to report gains (income) from installment sales of real or personal property by nondealers unless an election is made *not* to use the method.

If the sale results in a loss, the taxpayer may not use the installment method. If the loss is on an installment sale of business assets, it can be deducted only in the tax year of the sale.

WHAT AN EFFECTIVE AND COMPREHENSIVE BUY-SELL AGREEMENT SHOULD CONTAIN

Any transaction involving the purchase and sale of a corporation contains areas of potential and costly conflicts. The following checklist will enable purchasing and selling parties to deal with potential problem areas at the time the transaction is entered into so as to avoid possible future litigation.

Checklist for Buy-Sell Agreements

1. Should the buy-sell agreement apply to just current shareholders or to all new shareholders during the life of the new or existing corporation?
2. There should be a statement in the buy-sell agreement to the effect that it supersedes all other existing agreements to redeem stock or purchase stock executed by the shareholders.
3. Will the death of a shareholder in the corporation result in an automatic buy-out of his interest, or will the next of kin be allowed to become a shareholder in the corporation?
4. Will all of the death buy-out amount be funded by insurance, or just part of it? In the event of a death buy-out, will all the proceeds from the policy be used to redeem the stock of the deceased shareholder.

5. In the event of the death of a shareholder, what will be the disposition of shareholder receivables or payables?
6. What will be the price paid to an employee shareholder who resigns or is fired from the corporation?
7. In case an employee shareholder resigns or is fired from the corporation, will a covenant not to compete be involved, and if so, what will be its geographic area (fifty miles, for example) and for how long will it be in effect (for example, five years, or in conjunction with the installment payments of the buy-out if not paid in cash)?
8. How many days should the corporation have in which to pay off a terminated, disabled, or deceased shareholder?

OBSERVATION *As discussed in Chap. 15, certain arrangements, called either stock redemption or cross-purchase agreements, assure the further continuance of the corporation. These agreements may also give the corporation or shareholders the right of first refusal should the stock become available due to the death of a shareholder or because a shareholder wishes to sell her stock.*

EXAMPLE Marvin Gunn and Sima Parno are equal shareholders in Victor Heat Controls Inc. By prior written agreement, if either individual dies, retires, or becomes totally disabled, the other shareholder is required to purchase the shares, thus becoming the sole shareholder. This is an example of a cross-purchase agreement.

9. Disability buy-out is a sensitive subject for employee shareholders to discuss. However, a disabled corporate employee cannot be carried for very long in a small business. Most businesses use a disability buy-out period of between three and six months. In other words, if one of the employee shareholders becomes totally disabled for a period of three months, on the first day of the fourth month, the corporate employee's stock is automatically sold back to the corporation at a disability buy-out price.

10. The corporation needs to discuss the possibility of one of the shareholders finding a nonrelated third party to buy his stock. Does the corporation want shareholders to have the right to sell on the open market to any third party or only have the right of first refusal? Or does the corporation want to restrict rights and only allow the shareholders to sell back to the corporation itself. There is quite a danger in allowing for unrelated third parties to make offers on stock of closely held corporations. Obviously a competitor could make an offer, making it hard to tell if it was a bona fide offer or just a ploy to drive the stock price up so that the remaining shareholders would have to pay a higher price to repurchase the stock.

11. All shareholders in the corporation who sign buy-sell agreements should also have their spouses, if any, sign the agreement as well. It is best to do this at the attorney's office and have the signatures witnessed or notarized. This prevents later problems in the event of a marital dissolution.

12. Shareholders of a corporation must decide whether or not the corporation will guarantee obligations to a retiring or deceased shareholder. The obligations should be personally guaranteed by the remaining shareholders when a shareholder dies or retires because the corporation could eventually become insolvent. Since one of the most important functions of a corporation is to shield the shareholders from personal liability, the personal guarantee, in writing, of every shareholder would provide the best protection against pending obligations.

1. Q. Is it easier to form a sole proprietorship than a corporation?

A. Yes. A sole proprietorship requires few formalities, such as registering your business name if you do not use your own name. The new business also requires minimum assets, and allows ease of operation such as initially operating from your own home. The sole proprietor pays a personal income tax based upon his or net income for the year. If an owner has a loss for the year, that loss may be used to offset an owner's taxable income from other sources. Thus a sole proprietorship is cheap and uncomplicated.

2. Q. If a sole proprietorship looks so easy to form and operate, why don't all entrepreneurs elect to start out in this manner?

A. The owner of a sole proprietorship may not wish to start out in this way because it exposes his or her personal assets to business debts and other liabilities. In addition, if the owner of a sole proprietorship hires employees, and they get into an accident within the scope of their duties as employees, additional claims may be made against the sole proprietorship.

3. Q. If I elect to initially operate as a sole proprietorship and find that I prefer doing business in this manner, will I be able to pass the business on to my children?

A. Generally, unless the sole proprietorship contains assets such as inventory that will permit the continued operation of the sole proprietorship by a beneficiary, the death of a sole proprietor usually terminates the business.

4. Q. Would death of a sole stockholder (or shareholder) in a corporation terminate the corporation?

A. No. A corporation enjoys perpetual existence. Upon the death of a stockholder, the stock will pass under the terms of the owner's will to whomever is designated to receive the stock. Thus, the named beneficiary will become the new stockholder of the corporation.

5. Q. What are the advantages of a partnership?

A. Each partnership will share in the benefits and burdens of operating the partnership. A partnership also permits the partners to contribute additional capital when needed. Finally, two heads are better than one in that the success of the partnership is based on joint efforts and expertise, rather than the experience if one individual is a sole proprietor.

6. Q. If I decide to go into business with one or more other individuals, how long will the partnership last? Will it go on indefinitely?

A. No. All partnerships draw up a partnership agreement stipulating, among other things, the name of the partnership, required capital contributions, whether one or more partners are to receive a salary, and how long a partnership will last. The typical partnership agreement stipulates that a partnership shall last until it is dissolved by all of the partners, or when a partner leaves or dies.

7. Q. The benefits of a partnership sound very appealing. There must be drawbacks.

A. Yes. Each partner has unlimited personal liability. In addition, not all partners tend to agree with one another. It is very common to have friction among the partners if they do not agree on some aspect of the partnership's operations.

8. Q. Does a partnership pay an income tax?

A. No. There is a type of pass-through taxation. Each partner pays a personal income tax based upon his or her share of net income, *whether or not that income is actually distributed.* His or her share of a partnership's operating loss maybe used to offset a partner's other taxable income.

9. Q. If a new business carries substantial risks, what is the best way to run the business?

A. A risky business venture usually requires that a corporation be formed. A corporation will shield the stockholder's personal assets against any claims that may arise against the corporation. Thus a corporation, unlike a sole proprietorship or partnership, offers limited liability to its owner-stockholders.

10. Q. I've heard about an S corporation. What is it?

A. An S corporation allows a regular corporation to avoid tax liability at the corporate level. By electing S corporation status, the corporation is taxed as if it were a sole proprietorship or partnership. Thus, the profits pass through to the individual stockholders to be taxed on their personal tax returns.

11. Q. How do I become an S corporation?

A. The stockholders sign and file Form 2553. The election must be done by unanimous consent of all of the stockholders. Tax rules also require that there cannot be more than 75 stockholders in an S corporation.

12. Q. How does an S corporation differ from an LLC (Limited Liability Corporation)?

A. LLC's are very popular because Federal and state laws permit an LLC to be taxed just like a partnership, or for a one-owner LLC, just like a sole proprietorship. There are also "check-the-box" tax rules that permit the LLC to be taxed as if it was a corporation. The LLC electing corporate tax treatment files an annual corporate tax return (Form 1120). Also, unlike an S corporation, which limits stock ownership to 75 stockholders, any number of individuals may participate in the ownership and management of an LLC.

13. Q. Can I form a corporation myself?

A. Yes. Many incorporation kits are available as well as internet sites that will do the work for you. However, it is always wiser to have an experienced lawyer look over all of your documents before they are filed.

14. Q. If I plan to do business as a small corporation, do I need to register with the Securities and Exchange Commission (SEC)?

A. Yes. If you plan to make an initial public offering to the general public, or you plan to sell shares across state lines, you may first have to register with the SEC. There may also be state registration requirements.

15. Q. If I find that I have to file with the SEC, would I be exempt from a state registration of my securities?

A. It would depend on your state of incorporation. In most states, filing with the SEC would not exempt you from a state filing. In cases where you are exempt from filing with the SEC, you may still have to file with the proper state regulatory authority.

16. Q. What is the difference between debt and equity?

A. Debt represents the obligations of the corporation such as notes, accounts, and taxes payable. Equity represents stock ownership.

17. Q. What kinds of stock can a corporation issue?

A. A corporation can issue both common and preferred stock. Most new corporations begin doing business by issuing only common stock.

18. Q. What rights do common stock usually carry?

A. Common stockholders usually have the right to vote for directors and to receive dividends when declared by the directors.

19. Q. Suppose that the corporation is liquidated. What are the rights of a common stockholder?

A. The common stockholder receives any remaining assets of the corporation after all legal obligations of the corporation have been paid.

20. Q. What happens if there are no assets left after the payment of all corporate legal obligations?

A. Then the common stockholders will get nothing.

21. Q. As a common stockholder, are dividends guaranteed each year?

A. No. If the corporation never makes money, the stockholders will never receive dividends.

22. Q. If the corporation never makes money, won't it eventually face bankruptcy and be liquidated.

A. Yes. Most newly formed corporations, if they do not make money within the first three to five years of their existence, liquidate.

23. Q. For tax purposes, how does a stockholder treat the write-off of his or her stock investment?

A. Each stockholder may write off up to $3,000 of stock loss each year against ordinary income such as a salary, interest, and dividends from other sources.

24. Q. What is a capital gain?

A. A capital gain results from the sale of a stockholder's shares in a corporation at a profit. A capital loss results from the sale of stock at a loss.

25. Q. Suppose that a stockholder has capital gains from other stock holdings. For tax purposes, can the stock loss be used to offset other capital gains?

A. Yes. For example, if a stockholder has $10,000 of capital gains from the sale of other stock, and the newly formed corporation is liquidated with a resultant $6,000 loss, the stockholder may write off the entire $6,000 loss against the $10,000 capital gain, resulting in a net taxable gain of $4,000 ($10,000 – $6,000).

26. Q. Suppose that, in addition to common stock, a corporation is authorized to sell preferred stock. What rights do preferred shares have?

A. Preferred stockholders usually do not have the right to vote. In return, they are first to receive any dividends when they are declared, and are entitled to receive any remaining assets ahead of the common stockholders, in case of a corporate liquidation in bankruptcy.

27. Q. Suppose that I, as a stockholder, have two children that do not get along. Yet, I wish to leave half of the corporation to each child. How can I accomplish this objective without causing conflict among my children.

A. One possibility is to give each child half of your common voting shares.

28. Q. Suppose that I, as a stockholder, have two children that do not get along and one of them is in the business with me. I want her to continue the corporation and yet leave my other child, who is not involved in the corporation, a half interest in the company. How might I accomplish this?

A. One possibility is to give the child employed by the corporation the common shares while issuing an equal number of nonvoting preferred shares to the other child. This arrangement would guarantee that the child owning the preferred shares would be guaranteed half ownership as well as a share of any declared dividends.

29. Q. As incorporator, I do not want any shares to go to outsiders in the event of my death. I want to make sure that the stock remains in friendly hands when I die.

A. You might want to adopt a shareholders' buy-sell agreement giving either the surviving stockholders, or the corporation, the first option to buy back the shares at a stated price or at their fair market value at death.

30. Q. How would payment be made for the corporate shares discussed in question 29?

A. One possibility would be that the agreement would state that the purchase price for the shares would be made in a stated number of monthly payments; i.e., over 60 monthly payments at a stated rate of interest.

31. Q. I have heard about life insurance funding the buy-back. How does this work?

A. The corporation would take out a life insurance policy on the life of the shareholder. The proceeds of the policy would be payable to the corporation. The corporation would the use the proceeds to buy back the deceased stockholder's shares.

32. Q. What are retained earnings?

A. They are the accumulated profits of the corporation from the beginning of its corporate existence. Retained earnings are reduced by any operating annual losses and cash and stock dividends paid.

33. Q. Can a corporation pay dividends if there are no retained earnings?

A. No. It is illegal to do so.

34. Q. Suppose that the newly formed corporation does have retained earnings after its first or second year of operation. What are the chances of receiving a dividend?

A. It is highly unlikely for a new corporation to pay dividends during its first few years of operation. Most profits are put back into the corporation as the corporation grows.

35. Q. I have heard of incorporators, stockholders, directors, officers, and employees. What roles do they play in a corporation?

A. Incorporators bring people together who will invest in the corporation. Stockholders are the persons who will purchase and own the stock in the corporation. Directors are involved in long-term policy making decisions and hold regular and special meetings. Directors also decide when it is appropriate a declare a dividend. Officers run the day-to-day operations of the business including the making of sales, purchasing inventory, and the hiring and firing of employees. Employees work for the corporation in return for compensation.

36. Q. Can three incorporators, who are also equal stockholders, vote themselves as directors?

A. Yes.

37. Q. How might I fund my corporation once it comes into existence?

A. The stockholders, as equity owners, might contribute cash, valuable property, or services. For example, the sole stockholder of a newly formed corporation might contribute $10,000 in return for $10,000 of common stock.

38. Q. Suppose that I, as a stockholder, have insufficient assets with which to fund the corporation. Can the corporation borrow money?

A. Yes. However, most lenders, such as a bank, might require that the officers and stockholders personally guarantee to repay the debt in case the corporation is unable to do so.

39. Q. Can I form the corporation and make myself president of the corporation?

A. Yes. However, assuming that the president, as corporate officer, pays herself a salary, she will subject the corporation to payroll taxes such as federal and state unemployment, federal Social Security taxes, and disability taxes. In addition, the corporation will be required to withhold federal payroll taxes, federal withholding taxes, and possibly state and city withholding taxes if required by state and local laws.

40. Q. What is the difference between salary and a dividend?

A. A salary is paid to a corporate employee and must be paid whether or not the corporation is making a profit. A dividend is only paid out of corporate retained earnings, if there are any.

41. Q. Are both taxable to the recipient?

A. Yes.

42. Q. Are stock dividends taxable?

A. Generally no, unless the stockholders are given the choice of taking stock or cash. Should a stockholder elect to take the stock, the fair market value of the stock becomes taxable to him or her.

43. Q. As a corporate employee, can I receive workers' compensation if I am disabled on the job?

A. Yes. The benefit is not available to self-employed individuals operating as sole proprietorships.

44. Q. As a corporate officer, am I liable if the corporation's federal tax return contains material misstatements of fact?

A. Yes. Section 7206 of the Internal Revenue Code provides that anyone signing a corporate tax return that is not true or accurate in any material matter is liable for fraud.

45. Q. How could I, as a corporate officer, prevent this possible exposure to liability.

A. Upon completion of the corporate tax return and prior to its submission to the Internal Revenue Service, the entire return should be reviewed with the independent CPA who prepared the return to make sure that all the financial statements upon which the return is based, follow generally accepted accounting principles (GAAP), and that the tax return itself adheres to all applicable tax laws.

46. Q. Now that the corporation is formed, and the applicable tax laws have been reviewed, how do we go about electing directors?

A. In some states, the directors are listed in the articles of incorporation. In other states, the incorporators choose the first board of directors.

47. Q. What are bylaws?

A. Bylaws spell out the rights of the directors, officers, and stockholders of the corporation. For example, bylaws may contain the time and place for annual directors meetings, how many directors shall serve, how they are to be re-elected, and their compensation.

48. Q. How do I go about setting up a corporate bank account?

A. The board of directors, at their first meeting, should pass a resolution establishing a bank account at a designated bank. The bank will request the newly formed corporation's Employer EIN (Form SS-4, APPLICATION FOR EMPLOYER IDENTIFICATION NUMBER).

49. Q. How do I go about issuing stock?

A. Stock can be issued in return for cash, property, or services performed for the benefit of the corporation. If the stock is being issued for cash, payment should be received before the stock is issued. If the stock is being issued in return for property, such as a building, the person transferring the property should prepare a deed listing the corporation as purchaser before the stock is issued. Once services are performed on behalf of the corporation, such as legal or accounting services, the stock may be issued as payment.

50. Q. All of the above sounds complicated. Once the corporation is formed, will the corporation need an accountant?

A. Generally yes. Unless a corporate officer or employee is familiar with accounting principles, it might be wise to employ the services of a bookkeeper or accountant.

51. Q. If I need an accountant, should he or she be a Certified Public Accountant?

A. Initially probably not. Unless the business needs to borrow money from a bank, which will most likely require certified financial statements, a simple bookkeeping service should suffice. However, an outside accountant should also be hired to come in once every quarter, or perhaps on a monthly basis, as the activity of the newly formed corporation dictates. The accountant will review the books for any errors and might find it necessary to review any tax or financial problems that might arise.

52. Q. How do I go about finding a suitable bookkeeper?

A. Many newly formed corporations hire a part-time bookkeeper to come in a few days a week to record all the financial transactions such as the recording of sales, the payment of employees, and payment of liabilities.

One suggestion is to look in the Yellow Pages, or to seek the recommendation of an accountant. Family and friends are an excellent source for finding the right person.

53. Q. What questions should I ask the bookkeeper?

A. Ask about his or her prior experience, names of references, knowledge of basic payroll taxes, his or her days of availability, and whether he or she is computer literate since most record keeping today is done on computer. Ask about his or her expected rate of pay as well as whether payment is to be per hour or per day. Remember that if the bookkeeper is hired as an employee, the corporation will be subject to payroll taxes such as Social Security, and federal and state unemployment taxes.

54. Q. How do I go about finding a suitable CPA if I believe that I need one?

A. One suggestion is to look in the Yellow Pages, or to seek the recommendation of family or friends. Some newly formed corporations find it prudent not to hire a family member as the company CPA in order to promote objectivity.

55. Q. What questions should I ask the accountant?

A. Ask about his or her professional education (i.e., if he or she is a CPA), prior experience, rate of payment, whether the accountant feels that it will be necessary to come in on a monthly or quarterly basis, and any other fees in addition to their rate of payment. Also ask whether they return all calls promptly. Remember that since the newly formed corporation is small but will hopefully grow, it is not necessary to employ the service of a "big four" accounting firm. Most likely a small local practitioner will suffice.

56. Q. Must I separate corporate assets from my own personal assets?

A. Yes. The corporation must have its own bank account and assets. Do not use this account to pay any stockholder's personal expenses. Salaries paid to officers should be done on a regular basis with payroll records and the proper withholding of Social Security and federal taxes and applicable state and city taxes. Improper accounting records may lead to disregard of the corporate entity, personal liability for corporate debts, and additional personal tax liability.

57. Q. Why might I as a stockholder incur additional personal tax liability?

A. In effect, the Internal Revenue Code will treat a corporation's payment of personal expenses as additional taxable compensation.

58. Q. How can I avoid personal and tax liability when operating a corporation?

A. Quite simply, follow all corporate formalities such as issuing stock only when it is fully paid for, open a corporate bank account, keep accurate books and records, and do not use corporate funds to pay personal expenses. Finally, have an independent accountant review the corporation's books and records on a consistent monthly or quarterly basis as corporate activities may require.

59. Q. Who is usually authorized to sign corporate checks?

A. Usually the directors, or bylaws, authorize certain individuals, such as a corporate officer, to sign all corporate checks.

60. Q. Is it permissible to have a company bookkeeper sign all corporate checks?

A. Although permissible, it is not wise to have someone who has access to corporate records, to sign checks. There is always the possibility of fraud. That is why it is best to have a bookkeeper or company accountant prepare checks but have a corporate officer sign them. This represents a system of corporate control over all cash payments.

61. Q. Now that the corporation is organized and running, what is meant by the equation Assets = Liabilities + Capital?

A. Corporate assets are the resources that a corporation owns that are used to generate business. They may consist of cash, accounts receivable, equipment, and buildings. Liabilities are what the corporation owes. They may consist of accounts and notes payable, wages payable, and withholding taxes payable. Capital is simply outstanding stock purchased by investors as well as any profits retained by the business.

62. Q. What kind of expenses can a corporation be expected to incur?

A. Most corporations incur rent, telephone, car and truck expenses, insurance, depreciation, salaries, interest, and accounting and legal fees.

63. Q. What is inventory? Is it an asset?

A. Inventory is an asset that remains on the books of the corporation until sold. Inventory may be bought from others at a wholesale price and resold to customers at a higher price. The difference between sales and the cost of the goods sold is called gross profit.

64. Q. Do all corporations have inventory?

A. No. Corporations offering services such as a corporation performing painting services, or a dry cleaning store, do not have inventory since they are performing a service.

65. Q. What is depreciation?

A. Most fixed, or long-term, assets are subject to depreciation. This means that the assets, such as buildings and equipment, are written off over their useful lives, against a corporation's income, so as to arrive at net income.

66. Q. Does the IRS prescribe any type of format for keeping a corporation's business records?

A. No. The IRS does not require any particular method of record keeping so long as the records clearly reflect income and expenses.

67. Q. What are some of the methods for keeping track of income and expenses?

A. There are two systems: the single-entry system, and the double-entry system. The single-entry system, which is the simpler of the two, requires that a running total of all income and all expenses be kept for each month. At the end of the year, the twelve monthly totals are added together to determine whether the corporation has made money. A double-entry system, which is used by most businesses, requires the use of a debit and a credit entry on the books. The debits and credits are placed into the appropriate accounts and "closed" at the end of the year. All computer-based accounting programs use the double-entry system.

68. Q. What is a tax-year?

A. For tax purposes, all businesses must keep their books and records on a tax year basis, which is usually the period January 1 through December 31. Most businesses, including corporations and LLC's are required to use a December 31 tax year. An alternative year-end, such as a January 31, may also be elected by the new entity under certain circumstances.

69. Q. Suppose that the corporation has been funded with initial capital of, let us say $10,000, and additional money is needed. What are some sources of additional capital besides an incorporator's own personal funds?

A. One way is to borrow money from a bank by giving them a note. You promise to pay the bank back within a stated period of time, perhaps in installments, with interest. Another way is to sell additional shares to outside investors.

70. Q. What is a disadvantage of having the corporation borrow money by issuing notes?

A. Besides the interest element, notes are due at specified dates, i.e., the beginning of each month, whether or not the corporation is making money or has the cash funds available to make payment. Some lenders may also have a corporate officer personally sign the note so as to make them personally liable if the corporation fails to make timely payment.

71. Q. Is issuing stock to investors a better way to raise capital?

A. There is no definite answer. By selling stock in the corporation, other individuals now have the right to elect directors. There may also be SEC laws that must be complied with. Finally, it is absolutely necessary to advise potential investors of the risks involved in purchasing stock of the corporation. This advisory will reduce the possibility of a suit by other investors in case the corporation fails to make a profit and is eventually liquidated.

72. Q. How do I minimize the risk of, in the event of loss, being sued by the investors for giving misleading information?

A. Tell them to check with their own lawyer, accountant, or financial advisor as to the merits of the stock purchase.

73. Q. If I have a home, could I take out a second mortgage in order to raise additional funds?

A. Yes. Suppose that your home is now worth $300,000, and the original mortgage of $250,000 has been reduced to $100,000. You now have equity of $200,000 ($300,000 – $100,000) that can be used as security for a second mortgage.

74. Q. What about going to the Small Business Administration (SBA) for a loan?

A. The SBA's Micro Loan Program provides loans up to $25,000 through various non-profit agencies. Call 800-827-5722 for details or visit their website at http://www.sba.gov for more information.

75. Q. What type of insurance coverage will a corporation need?

A. A corporation will need property insurance coverage in case a fire destroys all furniture, fixtures, and equipment. A corporation also needs burglary insurance in case of theft. Finally, if the corporation is operating a restaurant, the corporation will need liability insurance in case a customer claims that she got sick from the food, or slipped while in your restaurant. The best course of action is to have a frank discussion with an insurance agent regarding the corporation's required insurance coverage.

76. Q. Historically, basic fire insurance covered either actual current value or replacement cost. Which should the corporation elect to take?

A. Replacement cost. For example, it usually costs more to replace a building that has burned to the ground than its current value (what someone would pay to buy the building).

77. Q. Are insurance premiums tax deductible?

A. Yes.

78. Q. What is product liability insurance?

A. Product liability insurance protects a corporation from liability if a product designed, manufactured, or sold by the corporation injures someone.

79. Q. What is workers' compensation insurance and how does it work?

A. All businesses, including corporations, by state law, must provide some kind of workers' compensation for injuries incurred on the job. Under workers' compensation laws, an employee cannot sue the corporation for negligence, but the corporation is automatically liable for benefits whether or not the business was negligent.

80. Q. Where can a corporation find a space from which to operate?

A. Many small businesses start out from a room in the stockholder's home until the business begins to grow. Other newly formed corporations lease a space either as a month-to-month tenant or sign a long-term lease of two years or more. Some corporations, as they become more and more profitable, purchase a building outright. Excess space can be then leased out to others, thereby providing additional income to the corporation.

81. Q. If the corporation decides to lease property, such as office space, which corporate officer signs the lease?

A. Usually the president of the corporation signs.

82. Q. Is a corporate officer personally liable for the lease payments?

A. No, as long as the president, (or possibly vice-president) signs as Judy Jones, President of Z Corp., indicating that they are signing in their capacity as a corporate officer, they are not personally liable.

83. Q. Is it wise for a corporate officer to personally guarantee the lease?

A. No. However, if the landlord demands a personal guarantee and the corporation absolutely must have the space because of its location or suitability for manufacturing operations, try to limit your liability to a lesser amount—say up to three or four months of unpaid rent, or the balance of the lease, whichever is less.

84. Q. What is key-person life insurance?

A. Key-person life insurance is insurance on the life of a key person in the corporation such as a major stockholder, officer, or high performing salesperson. Should that person die, the policy proceeds are payable to the corporation to compensate the business for any possible losses due to the death of the key person.

85. Q. Are the proceeds from a key-person life insurance policy taxable to the corporation?

A. No. Under the Internal Revenue Code, to be consistent, the premiums paid on this type of policy are not tax-deductible by the corporation.

86. Q. What is the difference between an independent contractor and a corporate employee?

A. Independent contractors are hired to perform a job based upon their individual expertise. They set their own rates, fees, and the way they perform the job. Basically, the corporation has no control over the work of an independent contractor.

87. Q. What type of people are typically independent contractors?

A. Lawyers, accountants who are hired to audit a corporation's books and records, and financial consultants.

88. Q. What is the advantage of hiring an independent contractor?

A. Payroll records must be kept for employees. In addition, Social Security must be paid for each employee. Social Security, federal, and applicable state and city withholding must be withheld from each employee's paycheck. Finally, at the end of the year, each employee must get a Form W-2 showing how much they earned together with all taxes withheld. In comparison, an independent contractor is merely given a Form 1099 MISC showing the amount paid if the contractor earned $600 or more for the year.

89. Q. How does a corporation protect itself from the possibility that the IRS will treat the independent contractor as an employee?

A. Draw up a contract, to be signed by both a corporate officer and the independent contractor, stating that the contract is one between the corporation and an independent contractor. Also specify the work to be done, the rate of payment, such as by the hour or by a flat fee, that the independent contractor shall use his or her own tools, and will carry his or her own insurance, including workers' compensation.

90. Q. Should a corporation permit payment by means of credit cards such as Visa and Mastercard?

A. It would depend on the preferences of the corporation's clientele. If the corporation is operating as a retail store, customers would probably expect the corporation to allow payment by credit card.

91. Q. Now that the corporation is growing, the stockholders may wish to elect more directors to the board. How is their compensation set?

A. Unless the corporate bylaws say otherwise, directors have the authority to fix their own compensation.

92. Q. What is a corporate director's legal liability?

A. Corporate directors have traditionally been held liable for gross negligence only and not for normal errors using reasonable business judgment.

93. Q. Who are the normal corporate officers?

A. The normal corporate officers are the president, vice president, secretary, treasurer, and general manager.

94. Q. Who appoints these officers?

A. The board of directors.

95. Q. Who fixes officers' compensation?

A. The board of directors.

96. Q. What is the role of the corporate secretary?

A. The corporate secretary attends all corporate meetings, keeps minutes, distributes notices, certifies corporate records, and keeps the corporate seal.

97. Q. What is the role of the corporate treasurer?

A. The corporate treasurer is the chief financial officer. He or she is responsible for signing or countersigning corporate notes, checks, and stock certificates.

98. Q. What is the role of the general manager?

A. The general manager administers the ordinary business of the corporation. This includes the hiring and firing of employees, the purchase of materials and supplies, and the payment of all corporate debts.

99. Q. Must every corporation have a general manager?

A. No. The corporate president, vice president, or treasurer can perform either part or all of these functions.

100. Q. I have been operating the corporation for many years and I feel that it is time to sell. How might I value the corporation for purposes of selling?

A. One method might be the book value of the corporation. A second might be to have an independent CPA or appraiser come in and put an appraisal value on the assets of the corporation.

101. Q. Which method is more realistic?

A. The appraisal method which takes into account any goodwill generated by the business. The weakness of the cost method is that it ignores any goodwill that has been generated by the corporation and would not appear in the corporate records.

102. Q. How might I sell the corporation?

A. One method is to sell the stock giving the seller capital gain treatment. A second method might be to sell the corporate assets and then liquidate. This method would also give rise to capital gain or loss.

103. Q. Suppose that after several years, the corporation has not proved profitable. Can it be dissolved?

A. Yes. A voluntary dissolution can be initiated by either the board of directors or the stockholders.

104. Q. What happens in case of a voluntary dissolution?

A. A certificate of dissolution is filed with the secretary of state, the corporate assets are sold, the creditors are paid off, and the stockholders are given any remaining assets.

105. Q. What happens when the directors of the corporation are so hopelessly deadlocked regarding the operation of the corporation that the entity cannot continue to function without the possibility of insolvency?

A. A group of stockholders can request an involuntary dissolution.

106. Q. What happens in case of involuntary dissolution?

A. A group of stockholders, usually less than 50%, petition a court of proper jurisdiction to dissolve the corporation. After a review of the facts, the court may grant the dissolution, and appoint a receiver to wind up the corporation's affairs.

107. Q. What's the difference between a Chapter 7 and Chapter 11 bankruptcy?

A. In a federal Bankruptcy Code Chapter 7, the corporate assets are sold and the creditors receive any available proceeds up to the amount owed them. In a Chapter 7 proceeding, the stockholders usually receive nothing. A Chapter 11 bankruptcy allows for a restructuring of the debts of the corporation and a continuation of the corporate business.

108. Q. Can a stockholder deduct the operating losses incurred by a C corporation?

A. No. Losses incurred by a C corporation cannot be deducted by a stockholder. In order to be able to deduct a corporation's losses, stockholders must elect S corporation status.

109. Q. What happens to a stockholder's shares if the stockholder dies?

A. If the corporation's outstanding shares are subject to a stock repurchase provision, the shares must first be offered back to the corporation for repurchase. If no such provision exists, or the corporation refuses to repurchase the shares, the individual designated in the decedent's will gets the shares and becomes a shareholder. If the decedent dies intestate (without a will), the shares will go to the individual designated by applicable state law to receive them.

110. Q. I have been asked to serve on the board of directors of a company. What issues are involved with my service as a board member?

A. Don't serve as a director if you cannot understand financial statements, or have ties to management. Don't rely solely on company management for information needed to oversee the company. Finally, don't ignore criticisms of the company's accounting methods. Do get a second opinion from other outside auditors if you have any questions regarding the financial statements.

111. Q. Can the members of an LLC split up the profits and losses any way they see fit?

A. Yes. While it is normal to distribute profits and losses according to the percentage of assets that each member contributes, there is no requirement that this rule be followed.

GLOSSARY

ACCOUNTING EQUATION Assets = Liabilities + Capital (or Shareholder's Equity)

ACCRUAL ACCOUNTING Based on the fundamental principle that all income earned for a period be matched with the expenses assignable to that period.

ACCUMULATED EARNINGS TAX A tax imposed on the accumulation of corporate earnings beyond the reasonable business needs of the corporation. The tax applies when corporate accumulated earnings exceeds $250,000 ($150,000 for personal service corporations).

ADOPTION In corporation law, the concept is applied when a newly formed corporation accepts a preincorporation contract made for its benefit by a promoter prior to the corporation's coming into existence. Adoption speaks only from the time such corporation agrees to accept the benefits of the preincorporation contract, in contrast to a "ratification," which relates back to the time the original contract was made.

ARTIFICIAL ENTITY A fictitious entity (or corporation) validly formed under state statutes applicable to corporations. Being an artificial person, it can only act through its directors, officers, employees, and agents.

ARTICLES OF INCORPORATION A certificate (or charter) filed with the state containing the name, purposes, and number of shares authorized for sale for a proposed corporation. The charter represents a contract between the state and its incorporators.

AUTHORIZED SHARES The shares described in the articles of incorporation, which a corporation can sell. Modern corporate practice recommends authorization of more shares than the corporation initially plans to issue.

BANKRUPTCY PROCEEDINGS A federal action permitting a corporation to either restructure itself or to liquidate. Bankruptcies filed under Chapter 7 of the federal bankruptcy code involve the liquidation of a business's or an individual's assets to pay outstanding debts. Typically, creditors receive only a portion of the amount that they are owed. Chapter 11 bankruptcies allow for a restructuring of the debts of a corporation.

BASIS In tax law, it is roughly the equivalent of the cost of the property by the taxpayer. To compute gain or loss on the sale or exchange of property, the basis of property is generally subtracted from the amount realized from the sale or exchange.

BENEFICIAL HOLDERS OF SECURITIES Individuals who have the equitable or legal title to shares but who have not registered the shares on the records of the corporation.

BLUE SKY LAWS State registration statutes that regulate the sale of securities within the state. Most blue sky laws require the registration of new issues of securities with a state agency that reviews selling documents for truth and completeness. The registration does not, however, guarantee that investors will earn a profit.

BONDS Long term (having a maturity life of more than one year) debt instruments. They can be either unsecured or secured by a lien on some or all of the corporate property. A bond, which pays interest on a semi-annual or annual basis, is payable to either its bearer or to its registered owner.

BUSINESS CORPORATION LAW (BCL) Used in New York State in place of the Model Business Corporation Act (MBCA) and the Revised Model Business Corporation Act (RMBCA).

BUSINESS JUDGMENT RULE Under this principle, a corporate director or officer can usually avoid liability for poor business judgment.

BYLAWS Govern the internal conduct of the corporation. The initial bylaws may be formulated by incorporators, shareholders, or board of directors.

C CORPORATION Pursuant to the Internal Revenue Code, a corporation that is subject to double taxation, once at the corporate level and again if there are profits that are distributed in the form of dividends.

CAFETERIA PLANS Employee benefit plans that offer workers the option of choosing cash or certain nontaxable fringe benefits (such as group term life insurance, accident and health benefits, or child care).

CALLABLE OR REDEEMABLE PREFERRED STOCK This type of stock is subject to involuntary redemption at the option of the board of directors at a fixed price at specific future dates.

CAPITAL GAINS AND LOSSES Under the Internal Revenue Code, stock held for longer than one year that is sold results in either a long-term gain or loss.

CAPITAL GAIN EXCLUSION FOR SMALL BUSINESS STOCK A non-corporate taxpayer who holds for more than five years qualified small business stock issued after August 10, 1993, can exclude 50 percent of any gain on the investor's sale or exchange of the stock.

CASH BASIS ACCOUNTING Under this system, income is recorded when received, and expenses are recorded when paid.

COMMON STOCK Represents the residual interest of the corporation. The common shareholders are the owners of shares who bear the risk of loss and enjoy the benefits of any profits in the form of dividend payments.

COMMON SHAREHOLDERS The owners of shares who bear the risk of loss and enjoy the benefits of any profits in the form of dividend payments. Their interest is said to be residual meaning that they are the last to be paid after creditors and preferred shareholders, if any.

CONSOLIDATION A consolidation is the union of two existing corporations to form a new corporation.

CONVERTIBLE SHARES Both common and other classes of shareholders may be given the option to exchange their shares into common stock and vice versa. This is known as the *convertibility* feature applicable to a particular class of shares.

CORPORATION BY ESTOPPEL This doctrine prevents a third party from holding a corporate director or officer or shareholder personally liable by denial of the corporate existence.

CRITERIA FOR CORPORATION NAME Name must include the word "corporation," "incorporated," "company," or "limited." Abbreviations such as "Corp.," "Inc.," "Co." and "Ltd." are also permitted.

CROSS-PURCHASE AGREEMENT An agreement that obligates each of the shareholders to buy each other's shares in case of the death of the shareholder or if one of the shareholders wishes to sell.

CUMULATIVE PREFERRED STOCK Cumulative preferred stock that gives the shareholder the right to receive a dividend, usually each quarter before the payment of any common dividends. If the dividends are not paid for a particular period, they accumulate as dividends in arrears.

CUMULATIVE VOTING A technique whereby minority shareholders concentrate all of their voting strength on one or more individual directors with the hope that they are elected. It is an excellent way of helping to preserve minority shareholder representation on the board of directors. The formula is the number of shares held times the number of individual directors to be elected.

DEADLOCK Occurs when there are an equal number of directors, and there is a tie vote that cannot be broken despite several attempts to do so, which may prevent the corporation from functioning.

DEATH TAX REDEMPTION A provision in the Internal Revenue Code stating that if the value of the stock redeemed is more than 35 percent of the decedent's gross estate with certain adjustments, the estate will *not recognize gain* from the redemption if the proceeds are used to pay all estate taxes, funeral and administration expenses imposed on the estate.

DE FACTO CORPORATION Arises when there has been a good faith attempt to comply fully with the state's statutory corporate laws and an exercise of corporate powers. A de facto corporation enjoys the same benefits as a properly formed corporation and cannot be challenged by third parties except for the state.

DEFERRED ARRANGEMENT PLANS Corporate executives can sign agreements calling for compensation to be paid at future dates. Such agreements result in a tax savings because the income will be spread over several future periods thereby resulting in the income being taxed at lower rates.

DE JURE CORPORATION A properly formed corporation that insulates the shareholders from personal liability.

DERIVATIVE ACTION The lawsuit is brought, usually by the minority shareholders, on the name of and on behalf of the corporation. The relief sought is in the form of compelling abusive directors and officers to account to the corporation for losses caused by their negligence, breach of fiduciary duty, or any other misconduct.

DILUTION A reduction in the percentage of outstanding shares owned, and also control of a corporation, resulting from the issuance of additional shares to other shareholders. For example, a shareholder owning 10 out of 100 common shares outstanding would own 10 percent of the corporation. If another shareholder bought an additional 100 shares, the original 10 percent shareholder would now own 5 percent (10/200) of the corporation. Dilution has occurred. Dilution also reduces earnings per share (EPS) because more shares are outstanding.

DIRECTORS Elected by the shareholders to represent the corporation and not the shareholders, directors, acting as a board, formulate the overall general policies of the corporation. The board of directors has final authority over all of the corporation's business activities. They are not involved in the day-to-day operations of the corporation unless they also serve as corporate officers.

DISSOLUTION The dissolution of a corporation requires that the entity file a certificate of dissolution. As a result, its operations are terminated, its assets distributed first to its creditors and then to its shareholders, and the corporation then ceases to exist.

DIVIDENDS IN ARREARS Dividends not paid in a particular year on preferred stock are said to be in arrears. All dividends in arrears must be paid before any dividends can be distributed to the common shareholders.

DOMESTIC CORPORATION A corporation doing business in the state where it is incorporated.

DOUBLE ENTRY BOOKKEEPING Under this system, debits and credits reflecting business transactions are entered into both journals and ledgers. The total amounts in the ledger are then added and adjusted at the end of the accounting period to create the financial statements.

EARNINGS PER SHARE (EPS) Net income divided by shares outstanding. Thus, if a corporation's net income is $100,000 and there are 100,000 common shares outstanding, EPS is $1 per share ($100,000/100,000).

EMPLOYER IDENTIFICATION NUMBER (EIN) A corporation must obtain an employer identification number (EIN) for tax purposes by obtaining and filing Form SS–4 with its local IRS office. The EIN is used on filed tax returns and correspondence with the IRS.

ESTATE TAX A transfer tax imposed on all assets of a decedent that exceed a certain amount. All property included in the gross estate is valued at either its fair market value (FMV) on the date of death or the alternate valuation date. The executor of the estate is required to file Form 706 with the Internal Revenue Service if the estate exceeds a certain statutory amount.

EX-DIVIDEND Meaning without the right to a dividend. A share goes "ex-dividend" on the date the seller becomes entitled to keep the dividend. This date is four business days before the date of record. The names of the holders of record are listed on a specific date on the corporation's books. Thus, if January 30 is the date of record, the stock goes "ex-dividend on January 26." If the purchaser buys the stock after January 26, the seller, or previous owner, is entitled to the dividend.

EXECUTIVE COMMITTEE Directors generally have the authority to designate executive committees composed of at least two directors, to exercise board authority in such matters as executive compensation, employee pension and retirement benefits, and accounting principles to be adopted by the corporation. Executive committees generally do not have the power to approve basic fundamental changes in the operation of the corporation, such as a merger or consolidation with another corporation, nor can they authorize the payment of dividends.

FAMILY AND MEDICAL LEAVE ACT (FMLA) OF 1993 Under this federal act, covered employers must provide access to up to 12 weeks' leave per calendar or fiscal year, for the employee's own illness, the illness of a close family member; or the birth or adoption of a child.

FIDUCIARY An individual who is in a trust relationship. Directors, officers, and majority stockholders have a fiduciary duty to the corporation. This means that they are not permitted to work on behalf of the corporation if their acts are motivated by self-interest.

FISCAL TAX YEAR A regular fiscal year is 12 consecutive months ending on the last day of any month except December. A 52–53 week year is a fiscal tax year that varies from 52 to 53 weeks.

FOREIGN CORPORATION A corporation doing business in a state where it is not incorporated. Thus, a corporation incorporated in Delaware but doing business in all other states is a domestic corporation if it does business in Delaware but foreign when doing business in any other state (e.g., California).

GENERAL MANAGER The role of this person is to administer the ordinary business of the corporation. Her general functions include hiring and firing employees, setting their compensation, purchasing materials and supplies, and paying corporate debts.

GENERAL PARTNERSHIP Composed of two or more individuals who contribute their capital and skills toward ongoing profit-directed activities. In a partnership, every partner is an agent of the partnership in dealing with third parties. Each partner is jointly (meaning that each copromisor is liable for the entire debt) and/or severally liable (meaning that each party is liable alone or individually) for the debts of the partnership.

ISSUED AND OUTSTANDING Shares sold by a corporation to its shareholders are called issued and outstanding shares.

JOINT VENTURE An undertaking by two or more persons or other entities, usually to accomplish a single objective. Aside from the single-objective feature, it is identical to a general partnership.

JUDICIAL LIQUIDATION An involuntary corporate dissolution, whereby a group of shareholders owning a specific percentage of the corporation's outstanding stock, usually less than 50 percent, petition a court of proper jurisdiction to dissolve the corporation. After review of all the facts, the court may grant dissolution and appoint a receiver to wind up the corporation's affairs.

LIABILITY FOR NEGLIGENCE Directors and officers are liable to the corporation for losses sustained by the business due to negligence in office.

LIMITED LIABILITY COMPANY (LLC) A recent form of organization that may offer greater business and tax advantages than a regular corporation. Profits and losses flow through to each individual owner on the personal level (called a "member" for LLC purposes). An LLC has the advantages of a partnership's nontaxable flow-through tax treatment, a corporate shareholder's limited liability, and a general partner's control of management (called a "manager" for LLC purposes).

LIMITED PARTNERSHIP The limited partnership form of doing business can only be created according to the formalities stated in the Uniform Limited Partnership Act (ULPA), which has been adopted in virtually all states. Every limited partnership must have at least one general and one limited partner.

LIQUIDATING DIVIDENDS Paid by a corporation that is in the process of liquidation. Such dividends are generally nontaxable under the Internal Revenue Code.

MAJORITY More than half the votes cast.

MERGER The absorption of one corporation (called the acquired or target corporation) by another corporation (called the acquiring corporation).

MODEL BUSINESS CORPORATION ACT (MBCA) A codification of today's modern corporation statutes. Used in many states as their statutory corporate law.

NATURAL BUSINESS YEAR Exists when a business has a peak period and a non-peak period.

NO PAR VALUE STOCK If no amount is designed for each share of stock in the articles of incorporation, the stock is called no par value stock. No par value stock can be given a stated value by the board of directors. The rights and privileges of the owners of no par value stock are generally the same as par value shareholders.

NONCUMULATIVE PREFERRED STOCK If a dividend is not declared on this type of stock for any given year, the obligation ceases for that particular year and there is no obligation to pay the dividend in future years.

NONPARTICIPATING PREFERRED STOCK Preferred stock that is entitled to its current annual dividend only, regardless of the dividends paid to the common shareholders.

OFFICERS Officers, unlike directors, are the true agents of the corporation. Each officer, i.e., president, vice-president, etc., has the power to bind the corporation by his individual acts within the actual or apparent scope of his authority.

OWNERS' OR SHAREHOLDERS' EQUITY Another name for the capital of the corporation. The capital of a corporation is composed of its outstanding preferred and common stock, and its surplus or retained earnings.

PAID-IN CAPITAL When a corporation receives payment for its shares in excess of its par or stated value, the excess is allocated to a capital account called paid-in capital. No such account exists where the corporation issues only no par value stock.

PAR VALUE Stock that is given an arbitrary value is called par value or stated value stock.

PARTICIPATING PREFERRED STOCK Participating preferred stock allows preferred shareholders to receive additional amounts of dividends after the dividends stipulated in the articles of incorporation are paid to both the preferred and common shareholders on a ratable basis.

PERSONAL HOLDING COMPANY A tax concept. To be considered a personal holding company (PHC), the corporation must satisfy two tests—the "adjusted ordinary gross income" test and the stock ownership test. The personal holding company (PHC) penalty tax is imposed in order to discourage the use of the corporate form as an "incorporated pocketbook" to shelter the income (meaning to offset other income) for later distribution when the individuals are in a lower tax bracket.

PIERCING THE CORPORATE VEIL Courts will sweep aside the dual personality concept applicable to the corporation by concluding that the entity and its shareholders are one and the same thereby making the shareholders personally liable for all corporate debts.

PLURALITY In some states, all directors can be chosen by a plurality (meaning the largest number of votes cast) of the shareholder votes cast providing that there is a quorum present.

PREEMPTIVE RIGHTS Allows an existing shareholder to purchase a new issue of shares in proportion to the amount of shares that he currently owns before it is offered to others. Thus, if the shareholder owns 1,000 common shares out of 10,000 common shares outstanding, he is permitted to purchase 10 percent of the new issue.

PREFERRED SHARES Shares that have preferential rights as to dividend payments and in case of corporate liquidation. Dividend payments on preferred shares are generally a stated amount of par, i.e., 6 percent of $100 par value preferred shares will result in a $6 dividend per year if declared and paid by the board of directors.

PREFERRED SHARES WITH A LIQUIDATING PREFERENCE In the event that the corporation is liquidated, the preferred shareholders are to receive assets up to a specified amount, for example, up to their par value. The effect of this preference is to make the preferred shares more attractive and less of a risk than the common shares.

PREFERRED STOCK ISSUED IN A SERIES (OR BLANK SHARES) A class of preferred shares that will be issued in installments over a period of time as fixed by the board of directors.

PRESIDENT Usually has the authority to manage the business of the corporation. These dealings include the signing of contracts, stock certificates, checks, notes, hiring key personnel, instituting corporate litigation, and making all other commitments on behalf of the corporation.

PRICE EARNINGS RATIO (P/E) The market value of the corporate shares divided by the earnings per share. Thus, if a corporation's market value is $100 and earnings per share (EPS) is $10, then the P/E ration is 10 to 1. The ratio is used as a measure of a potential investor's confidence in a company.

PROFESSIONAL SERVICE CORPORATIONS (PSCs) Members of the professions (e.g., those entities engaged in the practice of law, medicine, or accountancy) can form a professional service corporation (also called a professional association or PA in some states). By incorporating their practice, professionals and their employees can participate in employee fringe benefits and pension and profit-sharing plans. There are other legal benefits as well.

PROFIT-SHARING PLAN Under this arrangement, the employer allocates a share of corporate profits according to some predetermined formula. Incidental benefits such as disability, death, or medical insurance can also be provided. A profit-sharing plan can be established in addition to, or in lieu of, a pension plan.

PROMOTER An individual who provides the organizational initiative for forming the corporation for a specific purpose or purposes. Promoters are often called "insiders," as opposed to the "outsiders" or ultimate investors because their initial efforts and resources help establish the corporation.

PROXY A power of attorney given by a stockholder authorizing a designated person to cast the stockholder's ballot.

PUBLICLY HELD CORPORATION A corporation with shares held by numerous people. A corporation listed on an established stock exchange [e.g., New York, American, or over-the-counter (OTC)] is generally referred to as a publicly held corporation.

QUORUM The number of votes necessary to validate a meeting.

REASONABLE COMPENSATION Payments made to a shareholder-officer, such as a president or vice president, in the form of salary, bonus, or fringe benefits that are tax deductible. Compensation payments are deductible by the corporation as long as they are reasonable and necessary in amount.

RECORD OWNER The person in whose name the shares are registered on the books of the corporation.

REGISTERED AGENT A specific person who has been designated by the corporation as an agent to receive legal documents, including service of process.

RETAINED EARNINGS Another name required to be used by CPAs for listing surplus on the corporation's balance sheet. Retained earnings represents the total accumulated profits and losses of the corporation, less the payment of dividends, over the life of the corporation.

REVISED MODEL BUSINESS CORPORATION ACT (RMBCA) After several revisions, the MBCA is referred to as the Revised Model Business Corporation Act (RMBCA). Used in many states as statutory law.

REVISED UNIFORM LIMITED PARTNERSHIP ACT (RULPA) Both the Uniform Limited Partnership Act (ULPA) and RULPA form the basis for governing the limited partnership.

RIGHT OF FIRST REFUSAL Gives the corporation, or its shareholders, the opportunity to repurchase the shares of a selling shareholder by matching the best price that the shareholder can obtain on the open marketplace.

S CORPORATION Under the Internal Revenue Code, a corporation that avoids double taxation, once at the corporate level and again at the shareholder level, by electing to be taxed as if it was a partnership. S corporations cannot have more than 75 shareholders.

SCRIP Fractional shares of stock. Fractional shares may be turned in to the corporation for an equivalent number of full shares. For example, if a shareholder has 1/10 fractional share, he would need 9 more fractional shares to receive a full share.

SECRETARY The corporate secretary exercises authority equal to that of a general manager.

SECTION 1244 STOCK Section 1244 permits a special tax treatment for losses due to the sale of certain stock. Up to $100,000 for married couples filing jointly ($50,000 for single taxpayers) in Section 1244 stock losses can be deducted in one year against ordinary income.

SECURITIES AND EXCHANGE COMMISSION (SEC) An independent governmental regulatory agency whose function it is to administer the SEC Acts of 1933 and 1934. One if its major functions is to require disclosure of facts concerning offerings listed on national stock exchanges and certain securities traded over the counter (OTC).

SINGLE ENTRY ACCOUNTING SYSTEM A single entry bookkeeping system that is based on the company's profit or loss statement and includes only the corporation's business income and expense accounts.

SMALL BUSINESS ADMINISTRATION (SBA) An agency of the federal government set up to make credit available to small businesses that cannot reasonably obtain financing from private sources. The SBA makes direct loans, participation loans, and economic opportunity loans.

SOLE OR INDIVIDUAL PROPRIETORSHIP This is a natural form of doing business at lowest initial cost. The sole proprietor is the owner and "boss."

STATED VALUE STOCK No par value stock that is given a stated value (e.g., $1, $10 per share). Directors may vote to give no par value stock a stated value to give the stock a more meaningful value in the eyes of the investing public.

STERILIZATION OF THE BOARD OF DIRECTORS A restriction of the authority of the board of directors of a nonpublic, or closely-held corporation. This limitation must be set forth in the articles of incorporation. The effect of this provision is to relieve the directors of any liability for negligence on their part and to transfer such liability to all of the shareholders.

STOCK BONUS PLAN An arrangement whereby the employer's stock is contributed to a trust. The stock is allocated to each participant in the trust for eventual distribution to them.

STOCK DIVIDENDS A dividend payable in the stock of the corporation instead of cash or property.

STOCK REDEMPTION AGREEMENT This type of arrangement binds both the shareholders and the corporation. On the death of the shareholder, or in case the shareholder wishes to sell his stock back to the corporation, or in the event of a director deadlock that cannot be broken, the corporation is bound to repurchase the shares. See also the *cross purchase agreement*.

STOCK SPLIT Occurs when a corporation increases the number of issued shares of stock and reduces the par or stated value proportionally. When a corporation's stock is selling at a very low value, the corporation may perform a reverse stock split which reduces the number of shares outstanding and increases the market price of the stock.

STOCK SUBSCRIPTION A contract whereby an individual wishing to become a shareholder in a corporation to be organized or already organized makes an offer to subscribe to a specified number of shares at a stated price both before and after incorporation.

SURPLUS If net assets grow and exceed the corporation's capital there will be a *surplus* (called retained earnings by CPAs); if the net assets fall below capital due to operating losses, the corporation will have a *deficit* in its retained earnings account.

TAX-FREE INCORPORATION Where the incorporators contribute property, but not services, to the corporation and take back control of the corporation. Control under the Internal Revenue Code means at least 80 percent of the combined voting power of all classes of voting stock and, in addition, at least 80 percent of all other classes of the corporation.

TAX YEAR A corporation must calculate its net income on the basis of a tax year. The "tax year" is the annual accounting period the corporation uses for maintaining its records and reporting income and expenses. A corporation can use either a calendar year or a fiscal year.

TREASURER Chief financial officer of the corporation. As chief custodian of the corporate funds, she is frequently designated to countersign notes, checks, miscellaneous corporate instruments, and stock certificates.

TREASURY SHARES Issued and outstanding shares that are reacquired by the corporation. The corporation may reacquire shares to fund a company pension plan, to reduce the number of shareholders who have an interest in the corporation, to eliminate dissident or unhappy shareholders, to keep outsiders from gaining control of the corporation, to use the stock to acquire other companies, and for later reissuance as circumstances dictate.

UNIFORM LIMITED PARTNERSHIP ACT (ULPA) Both this act and RULPA (Revised Uniform Limited Partnership Act) form the basis for governing the limited partnership.

ULTRA VIRES Corporate acts that exceed the powers or stated purposes of the corporation. Modern corporate states generally validate most corporate acts if they are profit directed and are not in direct contravention of civil or criminal statutes.

UNISSUED SHARES Shares authorized by the articles of incorporation but not yet issued are called *unissued* shares.

VICE PRESIDENT A person who has no authority in his individual capacity, but is empowered to act in place of the president in case of the latter's death, illness, or incapacity.

VOTING AGREEMENT Two or more shareholders may enter into an agreement to vote their shares in a certain way. This "pooling agreement," which must be in writing and signed by the shareholders, requires that the members cast their votes in a certain way, such as which directors to elect.

VOTING TRUST An agreement by which shareholders surrender their voting power and place it irrevocably into the hands of others.

WARRANTS Stock options are usually evidenced by certificates known as "warrants."

WATERED STOCK Par value stock that is issued for less than its full value (e.g., discounted stock). The stockholder receiving watered stock is liable to the corporation for the difference between the price paid and the par value of the stock.

Where to File Incorporation Papers and Applicable Filing Fees

T he basic instrument that, upon filing, usually creates the corporation is called, in most states, "articles of incorporation" or "certificate of incorporation" or simply "the charter." Its contents are prescribed in the general incorporation statutes. In many jurisdictions, official forms are also prescribed. In most jurisdictions, corporate existence begins with the filing, usually with the secretary of state or other appropriate state officer. The following is a list of the appropriate state addresses and phone numbers for filing the corporate charter and all other required papers. Virtually every state has different standards that must be met for incorporation. It is also advisable for people seeking to incorporate to check with their secretary of state since the following filing fees, and various other required fees, are subject to change without notice. The following websites also offer information regarding incorporation in a particular state:

www.50states.com
www.Uslaw.com/library/article/noinx50states.html

State	Addresses & Fees
Alabama	Alabama Secretary of State Alabama Business Division Post Office Box 5616 Montgomery, AL 36103 (205) 242-5324 Controlling State Law: Alabama Business Corporation Act **Filing Fee:** $40 to Secretary of State
Alaska	Alaska Department of Community and Economic Development Division of Banking, Securities, and Corporations Post Office Box D Juneau, AK 99801 (907) 465-2530 Controlling State Law: Alaska Statutes, Section 10 **Filing Fee:** $150

State	Addresses & Fees	State	Addresses & Fees
Arizona	Arizona Corporation Commission 1200 West Washington Post Office Box 6019 Phoenix, AZ 85005 (602) 542-3135 Controlling State Law: Arizona Revised Statutes, Section 10 Filing Fee: $50	*Delaware*	Delaware Department of State Corporation Division Post Office Box 898 Dover, DE 19903 (302) 739-3073 Controlling State Law: Delaware Code, Chapter 1, Title 8 Filing Fee: $25
Arkansas	Arkansas Secretary of State Corporation Department State Capital Room 256 Little Rock, AK 72201 (501) 682-5160 Controlling State Law: Arkansas Code, Section 4-27-400+ Filing Fee: $50	*District of Columbia*	Recorder of Deeds Superintendent of Corporations 515 D Street NW Washington, DC 20001 (202) 727-7278 Controlling State Law: District of Columbia Code, Section 29-. Filing Fee: $20
California	California Secretary of State Corporation Division 1560 Broadway Sacramento, CA 95814 (916) 445-0620 Controlling State Law: California Corporation Code, Section 200+ Filing Fee: $100	*Florida*	Florida Department of State Corporation Division Post Office Box 6327 Tallahassee, FL 32304 (904) 488-9000 Controlling State Law: Florida Statutes, Section 607.+ Filing Fee: $35
Colorado	Colorado Secretary of State Corporations Section 1560 Broadway Suite 200 Denver, CO 80202 (303) 894-2251 Controlling State Law: Colorado Revised Statutes Filing Fee: $50	*Georgia*	Georgia Secretary of State Corporation Division 2 Martin Luther King Drive SE Atlanta, GA 30334 (404) 656-2817 Controlling State Law: Official Code of Georgia Annotated, Sections 14-2-. Filing Fee: $60
Connecticut	Connecticut Secretary of State Corporate Division 36 Trinity Street Hartford, CT 06115 (203) 566-4128 Controlling State Law: General Statutes of Connecticut, Section 33-. Filing Fee: $45		

State	Addresses & Fees	State	Addresses & Fees
Hawaii	Hawaii Department of Commerce and Consumer Affairs Business Registration Division Post Office Box 40 Honolulu, HI 96813 (808) 586-2727 Controlling State Law: Hawaii Revised Statutes, Section 415-. Filing Fee: $50	*Iowa*	Iowa Secretary of State Corporation Division Hoover Building, 2nd Floor Des Moines, IA 50319 (515) 281-5204 Controlling State Law: Iowa Code Annotated, Section 49.3B. Filing Fee: $50
Idaho	Idaho Secretary of State Corporation Division Statehouse Room 203 Boise, ID 83720 (204) 334-2300 Controlling State Law: Idaho Code, Section 30-. Filing Fee: $60	*Kansas*	Kansas Secretary of State Corporation Division State Capitol, 2nd Floor Topeka, KS 66612 (913) 296-4564 Controlling State Law: Kansas Statutes Annotated, Section 17-. Filing Fee: $75
Illinois	Illinois Secretary of State Corporation Division Centennial Building 3rd Floor Springfield, IL 62756 (217) 782-7880 Controlling State Law: Illinois Annotated Statutes, Chapter 32 Filing Fee: $75	*Kentucky*	Kentucky Secretary of State Corporation Division New Capitol Building Frankfort, KY 40601 (502) 564-2848 Controlling State Law: Kentucky Revised Statutes, Section 271B-. Filing Fee: $40
Indiana	Indiana Secretary of State Corporation Division 201 State House Indianapolis, IN 46204 (317) 232-6576 Controlling State Law: Indiana Business Corporation Law, Section 23-1-. Filing Fee: $90	*Louisiana*	Administrator Corporations, Trademarks, and Partnerships Post Office Box 94125 Baton Rouge, LA 70804 (504) 925-4704 Controlling State Law: Business Corporation Law Chapter 1 of Title 12 Filing Fee: $60

State	Addresses & Fees	State	Addresses & Fees
Maine	Maine Secretary of State Corporation Division State House Station 101 Augusta, ME 04333 (207) 287-4180 Controlling State Law: Maine Revised Statutes, Title 13-A. Filing Fee: $75	*Minnesota*	Minnesota Secretary of State Corporation Division State Office Building #180 St. Paul, MN 55155 (612) 296-2803 Controlling State Law: Minnesota Statutes, Section 320A. Filing Fee: $135
Maryland	Maryland State Department of Assessments and Taxation Corporation Division 301 West Preston Street, Room 809 Baltimore, MD 21201 (410) 225-1340 Controlling State Law: Annotated Code of Maryland, Corporation and Association Articles Filing Fee: $40	*Mississippi*	Mississippi Secretary of State Corporation Division Post Office Box 136 Jackson, MS 39205 (601) 359-1633 Controlling State Law: Mississippi Code Annotated, Section 79-4-. Filing Fee: $50
Massachusetts	Massachusetts Secretary of Commonwealth Corporation Division/State House Boston, MA 02133 (617) 727-9640 Controlling State Law: Massachu- setts Business Corporation Law, Chapter 156B Filing Fees: Based upon the amount of authorized stock with a minimum fee of $200.	*Missouri*	Secretary of State Corporation Division Post Office Box 0778 Jefferson City, MO 65102 (314) 751-3827 Controlling State Law: Revised Statutes of Missouri, Section 351. Filing Fees: Based upon the amount of authorized stock with a minimum fee of $53.
Michigan	Michigan Department of Commerce Corporation Bureau Post Office Box 30054 Lansing, MI 48926 (517) 334-6302 Controlling State Law: Michigan Compiled Laws, Section 450 Filing Fee: $10	*Montana*	Montana Secretary of State Corporation Division State Capitol Helena, MT 59601 (406) 444-3665 Controlling State Law: Montana Code Annotated, Title 35. Filing Fee: $20

State	Addresses & Fees	State	Addresses & Fees
Nebraska	Nebraska Secretary of State Corporation Division State Capitol Building, Room 2300 Lincoln, NE 68509 (402) 471-4079 Controlling State Law: Revised Statutes of Nebraska, Section 21-. Filing Fees: Based upon the amount of authorized stock with a minimum fee of $40.	New Mexico	New Mexico Department of State Corporation Division Post Office Box 1269 Santa Fe, NM 87504 (505) 827-4511 Controlling State Law: New Mex- ico Statutes Annotated, Section 53. Filing Fees: Based upon the amount of authorized stock with a minimum fee of $50.
Nevada	Nevada Secretary of State Corporation Division Capitol Complex Carson City, NV 89701 (702) 687-5203 Controlling State Law: Nevada Revised Statutes, Section 78. Filing Fees: Based upon the amount of authorized stock with a minimum fee of $125.	New York	New York Department of State Corporation Bureau 125 Washington Street Albany, NY 12231 (518) 473-2492 Controlling State Law: New York Business Corporation Law Filing Fee: $125
New Hampshire	New Hampshire Department of State Corporation Division 107 North Main Street Concord, NH 00301 (603) 271-3244 Controlling State Law: New Hampshire Revised Statutes Annotated, Section 293A. Filing Fee: $35.	North Carolina	North Carolina Secretary of State Corporation Division Capitol Building Raleigh, NC 27603 (919) 733-4201 Controlling State Law: General Statutes of North Carolina, Section 55. Filing Fee: $100.
New Jersey	New Jersey Department of State Corporation Division CN 308 Trenton, NJ 08625 (609) 530-6400 Controlling State Law: New Jersey Statutes, Section 14A. Filing Fee: $100.	North Dakota	North Dakota Secretary of State Main Capitol Building 600 East Boulevard Avenue Bismark, ND 58505-0500 (701) 224-4284 Controlling State Law: North Dakota Century Code, Chapter 10–19. Filing Fee: $90.

State	Addresses & Fees	State	Addresses & Fees

Ohio	Ohio Secretary of State
	Corporation Division
	30 East Broad Street
	Columbus, OH 43266
	(614) 466-3910
	Controlling State Law: Ohio
	  Revised Code, Section 1701.
	Filing Fees: Based upon the
	  amount of authorized stock with
	  a minimum fee of $75.
		Rhode Island	Rhode Island Secretary of State
			Corporation Division
			100 North Main Street
			Providence, RI 20903
			(401) 277-3040
			Controlling State Law: General
			  Laws of Rhode Island, Section 7-1.
			Filing Fee: $70

Oklahoma	Oklahoma Secretary of State
	Corporation Division
	101 State Capitol Building
	Oklahoma City, OK 73105
	(405) 521-3911
	Controlling State Law: Oklahoma
	  Statutes, Title 18.
	Filing Fees: Based upon the
	  amount of authorized stock with
	  a minimum fee of $50.
		South Carolina	South Carolina Secretary of State
			Corporation Division
			Post Office Box 11350
			Columbia, SC 29211
			(803) 734-2158
			Controlling State Law: Code of
			  Laws of South Carolina, Section
			  33.
			Filing Fee: $10

Oregon	Oregon Secretary of State
	Corporation Division
	158 NE 12th
	Salem, OR 97310
	(503) 986-2200
	Controlling State Law: Oregon
	  Business Corporation Act.
	Filing Fee: $75
		South Dakota	South Dakota Secretary of State
			Corporation Division
			Capitol Building
			Pierre, SD 57501
			(605) 773-4845
			Controlling State Law: South
			  Dakota Compiles Laws, Section 47.
			Filing Fees: Based upon the
			  amount of authorized stock with
			  a minimum fee of $40.

Pennsylvania	Pennsylvania Department of State
	Corporation Bureau
	308 North Office Building
	Harrisburg, PA 17120
	(717) 787-1057
	Controlling State Law: Pennsylva-
	  nia Consolidated Statutes, Sec-
	  tion 1300-.
	Filing Fee: $100
		Tennessee	Tennessee Secretary of State
			Corporation Division
			State Capitol Building
			Nashville, TN 37219
			(615) 741-0537
			Controlling State Law: Tennessee
			  Code Annotated, Section 48.
			Filing Fee: $50

State	Addresses & Fees	State	Addresses & Fees
Texas	Texas Secretary of State Corporation Section Post Office Box 13697-3697 Austin, TX 78711 (512) 463-5555 Controlling State Law: Texas Business Corporation Act **Filing Fee:** $300	*Washington*	Washington Secretary of State Corporation Division 505 East Union Street Olympia, WA 98504 (206) 753-7115 Controlling State Law: Revised Code of Washington, Title 23-B. **Filing Fee:** $175
Utah	Utah Department of Commerce Division of Corporations and Commercial Code Post Office Box 45801 Salt Lake City, UT 84145-0801 (801) 530-4849 Controlling State Law: Utah Code Annotated, Section 16-10. **Filing Fee:** $50	*West Virginia*	West Virginia Secretary of State Corporation Division State Capital Building Charleston, WV 25305 (304) 528-8000 Controlling State Law: West Virginia Code, Chapter 31, Article 1. **Filing Fee:** $10
Vermont	Vermont Secretary of State Redstone Building 26 Terrace Street Drawer 09 Montpelier, VT 05609-1101 (802) 828-2363 Controlling State Law: Vermont Statutes Annotated, Title 11 **Filing Fees:** Based upon the amount of authorized stock with a minimum fee of $35.	*Wisconsin*	Wisconsin Secretary of State Corporation Division Post Office Box 7846 Madison, WI 53701 (608) 266-3590 Controlling State Law: Wisconsin Statutes Annotated, Section 180. **Filing Fees:** Based upon the amount of authorized stock with a minimum fee of $90.
Virginia	Virginia State Corporation Commission 1220 Bank Street Post Office Box 1197 Richmond, VA 23219 (804) 371-9733 Controlling State Law: Code of Virginia, Title 13.1 **Filing Fee:** $25	*Wyoming*	Wyoming Secretary of State Corporation Division State Capitol Building Cheyenne, WY 82002 (307) 777-7311 Controlling State Law: Wyoming Statutes, Section 17-16. **Filing Fees:** $90. There is a $30 credit if filed when reserving a corporate name.

APPENDIX 2   Sample Tax Forms

The forms in this appendix (accompanied by their respective instructions) represent some of the information needed to be prepared by a corporation for income tax purposes. They have been filled in with information from a fictional corporation in order to help you understand how they need to be prepared. You will, of course, need to determine which forms you will need and supply your own corporation's personal information on current tax forms, which can be obtained from your local IRS office.

Form **940-EZ**	Employer's Annual Federal	OMB No. 1545-1110
(1)	Unemployment (FUTA) Tax Return	**2002**
Department of the Treasury Internal Revenue Service	▶ See separate Instructions for Form 940-EZ for information on completing this form.	

				T
	Name (as distinguished from trade name)		Calendar year	FF
				FD
You must complete this section. ▶	Trade name, if any Peter Cone			FP
				I
	Address and ZIP code 362 Main Street Pine Town, VA 3000		Employer identification number	T

*Answer the questions under **Who May Use Form 940-EZ** on page 2. If you cannot use Form 940-EZ, you must use Form 940.*

A Enter the amount of contributions paid to your state unemployment fund. (see separate instructions) . . . ▶ $ ___630.00___

B (1) Enter the name of the state where you have to pay contributions . . . . ▶ VIRGINIA

  (2) Enter your state reporting number as shown on your state unemployment tax return ▶ 98765432

If you will not have to file returns in the future, check here (see **Who Must File** in separate instructions) **and complete and sign the return.** ▶ ☐

If this is an Amended Return, check here (see **Amended Returns** on page 2 of the separate instructions) . . . . ▶ ☐

Part I Taxable Wages and FUTA Tax

1	Total payments (including payments shown on lines 2 and 3) during the calendar year for services of employees	**1**	78,000	00
2	Exempt payments. (Explain all exempt payments, attaching additional sheets if necessary.) ▶ --- ---	**2**		
3	Payments of more than $7,000 for services. Enter only amounts over the first $7,000 paid to each employee. (see separate instructions)	**3** 57,000 00		
4	Add lines 2 and 3	**4**	57,000	00
5	Total taxable wages (subtract line 4 from line 1)	**5**	21,000	00
6	**FUTA tax.** Multiply the wages on line 5 by .008 and enter here. (**If the result is over $100, also complete Part II.**)	**6**	168	00
7	Total FUTA tax deposited for the year, including any overpayment applied from a prior year	**7**	149	60
8	**Balance due** (subtract line 7 from line 6). Pay to the "United States Treasury." . . . . ▶	**8**	18	40
	If you owe more than $100, see **Depositing FUTA tax** in separate instructions.			
9	**Overpayment** (subtract line 6 from line 7). Check if it is to be: ☐ **Applied to next return** or ☐ **Refunded** ▶	**9**		

Part II Record of Quarterly Federal Unemployment Tax Liability (Do not include state liability.) Complete only if line 6 is over $100.

Quarter	First (Jan. 1 – Mar. 31)	Second (Apr. 1 – June 30)	Third (July 1 – Sept. 30)	Fourth (Oct. 1 – Dec. 31)	Total for year
Liability for quarter	149.60	18.40			168.00

Third Party Designee	Do you want to allow another person to discuss this return with the IRS (see instructions page 5)? ☐ **Yes.** Complete the following.		☐ **No**
	Designee's name ▶	Phone no. ▶ ( )	Personal identification number (PIN) ▶ ☐☐☐☐☐

Under penalties of perjury, I declare that I have examined this return, including accompanying schedules and statements, and, to the best of my knowledge and belief, it is true, correct, and complete, and that no part of any payment made to a state unemployment fund claimed as a credit was, or is to be, deducted from the payments to employees.

Signature ▶ *Peter Cone*   Title (Owner, etc.) ▶ *Owner*   Date ▶ 1/25/XX

For Privacy Act and Paperwork Reduction Act Notice, see separate instructions.   ▼ **DETACH HERE** ▼   Cat. No. 10983G   Form **940-EZ** (2002)

Form **940-EZ(V)**	**Form 940-EZ Payment Voucher**	OMB No. 1545-1110
Department of the Treasury Internal Revenue Service	**Use this voucher only when making a payment with your return.**	**2002**

Complete boxes 1, 2, and 3. Do not send cash, and do not staple your payment to this voucher. Make your check or money order payable to the "United States Treasury." Be sure to enter your employer identification number, "Form 940-EZ," and "2002" on your payment.

1 Enter your employer identification number.	2		Dollars	Cents
	Enter the amount of your payment. ▶			
	3 Enter your business name (individual name for sole proprietors).			
	Enter your address.			
	Enter your city, state, and ZIP code.			

Who May Use Form 940-EZ

The following chart will lead you to the right form to use—

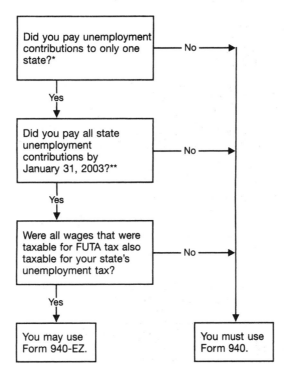

Did you pay unemployment contributions to only one state?* — No →

↓ Yes

Did you pay all state unemployment contributions by January 31, 2003?** — No →

↓ Yes

Were all wages that were taxable for FUTA tax also taxable for your state's unemployment tax? — No →

↓ Yes

You may use Form 940-EZ.

You must use Form 940.

* Do not file Form 940-EZ if—
● **You owe FUTA tax only for household work in a private home. See Schedule H (Form 1040).**
● **You are a successor employer claiming a credit for state unemployment contributions paid by a prior employer. File Form 940.**

**If you deposited all FUTA tax when due, you may answer "Yes" if you paid all state unemployment contributions by February 10, 2003. ★ U.S. GPO 2002 490-030

2002

Instructions for Forms 1120 and 1120-A

Section references are to the Internal Revenue Code unless otherwise noted.

Department of the Treasury
Internal Revenue Service

Changes To Note

- If the corporation's total receipts for the tax year (line 1a plus lines 4 through 10 on page 1 of Form 1120 or 1120-A) **and** its total assets at the end of the year are less than $250,000, it is not required to complete Schedules L, M-1, and M-2 on page 4 of Form 1120 (Parts III and IV on page 2 of Form 1120-A).
- Additional guidance has been issued allowing qualifying small businesses to adopt or change to the cash method of accounting. For details, see **Cost of Goods Sold** on page 14.
- Guidance has been issued regarding the nonaccrual experience method of accounting. See page 6.
- For tax years ending on or after December 31, 2001, if the corporation must make a section 481(a) adjustment because of an accounting method change, the adjustment period is 1 year for negative adjustments. For details, including special rules and exceptions, see Rev. Proc. 2002-19, 2002-13 I.R.B. 696 and Rev. Proc. 2002-54, 2002-35 I.R.B. 432. Also see **Change in accounting method** on page 6.
- Additional guidance has been issued regarding the rules for adopting, changing, and retaining an accounting period. See Regulations sections 1.441 and 1.442. Also, personal service corporations should see **Accounting period** on page 8.
- New procedures for certain corporations, including personal service corporations, to obtain automatic approval to adopt, change, or retain an accounting period have been issued. See Rev. Proc. 2002-37, 2002-22 I.R.B. 1030; Rev. Proc. 2002-38, 2002-22 I.R.B. 1037; and Rev. Proc. 2002-39, 2002-22 I.R.B. 1046.
- As a result of changes to the North American Industry Classification System (NAICS), some of the principal business activity codes listed on pages 21 through 23 have changed, mainly in the Construction, Wholesale Trade, and Information sectors.
- The corporation must file a disclosure statement for each reportable tax shelter transaction in which it participated, directly or indirectly, if the transaction affects the corporation's Federal tax liability. See **Tax shelter disclosure statement** on page 5 for details.

Photographs of Missing Children

The Internal Revenue Service is a proud partner with the National Center for Missing and Exploited Children. Photographs of missing children selected by the Center may appear in instructions on pages that would otherwise be blank. You can help bring these children home by looking at the photographs and calling **1-800-THE-LOST** (1-800-843-5678) if you recognize a child.

Unresolved Tax Issues

If the corporation has attempted to deal with an IRS problem unsuccessfully, it should contact the Taxpayer Advocate. The Taxpayer Advocate independently represents the corporation's interests and concerns within the IRS by protecting its rights and resolving problems that have not been fixed through normal channels.

While Taxpayer Advocates cannot change the tax law or make a technical tax decision, they can clear up problems that resulted from previous contacts and ensure that the corporation's case is given a complete and impartial review.

The corporation's assigned personal advocate will listen to its point of view and will work with the corporation to address its concerns. The corporation can expect the advocate to provide:

- A "fresh look" at a new or on-going problem.
- Timely acknowledgment.
- The name and phone number of the individual assigned to its case.
- Updates on progress.
- Timeframes for action.
- Speedy resolution.
- Courteous service.
    When contacting the Taxpayer Advocate, the corporation should provide the following information:
- The corporation's name, address, and employer identification number (EIN).
- The name and telephone number of an authorized contact person and the hours he or she can be reached.
- The type of tax return and year(s) involved.
- A detailed description of the problem.
- Previous attempts to solve the problem and the office that had been contacted.
- A description of the hardship the corporation is facing (if applicable).

The corporation may contact a Taxpayer Advocate by calling **1-877-777-4778** (toll free). Persons who have access to TTY/TDD equipment may call 1-800-829-4059 and ask for Taxpayer Advocate assistance. If the corporation prefers, it may call, write, or fax the Taxpayer Advocate office in its area. See **Pub. 1546,** The Taxpayer Advocate Service of the IRS, for a list of addresses and fax numbers.

Direct Deposit of Refund

To request a direct deposit of the corporation's income tax refund, attach Form 8050 (see pages 4 and 14).

Cat. No. 11455T

How To Make a Contribution To Reduce the Public Debt

To help reduce the public debt, make a check payable to the: "Bureau of the Public Debt." Send it to Bureau of the Public Debt, Department G, P.O. Box 2188, Parkersburg, WV 26106-2188. Or, enclose a check with the income tax return. Contributions to reduce the public debt are deductible subject to the rules and limitations for charitable contributions.

How To Get Forms and Publications

Personal computer. You can access the IRS web site 24 hours a day, 7 days a week at **www.irs.gov** to:
● Order IRS products on-line.
● Download forms, instructions, and publications.
● See answers to frequently asked tax questions.
● Search publications on-line by topic or keyword.
● Send us comments or request help by e-mail.
● Sign up to receive local and national tax news by e-mail.
   You can also reach us using file transfer protocol at **ftp.irs.gov**.

CD-ROM. Order **Pub. 1796**, Federal Tax Products on CD-ROM, and get:

● Current year forms, instructions, and publications.
● Prior year forms, instructions, and publications.
● Frequently requested tax forms that may be filled in electronically, printed out for submission, and saved for recordkeeping.
● The Internal Revenue Bulletin.
   Buy the CD-ROM on the Internet at **www.irs.gov/cdorders** from the National Technical Information Service (NTIS) for $22 (no handling fee), or call **1-877-CDFORMS** (1-877-233-6767) toll free to buy the CD-ROM for $22 (plus a $5 handling fee).

By phone and in person. You can order forms and publications 24 hours a day, 7 days a week, by calling **1-800-TAX-FORM** (1-800-829-3676). You can also get most forms and publications at your local IRS office.

General Instructions

Purpose of Form

Use **Form 1120**, U.S. Corporation Income Tax Return, or **Form 1120-A**, U.S. Corporation Short-Form Income Tax Return, to report the income, gains, losses, deductions, credits, and to figure the income tax liability of a corporation. Also see **Pub. 542**, Corporations, for more information.

Who Must File

Unless exempt under section 501, all domestic corporations (including corporations in bankruptcy) must file whether or not they have taxable income. Domestic corporations must file Form 1120 or, if they qualify, Form 1120-A, unless they are required to file a special return (see

Special Returns for Certain Organizations on this page).

Limited liability companies. If an entity was formed as a limited liability company under state law and is treated as a partnership for Federal income tax purposes, it should not file Form 1120 or 1120-A. Instead, file **Form 1065**, U.S. Return of Partnership Income. For the definition of a limited liability company, see the Instructions for Form 1065.

Corporations engaged in farming. Any corporation that engages in farming should use Form 1120 or, if they qualify, Form 1120-A to report the income (loss) from such activities. Enter the income and deductions of the corporation in accordance with the instructions for lines 1 through 10 and 12 through 29.

Who May File Form 1120-A

Form 1120-A may be filed by a corporation if it met **all** of the following requirements during the tax year:

● Its gross receipts (line 1a on page 1) are under $500,000.

● Its total income (line 11 on page 1) is under $500,000.

● Its total assets (Item D on page 1) are under $500,000.

● Its only dividend income is from domestic corporations and those dividends **(a)** qualify for the 70% dividends-received deduction and **(b)** are not from debt-financed securities.

● It is a small corporation exempt from the alternative minimum tax (AMT) under section 55(e) or it does not owe any AMT on **Form 4626**, Alternative Minimum Tax— Corporations.

● It does not have any of the "write-in" additions to tax listed in the Instructions for Form 1120, Schedule J, line 3 or line 11.

● It has no nonrefundable tax credits other than the general business credit or the credit for prior year minimum tax.

● It is not: **(a)** a member of a controlled group, **(b)** a personal holding company, **(c)** filing a consolidated return, **(d)** filing its final return, **(e)** dissolving or liquidating, **(f)** electing to forego the entire carryback period for any NOL, or **(g)** required to file one of the returns listed under **Special Returns for Certain Organizations** below.

● It does not have: **(a)** any ownership in a foreign corporation or foreign partnership, **(b)** foreign shareholders that directly or indirectly own 25% or more of its stock, or **(c)** any ownership in, or transactions with, a foreign trust.

Special Returns for Certain Organizations

Instead of filing Form 1120 or Form 1120-A, certain organizations, as shown below, have to file special returns.

If the organization is a	File Form
Farmers' cooperative (sec. 1381)	**990-C**
Exempt organization with unrelated trade or business income	**990-T**
Religious or apostolic organization exempt under section 501(d)	**1065**
Entity formed as a limited liability company under state law and treated as a partnership for Federal income tax purposes	**1065**
Entity that elects to be treated as a real estate mortgage investment conduit (REMIC) under sec. 860D	**1066**
Interest charge domestic international sales corporation (section 992)	**1120-IC-DISC**
Foreign corporation (other than life and property and casualty insurance company filing Form 1120-L or Form 1120-PC)	**1120-F**
Foreign sales corporation (sec. 922)	**1120-FSC**
Condominium management association or residential real estate management association that elects to be treated as a homeowners association under section 528	**1120-H**
Life insurance company (sec. 801)	**1120-L**
Fund set up to pay for nuclear decommissioning costs (sec. 468A)	**1120-ND**
Property and casualty insurance company (section 831)	**1120-PC**
Political organization (section 527)	**1120-POL**
Real estate investment trust (section 856)	**1120-REIT**
Regulated investment company (section 851)	**1120-RIC**
S corporation (section 1361)	**1120S**
Settlement fund (section 468B)	**1120-SF**

Ownership Interest in a FASIT

If a corporation holds an ownership interest in a **financial asset securitization investment trust (FASIT)**, it must report all items of income, gain, deductions, losses, and credits on the corporation's income tax return (except as provided in section 860H). Show a breakdown of the items on an attached schedule. For more information, see sections 860H and 860L.

When To File

Generally, a corporation must file its income tax return by the 15th day of the 3rd month after the end of the tax year. A new corporation filing a short-period return must generally file by the 15th day of the 3rd month after the short period ends. A corporation that has dissolved must generally file by the 15th day of the 3rd month after the date it dissolved.

-2-

Instructions for Forms 1120 and 1120-A

If the due date falls on a Saturday, Sunday, or legal holiday, the corporation may file on the next business day.

Private delivery services. Corporations can use certain private delivery services designated by the IRS to meet the "timely mailing as timely filing/paying" rule for tax returns and payments. The most recent list of designated private delivery services was published by the IRS in September 2002.

The list includes only the following.
- Airborne Express (Airborne): Overnight Air Express Service, Next Afternoon Service, Second Day Service.
- DHL Worldwide Express (DHL): DHL "Same Day" Service, DHL USA Overnight.
- Federal Express (FedEx): FedEx Priority Overnight, FedEx Standard Overnight, FedEx 2Day, FedEx International Priority, and Fed Ex International First.
- United Parcel Service (UPS): UPS Next Day Air, UPS Next Day Air Saver, UPS 2nd Day Air, UPS 2nd Day Air A.M., UPS Worldwide Express Plus, and UPS Worldwide Express.

The private delivery service can tell you how to get written proof of the mailing date.

Extension. File **Form 7004,** Application for Automatic Extension of Time To File Corporation Income Tax Return, to request a 6-month extension of time to file.

Who Must Sign

The return must be signed and dated by:
- The president, vice president, treasurer, assistant treasurer, chief accounting officer or
- Any other corporate officer (such as tax officer) authorized to sign.

Receivers, trustees, or assignees must also sign and date any return filed on behalf of a corporation.

If an employee of the corporation completes Form 1120 or Form 1120-A, the paid preparer's space should remain blank. In addition, anyone who prepares Form 1120 or Form 1120-A but does not charge the corporation should not complete that section. Generally, anyone who is paid to prepare the return must sign it and fill in the "Paid Preparer's Use Only" area.

The **paid preparer** must complete the required preparer information and—
- Sign the return, by hand, in the space provided for the preparer's signature (signature stamps and labels are not acceptable).
- Give a copy of the return to the taxpayer.

Paid Preparer Authorization

If the corporation wants to allow the IRS to discuss its 2002 tax return with the paid preparer who signed it, check the "Yes" box in the signature area of the return. This authorization applies only to the individual whose signature appears in the "Paid

Preparer's Use Only" section of the corporation's return. It does not apply to the firm, if any, shown in that section.

If the "Yes" box is checked, the corporation is authorizing the IRS to call the paid preparer to answer any questions that may arise during the processing of its return. The corporation is also authorizing the paid preparer to:
- Give the IRS any information that is missing from the return,
- Call the IRS for information about the processing of the return or the status of any related refund or payment(s), and
- Respond to certain IRS notices that the corporation has shared with the preparer about math errors, offsets, and return preparation. The notices will not be sent to the preparer.

The corporation is not authorizing the paid preparer to receive any refund check, bind the corporation to anything (including any additional tax liability), or otherwise represent the corporation before the IRS. If the corporation wants to expand the paid preparer's authorization, see **Pub. 947,** Practice Before the IRS and Power of Attorney.

The authorization cannot be revoked. However, the authorization will automatically end no later than the due date (excluding extensions) for filing the corporation's 2003 tax return.

Other Forms, Returns, and Statements That May Be Required

Forms

The corporation may have to file some of the following forms. See the form for more information.
- **Form W-2,** Wage and Tax Statement, and **Form W-3,** Transmittal of Wage and Tax Statements. Use these forms to report wages, tips, and other compensation, and withheld income, social security, and Medicare taxes for employees.
- **Form W-2G,** Certain Gambling Winnings. Use this form to report gambling winnings from horse racing, dog racing, jai alai, lotteries, keno, bingo, slot machines, sweepstakes, wagering pools, etc.
- **Form 720,** Quarterly Federal Excise Tax Return. Use this form to report and pay the luxury tax on passenger vehicles, environmental taxes, communications and air transportation taxes, fuel taxes, manufacturers taxes, ship passenger taxes, and certain other excise taxes.
- **Form 851,** Affiliations Schedule. The parent corporation of an **affiliated group** of corporations must attach this form to its consolidated return. If this is the first year one or more subsidiaries are being included in a consolidated return, also see **Form 1122,** Authorization and Consent of Subsidiary Corporation To Be Included in a Consolidated Income Tax Return, on page 4.
- **Form 926,** Return by a U.S. Transferor of Property to a Foreign Corporation. Use this form to report certain transfers to foreign corporations under section 6038B.
- **Form 940** or **Form 940-EZ,** Employer's Annual Federal Unemployment (FUTA) Tax Return. The corporation may be liable for

Where To File

File the corporation's return at the applicable IRS address listed below.

If the corporation's principal business, office, or agency is located in:	And the total assets at the end of the tax year (Form 1120, page 1, item D) are:	Use the following Internal Revenue Service Center address:
Connecticut, Delaware, District of Columbia, Illinois, Indiana, Kentucky, Maine, Maryland, Massachusetts, Michigan, New Hampshire, New Jersey, New York, North Carolina, Ohio, Pennsylvania, Rhode Island, South Carolina, Vermont, Virginia, West Virginia, Wisconsin	Less than $10 million	Cincinnati, OH 45999-0012
	$10 million or more	Ogden, UT 84201-0012
Alabama, Alaska, Arizona, Arkansas, California, Colorado, Florida, Georgia, Hawaii, Idaho, Iowa, Kansas, Louisiana, Minnesota, Mississippi, Missouri, Montana, Nebraska, Nevada, New Mexico, North Dakota, Oklahoma, Oregon, South Dakota, Tennessee, Texas, Utah, Washington, Wyoming	Any amount	Ogden, UT 84201-0012
A foreign country or U.S. possession (or the corporation is claiming the possessions corporation tax credit under sections 30A and 936)	Any amount	Philadelphia, PA 19255-0012

A group of corporations with members located in more than one service center area will often keep all the books and records at the principal office of the managing corporation. In this case, the tax returns of the corporations may be filed with the service center for the area in which the principal office of the managing corporation is located.

Instructions for Forms 1120 and 1120-A   -3-

FUTA tax and may have to file Form 940 or Form 940-EZ if it either:

1. Paid wages of $1,500 or more in any calendar quarter in 2001 or 2002 or

2. Had one or more employees who worked for the corporation for at least some part of a day in any 20 or more different weeks in 2001 or 20 or more different weeks in 2002.

• **Form 941,** Employer's Quarterly Federal Tax Return, or **Form 943,** Employer's Annual Tax Return for Agricultural Employees. Employers must file these forms to report income tax withheld, and employer and employee social security and Medicare taxes. Also, see **Trust fund recovery penalty** on page 7.

• **Form 945,** Annual Return of Withheld Federal Income Tax. File Form 945 to report income tax withheld from nonpayroll distributions or payments, including pensions, annuities, IRAs, gambling winnings, and backup withholding. See **Trust fund recovery penalty** on page 7.

• **Form 952,** Consent To Extend the Time To Assess Tax Under Section 332(b). This form is filed to extend the period of assessment of all income taxes of the receiving corporation on the complete liquidation of a subsidiary under section 332.

• **Form 966,** Corporate Dissolution or Liquidation. Use this form to report the adoption of a resolution or plan to dissolve the corporation or liquidate any of its stock.

• **Form 1042,** Annual Withholding Tax Return for U.S. Source Income of Foreign Persons;

• **Form 1042-S,** Foreign Person's U.S. Source Income Subject to Withholding; and

• **Form 1042-T,** Annual Summary and Transmittal of Forms 1042-S. Use these forms to report and send withheld tax on payments or distributions made to nonresident alien individuals, foreign partnerships, or foreign corporations to the extent these payments constitute gross income from sources within the United States (see sections 861 through 865).

Also see **Pub. 515,** Withholding of Tax on Nonresident Aliens and Foreign Entities, and sections 1441 and 1442.

• **Form 1096,** Annual Summary and Transmittal of U.S. Information Returns.

• **Form 1098,** Mortgage Interest Statement. Use this form to report the receipt from any individual of $600 or more of mortgage interest (including points) in the course of the corporation's trade or business and reimbursements of overpaid interest.

• **Form 1098-E,** Student Loan Interest Statement. Use this form to report the receipt of $600 or more of student loan interest in the course of the corporation's trade or business.

• **Forms 1099.** Use these information returns to report the following.

1. **1099-A,** Acquisition or Abandonment of Secured Property.

2. **1099-B,** Proceeds From Broker and Barter Exchange Transactions.

3. **1099-C,** Cancellation of Debt.

4. **1099-DIV,** Dividends and Distributions.

5. **1099-INT,** Interest Income.

6. **1099-LTC,** Long-Term Care and Accelerated Death Benefits.

7. **1099-MISC,** Miscellaneous Income. Use this form to report payments: to certain fishing boat crew members, to providers of health and medical services, of rent or royalties, of nonemployee compensation, etc.

Note: *Every corporation must file Form 1099-MISC if it makes payments of rents, commissions, or other fixed or determinable income (see section 6041) totaling $600 or more to any one person in the course of its trade or business during the calendar year.*

8. **1099-MSA,** Distributions From an Archer MSA or Medicare+Choice MSA.

9. **1099-OID,** Original Issue Discount.

10. **1099-PATR,** Taxable Distributions Received From Cooperatives.

11. **1099-R,** Distributions From Pensions, Annuities, Retirement or Profit-Sharing Plans, IRAs, Insurance Contracts, etc.

12. **1099-S,** Proceeds From Real Estate Transactions.

Also use these returns to report amounts received as a nominee for another person.

• **Form 1122,** Authorization and Consent of Subsidiary Corporation To Be Included in a Consolidated Income Tax Return. For the first year a subsidiary corporation is being included in a consolidated return, attach the completed form to the parent's consolidated return. Attach a separate Form 1122 for each subsidiary being included in the consolidated return.

• **Form 3520,** Annual Return To Report Transactions With Foreign Trusts and Receipt of Certain Foreign Gifts. Use this form to report a distribution received from a foreign trust; or, if the corporation was the grantor of, transferor of, or transferor to, a foreign trust that existed during the tax year. See Question 5 of Schedule N (Form 1120).

• **Form 5452,** Corporate Report of Nondividend Distributions. Use this form to report nondividend distributions.

• **Form 5471,** Information Return of U.S. Persons With Respect to Certain Foreign Corporations. This form is required if the corporation controls a foreign corporation; acquires, disposes of, or owns 10% or more in value or vote of the outstanding stock of a foreign corporation; or had control of a foreign corporation for an uninterrupted period of at least 30 days during the annual accounting period of the foreign corporation. See Question 4 of Schedule N (Form 1120).

• **Form 5472,** Information Return of a 25% Foreign-Owned U.S. Corporation or a Foreign Corporation Engaged in a U.S. Trade or Business. This form is filed if the corporation is 25% or more foreign-owned. See Question 7 on page 19.

• **Form 5498,** IRA and Coverdell ESA Contribution Information. Use this form to report contributions (including rollover contributions) to any IRA, including a SEP, SIMPLE, or Roth IRA, or a Coverdell ESA, and to report Roth IRA conversions, IRA recharacterizations, and the fair market value of the account.

• **Form 5498-MSA,** Archer MSA or Medicare+Choice MSA Information. Use this form to report contributions to an Archer MSA and the fair market value of an Archer MSA or Medicare+Choice MSA.

For more information, see the general and specific Instructions for Forms 1099, 1098, 5498, and W-2G.

• **Form 5713,** International Boycott Report. Corporations that had operations in, or related to, certain "boycotting" countries file Form 5713.

• **Form 8023,** Elections Under Section 338 for Corporations Making Qualified Stock Purchases. Corporations file this form to make elections under section 338 for a "target" corporation if the purchasing corporation has made a qualified stock purchase of the target corporation.

• **Form 8027,** Employer's Annual Information Return of Tip Income and Allocated Tips. Use this form to report receipts from large food or beverage operations, tips reported by employees, and allocated tips.

• **Form 8050,** Direct Deposit of Corporate Tax Refund. File Form 8050 to request that the IRS deposit a corporate tax refund (including a refund of $1 million or more) directly into an account at any U.S. bank or other financial institution (such as a mutual fund or brokerage firm) that accepts direct deposits.

• **Form 8264,** Application for Registration of a Tax Shelter. Tax shelter organizers use this form to receive a tax shelter registration number from the IRS.

• **Form 8271,** Investor Reporting of Tax Shelter Registration Number. Corporations, which have acquired an interest in a tax shelter that is required to be registered, use this form to report the tax shelter's registration number. Attach Form 8271 to any tax return (including an application for tentative refund (Form 1139) and an amended return) on which a deduction, credit, loss, or other tax benefit attributable to a tax shelter is taken or any income attributable to a tax shelter is reported.

• **Form 8275,** Disclosure Statement, and **Form 8275-R,** Regulation Disclosure Statement. Disclose items or positions taken on a tax return that are not otherwise adequately disclosed on a tax return or that are contrary to Treasury regulations (to avoid parts of the accuracy-related penalty or certain preparer penalties).

• **Form 8281,** Information Return for Publicly Offered Original Issue Discount Instruments. Use this form to report the issuance of public offerings of debt instruments (obligations).

• **Form 8288,** U.S. Withholding Tax Return for Dispositions by Foreign Persons of U.S. Real Property Interests, and **Form 8288-A,** Statement of Withholding on Dispositions by Foreign Persons of U.S. Real Property Interests. Use these forms to report and transmit withheld tax on the purchase of a U.S. real property interest from a foreign person. See section 1445 and the related regulations for more information.

• **Form 8300,** Report of Cash Payments Over $10,000 Received in a Trade or Business. Use this form to report the receipt of more than $10,000 in cash or foreign currency in one transaction or a series of related transactions.

• **Form 8594,** Asset Acquisition Statement Under Section 1060. Corporations file this form to report the purchase or sale of a group of assets that make up a trade or business if goodwill or going concern value attaches or could attach to the assets and if the buyer's basis is determined only by the amount paid for the assets.

• **Form 8621,** Return by a Shareholder of a Passive Foreign Investment Company or Qualified Electing Fund. Use this form to make certain elections by shareholders in a passive foreign investment company and to figure certain deferred taxes.

-4-

Instructions for Forms 1120 and 1120-A

- **Form 8697,** Interest Computation Under the Look-Back Method for Completed Long-Term Contracts. Use this form to figure the interest due or to be refunded under the look-back method of section 460(b)(2). The look-back method applies to certain long-term contracts accounted for under the either percentage of completion method or the percentage of completion-capitalized cost method.
- **Form 8810,** Corporate Passive Activity Loss and Credit Limitations. Closely held corporations (and corporations that are personal service corporations) must use this form to compute the passive activity loss and credit allowed under section 469.
- **Form 8817,** Allocation of Patronage and Nonpatronage Income and Deductions. Use this form to figure and report patronage and nonpatronage income and deductions (used by taxable cooperatives).
- **Form 8842,** Election To Use Different Annualization Periods for Corporate Estimated Tax. Corporations use Form 8842 for each year they want to elect one of the annualization periods in section 6655(e)(2) for figuring estimated tax payments under the annualized income installment method.
- **Form 8849,** Claim for Refund of Excise Taxes. Corporations use this form to claim a refund of certain excise taxes.
- **Form 8865,** Return of U.S. Persons With Respect to Certain Foreign Partnerships. A domestic corporation may have to file Form 8865 if it:

    1. Controlled a foreign partnership (i.e., owned more than a 50% direct or indirect interest in the partnership).

    2. Owned at least a 10% direct or indirect interest in a foreign partnership while U.S. persons controlled that partnership.

    3. Had an acquisition, disposition, or change in proportional interest in a foreign partnership that:

    a. Increased its direct interest to at least 10% or reduced its direct interest of at least 10% to less than 10%.

    b. Changed its direct interest by at least a 10% interest.

    4. Contributed property to a foreign partnership in exchange for a partnership interest if:

    a. Immediately after the contribution, the corporation owned, directly or indirectly, at least a 10% interest in the foreign partnership or

    b. The fair market value of the property the corporation contributed to the foreign partnership, when added to other contributions of property made to the foreign partnership during the preceding 12-month period, exceeds $100,000.

    Also, the domestic corporation may have to file Form 8865 to report certain dispositions by a foreign partnership of property it previously contributed to that partnership if it was a partner at the time of the disposition.

    For more details, including penalties for failing to file Form 8865, see Form 8865 and its separate instructions.
- **Form 8866,** Interest Computation Under the Look-Back Method for Property Depreciated Under the Income Forecast Method. Figure the interest due or to be refunded under the look-back method of section 167(g)(2) for property placed in service after September 13, 1995, that is depreciated under the income forecast method.
- **Form 8876,** Excise Tax on Structured Settlement Factoring Transactions. Use this form to report and pay the 40% excise tax imposed under section 5891.
- **Form 8883,** Asset Allocation Statement Under Section 338. Corporations file this form to report information about transactions involving the deemed sale of corporate assets under section 338.

Amended Return

Use **Form 1120X,** Amended U.S. Corporation Income Tax Return, to correct a previously filed Form 1120 or Form 1120-A.

Statements

Consolidated returns. File supporting statements for each corporation included in the consolidated return. Do not use Form 1120 as a supporting statement. On the supporting statement, use columns to show the following, both before and after adjustments:

1. Items of gross income and deductions.

2. A computation of taxable income.

3. Balance sheets as of the beginning and end of the tax year.

4. A reconciliation of income per books with income per return.

5. A reconciliation of retained earnings.

Enter the totals for the consolidated group on Form 1120. Attach consolidated balance sheets and a reconciliation of consolidated retained earnings. For more information on consolidated returns, see the regulations under section 1502.

Tax shelter disclosure statement. For each reportable tax shelter transaction entered into **prior to January 1, 2003,** in which the corporation participated, directly or indirectly, the corporation must attach a disclosure statement to its return for each tax year that its Federal income tax liability is affected by its participation in the transaction. In addition, for the first tax year a disclosure statement is attached to its return, the corporation must send a copy of the disclosure statement to the Internal Revenue Service, LM:PFTG:OTSA, Large & Mid-Size Business Division, 1111 Constitution Ave., NW, Washington, DC 20224. If a transaction becomes a reportable transaction after the corporation files its return, it must attach a statement to the following year's return (whether or not its tax liability is affected for that year). The corporation is considered to have indirectly participated if it participated as a partner in a partnership or if it knows or has reason to know that the tax benefits claimed were derived from a reportable transaction.

Disclosure is required for a reportable transaction that is a listed transaction. A transaction is a listed transaction if it is the same as or substantially similar to a transaction that the IRS has determined to be a tax avoidance transaction and has identified as a listed transaction by notice, regulation, or other published guidance. See Notice 2001-51, 2001-34 I.R.B. 190, for transactions identified by the IRS as listed transactions. The listed transactions identified in this notice will be updated in future published guidance.

See Temporary Regulations section 1.6011-4T for details, including:

1. Definitions of reportable transaction, listed transaction, and substantially similar.

2. Form and content of the disclosure statement.

3. Filing requirements for the disclosure statement.

For reportable transactions entered into **after December 31, 2002,** use **Form 8886,** Reportable Transaction Disclosure Statement, to disclose information for each reportable transaction in which the corporation participated, directly or indirectly. Form 8886 must be filed for each tax year that the Federal income tax liability of the corporation is affected by its participation in the transaction. The following are reportable transactions.

- Any transaction that is the same as or substantially similar to tax avoidance transactions identified by the IRS.
- Any transaction offered under conditions of confidentiality.
- Any transaction for which the corporation has contractual protection against disallowance of the tax benefits.
- Any transaction resulting in a loss of at least $10 million in any single year or $20 million in any combination of years.
- Any transaction resulting in a book-tax difference of more than $10 million on a gross basis.
- Any transaction resulting in a tax credit of more than $250,000, if the corporation held the asset generating the credit for less than 45 days.

See the Instructions for Form 8886 for more details.

Stock ownership in foreign corporations. Attach the statement required by section 551(c) if:

- The corporation owned 5% or more in value of the outstanding stock of a foreign personal holding company and
- The corporation was required to include in its gross income any undistributed foreign personal holding company income from a foreign personal holding company.

Transfers to a corporation controlled by the transferor. If a person receives stock of a corporation in exchange for property, and no gain or loss is recognized under section 351, the person (transferor) and the transferee must each attach to their tax returns the information required by Regulations section 1.351-3.

Dual consolidated losses. If a domestic corporation incurs a dual consolidated loss (as defined in Regulations section 1.1503-2(c)(5)), the corporation (or consolidated group) may need to attach an elective relief agreement and/or an annual certification as provided in Regulations section 1.1503-2(g)(2).

Assembling the Return

To ensure that the corporation's tax return is correctly processed, attach all schedules and other forms after page 4, Form 1120 (or page 2, Form 1120-A), and in the following order.

1. Schedule N (Form 1120).

2. Form 8050.

3. Form 4136.

4. Form 4626.

5. Form 851.

Instructions for Forms 1120 and 1120-A

-5-

6. Additional schedules in alphabetical order.

7. Additional forms in numerical order.

Complete every applicable entry space on Form 1120 or Form 1120-A. Do not write "See Attached" instead of completing the entry spaces. If more space is needed on the forms or schedules, attach separate sheets using the same size and format as the printed forms. If there are supporting statements and attachments, arrange them in the same order as the schedules or forms they support and attach them last. Show the totals on the printed forms. Also, be sure to enter the corporation's name and EIN on each supporting statement or attachment.

Accounting Methods

An accounting method is a set of rules used to determine when and how income and expenses are reported. Figure taxable income using the method of accounting regularly used in keeping the corporation's books and records. In all cases, the method used must clearly show taxable income.

Generally, permissible methods include:
- Cash,
- Accrual, or
- Any other method authorized by the Internal Revenue Code.

Accrual method. Generally, a corporation (other than a qualified personal service corporation) must use the accrual method of accounting if its average annual gross receipts exceed $5 million. See section 448(c). A corporation engaged in farming operations also must use the accrual method. For exceptions, see section 447.

If inventories are required, the accrual method generally must be used for sales and purchases of merchandise. However, qualifying taxpayers and eligible businesses of qualifying small business taxpayers are excepted from using the accrual method for eligible trades or businesses and may account for inventoriable items as materials and supplies that are not incidental. For details, see **Cost of Goods Sold** on page 14.

Under the accrual method, an amount is includible in income when:
- All the events have occurred that fix the right to receive the income, which is the earliest of the date: **(a)** the required performance takes place, **(b)** payment is due, or **(c)** payment is received and
- The amount can be determined with reasonable accuracy.

See Regulations section 1.451-1(a) for details.

Generally, an accrual basis taxpayer can deduct accrued expenses in the tax year when:
- All events that determine the liability have occurred,
- The amount of the liability can be figured with reasonable accuracy, and
- Economic performance takes place with respect to the expense.

There are exceptions to the economic performance rule for certain items, including recurring expenses. See section 461(h) and the related regulations for the rules for determining when economic performance takes place.

Nonaccrual experience method. Accrual method corporations are not required to accrue certain amounts to be received from the performance of services that, on the basis of their experience, will not be collected, if:
- The services are in the fields of health, law, engineering, architecture, accounting, actuarial science, performing arts, or consulting or
- The corporation's average annual gross receipts for the 3 prior tax years does not exceed $5 million.

This provision does not apply to any amount if interest is required to be paid on the amount or if there is any penalty for failure to timely pay the amount. For more information, see section 448(d)(5). For reporting requirements, see the instructions for line 1 on page 8.

Percentage-of-completion method. Long-term contracts (except for certain real property construction contracts) must generally be accounted for using the percentage of completion method described in section 460. See section 460 and the underlying regulations for rules on long-term contracts.

Mark-to-market accounting method. Generally, dealers in securities must use the mark-to-market accounting method described in section 475. Under this method, any security that is inventory to the dealer must be included in inventory at its fair market value (FMV). Any security held by a dealer that is not inventory and that is held at the close of the tax year is treated as sold at its FMV on the last business day of the tax year. Any gain or loss must be taken into account in determining gross income. The gain or loss taken into account is generally treated as ordinary gain or loss. For details, including exceptions, see section 475, the related regulations, and Rev. Rul. 94-7, 1994-1 C.B. 151.

Dealers in commodities and traders in securities and commodities may elect to use the mark-to-market accounting method. To make the election, the corporation must file a statement describing the election, the first tax year the election is to be effective, and, in the case of an election for traders in securities or commodities, the trade or business for which the election is made. Except for new taxpayers, the statement must be filed by the due date (not including extensions) of the income tax return for the tax year immediately **preceding** the election year and attached to that return, or if applicable, to a request for an extension of time to file that return. For more details, see sections 475(e) and (f) and Rev. Proc. 99-17, 1999-1 C.B. 503.

Change in accounting method. Generally, the corporation must get IRS consent to change the method of accounting used to report taxable income (for income as a whole or for any material item). To do so, it must file **Form 3115,** Application for Change in Accounting Method. For more information, see Form 3115 and **Pub. 538,** Accounting Periods and Methods. However, there are new procedures under which a corporation may obtain automatic consent for certain changes in accounting method. See Rev. Proc. 2002-9, 2002-3 I.R.B. 327, as modified by Rev. Proc. 2002-19 and Rev. Proc. 2002-54.

Certain qualifying taxpayers or qualifying small business taxpayers (described on page 14) that want to use the cash method for an eligible trade or business may get an automatic consent to change their method of accounting. For details, see Rev. Proc. 2002-10, 2001-2 I.R.B. 272, Rev. Proc. 2002-28, 2002-18 I.R.B. 815, and Form 3115.

Section 481(a) adjustment. The corporation may have to make an adjustment under section 481(a) to prevent amounts of income or expense from being duplicated or omitted. The section 481(a) adjustment period is generally 1 year for a net negative adjustment and 4 years for a net positive adjustment. However, a corporation may elect to use a 1-year adjustment period if the net section 481(a) adjustment for the change is less than $25,000. The corporation must complete the appropriate lines of Form 3115 to make the election. For more details on the section 481(a) adjustment, see Rev. Proc. 2002-9, 2002-19, and 2002-54.

Include any net positive section 481(a) adjustment on page 1, line 10. If the net section 481(a) adjustment is negative, report it on Form 1120, line 26 (Form 1120-A, line 22).

Accounting Periods

A corporation must figure its taxable income on the basis of a tax year. The tax year is the annual accounting period the corporation uses to keep its records and report its income and expenses. Generally, corporations can use a calendar year or a fiscal year. Personal service corporations, however, must use a calendar year unless they meet one of the exceptions discussed in **Accounting period** on page 8.

For more information about accounting periods, see Regulations sections 1.441-1 and 1.441-2 and Pub. 538.

Calendar year. If the calendar year is adopted as the annual accounting period, the corporation must maintain its books and records and report its income and expenses for the period from January 1 through December 31 of each year.

Fiscal year. A fiscal year is 12 consecutive months ending on the last day of any month except December. A 52–53-week year is a fiscal year that varies from 52 to 53 weeks.

Adoption of tax year. A corporation adopts a tax year when it files its first income tax return. It must adopt a tax year by the due date (not including extensions) of its first income tax return.

Change of tax year. Generally, a corporation must get the consent of the IRS before changing its tax year by filing **Form 1128,** Application To Adopt, Change, or Retain a Tax Year. However, under certain conditions, a corporation may change its tax year without getting the consent.

For more information on change in tax year, see Form 1128, Regulations section 1.442-1, Pub. 538, and Rev. Proc. 2002-37 and 2002-39. Personal service corporations should also see **Accounting period** on page 8.

Rounding Off to Whole Dollars

The corporation may show amounts on the return and accompanying schedules as whole dollars. To do so, drop amounts less than 50 cents and increase amounts from

-6-

Instructions for Forms 1120 and 1120-A

50 cents through 99 cents to the next higher dollar.

Recordkeeping

Keep the corporation's records for as long as they may be needed for the administration of any provision of the Internal Revenue Code. Usually, records that support an item of income, deduction, or credit on the return must be kept for 3 years from the date the return is due or filed, whichever is later. Keep records that verify the corporation's basis in property for as long as they are needed to figure the basis of the original or replacement property.

The corporation should keep copies of all filed returns. They help in preparing future and amended returns.

Depository Method of Tax Payment

The corporation must pay the tax due in full no later than the 15th day of the 3rd month after the end of the tax year. The two methods of depositing corporate income taxes are discussed below.

Electronic Deposit Requirement

The corporation must make electronic deposits of **all** depository taxes (such as employment tax, excise tax, and corporate income tax) using the Electronic Federal Tax Payment System (EFTPS) in 2003 if:
● The total deposits of such taxes in 2001 were more than $200,000 or
● The corporation was required to use EFTPS in 2002.

If the corporation is required to use EFTPS and fails to do so, it may be subject to a 10% penalty. If the corporation is not required to use EFTPS, it may participate voluntarily. To enroll in or get more information about EFTPS, call 1-800-555-4477 or 1-800-945-8400. To enroll online, visit **www.eftps.gov**.

Depositing on time. For EFTPS deposits to be made timely, the corporation must initiate the transaction at least 1 business day before the date the deposit is due.

Deposits With Form 8109

If the corporation does not use EFTPS, deposit corporation income tax payments (and estimated tax payments) with **Form 8109,** Federal Tax Deposit Coupon. If you do not have a preprinted Form 8109, use Form 8109-B to make deposits. You can get this form by calling 1-800-829-4933. Be sure to have your EIN ready when you call.

Do not send deposits directly to an IRS office; otherwise, the corporation may have to pay a penalty. Mail or deliver the completed Form 8109 with the payment to an authorized depositary, i.e., a commercial bank or other financial institution authorized to accept Federal tax deposits. Make checks or money orders payable to the depositary.

If the corporation prefers, it may mail the coupon and payment to: Financial Agent, Federal Tax Deposit Processing, P.O. Box 970030, St. Louis, MO 63197. Make the check or money order payable to "Financial Agent."

To help ensure proper crediting, write the corporation's EIN, the tax period to which the deposit applies, and "Form 1120" on the check or money order. Be sure to

darken the "1120" box on the coupon. Records of these deposits will be sent to the IRS.

For more information on deposits, see the instructions in the coupon booklet (Form 8109) and **Pub. 583,** Starting a Business and Keeping Records.

 If the corporation owes tax when it files Form 1120 or Form 1120-A, do not include the payment with the tax return. Instead, mail or deliver the payment with Form 8109 to an authorized depositary, or use EFTPS, if applicable.

Estimated Tax Payments

Generally, the following rules apply to the corporation's payments of estimated tax.
● The corporation must make installment payments of estimated tax if it expects its total tax for the year (less applicable credits) to be $500 or more.
● The installments are due by the 15th day of the 4th, 6th, 9th, and 12th months of the tax year. If any date falls on a Saturday, Sunday, or legal holiday, the installment is due on the next regular business day.
● Use **Form 1120-W,** Estimated Tax for Corporations, as a worksheet to compute estimated tax.
● If the corporation does not use EFTPS, use the deposit coupons (Forms 8109) to make deposits of estimated tax.

For more information on estimated tax payments, including penalties that apply if the corporation fails to make required payments, see the instructions for line 33 on page 14.

Overpaid estimated tax. If the corporation overpaid estimated tax, it may be able to get a quick refund by filing **Form 4466,** Corporation Application for Quick Refund of Overpayment of Estimated Tax. The overpayment must be at least 10% of the corporation's expected income tax liability and at least $500. File Form 4466 after the end of the corporation's tax year, and no later than the 15th day of the third month after the end of the tax year. Form 4466 must be filed before the corporation files its tax return.

Interest and Penalties

Interest. Interest is charged on taxes paid late even if an extension of time to file is granted. Interest is also charged on penalties imposed for failure to file, negligence, fraud, gross valuation overstatements, and substantial understatements of tax from the due date (including extensions) to the date of payment. The interest charge is figured at a rate determined under section 6621.

Penalty for late filing of return. A corporation that does not file its tax return by the due date, including extensions, may be penalized 5% of the unpaid tax for each month or part of a month the return is late, up to a maximum of 25% of the unpaid tax. The minimum penalty for a return that is over 60 days late is the smaller of the tax due or $100. The penalty will not be imposed if the corporation can show that the failure to file on time was due to reasonable cause. Corporations that file late must attach a statement explaining the reasonable cause.

Penalty for late payment of tax. A corporation that does not pay the tax when due generally may be penalized $\frac{1}{2}$ of 1% of the unpaid tax for each month or part of a month the tax is not paid, up to a maximum of 25% of the unpaid tax. The penalty will not be imposed if the corporation can show that the failure to pay on time was due to reasonable cause.

Trust fund recovery penalty. This penalty may apply if certain excise, income, social security, and Medicare taxes that must be collected or withheld are not collected or withheld, or these taxes are not paid. These taxes are generally reported on Forms 720, 941, 943, or 945 (see **Other Forms, Returns, and Statements That May Be Required** on page 3). The trust fund recovery penalty may be imposed on all persons who are determined by the IRS to have been responsible for collecting, accounting for, and paying over these taxes, and who acted willfully in not doing so. The penalty is equal to the unpaid trust fund tax. See the Instructions for Form 720, **Pub. 15** (Circular E), Employer's Tax Guide, or **Pub. 51** (Circular A), Agricultural Employer's Tax Guide, for details, including the definition of responsible persons.

Other penalties. Other penalties can be imposed for negligence, substantial understatement of tax, and fraud. See sections 6662 and 6663.

Specific Instructions

Period Covered

File the 2002 return for calendar year 2002 and fiscal years that begin in 2002 and end in 2003 For a fiscal year return, fill in the tax year space at the top of the form.

Note: *The 2002 Form 1120 may also be used if:*
● *The corporation has a tax year of less than 12 months that begins and ends in 2003 and*
● *The 2003 Form 1120 is not available at the time the corporation is required to file its return.*

The corporation must show its 2003 tax year on the 2002 Form 1120 and take into account any tax law changes that are effective for tax years beginning after December 31, 2002.

Name

Use the preprinted label on the tax package information form (Form 8160-A) or the Form 1120 package that was mailed to the corporation. Cross out any errors and print the correct information on the label. If the corporation did not receive a label, print or type the corporation's true name (as set forth in the charter or other legal document creating it), address, and EIN on the appropriate lines.

Address

Include the suite, room, or other unit number after the street address. If a preaddressed label is used, include this information on the label. If the Post Office does not deliver mail to the street address and the corporation has a P.O. box, show the box number instead.

Instructions for Forms 1120 and 1120-A

Item A

Consolidated Return (Form 1120 Only)

Corporations filing a consolidated return must attach Form 851 and other supporting statements to the return. For details, see **Other Forms, Returns, and Statements That May Be Required** on page 3, and **Statements** on page 5.

Personal Holding Company (Form 1120 Only)

A personal holding company must attach to Form 1120 a **Schedule PH (Form 1120)**, U.S. Personal Holding Company (PHC) Tax. See the instructions for that form for details.

Personal Service Corporation

A personal service corporation is a corporation whose principal activity (defined below) for the testing period for the tax year is the performance of personal services. The services must be substantially performed by employee-owners. Employee-owners must own more than 10% of the fair market value of the corporation's outstanding stock on the last day of the testing period.

Testing period. Generally, the testing period for a tax year is the prior tax year. The testing period for a new corporation starts with the first day of its first tax year and ends on the **earlier** of:
- The last day of its first tax year or
- The last day of the calendar year in which the first tax year began.

Principal activity. The principal activity of a corporation is considered to be the performance of personal services if, during the testing period, the corporation's compensation costs for the performance of personal services (defined below) are more than 50% of its total compensation costs.

Performance of personal services. The term "performance of personal services" includes any activity involving the performance of personal services in the field of: health, law, engineering, architecture, accounting, actuarial science, performing arts, or consulting (as defined in Temporary Regulations section 1.448-1T(e)).

Substantial performance by employee-owners. Personal services are substantially performed by employee-owners if, for the testing period, more than 20% of the corporation's compensation costs for the performance of personal services are for services performed by employee-owners.

Employee-owner. A person is considered to be an employee-owner if the person:
- Is an employee of the corporation on any day of the testing period **and**
- Owns any outstanding stock of the corporation on any day of the testing period. Stock ownership is determined under the attribution rules of section 318, except that "any" is substituted for "50%" in section 318(a)(2)(C).

Accounting period. A personal service corporation must use a calendar tax year unless:
- It elects to use a 52–53-week tax year that ends with reference to the calendar year or tax year elected under section 444;
- It can establish a business purpose for a different tax year and obtains the approval of the IRS (see Rev. Proc. 2002-38, Rev. Proc. 2002-39, and Rev. Rul. 87-57, 1987-2 C.B. 117); or
- It elects under section 444 to have a tax year other than a calendar year. To make the election, see **Form 8716**, Election To Have a Tax Year Other Than a Required Tax Year.

If a corporation makes the section 444 election, its deduction for certain amounts paid to employee-owners may be limited. See **Schedule H (Form 1120)**, Section 280H Limitations for a Personal Service Corporation (PSC), to figure the maximum deduction.

If a section 444 election is terminated and the termination results in a short tax year, type or print at the top of the first page of Form 1120 or 1120-A for the short tax year "SECTION 444 ELECTION TERMINATED." See Temporary Regulations section 1.444-1T(a)(5) for more information.

Personal service corporations that want to change their tax year must file Form 1128 to get IRS consent. For more information about personal service corporations, see Regulations section 1.441-3. For rules and procedures on adopting, changing, or retaining an accounting period for a personal service corporation, see Form 1128, Rev. Proc. 2002-38, and Rev. Proc. 2002-39.

Other rules. For other rules that apply to personal service corporations, see **Passive activity limitations** on page 10 and **Contributions of property other than cash** on page 11.

Item B—Employer Identification Number (EIN)

Enter the corporation's EIN. If the corporation does not have an EIN, it must apply for one on **Form SS-4**, Application for Employer Identification Number. If the corporation has not received its EIN by the time the return is due, write "Applied for" in the space for the EIN. See Pub. 583 for details.

Item D—Total Assets

Enter the corporation's total assets (as determined by the accounting method regularly used in keeping the corporation's books and records) at the end of the tax year. If there are no assets at the end of the tax year, enter -0-.

Item E—Initial Return, Final Return, Name Change, or Address Change

- If this is the corporation's first return, check the "Initial return" box.
- If the corporation ceases to exist, file Form 1120 and check the "Final return" box. Do not file Form 1120-A.
- If the corporation changed its name since it last filed a return, check the box for "Name change." Generally, a corporation also must have amended its articles of incorporation and filed the amendment with the state in which it was incorporated.

- If the corporation has changed its address since it last filed a return, check the box for "Address change."

Note: *If a change in address occurs after the return is filed, use Form 8822, Change of Address, to notify the IRS of the new address.*

Income

Except as otherwise provided in the Internal Revenue Code, gross income includes all income from whatever source derived. Gross income, however, does not include **extraterritorial income** that is qualifying foreign trade income. Use **Form 8873**, Extraterritorial Income Exclusion, to figure the exclusion. Include the exclusion in the total for "Other deductions" on Line 26, Form 1120 (line 22, Form 1120-A).

Line 1

Gross Receipts

Enter gross receipts or sales from all business operations except those that must be reported on lines 4 through 10. In general, advance payments are reported in the year of receipt. To report income from long-term contracts, see section 460. For special rules for reporting certain advance payments for goods and long-term contracts, see Regulations section 1.451-5. For permissible methods for reporting advance payments for services by an accrual method corporation, see Rev. Proc. 71-21, 1971-2 C.B. 549.

Installment sales. Generally, the installment method cannot be used for dealer dispositions of property. A "dealer disposition" is: **(a)** any disposition of personal property by a person who regularly sells or otherwise disposes of personal property of the same type on the installment plan or **(b)** any disposition of real property held for sale to customers in the ordinary course of the taxpayer's trade or business.

These restrictions on using the installment method do not apply to dispositions of property used or produced in a farming business or sales of timeshares and residential lots for which the corporation elects to pay interest under section 453(l)(3).

For sales of timeshares and residential lots reported under the installment method, the corporation's income tax is increased by the interest payable under section 453(l)(3). To report this addition to the tax, see the instructions for line 10, Schedule J, Form 1120.

Enter on line 1 (and carry to line 3), the gross profit on collections from installment sales for any of the following:
- Dealer dispositions of property before March 1, 1986.
- Dispositions of property used or produced in the trade or business of farming.
- Certain dispositions of timeshares and residential lots reported under the installment method.

Attach a schedule showing the following information for the current and the 3 preceding years: **(a)** gross sales, **(b)** cost of goods sold, **(c)** gross profits, **(d)** percentage of gross profits to gross sales, **(e)** amount collected, and **(f)** gross profit on the amount collected.

-8-

Instructions for Forms 1120 and 1120-A

Nonaccrual experience method. Corporations that qualify to use the nonaccrual experience method (described on page 6) should attach a schedule showing total gross receipts, the amount not accrued as a result of the application of section 448(d)(5), and the net amount accrued. Enter the net amount on line 1a.

Line 2

Cost of Goods Sold

Enter the cost of goods sold on line 2, page 1. Before making this entry, a Form 1120 filer must complete Schedule A on page 2 of Form 1120. See the Schedule A instructions on page 14. Form 1120-A filers may use the worksheet on page 14 to figure the amount to enter on line 2.

Line 4

Dividends

Form 1120 filers. See the instructions for Schedule C on page 15. Then, complete Schedule C and enter on line 4 the amount from Schedule C, line 19.

Form 1120-A filers. Enter the total dividends received (that are not from debt-financed stock) from domestic corporations that qualify for the 70% dividends-received deduction.

Line 5

Interest

Enter taxable interest on U.S. obligations and on loans, notes, mortgages, bonds, bank deposits, corporate bonds, tax refunds, etc. Do not offset interest expense against interest income. Special rules apply to interest income from certain below-market-rate loans. See section 7872 for more information.

Line 6

Gross Rents

Enter the gross amount received for the rental of property. Deduct expenses such as repairs, interest, taxes, and depreciation on the proper lines for deductions. A rental activity held by a closely held corporation or a personal service corporation may be subject to the passive activity loss rules. See Form 8810 and its instructions.

Line 8

Capital Gain Net Income

Every sale or exchange of a capital asset must be reported in detail on **Schedule D (Form 1120),** Capital Gains and Losses, even if there is no gain or loss.

Line 9

Net Gain or (Loss)

Enter the net gain or (loss) from line 18, Part II, **Form 4797,** Sales of Business Property.

Line 10

Other Income

Enter any other taxable income not reported on lines 1 through 9. List the type and amount of income on an attached schedule. If the corporation has only one item of other income, describe it in parentheses on line

10. Examples of other income to report on line 10 are:
• Recoveries of bad debts deducted in prior years under the specific charge-off method.
• The amount of credit for alcohol used as fuel (determined without regard to the limitation based on tax) entered on **Form 6478,** Credit for Alcohol Used as Fuel.
• Refunds of taxes deducted in prior years to the extent they reduced income subject to tax in the year deducted (see section 111). Do not offset current year taxes against tax refunds.
• The amount of any deduction previously taken under section 179A that is subject to recapture. The corporation must recapture the benefit of any allowable deduction for clean-fuel vehicle property (or clean-fuel vehicle refueling property), if the property later ceases to qualify. See Regulations section 1.179A-1 for details.
• Ordinary income from trade or business activities of a partnership (from Schedule K-1 (Form 1065 or 1065-B)). Do not offset ordinary losses against ordinary income. Instead, include the losses on line 26, Form 1120, or line 22, Form 1120-A. Show the partnership's name, address, and EIN on a separate statement attached to this return. If the amount entered is from more than one partnership, identify the amount from each partnership.
• Any **LIFO recapture amount** under section 1363(d). The corporation may have to include a LIFO recapture amount in income if it:
   1. Used the LIFO inventory method for its last tax year before the first tax year for which it elected to become an S corporation or
   2. Transferred LIFO inventory assets to an S corporation in a nonrecognition transaction in which those assets were transferred basis property.

The LIFO recapture amount is the amount by which the C corporation's inventory under the FIFO method exceeds the inventory amount under the LIFO method at the close of the corporation's last tax year as a C corporation (or for the year of the transfer, if **2** above applies). For more information, see Regulations section 1.1363-2 and Rev. Proc. 94-61, 1994-2 C.B. 775. Also see the instructions for Schedule J, line 11.

Deductions

Limitations on Deductions

Section 263A uniform capitalization rules. The uniform capitalization rules of section 263A require corporations to capitalize, or include in inventory, certain costs incurred in connection with:
• The production of real property and tangible personal property held in inventory or held for sale in the ordinary course of business.
• Real property or personal property (tangible and intangible) acquired for resale.
• The production of real property and tangible personal property by a corporation for use in its trade or business or in an activity engaged in for profit.
   Tangible personal property produced by a corporation includes a film, sound recording, videotape, book, or similar property.

Corporations subject to the section 263A uniform capitalization rules are required to capitalize:
   1. Direct costs and
   2. An allocable part of most indirect costs (including taxes) that **(a)** benefit the assets produced or acquired for resale or **(b)** are incurred by reason of the performance of production or resale activities.

For inventory, some of the **indirect expenses** that must be capitalized are:
• Administration expenses.
• Taxes.
• Depreciation.
• Insurance.
• Compensation paid to officers attributable to services.
• Rework labor.
• Contributions to pension, stock bonus, and certain profit-sharing, annuity, or deferred compensation plans.
   Regulations section 1.263A-1(e)(3) specifies other indirect costs that relate to production or resale activities that must be capitalized and those that may be currently deductible.

   Interest expense paid or incurred during the production period of designated property must be capitalized and is governed by special rules. For more details, see Regulations sections 1.263A-8 through 1.263A-15.

The costs required to be capitalized under section 263A are not deductible until the property (to which the costs relate) is sold, used, or otherwise disposed of by the corporation.

Exceptions. Section 263A **does not** apply to:
• Personal property acquired for resale if the corporation's average annual gross receipts for the 3 prior tax years were $10 million or less.
• Timber.
• Most property produced under a long-term contract.
• Certain property produced in a farming business.
• Research and experimental costs under section 174.
• Intangible drilling costs for oil, gas, and geothermal property.
• Mining exploration and development costs.
• Inventoriable items accounted for in the same manner as materials and supplies that are not incidental. See **Cost of Goods Sold** on page 14 for details.

For more details on the uniform capitalization rules, see Regulations sections 1.263A-1 through 1.263A-3. See Regulations section 1.263A-4 for rules for property produced in a farming business.

Transactions between related taxpayers. Generally, an accrual basis taxpayer may only deduct business expenses and interest owed to a related party in the year the payment is included in the income of the related party. See sections 163(e)(3),163(j), and 267 for limitations on deductions for unpaid interest and expenses.

Section 291 limitations. Corporations may be required to adjust deductions for depletion of iron ore and coal, intangible drilling and exploration and development costs, certain deductions for financial institutions, and the amortizable basis of

Instructions for Forms 1120 and 1120-A

pollution control facilities. See section 291 to determine the amount of the adjustment. Also see section 43.

Golden parachute payments. A portion of the payments made by a corporation to key personnel that exceeds their usual compensation may not be deductible. This occurs when the corporation has an agreement (golden parachute) with these key employees to pay them these excess amounts if control of the corporation changes. See section 280G.

Business startup expenses. Business startup expenses must be capitalized unless an election is made to amortize them over a period of 60 months. See section 195 and Regulations section 1.195-1.

Passive activity limitations. Limitations on passive activity losses and credits under section 469 apply to personal service corporations (see **Personal Service Corporation** on page 8) and closely held corporations (see below).

Generally, the two kinds of passive activities are:
● Trade or business activities in which the corporation did not materially participate for the tax year and
● Rental activities, regardless of its participation.

For exceptions, see Form 8810. An activity is a trade or business activity if it is not a rental activity and:
● The activity involves the conduct of a trade or business (i.e., deductions from the activity would be allowable under section 162 if other limitations, such as the passive loss rules, did not apply) or
● The activity involves research and experimental costs that are deductible under section 174 (or would be deductible if the corporation chose to deduct rather than capitalize them).

Corporations subject to the passive activity limitations must complete Form 8810 to compute their allowable passive activity loss and credit. Before completing Form 8810, see Temporary Regulations section 1.163-8T, which provides rules for allocating interest expense among activities. If a passive activity is also subject to the earnings stripping rules of section 163(j) or the at-risk rules of section 465, those rules apply before the passive loss rules. For more information, see section 469, the related regulations, and **Pub. 925**, Passive Activity and At-Risk Rules.

Closely held corporations. A corporation is a closely held corporation if:
● At any time during the last half of the tax year more than 50% in value of its outstanding stock is owned, directly or indirectly, by or for not more than five individuals and
● The corporation is not a personal service corporation.

Certain organizations are treated as individuals for purposes of this test. See section 542(a)(2). For rules for determining stock ownership, see section 544 (as modified by section 465(a)(3)).

Reducing certain expenses for which credits are allowable. For each credit listed below, the corporation must reduce the otherwise allowable deductions for expenses used to figure the credit by the amount of the current year credit.

● Work opportunity credit.
● Research credit.
● Enhanced oil recovery credit.
● Disabled access credit.
● Empowerment zone and renewal community employment credit.
● Indian employment credit.
● Employer credit for social security and Medicare taxes paid on certain employee tips.
● Orphan drug credit.
● Welfare-to-work credit.
● New York Liberty Zone business employee credit.

If the corporation has any of these credits, figure each current year credit before figuring the deduction for expenses on which the credit is based.

Line 12

Compensation of Officers

Enter deductible officers' compensation on line 12. Form 1120 filers must complete Schedule E if their total receipts (line 1a, plus lines 4 through 10) are $500,000 or more. Do not include compensation deductible elsewhere on the return, such as amounts included in cost of goods sold, elective contributions to a section 401(k) cash or deferred arrangement, or amounts contributed under a salary reduction SEP agreement or a SIMPLE IRA plan.

Include only the deductible part of each officer's compensation on Schedule E. See **Disallowance of deduction for employee compensation in excess of $1 million** below. Complete Schedule E, line 1, columns (a) through (f), for all officers. The corporation determines who is an officer under the laws of the state where it is incorporated.

If a consolidated return is filed, each member of an affiliated group must furnish this information.

Disallowance of deduction for employee compensation in excess of $1 million. Publicly held corporations may not deduct compensation to a "covered employee" to the extent that the compensation exceeds $1 million. Generally, a covered employee is:
● The chief executive officer of the corporation (or an individual acting in that capacity) as of the end of the tax year or
● An employee whose total compensation must be reported to shareholders under the Securities Exchange Act of 1934 because the employee is among the four highest compensated officers for that tax year (other than the chief executive officer).

For this purpose, compensation does not include the following:
● Income from certain employee trusts, annuity plans, or pensions and
● Any benefit paid to an employee that is excluded from the employee's income.
The deduction limit does not apply to:
● Commissions based on individual performance,
● Qualified performance-based compensation, and
● Income payable under a written, binding contract in effect on February 17, 1993.
The $1-million limit is reduced by amounts disallowed as excess parachute payments under section 280G.

For details, see section 162(m) and Regulations section 1.162-27.

Line 13

Salaries and Wages

Enter the amount of salaries and wages paid for the tax year, reduced by:
● Any work opportunity credit from Form 5884,
● Any empowerment zone and renewal community employment credit from Form 8844,
● Any Indian employment credit from Form 8845,
● Any welfare-to-work credit from Form 8861, and
● Any New York Liberty Zone business employee credit from Form 8884.

See the instructions for these forms for more information. Do not include salaries and wages deductible elsewhere on the return, such as amounts included in cost of goods sold, elective contributions to a section 401(k) cash or deferred arrangement, or amounts contributed under a salary reduction SEP agreement or a SIMPLE IRA plan.

 If the corporation provided taxable fringe benefits to its employees, such as personal use of a car, do not deduct as wages the amount allocated for depreciation and other expenses claimed on lines 20 and 26, Form 1120, or lines 20 and 22, Form 1120-A.

Line 14

Repairs and Maintenance

Enter the cost of incidental repairs and maintenance not claimed elsewhere on the return, such as labor and supplies, that do not add to the value of the property or appreciably prolong its life. New buildings, machinery, or permanent improvements that increase the value of the property are not deductible. They must be depreciated or amortized.

Line 15

Bad Debts

Enter the total debts that became worthless in whole or in part during the tax year. A small bank or thrift institution using the reserve method of section 585 should attach a schedule showing how it figured the current year's provision. A cash basis taxpayer may not claim a bad debt deduction unless the amount was previously included in income.

Line 16

Rents

If the corporation rented or leased a vehicle, enter the total annual rent or lease expense paid or incurred during the year. Also complete Part V of **Form 4562**, Depreciation and Amortization. If the corporation leased a vehicle for a term of 30 days or more, the deduction for vehicle lease expense may have to be reduced by an amount called the **inclusion amount.** The corporation may have an inclusion amount if:

-10-

Instructions for Forms 1120 and 1120-A

The lease term began:	And the vehicle's FMV on the first day of the lease exceeded:
After 12/31/98 and before 1/1/03 . . .	$15,500
After 12/31/96 but before 1/1/99	$15,800
After 12/31/94 but before 1/1/97	$15,500
After 12/31/93 but before 1/1/95	$14,600

If the lease term began before January 1, 1994, or, the leased vehicle was an electric vehicle, see **Pub. 463**, Travel, Entertainment, Gift, and Car Expenses, to find out if the corporation has an inclusion amount. The inclusion amount for lease terms beginning in 2003 will be published in the Internal Revenue Bulletin in early 2003.

See Pub. 463 for instructions on figuring the inclusion amount.

Line 17

Taxes and Licenses

Enter taxes paid or accrued during the tax year, but do not include the following.
• Federal income taxes.
• Foreign or U.S. possession income taxes if a tax credit is claimed (however, see the Instructions for Form 5735 for special rules for possession income taxes).
• Taxes not imposed on the corporation.
• Taxes, including state or local sales taxes, that are paid or incurred in connection with an acquisition or disposition of property (these taxes must be treated as a part of the cost of the acquired property or, in the case of a disposition, as a reduction in the amount realized on the disposition).
• Taxes assessed against local benefits that increase the value of the property assessed (such as for paving, etc.).
• Taxes deducted elsewhere on the return, such as those reflected in cost of goods sold.

See section 164(d) for apportionment of taxes on real property between seller and purchaser.

Line 18

Interest

Note: *The deduction for interest is limited when the corporation is a policyholder or beneficiary with respect to a life insurance, endowment, or annuity contract issued after June 8, 1997. For details, see section 264(f). Attach a statement showing the computation of the deduction.*

The corporation must make an interest allocation if the proceeds of a loan were used for more than one purpose (e.g., to purchase a portfolio investment and to acquire an interest in a passive activity). See Temporary Regulations section 1.163-8T for the interest allocation rules.

Mutual savings banks, building and loan associations, and cooperative banks can deduct the amounts paid or credited to the accounts of depositors as dividends, interest, or earnings. See section 591.

Do not deduct the following interest.
• Interest on indebtedness incurred or continued to purchase or carry obligations if the interest is wholly exempt from income tax. For exceptions, see section 265(b).
• For cash basis taxpayers, prepaid interest allocable to years following the current tax

year (e.g., a cash basis calendar year taxpayer who in 2002 prepaid interest allocable to any period after 2002 can deduct only the amount allocable to 2002).
• Interest and carrying charges on straddles. Generally, these amounts must be capitalized. See section 263(g).
• Interest on debt allocable to the production of designated property by a corporation for its own use or for sale. The corporation must capitalize this interest. Also capitalize any interest on debt allocable to an asset used to produce the property. See section 263A(f) and Regulations section 1.263A-8 through 1.263A-15 for definitions and more information.

Special rules apply to:
• Interest on which no tax is imposed (see section 163(j)).
• Foregone interest on certain below-market-rate loans (see section 7872).
• Original issue discount on certain high-yield discount obligations. (See section 163(e) to figure the disqualified portion.)

Line 19

Charitable Contributions

Enter contributions or gifts actually paid within the tax year to or for the use of charitable and governmental organizations described in section 170(c) and any unused contributions carried over from prior years.

Corporations reporting taxable income on the accrual method may elect to treat as paid during the tax year any contributions paid by the 15th day of the 3rd month after the end of the tax year if the contributions were authorized by the board of directors during the tax year. Attach a declaration to the return, signed by an officer, stating that the resolution authorizing the contributions was adopted by the board of directors during the tax year. Also attach a copy of the resolution.

Limitation on deduction. The total amount claimed may not be more than 10% of taxable income (line 30, Form 1120, or line 26, Form 1120-A) computed without regard to the following:
• Any deduction for contributions,
• The special deductions on line 29b, Form 1120 (line 25b, Form 1120-A),
• The deduction allowed under section 249,
• Any net operating loss (NOL) carryback to the tax year under section 172, and
• Any capital loss carryback to the tax year under section 1212(a)(1).

Carryover. Charitable contributions over the 10% limitation may not be deducted for the tax year but may be carried over to the next 5 tax years.

Special rules apply if the corporation has an NOL carryover to the tax year. In figuring the charitable contributions deduction for the tax year, the 10% limit is applied using the taxable income after taking into account any deduction for the NOL.

To figure the amount of any remaining NOL carryover to later years, taxable income must be modified (see section 172(b)). To the extent that contributions are used to reduce taxable income for this purpose and increase an NOL carryover, a contributions carryover is not allowed. See section 170(d)(2)(B).

Substantiation requirements. Generally, no deduction is allowed for any contribution

of $250 or more unless the corporation gets a written acknowledgment from the donee organization that shows the amount of cash contributed, describes any property contributed, and, either gives a description and a good faith estimate of the value of any goods or services provided in return for the contribution or states that no goods or services were provided in return for the contribution. The acknowledgment must be obtained by the due date (including extensions) of the corporation's return, or, if earlier, the date the return is filed. Do not attach the acknowledgment to the tax return, but keep it with the corporation's records. These rules apply in addition to the filing requirements for **Form 8283**, Noncash Charitable Contributions, described below.

For more information on substantiation and recordkeeping requirements, see the regulations under section 170 and **Pub. 526**, Charitable Contributions.

Contributions to organizations conducting lobbying activities. Contributions made to an organization that conducts lobbying activities are not deductible if:
• The lobbying activities relate to matters of direct financial interest to the donor's trade or business and
• The principal purpose of the contribution was to avoid Federal income tax by obtaining a deduction for activities that would have been nondeductible under the lobbying expense rules if conducted directly by the donor.

Contributions of property other than cash. If a corporation (other than a closely held or personal service corporation) contributes property other than cash and claims over a $500 deduction for the property, it must attach a schedule to the return describing the kind of property contributed and the method used to determine its fair market value (FMV). Closely held corporations and personal service corporations must complete Form 8283 and attach it to their returns. All other corporations generally must complete and attach Form 8283 to their returns for contributions of property (other than money) if the total claimed deduction for all property contributed was more than $5,000.

If the corporation made a "qualified conservation contribution" under section 170(h), also include the FMV of the underlying property before and after the donation, as well as the type of legal interest contributed, and describe the conservation purpose benefited by the donation. If a contribution carryover is included, show the amount and how it was determined.

Reduced deduction for contributions of certain property. For a charitable contribution of property, the corporation must reduce the contribution by the sum of:
• The ordinary income and short-term capital gain that would have resulted if the property were sold at its FMV and
• For certain contributions, the long-term capital gain that would have resulted if the property were sold at its FMV.

The reduction for the long-term capital gain applies to:
• Contributions of tangible personal property for use by an exempt organization for a purpose or function unrelated to the basis for its exemption and

Instructions for Forms 1120 and 1120-A

-11-

- Contributions of any property to or for the use of certain private foundations except for stock for which market quotations are readily available (section 170(e)(5)).

Larger deduction. A larger deduction is allowed for certain contributions of:
- Inventory and other property to certain organizations for use in the care of the ill, needy, or infants (see section 170(e)(3) and Regulations section 1.170A-4A);
- Scientific equipment used for research to institutions of higher learning or to certain scientific research organizations (other than by personal holding companies and service organizations) (see section 170(e)(4)); and
- Computer technology and equipment for educational purposes.

Contributions of computer technology and equipment for educational purposes. A corporation may take an increased deduction under section 170(e)(6) for qualified contributions of computer technology or equipment for educational purposes. **Computer technology or equipment** means computer software, computer or peripheral equipment, and fiber optic cable related to computer use. A contribution is a qualified contribution if:
- It is made to an eligible donee (see below);
- Substantially all of the donee property's use is:
    1. Related to the purpose or function of the donee,
    2. For use within the United States, and
    3. For educational purposes.
- The contribution is made not later than 3 years after the date the taxpayer acquired or substantially completed the construction of the property;
- The original use of the property is by the donor or the donee;
- The property is not transferred by the donee for money, services, or other property, except for shipping, transfer, and installation costs;
- The property fits productively into the donee's education plan; and
- The property meets standards, if any, that may be prescribed by future regulations, to assure it meets minimum functionality and suitability for educational purposes.

Eligible donee. The term "eligible donee" means:
- An educational organization that normally maintains a regular faculty and curriculum and has a regularly enrolled body of pupils in attendance at the place where its educational activities are regularly conducted,
- A section 501(c)(3) entity organized primarily for purposes of supporting elementary and secondary education, or
- A public library (as described in section 170(e)(6)(B)(i)(III)).

Exceptions. The following exceptions apply to the above rules for computer technology and equipment:
- Contributions to private foundations may qualify if the foundation contributes the property to an eligible donee within 30 days after the contribution and notifies the donor of the contribution. For more details, see section 170(e)(6)(C).
- For contributions of property reacquired by the manufacturer of the property, the 3 year period begins on the date that the original construction of the property was substantially completed. Also, the original use of the property may be by someone other than the donor or the donee.

Line 20

Depreciation

Besides depreciation, include on line 20 the part of the cost that the corporation elected to expense under section 179 for certain tangible property placed in service during tax year 2002 or carried over from 2001. See Form 4562 and its instructions.

Line 22 (Form 1120 Only)

Depletion

See sections 613 and 613A for percentage depletion rates applicable to natural deposits. Also, see section 291 for the limitation on the depletion deduction for iron ore and coal (including lignite).

Attach **Form T (Timber)**, Forest Activities Schedule, if a deduction for depletion of timber is taken.

Foreign intangible drilling costs and foreign exploration and development costs must either be added to the corporation's basis for cost depletion purposes or be deducted ratably over a 10-year period. See sections 263(i), 616, and 617 for details.

Line 24 (Form 1120 Only)

Pension, Profit-Sharing, etc., Plans

Enter the deduction for contributions to qualified pension, profit-sharing, or other funded deferred compensation plans. Employers who maintain such a plan generally must file one of the forms listed below, even if the plan is not a qualified plan under the Internal Revenue Code. The filing requirement applies even if the corporation does not claim a deduction for the current tax year. There are penalties for failure to file these forms on time and for overstating the pension plan deduction. See sections 6652(e) and 6662(f).

Form 5500, Annual Return/Report of Employee Benefit Plan. File this form for a plan that is not a one-participant plan (see below).

Form 5500-EZ, Annual Return of One-Participant (Owners and Their Spouses) Retirement Plan. File this form for a plan that only covers the owner (or the owner and his or her spouse) but only if the owner (or the owner and his or her spouse) owns the entire business.

Line 25 (Form 1120 Only)

Employee Benefit Programs

Enter contributions to employee benefit programs not claimed elsewhere on the return (e.g., insurance, health and welfare programs, etc.) that are not an incidental part of a pension, profit-sharing, etc., plan included on line 24.

Line 26, Form 1120 (Line 22, Form 1120-A)

Other Deductions

Attach a schedule, listing by type and amount, all allowable deductions that are not deductible elsewhere on Form 1120 or Form 1120-A. Form 1120-A filers should include amounts described in the instructions above for lines 22, 24, and 25 of Form 1120. Enter the total of other deductions on line 26, Form 1120 (line 22, Form 1120-A).

Examples of other deductions include:
- Amortization of pollution control facilities, organization expenses, etc. (see Form 4562).
- Insurance premiums.
- Legal and professional fees.
- Supplies used and consumed in the business.
- Utilities.
- Ordinary losses from trade or business activities of a partnership (from Schedule K-1 (Form 1065 or 1065-B). Do not offset ordinary income against ordinary losses. Instead, include the income on line 10. Show the partnership's name, address, and EIN on a separate statement attached to this return. If the amount is from more than one partnership, identify the amount from each partnership.
- Extraterritorial income exclusion (from Form 8873, line 55).
- Dividends paid in cash on stock held by an employee stock ownership plan. However, a deduction may only be taken if, according to the plan, the dividends are:
    1. Paid in cash directly to the plan participants or beneficiaries;
    2. Paid to the plan, which distributes them in cash to the plan participants or their beneficiaries no later than 90 days after the end of the plan year in which the dividends are paid;
    3. At the election of such participants or their beneficiaries (a) payable as provided under 1 or 2 above or (b) paid to the plan and reinvested in qualifying employer securities; or
    4. Used to make payments on a loan described in section 404(a)(9).

See section 404(k) for more details and the limitation on certain dividends.

Also see **Special rules** below for limits on certain other deductions.

Do not deduct:
- Fines or penalties paid to a government for violating any law.
- Any amount that is allocable to a class of exempt income. See section 265(b) for exceptions.

Special rules apply to the following expenses:

Travel, meals, and entertainment. Subject to limitations and restrictions discussed below, a corporation can deduct ordinary and necessary travel, meals, and entertainment expenses paid or incurred in its trade or business. Also, special rules apply to deductions for gifts, skybox rentals, luxury water travel, convention expenses, and entertainment tickets. See section 274 and Pub. 463 for more details.

Travel. The corporation cannot deduct travel expenses of any individual accompanying a corporate officer or employee, including a spouse or dependent of the officer or employee, unless:
- That individual is an employee of the corporation and
- His or her travel is for a bona fide business purpose and would otherwise be deductible by that individual.

Meals and entertainment. Generally, the corporation can deduct only 50% of the amount otherwise allowable for meals and

-12-

Instructions for Forms 1120 and 1120-A

entertainment expenses paid or incurred in its trade or business. In addition (subject to exceptions under section 274(k)(2)):

• Meals must not be lavish or extravagant;
• A bona fide business discussion must occur during, immediately before, or immediately after the meal; and
• An employee of the corporation must be present at the meal.

See section 274(n)(3) for a special rule that applies to expenses for meals consumed by individuals subject to the hours of service limits of the Department of Transportation.

Membership dues. The corporation may deduct amounts paid or incurred for membership dues in civic or public service organizations, professional organizations (such as bar and medical associations), business leagues, trade associations, chambers of commerce, boards of trade, and real estate boards. However, no deduction is allowed if a principal purpose of the organization is to entertain, or provide entertainment facilities for, members or their guests. In addition, corporations may not deduct membership dues in any club organized for business, pleasure, recreation, or other social purpose. This includes country clubs, golf and athletic clubs, airline and hotel clubs, and clubs operated to provide meals under conditions favorable to business discussion.

Entertainment facilities. The corporation cannot deduct an expense paid or incurred for a facility (such as a yacht or hunting lodge) used for an activity usually considered entertainment, amusement, or recreation.

Note: *The corporation may be able to deduct otherwise nondeductible meals, travel, and entertainment expenses if the amounts are treated as compensation and reported on Form W-2 for an employee or on Form 1099-MISC for an independent contractor.*

Deduction for clean-fuel vehicles and certain refueling property. Section 179A allows a deduction for part of the cost of qualified clean-fuel vehicle property and qualified clean-fuel vehicle refueling property placed in service during the tax year. For more information, see Pub. 535.

Lobbying expenses. Generally, lobbying expenses are not deductible. These expenses include:
• Amounts paid or incurred in connection with influencing Federal or state legislation (but not local legislation) or
• Amounts paid or incurred in connection with any communication with certain Federal executive branch officials in an attempt to influence the official actions or positions of the officials. See Regulations section 1.162-29 for the definition of "influencing legislation."

Dues and other similar amounts paid to certain tax-exempt organizations may not be deductible. See section 162(e)(3). If certain in-house lobbying expenditures do not exceed $2,000, they are deductible. For information on contributions to charitable organizations that conduct lobbying activities, see the instructions for line 19. For more information on lobbying expenses, see section 162(e).

Line 28, Form 1120 (Line 24, Form 1120-A)

Taxable Income Before NOL Deduction and Special Deductions

At-risk rules. Generally, special at-risk rules under section 465 apply to closely held corporations (see **Passive activity limitations** on page 10) engaged in any activity as a trade or business or for the production of income. These corporations may have to adjust the amount on line 28, Form 1120, or line 24, Form 1120-A. (See below.)

The at-risk rules do not apply to:
• Holding real property placed in service by the taxpayer before 1987;
• Equipment leasing under sections 465(c)(4), (5), and (6); or
• Any qualifying business of a qualified corporation under section 465(c)(7).

However, the at-risk rules do apply to the holding of mineral property.

If the at-risk rules apply, adjust the amount on this line for any section 465(d) losses. These losses are limited to the amount for which the corporation is at risk for each separate activity at the close of the tax year. If the corporation is involved in one or more activities, any of which incurs a loss for the year, report the losses for each activity separately. Attach **Form 6198,** At-Risk Limitations, showing the amount at risk and gross income and deductions for the activities with the losses.

If the corporation sells or otherwise disposes of an asset or its interest (either total or partial) in an activity to which the at-risk rules apply, determine the net profit or loss from the activity by combining the gain or loss on the sale or disposition with the profit or loss from the activity. If the corporation has a net loss, it may be limited because of the at-risk rules.

Treat any loss from an activity not allowed for the tax year as a deduction allocable to the activity in the next tax year.

Line 29a, Form 1120 (Line 25a, Form 1120-A)

Net Operating Loss Deduction

A corporation may use the NOL incurred in one tax year to reduce its taxable income in another tax year. Enter on line 29a (line 25a, Form 1120-A), the total NOL carryovers from other tax years, but do not enter more than the corporation's taxable income (after special deductions). Attach a schedule showing the computation of the NOL deduction. Form 1120 filers must also complete item 12 on Schedule K.

The following special rules apply.
• A personal service corporation may not carry back an NOL to or from any tax year to which an election under section 444 to have a tax year other than a required tax year applies.
• A corporate equity reduction interest loss may not be carried back to a tax year preceding the year of the equity reduction transaction (see section 172(b)(1)(E)).
• If an ownership change occurs, the amount of the taxable income of a loss corporation that may be offset by the pre-change NOL carryovers may be limited (see section 382 and the related

regulations). A loss corporation must file an information statement with its income tax return for each tax year that certain ownership shifts occur (see Temporary Regulations section 1.382-2T(a)(2)(ii) for details). See Regulations section 1.382-6(b) for details on how to make the closing-of-the-books election.
• If a corporation acquires control of another corporation (or acquires its assets in a reorganization), the amount of pre-acquisition losses that may offset recognized built-in gain may be limited (see section 384).

For details on the NOL deduction, see Pub. 542, section 172, and **Form 1139,** Corporation Application for Tentative Refund.

Line 29b, Form 1120 (Line 25b, Form 1120-A)

Special Deductions

Form 1120 filers. See the instructions for Schedule C on page 15.

Form 1120-A filers. Generally, enter 70% of line 4, page 1, on line 25b. However, this deduction may not be more than 70% of line 24, page 1. Compute line 24 without regard to any adjustment under section 1059 and without regard to any capital loss carryback to the tax year under section 1212(a)(1).

In a year in which an NOL occurs, this 70% limitation does not apply even if the loss is created by the dividends-received deduction. See sections 172(d) and 246(b).

Line 30, Form 1120 (Line 26, Form 1120-A)

Taxable Income

Net operating loss (NOL). If line 30 is zero or less, the corporation may have an NOL that can be carried back or forward as a deduction to other tax years. Generally, a corporation first carries back an NOL 2 tax years (5 tax years for NOLs incurred in tax years ending in 2001 or 2002). However, the corporation may elect to waive the carryback period and instead carry the NOL forward to future tax years. To make the election, see the instructions for Schedule K, item 11, on page 20.

See Form 1139 for details, including other elections that may be available, which must be made no later than 6 months after the due date (excluding extensions) of the corporation's tax return.

Capital construction fund. To take a deduction for amounts contributed to a capital construction fund (CCF), reduce the amount that would otherwise be entered on line 30 (line 26, Form 1120-A) by the amount of the deduction. On the dotted line next to the entry space, write "CCF" and the amount of the deduction. For more information, see **Pub. 595,** Tax Highlights for Commercial Fishermen.

Line 32b, Form 1120 (Line 28b, Form 1120-A)

Estimated Tax Payments

Enter any estimated tax payments the corporation made for the tax year.

Beneficiaries of trusts. If the corporation is the beneficiary of a trust, and the trust makes a section 643(g) election to credit its estimated tax payments to its beneficiaries, include the corporation's share of the payment in the total for line 32b, Form 1120 (line 28b, Form 1120-A). Write "T" and the amount on the dotted line next to the entry space.

Special estimated tax payments for certain life insurance companies. If the corporation is required to make or apply special estimated tax payments (SETP) under section 847 in addition to its regular estimated tax payments, enter on line 32b (line 28b, Form 1120-A), the corporation's total estimated tax payments. In the margin near line 32b, write "Form 8816" and the amount. Attach a schedule showing your computation of estimated tax payments. See sections 847(2) and 847(8) and **Form 8816,** Special Loss Discount Account and Special Estimated Tax Payments for Insurance Companies, for more information.

Line 32f, Form 1120 (Line 28f, Form 1120-A)

Enter the credit (from **Form 2439,** Notice to Shareholder of Undistributed Long-Term Capital Gains) for the corporation's share of the tax paid by a regulated investment company (RIC) or a real estate investment trust (REIT) on undistributed long-term capital gains included in the corporation's income. Attach Form 2439 to Form 1120 or 1120-A.

Line 32g, Form 1120 (Line 28g, Form 1120-A)

Credit for Federal Tax on Fuels

Enter the credit from **Form 4136,** Credit for Federal Tax Paid on Fuels, if the corporation qualifies to take this credit. Attach Form 4136 to Form 1120 or 1120-A.

Credit for tax on ozone-depleting chemicals. Include on line 32g (line 28g, Form 1120-A) any credit the corporation is claiming under section 4682(g)(2) for tax on ozone-depleting chemicals. Write "ODC" to the left of the entry space.

Line 32h, Form 1120 (Line 28h, Form 1120-A)

Total Payments

On Form 1120, add the amounts on lines 32d through 32g and enter the total on line

32h. On Form 1120-A, add the amounts on lines 28d through 28g and enter the total on line 28h.

Backup withholding. If the corporation had income tax withheld from any payments it received because, for example, it failed to give the payer its correct EIN, include the amount withheld in the total for line 32h, Form 1120 (line 28h, Form 1120-A). This type of withholding is called backup withholding. On Form 1120, show the amount withheld in the blank space in the right-hand column between lines 31 and 32h, and write "Backup Withholding." On Form 1120-A, show the amount withheld on the dotted line to the left of line 28h, and write "Backup Withholding."

Line 33, Form 1120 (Line 29, Form 1120-A)

Estimated Tax Penalty

A corporation that does not make estimated tax payments when due may be subject to an underpayment penalty for the period of underpayment. Generally, a corporation is subject to the penalty if its tax liability is $500 or more and it did not timely pay the smaller of:
- Its tax liability for 2002 or
- Its prior year's tax.

See section 6655 for details and exceptions, including special rules for large corporations.

Use **Form 2220,** Underpayment of Estimated Tax by Corporations, to see if the corporation owes a penalty and to figure the amount of the penalty. Generally, the corporation does not have to file this form because the IRS can figure the amount of any penalty and bill the corporation for it. However, even if the corporation does not owe the penalty, complete and attach Form 2220 if:
- The annualized income or adjusted seasonal installment method is used or
- The corporation is a large corporation computing its first required installment based on the prior year's tax. (See the Instructions for Form 2220 for the definition of a large corporation.)

If Form 2220 is attached, check the box on line 33, Form 1120 (line 29, Form 1120-A), and enter the amount of any penalty on this line.

Line 36, Form 1120 (Line 32, Form 1120-A)

Direct Deposit of Refund

If the corporation wants its refund directly deposited into its checking or savings account at any U.S. bank or other financial institution instead of having a check sent to the corporation, complete Form 8050 and attach it to the corporation's tax return.

Schedule A, Form 1120 (Worksheet, Form 1120-A)

Cost of Goods Sold

Generally, inventories are required at the beginning and end of each tax year if the production, purchase, or sale of merchandise is an income-producing factor. See Regulations section 1.471-1.

However, if the corporation is a qualifying taxpayer or a qualifying small business taxpayer, it may adopt or change its accounting method to account for inventoriable items in the same manner as materials and supplies that are not incidental.

A **qualifying taxpayer** is a taxpayer **(a)** whose average annual gross receipts for the 3 prior tax years are $1 million or less and **(b)** whose business is not a tax shelter (as defined in section 448(d)(3)).

A **qualifying small business taxpayer** is a taxpayer **(a)** whose average annual gross receipts for the 3 prior tax years are more than $1 million but not more than $10 million, **(b)** whose business is not a tax shelter (as defined in section 448(d)(3)), and **(c)** whose principal business activity is not an ineligible business as explained in Rev. Proc. 2002-28.

Under this accounting method, inventory costs for raw materials purchased for use in producing finished goods and merchandise purchased for resale are deductible in the year the finished goods or merchandise are sold (but not before the year the corporation paid for the raw materials or merchandise, if it is also using the cash method).

For additional guidance on this method of accounting for inventoriable items, see Rev. Proc. 2001-10 if the corporation is a qualifying taxpayer or Rev. Proc. 2002-28 if the corporation is a qualifying small business taxpayer.

Enter amounts paid for all raw materials and merchandise during the tax year on line 2. The amount the corporation can deduct for the tax year is figured on line 8.

All filers not using the cash method of accounting should see **Section 263A uniform capitalization rules** on page 9 before completing Schedule A or the worksheet. The instructions for lines 4 through 7 that follow apply to Schedule A (Form 1120) and the worksheet for Form 1120-A on this page.

Line 1

Inventory at Beginning of Year

If the corporation is changing its method of accounting for the current tax year, it must refigure last year's closing inventory using its new method of accounting and enter the

---

Cost of Goods Sold Worksheet

Form 1120-A
(keep for your records)

1. Inventory at start of year. Enter here and in Part III, line 3, column (a), Form 1120-A . . . . 1. _____
2. Purchases. Enter here and in Part II, line 5a(1), Form 1120-A . 2. _____
3. Cost of labor. Enter here and include in total in Part II, line 5a(3), Form 1120-A . . . . 3. _____
4. Additional section 263A costs. Enter here and in Part II, line 5a(2), Form 1120-A (see instructions for line 4). . . . . 4. _____
5. Other costs. Enter here and include in Part II, line 5a(3), Form 1120-A . . . . 5. _____
6. Total. Add lines 1 through 5 . . . . 6. _____
7. Inventory at end of year. Enter here and in Part III, line 3, column (b), Form 1120-A. . . . . 7. _____
8. **Cost of goods sold.** Subtract line 7 from line 6. Enter the result here and on page 1, line 2, Form 1120-A . . . . 8. _____

-14-

Instructions for Forms 1120 and 1120-A

result on line 1. If there is a difference between last year's closing inventory and the refigured amount, attach an explanation and take it into account when figuring the corporation's section 481(a) adjustment (explained on page 6).

Line 4

Additional Section 263A Costs

An entry is required on this line only for corporations that have elected a simplified method of accounting.

For corporations that have elected the **simplified production method**, additional section 263A costs are generally those costs, other than interest, that were not capitalized under the corporation's method of accounting immediately prior to the effective date of section 263A but are now required to be capitalized under section 263A. For details, see Regulations section 1.263A-2(b).

For corporations that have elected the **simplified resale method**, additional section 263A costs are generally those costs incurred with respect to the following categories.
• Off-site storage or warehousing.
• Purchasing; handling, such as processing, assembling, repackaging, and transporting.
• General and administrative costs (mixed service costs).
For details, see Regulations section 1.263A-3(d).

Enter on line 4 the balance of section 263A costs paid or incurred during the tax year not includible on lines 2, 3, and 5.

Line 5

Other Costs

Enter on line 5 any costs paid or incurred during the tax year not entered on lines 2 through 4.

Line 7

Inventory at End of Year

See Regulations section 1.263A-1 through 1.263A-3 for details on figuring the amount of additional section 263A costs to be included in ending inventory. If the corporation accounts for inventoriable items in the same manner as materials and supplies that are not incidental, enter on line 7 the portion of its raw materials and merchandise purchased for resale that are included on line 6 and were not sold during the year.

Lines 9a through 9f (Schedule A)

Inventory Valuation Methods

Inventories can be valued at:
• Cost;
• Cost or market value (whichever is lower); or
• Any other method approved by the IRS that conforms to the requirements of the applicable regulations cited below.
However, if the corporation is using the cash method of accounting, it is required to use cost.

Corporations that account for inventoriable items in the same manner as materials and supplies that are not incidental may currently deduct expenditures for direct labor and all indirect costs that would otherwise be included in inventory costs.

The average cost (rolling average) method of valuing inventories generally does not conform to the requirements of the regulations. See Rev. Rul. 71-234, 1971-1 C.B. 148.

Corporations that use erroneous valuation methods must change to a method permitted for Federal income tax purposes. To make this change, use Form 3115.

On line 9a, check the method(s) used for valuing inventories. Under lower of cost or market, the term "market" (for normal goods) means the current bid price prevailing on the inventory valuation date for the particular merchandise in the volume usually purchased by the taxpayer. For a manufacturer, market applies to the basic elements of cost—raw materials, labor, and burden. If section 263A applies to the taxpayer, the basic elements of cost must reflect the current bid price of all direct costs and all indirect costs properly allocable to goods on hand at the inventory date.

Inventory may be valued below cost when the merchandise is unsalable at normal prices or unusable in the normal way because the goods are subnormal due to damage, imperfections, shopwear, etc., within the meaning of Regulations section 1.471-2(c). The goods may be valued at the current bona fide selling price, minus direct cost of disposition (but not less than scrap value) if such a price can be established.

If this is the first year the Last-in, First-out (LIFO) inventory method was either adopted or extended to inventory goods not previously valued under the LIFO method provided in section 472, attach **Form 970,** Application To Use LIFO Inventory Method, or a statement with the information required by Form 970. Also check the LIFO box on line 9c. On line 9d, enter the amount or the percent of total closing inventories covered under section 472. Estimates are acceptable.

If the corporation changed or extended its inventory method to LIFO and had to write up the opening inventory to cost in the year of election, report the effect of the write-up as other income (line 10, page 1), proportionately over a 3-year period that begins with the year of the LIFO election (section 472(d)).

Note: *Corporations using the LIFO method that make an S corporation election or transfer LIFO inventory to an S corporation in a nonrecognition transaction may be subject to an additional tax attributable to the LIFO recapture amount. See the instructions for line 11, Schedule J, on page 19, and for line 10, **Other Income**, on page 9.*

For more information on inventory valuation methods, see Pub. 538.

Schedule C (Form 1120 Only)

For purposes of the 20% ownership test on lines 1 through 7, the percentage of stock owned by the corporation is based on voting power and value of the stock. Preferred stock described in section 1504(a)(4) is not taken into account. Corporations filing a consolidated return should see Regulations sections 1.1502-13, 1.1502-26, and 1.1502-27 before completing Schedule C.

Line 1, Column (a)

Enter dividends (except those received on debt-financed stock acquired after July 18, 1984—see section 246A) that:
• Are received from less-than-20%-owned domestic corporations subject to income tax and
• Qualify for the 70% deduction under section 243(a)(1).
Also include on line 1:
• Taxable distributions from an IC-DISC or former DISC that are designated as eligible for the 70% deduction and certain dividends

---

Worksheet for Schedule C, line 9
(keep for your records)

1. Refigure line 28, page 1, Form 1120, without any adjustment under section 1059 and without any capital loss carryback to the tax year under section 1212(a)(1) . . . .   1. _____
2. Complete lines 10, 11, and 12, column (c), and enter the total here   2. _____
3. Subtract line 2 from line 1 . . . .   3. _____
4. Multiply line 3 by 80% . . . .   4. _____
5. Add lines 2, 5, 7, and 8, column (c), and the part of the deduction on line 3, column (c), that is attributable to dividends from 20%-or-more-owned corporations . . . .   5. _____
6. Enter the smaller of line 4 or 5. If line 5 is greater than line 4, stop here; enter the amount from line 6 on line 9, column (c), and do not complete the rest of this worksheet . . . .   6. _____
7. Enter the total amount of dividends from 20%-or-more-owned corporations that are included on lines 2, 3, 5, 7, and 8, column (a)   7. _____
8. Subtract line 7 from line 3 . . . .   8. _____
9. Multiply line 8 by 70% . . . .   9. _____
10. Subtract line 5 above from line 9, column (c). . . . . . .   10. _____
11. Enter the smaller of line 9 or line 10 . . . .   11. _____
12. **Dividends-received deduction after limitation** (sec. 246(b)). Add lines 6 and 11. Enter the result here and on line 9, column (c) .   12. _____

---

of Federal Home Loan Banks. See section 246(a)(2).

- Dividends (except those received on debt-financed stock acquired after July 18, 1984) from a regulated investment company (RIC). The amount of dividends eligible for the dividends-received deduction under section 243 is limited by section 854(b). The corporation should receive a notice from the RIC specifying the amount of dividends that qualify for the deduction.

Report so-called dividends or earnings received from mutual savings banks, etc., as interest. Do not treat them as dividends.

Line 2, Column (a)

Enter on line 2:
- Dividends (except those received on debt-financed stock acquired after July 18, 1984) that are received from 20%-or-more-owned domestic corporations subject to income tax and that are subject to the 80% deduction under section 243(c) and
- Taxable distributions from an IC-DISC or former DISC that are considered eligible for the 80% deduction.

Line 3, Column (a)

Enter dividends that are:
- Received on debt-financed stock acquired after July 18, 1984, from domestic and foreign corporations subject to income tax that would otherwise be subject to the dividends-received deduction under section 243(a)(1), 243(c), or 245(a). Generally, debt-financed stock is stock that the corporation acquired by incurring a debt (e.g., it borrowed money to buy the stock).
- Received from a RIC on debt-financed stock. The amount of dividends eligible for the dividends-received deduction is limited by section 854(b). The corporation should receive a notice from the RIC specifying the amount of dividends that qualify for the deduction.

Line 3, Columns (b) and (c)

Dividends received on debt-financed stock acquired after July 18, 1984, are not entitled to the full 70% or 80% dividends-received deduction. The 70% or 80% deduction is reduced by a percentage that is related to the amount of debt incurred to acquire the stock. See section 246A. Also, see section 245(a) before making this computation for an additional limitation that applies to dividends received from foreign corporations. Attach a schedule to Form 1120 showing how the amount on line 3, column (c), was figured.

Line 4, Column (a)

Enter dividends received on the preferred stock of a less-than-20%-owned public utility that is subject to income tax and is allowed the deduction provided in section 247 for dividends paid.

Line 5, Column (a)

Enter dividends received on preferred stock of a 20%-or-more-owned public utility that is subject to income tax and is allowed the deduction provided in section 247 for dividends paid.

Line 6, Column (a)

Enter the U.S.–source portion of dividends that:
- Are received from less-than-20%-owned foreign corporations and

- Qualify for the 70% deduction under section 245(a). To qualify for the 70% deduction, the corporation must own at least 10% of the stock of the foreign corporation by vote and value.

Also include dividends received from a less-than-20%-owned FSC that:
- Are attributable to income treated as effectively connected with the conduct of a trade or business within the United States (excluding foreign trade income) and
- Qualify for the 70% deduction provided in section 245(c)(1)(B).

Line 7, Column (a)

Enter the U.S.-source portion of dividends that are received from 20%-or-more-owned foreign corporations that qualify for the 80% deduction under section 245(a). Also include dividends received from a 20%-or-more-owned FSC that:
- Are attributable to income treated as effectively connected with the conduct of a trade or business within the United States (excluding foreign trade income) and
- Qualify for the 80% deduction provided in section 245(c)(1)(B).

Line 8, Column (a)

Enter dividends received from wholly owned foreign subsidiaries that are eligible for the 100% deduction provided in section 245(b).

In general, the deduction under section 245(b) applies to dividends paid out of the earnings and profits of a foreign corporation for a tax year during which:
- All of its outstanding stock is owned (directly or indirectly) by the domestic corporation receiving the dividends and
- All of its gross income from all sources is effectively connected with the conduct of a trade or business within the United States.

Line 9, Column (c)

Generally, line 9, column (c), may not exceed the amount from the worksheet on page 15. However, in a year in which an NOL occurs, this limitation does not apply even if the loss is created by the dividends-received deduction. See sections 172(d) and 246(b).

Line 10, Columns (a) and (c)

Small business investment companies operating under the Small Business Investment Act of 1958 (15 U.S.C. 661 and following) must enter dividends that are received from domestic corporations subject to income tax even though a deduction is allowed for the entire amount of those dividends. To claim the 100% deduction on line 10, column (c), the company must file with its return a statement that it was a Federal licensee under the Small Business Investment Act of 1958 at the time it received the dividends.

Line 11, Column (a)

Enter dividends from FSCs that are attributable to foreign trade income and that are eligible for the 100% deduction provided in section 245(c)(1)(A).

Line 12, Columns (a) and (c)

Enter only those dividends that qualify under section 243(b) for the 100% dividends-received deduction described in section 243(a)(3). Corporations taking this

deduction are subject to the provisions of section 1561.

The 100% deduction does not apply to affiliated group members that are joining in the filing of a consolidated return.

Line 13, Column (a)

Enter foreign dividends not reportable on lines 3, 6, 7, 8, or 11 of column (a). Include on line 13 the corporation's share of the ordinary earnings of a qualified electing fund from Form 8621, line 1c. Exclude distributions of amounts constructively taxed in the current year or in prior years under subpart F (sections 951 through 964).

Line 14, Column (a)

Include income constructively received from controlled foreign corporations under subpart F. This amount should equal the total subpart F income reported on Schedule I, Form 5471.

Line 15, Column (a)

Include gross-up for taxes deemed paid under sections 902 and 960.

Line 16, Column (a)

Enter taxable distributions from an IC-DISC or former DISC that are designated as not eligible for a dividends-received deduction.

No deduction is allowed under section 243 for a dividend from an IC-DISC or former DISC (as defined in section 992(a)) to the extent the dividend:
- Is paid out of the corporation's accumulated IC-DISC income or previously taxed income or
- Is a deemed distribution under section 995(b)(1).

Line 17, Column (a)

Include the following:

1. Dividends (other than capital gain distributions reported on Schedule D (Form 1120) and exempt-interest dividends) that are received from RICs and that are not subject to the 70% deduction.

2. Dividends from tax-exempt organizations.

3. Dividends (other than capital gain distributions) received from a REIT that, for the tax year of the trust in which the dividends are paid, qualifies under sections 856 through 860.

4. Dividends not eligible for a dividends-received deduction because of the holding period of the stock or an obligation to make corresponding payments with respect to similar stock.

Two situations in which the dividends-received deduction will not be allowed on any share of stock are:
- If the corporation held it less than 46 days during the 90-day period beginning 45 days before the stock became ex-dividend with respect to the dividend (see section 246(c)(1)(A)) or
- To the extent the corporation is under an obligation to make related payments for substantially similar or related property.

5. Any other taxable dividend income not properly reported above (including distributions under section 936(h)(4)).

If patronage dividends or per-unit retain allocations are included on line 17, identify the total of these amounts in a schedule attached to Form 1120.

-16-

Instructions for Forms 1120 and 1120-A

Line 18, Column (c)

Section 247 allows public utilities a deduction of 40% of the smaller of (a) dividends paid on their preferred stock during the tax year or (b) taxable income computed without regard to this deduction. In a year in which an NOL occurs, compute the deduction without regard to section 247(a)(1)(B). See section 172(d).

Schedule J, Form 1120 (Part I, Form 1120-A)

Lines 1 and 2 (Form 1120 Only)

Members of a controlled group. A member of a controlled group, as defined in section 1563, must check the box on line 1 and complete lines 2a and 2b of Schedule J, Form 1120.

Line 2a. Members of a controlled group are entitled to one $50,000, one $25,000, and one $9,925,000 taxable income bracket amount (in that order) on line 2a.

When a controlled group adopts or later amends an apportionment plan, each member must attach to its tax return a copy of its consent to this plan. The copy (or an attached statement) must show the part of the amount in each taxable income bracket apportioned to that member. See Regulations section 1.1561-3(b) for other requirements and for the time and manner of making the consent.

Unequal apportionment plan.
Members of a controlled group may elect an unequal apportionment plan and divide the taxable income brackets as they want. There is no need for consistency among taxable income brackets. Any member may be entitled to all, some, or none of the taxable income bracket. However, the total amount for all members cannot be more than the total amount in each taxable income bracket.

Equal apportionment plan. If no apportionment plan is adopted, members of a controlled group must divide the amount in each taxable income bracket equally among themselves. For example, Controlled Group AB consists of Corporation A and Corporation B. They do not elect an apportionment plan. Therefore, each corporation is entitled to:
• $25,000 (one-half of $50,000) on line 2a(1),
• $12,500 (one-half of $25,000) on line 2a(2), and
• $4,962,500 (one-half of $9,925,000) on line 2a(3).

Line 2b. Members of a controlled group are treated as one group to figure the applicability of the additional 5% tax and the additional 3% tax. If an additional tax applies, each member will pay that tax based on the part of the amount used in each taxable income bracket to reduce that member's tax. See section 1561(a). If an additional tax applies, attach a schedule showing the taxable income of the entire group and how the corporation figured its share of the additional tax.

Line 2b(1). Enter the corporation's share of the additional 5% tax on line 2b(1).

Line 2b(2). Enter the corporation's share of the additional 3% tax on line 2b(2).

Instructions for Forms 1120 and 1120-A

Tax Computation Worksheet for Members of a Controlled Group
(keep for your records)

Note: *Each member of a controlled group (except a qualified personal service corporation) must compute the tax using this worksheet.*

1. Enter taxable income (line 30, page 1, Form 1120) . . . . .   1. _____
2. Enter line 1 or the corporation's share of the $50,000 taxable income bracket, whichever is less . . . .   2. _____
3. Subtract line 2 from line 1 . . . .   3. _____
4. Enter line 3 or the corporation's share of the $25,000 taxable income bracket, whichever is less . . . .   4. _____
5. Subtract line 4 from line 3 . . . .   5. _____
6. Enter line 5 or the corporation's share of the $9,925,000 taxable income bracket, whichever is less . . . .   6. _____
7. Subtract line 6 from line 5 . . . .   7. _____
8. Multiply line 2 by 15% . . . .   8. _____
9. Multiply line 4 by 25% . . . .   9. _____
10. Multiply line 6 by 34% . . . .   10. _____
11. Multiply line 7 by 35% . . . .   11. _____
12. If the taxable income of the controlled group exceeds $100,000, enter this member's share of the smaller of: 5% of the taxable income in excess of $100,000, or $11,750 (See the instructions for Schedule J, line 2b.) . . . .   12. _____
13. If the taxable income of the controlled group exceeds $15 million, enter this member's share of the smaller of: 3% of the taxable income in excess of $15 million, or $100,000 (See the instructions for Schedule J, line 2b.) . . . .   13. _____
14. **Total.** Add lines 8 through 13. Enter here and on line 3, Schedule J, Form 1120 . . . .   14. _____

Line 3, Form 1120 (Line 1, Form 1120-A)

Members of a controlled group should use the worksheet above to figure the tax for the group. In addition, members of a controlled group **must** attach to Form 1120 a statement showing the computation of the tax entered on line 3.

Most corporations not filing a consolidated return figure their tax by using the Tax Rate Schedule below. Qualified personal service corporations should see the instructions below.

Tax Rate Schedule

If taxable income (line 30, Form 1120, or line 26, Form 1120-A) on page 1 is:

Over—	But not over—	Tax is:	Of the amount over—
$0	$50,000	15%	$0
50,000	75,000	$ 7,500 + 25%	50,000
75,000	100,000	13,750 + 34%	75,000
100,000	335,000	22,250 + 39%	100,000
335,000	10,000,000	113,900 + 34%	335,000
10,000,000	15,000,000	3,400,000 + 35%	10,000,000
15,000,000	18,333,333	5,150,000 + 38%	15,000,000
18,333,333	- - - - -	35%	0

Qualified personal service corporation. A qualified personal service corporation is taxed at a flat rate of 35% on taxable income. If the corporation is a qualified personal service corporation, check the box on line 3, Schedule J, Form 1120 (or line 1, Part I, Form 1120-A) even if the corporation has no tax liability.

A corporation is a qualified personal service corporation if it meets **both** of the following tests:
• Substantially all of the corporation's activities involve the performance of

services in the fields of health, law, engineering, architecture, accounting, actuarial science, performing arts, or consulting and
• At least 95% of the corporation's stock, by value, is owned, directly or indirectly, by (a) employees performing the services, (b) retired employees who had performed the services listed above, (c) any estate of the employee or retiree described above, or (d) any person who acquired the stock of the corporation as a result of the death of an employee or retiree (but only for the 2-year period beginning on the date of the employee or retiree's death). See Temporary Regulations section 1.448-1T(e) for details.

Mutual savings bank conducting life insurance business. The tax under section 594 consists of the sum of (a) a partial tax computed on Form 1120 on the taxable income of the bank determined without regard to income or deductions allocable to the life insurance department and (b) a partial tax on the taxable income computed on Form 1120-L of the life insurance department. Enter the combined tax on line 3 of Schedule J, Form 1120. Attach Form 1120-L as a schedule (and identify it as such) or a statement showing the computation of the taxable income of the life insurance department.

Deferred tax under section 1291. If the corporation was a shareholder in a passive foreign investment company (PFIC) and received an excess distribution or disposed of its investment in the PFIC during the year, it must include the increase in taxes due under section 1291(c)(2) in the total for line 3, Schedule J, Form 1120. On the dotted line next to line 3, write "Section 1291" and the amount.

Do not include on line 3 any interest due under section 1291(c)(3). Instead, show the amount of interest owed in the bottom

-17-

margin of page 1, Form 1120, and write "Section 1291 interest." For details, see **Form 8621,** Return by a Shareholder of a Passive Foreign Investment Company or Qualified Electing Fund.

Additional tax under section 197(f). A corporation that elects to pay tax on the gain from the sale of an intangible under the related person exception to the anti-churning rules should include any additional tax due under section 197(f)(9)(B) in the total for line 3. On the dotted line next to line 3, write "Section 197" and the amount. For more information, see **Pub. 535,** Business Expenses.

Line 4 (Form 1120 Only)

Note: *A corporation filing Form 1120-A that is not a small corporation exempt from the AMT (see below) may be required to file Form 4626, Alternative Minimum Tax— Corporations, if it claims any credits, even though it does not owe any AMT. See Form 4626 for details.*

Unless the corporation is treated as a small corporation exempt from the AMT, it may owe the AMT if it has any of the adjustments and tax preference items listed on Form 4626. The corporation must file Form 4626 if its taxable income (or loss) before the NOL deduction, combined with these adjustments and tax preference items is more than the smaller of $40,000 or the corporation's allowable exemption amount (from Form 4626).

For this purpose, taxable income does not include the NOL deduction. See Form 4626 for details.

Exemption for small corporations. A corporation is treated as a small corporation exempt from the AMT for its tax year beginning in 2002 if that year is the corporation's first tax year in existence (regardless of its gross receipts) **or:**

1. It was treated as a small corporation exempt from the AMT for all prior tax years beginning after 1997 **and**

2. Its average annual gross receipts for the 3-tax-year period (or portion thereof during which the corporation was in existence) ending before its tax year beginning in 2002 did not exceed $7.5 million ($5 million if the corporation had only 1 prior tax year).

Line 6a (Form 1120 Only)

To find out when a corporation can take the credit for payment of income tax to a foreign country or U.S. possession, see **Form 1118,** Foreign Tax Credit—Corporations.

Line 6b (Form 1120 Only)

The Small Business Job Protection Act of 1996 repealed the possessions credit. However, existing credit claimants may qualify for a credit under the transitional rules. See **Form 5735,** Possessions Corporation Tax Credit (Under Sections 936 and 30A).

Line 6c (Form 1120 Only)

If the corporation can take either of the following credits, check the appropriate box(es) and include the amount of the credits in the total for line 6c.

Nonconventional source fuel credit. A credit is allowed for the sale of qualified fuels produced from a nonconventional

source. Section 29 contains a definition of qualified fuels, provisions for figuring the credit, and other special rules. Attach a separate schedule to the return showing the computation of the credit.

Qualified electric vehicle (QEV) credit. Use **Form 8834,** Qualified Electric Vehicle Credit, if the corporation can claim a credit for the purchase of a new qualified electric vehicle. Vehicles that qualify for this credit are not eligible for the deduction for clean-fuel vehicles under section 179A.

Line 6d, Form 1120 (Line 2a, Form 1120-A)

Enter on line 6d (line 2a of Form 1120-A) the corporation's total general business credit.

If the corporation is filing **Form 8844,** Empowerment Zone and Renewal Community Employment Credit, or **Form 8884,** New York Liberty Zone Business Employee Credit, check the "Form(s) " box, write the form number in the space provided, and include the allowable credit on line 6d (line 2a of Form 1120-A).

If the corporation is required to file Form 3800, General Business Credit, check the "Form 3800" box and include the allowable credit on line 6d (line 2a of Form 1120-A).

If the corporation is not required to file Form 3800, check the "Form(s)" box, write the form number in the space provided, and include on line 6d (line 2a of Form 1120-A) the allowable credit from the applicable form listed below.

- Investment Credit (Form 3468).
- Work Opportunity Credit (Form 5884).
- Credit for Alcohol Used as Fuel (Form 6478).
- Credit for Increasing Research Activities (Form 6765).
- Low-Income Housing Credit (Form 8586).
- Orphan Drug Credit (Form 8820).
- Disabled Access Credit (Form 8826).
- Enhanced Oil Recovery Credit (Form 8830).
- Renewable Electricity Production Credit (Form 8835).
- Indian Employment Credit (Form 8845).
- Credit for Employer Social Security and Medicare Taxes Paid on Certain Employee Tips (Form 8846).
- Credit for Contributions to Selected Community Development Corporations (Form 8847).
- Welfare-to-Work Credit (Form 8861).
- New Markets Credit (Form 8874).
- Credit for Small Employer Pension Plan Startup Costs (Form 8881).
- Credit for Employer-Provided Child Care Facilities and Services (Form 8882).

Line 6e, Form 1120 (Line 2b, Form 1120-A)

To figure the minimum tax credit and any carryforward of that credit, use **Form 8827,** Credit for Prior Year Minimum Tax— Corporations. Also see Form 8827 if any of the corporation's 2001 nonconventional source fuel credit or qualified electric vehicle credit was disallowed solely because of the tentative minimum tax limitation. See section 53(d).

Line 6f (Form 1120 Only)

Enter the amount of any credit from **Form 8860,** Qualified Zone Academy Bond Credit.

Line 9 (Form 1120 Only)

A corporation is taxed as a personal holding company under section 542 if:
- At least 60% of its adjusted ordinary gross income for the tax year is personal holding company income and
- At any time during the last half of the tax year more than 50% in value of its outstanding stock is owned, directly or indirectly, by five or fewer individuals.

See Schedule PH (Form 1120) for definitions and details on how to figure the tax.

Line 10, Form 1120 (Line 5, Form 1120-A)

Include any of the following taxes and interest in the total on line 10 (line 5, Part I, Form 1120-A). Check the appropriate box(es) for the form, if any, used to compute the total.

Recapture of investment credit. If the corporation disposed of investment credit property or changed its use before the end of its useful life or recovery period, it may owe a tax. See **Form 4255,** Recapture of Investment Credit, for details.

Recapture of low-income housing credit. If the corporation disposed of property (or there was a reduction in the qualified basis of the property) for which it took the low-income housing credit, it may owe a tax. See **Form 8611,** Recapture of Low-Income Housing Credit.

Interest due under the look-back methods. If the corporation used the look-back method for certain long-term contracts, see Form 8697 for information on figuring the interest the corporation may have to include. The corporation may also have to include interest due under the look-back method for property depreciated under the income forecast method. See Form 8866.

Other. Additional taxes and interest amounts may be included in the total entered on line 10 (line 5, Part I, Form 1120-A). Check the box for "Other" if the corporation includes any of the taxes and interest discussed below. See *How to report* on page 19 for details on reporting these amounts on an attached schedule.
- Recapture of qualified electric vehicle (QEV) credit. The corporation must recapture part of the QEV credit it claimed in a prior year if, within 3 years of the date the vehicle was placed in service, it ceases to qualify for the credit. See Regulations section 1.30-1 for details on how to figure the recapture.
- Recapture of Indian employment credit. Generally, if an employer terminates the employment of a qualified employee less than 1 year after the date of initial employment, any Indian employment credit allowed for a prior tax year because of wages paid or incurred to that employee must be recaptured. For details, see Form 8845 and section 45A.
- Recapture of new markets credit (see Form 8874).
- Tax and interest on a nonqualified withdrawal from a capital construction fund (section 7518).
- Interest on deferred tax attributable to **(a)** installment sales of certain timeshares and residential lots (section 453(l)(3)) and

Instructions for Forms 1120 and 1120-A

(b) certain nondealer installment obligations (section 453A(c)).
• Interest due on deferred gain (section 1260(b)).

How to report. If the corporation checked the "Other" box, attach a schedule showing the computation of each item included in the total for line 10 (line 5, Part I, Form 1120-A) and identify the applicable Code section and the type of tax or interest.

Line 11 (Form 1120 Only)

Include any deferred tax on the termination of a section 1294 election applicable to shareholders electing fund in the amount entered on line 11. See Form 8621, Part V, and **How to report,** below.

Subtract the following amounts from the total for line 11.
• Deferred tax on the corporation's share of undistributed earnings of a qualified electing fund (see Form 8621, Part II).
• Deferred LIFO recapture tax (section 1363(d)). This tax is the part of the LIFO recapture tax that will be deferred and paid with Form 1120S in the future. To figure the deferred tax, first figure the total LIFO recapture tax. Follow the steps below to figure the total LIFO recapture tax and the deferred amount. Also see the instructions regarding LIFO recapture amount under **Line 10, Other Income,** on page 9.

Step 1. Figure the tax on the corporation's income including the LIFO recapture amount. (Complete Schedule J through line 10, but do not enter a total on line 11 yet.)

Step 2. Using a separate worksheet, complete Schedule J again, but **do not** include the LIFO recapture amount in the corporation's taxable income.

Step 3. Compare the tax in Step 2 to the tax in Step 1. (The difference between the two is the **LIFO recapture tax.**)

Step 4. Multiply the amount figured in Step 3 by 75%. (The result is the **deferred LIFO recapture tax.**)

How to report. Attach a schedule showing the computation of each item included in, or subtracted from, the total for line 11. On the dotted line next to line 11, specify **(a)** the applicable Code section, **(b)** the type of tax, and **(c)** enter the amount of tax. For example, if the corporation is deferring $100 LIFO recapture tax, subtract this amount from the total on line 11, then enter "Section 1363-Deferred Tax-$100" on the dotted line next to line 11.

Schedule K, Form 1120 (Part II, Form 1120-A)

The following instructions apply to Form 1120, page 3, Schedule K, or Form 1120-A, page 2, Part II. Be sure to complete all the items that apply to the corporation.

Question 4 (Form 1120 Only)

Check the "Yes" box for question 4 if:
• The corporation is a subsidiary in an affiliated group (defined below), but is not filing a consolidated return for the tax year with that group or
• The corporation is a subsidiary in a parent-subsidiary controlled group (defined below).

Any corporation that meets either of the requirements above should check the "Yes" box. This applies even if the corporation is a subsidiary member of one group and the parent corporation of another.

Note: *If the corporation is an "excluded member" of a controlled group (see section 1563(b)(2)), it is still considered a member of a controlled group for this purpose.*

Affiliated group. The term "affiliated group" means one or more chains of includible corporations (section 1504(a)) connected through stock ownership with a common parent corporation. The common parent must be an includible corporation and the following requirements **must** be met:

1. The common parent must own directly stock that represents at least 80% of the total voting power and at least 80% of the total value of the stock of at least one of the other includible corporations and

2. Stock that represents at least 80% of the total voting power and at least 80% of the total value of the stock of each of the other corporations (except for the common parent) must be owned directly by one or more of the other includible corporations.

For this purpose, the term "stock" generally does not include any stock that **(a)** is nonvoting, **(b)** is nonconvertible, **(c)** is limited and preferred as to dividends and does not participate significantly in corporate growth, and **(d)** has redemption and liquidation rights that do not exceed the issue price of the stock (except for a reasonable redemption or liquidation premium). See section 1504(a)(4).

Parent-subsidiary controlled group. The term "parent-subsidiary controlled group" means one or more chains of corporations connected through stock ownership (section 1563(a)(1)). Both of the following requirements **must** be met:

1. At least 80% of the total combined voting power of all classes of voting stock, or at least 80% of the total value of all classes of stock of each corporation in the group (except the parent) must be owned by one or more of the other corporations in the group and

2. The common parent must own at least 80% of the total combined voting power of all classes of stock entitled to vote or at least 80% of the total value of all classes of stock of one or more of the other corporations in the group. Stock owned directly by other members of the group is not counted when computing the voting power or value.

See section 1563(d)(1) for the definition of "stock" for purposes of determining stock ownership above.

Question 6 (Form 1120-A Only)

Foreign financial accounts. Check the "Yes" box for question 6 if either **1** or **2** below applies to the corporation. Otherwise, check the "No" box:

1. At any time during the 2002 calendar year, the corporation had an interest in or signature or other authority over a bank, securities, or other financial account in a foreign country (see **Form TD F 90-22.1,**

Report of Foreign Bank and Financial Accounts); and
• The combined value of the accounts was more than $10,000 at any time during the calendar year and
• The account was **not** with a U.S. military banking facility operated by a U.S. financial institution.

2. The corporation owns more than 50% of the stock in any corporation that would answer "Yes" to item **1** above.

If the "Yes" box is checked for the question:
• Enter the name of the foreign country or countries. Attach a separate sheet if more space is needed.
• File Form TD F 90-22.1 by June 30, 2003, with the Department of the Treasury at the address shown on the form. Because Form TD F 90-22.1 is not a tax form, do not file it with Form 1120-A. You can order Form TD F 90-22.1 by calling 1-800-TAX-FORM (1-800-829-3676) or you can download it from the IRS web site at **www.irs.gov.**

Question 7 (Form 1120 Only)

Check the "Yes" box if one foreign person owned at least 25% of **(a)** the total voting power of all classes of stock of the corporation entitled to vote or **(b)** the total value of all classes of stock of the corporation.

The constructive ownership rules of section 318 apply in determining if a corporation is foreign owned. See section 6038A(c)(5) and the related regulations.

Enter on line 7a the percentage owned by the foreign person specified in question 7. On line 7b, write the name of the owner's country.

Note: *If there is more than one 25%-or-more foreign owner, complete lines 7a and 7b for the foreign person with the highest percentage of ownership.*

Foreign person. The term "foreign person" means:
• A foreign citizen or nonresident alien.
• An individual who is a citizen of a U.S. possession (but who is not a U.S. citizen or resident).
• A foreign partnership.
• A foreign corporation.
• Any foreign estate or trust within the meaning of section 7701(a)(31).
• A foreign government (or one of its agencies or instrumentalities) to the extent that it is engaged in the conduct of a commercial activity as described in section 892.

Owner's country. For individuals, the term "owner's country" means the country of residence. For all others, it is the country where incorporated, organized, created, or administered.

Requirement to file Form 5472. If the corporation checked "Yes," it may have to file Form 5472. Generally, a 25% foreign-owned corporation that had a reportable transaction with a foreign or domestic related party during the tax year must file Form 5472.

See Form 5472 for filing instructions and penalties for failure to file.

Instructions for Forms 1120 and 1120-A

-19-

Item 9, Form 1120
(Item 3, Form 1120-A)

Show any **tax-exempt interest** received or accrued. Include any exempt-interest dividends received as a shareholder in a mutual fund or other RIC.

Item 11 (Form 1120 Only)

If the corporation has an NOL for its 2002 tax year, it may elect under section 172(b)(3) to waive the entire carryback period for the NOL and instead carry the NOL forward to future tax years. To do so, check the box on line 11 and file the tax return by its due date, including extensions (do not attach the statement described in Temporary Regulations section 301.9100-12T). Once made, the election is irrevocable. See Pub. 542, section 172, and Form 1139 for more details.

Corporations filing a **consolidated return** must also attach the statement required by Regulations section 1.1502-21(b)(3)(i) or (ii).

Item 12 (Form 1120 Only)

Enter the amount of the NOL carryover to the tax year from prior years, even if some of the loss is used to offset income on this return. The amount to enter is the total of all NOLs generated in prior years but not used to offset income (either as a carryback or carryover) to a tax year prior to 2002. Do not reduce the amount by any NOL deduction reported on line 29a.

Schedule L, Form 1120
(Part III, Form 1120-A)

The balance sheet should agree with the corporation's books and records. Include certificates of deposit as cash on line 1, Schedule L.

Line 5

Include on this line:

1. State and local government obligations, the interest on which is excludable from gross income under section 103(a) and

2. Stock in a mutual fund or other RIC that distributed exempt-interest dividends during the tax year of the corporation.

Line 26, Form 1120
(Line 21, Form 1120-A)

Some examples of adjustments to report on this line include:

• Unrealized gains and losses on securities held "available for sale."

• Foreign currency translation adjustments.

• The excess of additional pension liability over unrecognized prior service cost.

• Guarantees of employee stock (ESOP) debt.

• Compensation related to employee stock award plans.

If the total adjustment to be entered on line 26 (line 21, Form 1120-A) is a negative amount, enter the amount in parentheses.

Schedule M-1, Form 1120
(Part IV, Form 1120-A)

Line 5c, Form 1120
(Line 5, Form 1120-A)

Include any of the following:
• Meal and entertainment expenses not deductible under section 274(n).
• Expenses for the use of an entertainment facility.
• The part of business gifts over $25.
• Expenses of an individual over $2,000, which are allocable to conventions on cruise ships.
• Employee achievement awards over $400.
• The cost of entertainment tickets over face value (also subject to 50% limit under section 274(n)).
• The cost of skyboxes over the face value of nonluxury box seat tickets.
• The part of luxury water travel expenses not deductible under section 274(m).
• Expenses for travel as a form of education.
• Other nondeductible travel and entertainment expenses.
For more information, see Pub. 542.

Line 7, Form 1120
(Line 6, Form 1120-A)

Include as interest on line 7 (line 6, Form 1120-A), any exempt-interest dividends received as a shareholder in a mutual fund or other RIC.

Paperwork Reduction Act Notice. We ask for the information on these forms to carry out the Internal Revenue laws of the United States. You are required to give us the information. We need it to ensure that you are complying with these laws and to allow us to figure and collect the right amount of tax.

You are not required to provide the information requested on a form that is subject to the Paperwork Reduction Act unless the form displays a valid OMB control number. Books or records relating to a form or its instructions must be retained as long as their contents may become material in the administration of any Internal Revenue law. Generally, tax returns and return information are confidential, as required by section 6103.

The time needed to complete and file the following forms will vary depending on individual circumstances. The estimated average times are:

Form	Recordkeeping	Learning about the law or the form	Preparing the form	Copying, assembling, and sending the form to the IRS
1120	71 hr., 18 min.	43 hr., 29 min.	75 hr., 24 min.	8 hr., 18 min.
1120-A	43 hr., 45 min.	24 hr., 34 min.	49 hr., 3 min.	5 hr., 5 min.
Sch. D (1120)	7 hr., 10 min.	4 hr., 6 min.	6 hr., 16 min.	32 min.
Sch. H (1120)	5 hr., 58 min.	35 min.	43 min.	- - - - -
Sch. N (1120)	3 hr., 35 min.	1 hr., 7 min.	3 hr., 6 min.	32 min.
Sch. PH (1120)	15 hr., 18 min.	6 hr., 12 min.	8 hr., 35 min.	32 min.

If you have comments concerning the accuracy of these time estimates or suggestions for making this form and related schedules simpler, we would be happy to hear from you. You can write to the Tax Forms Committee, Western Area Distribution Center, Rancho Cordova, CA 95743-0001. **Do not** send the tax form to this address. Instead, see **Where To File** on page 3.

Forms 1120 and 1120-A

Codes for Principal Business Activity

This list of principal business activities and their associated codes is designed to classify an enterprise by the type of activity in which it is engaged to facilitate the administration of the Internal Revenue Code. These principal business activity codes are based on the North American Industry Classification System.

Using the list of activities and codes below, determine from which activity the company derives the largest percentage of its "total receipts." Total receipts is defined as the sum of gross receipts or sales (page 1, line 1a) plus all other income (page 1, lines 4 through 10). If the company purchases raw materials and supplies them to a subcontractor to produce the finished product, but retains title to the product, the company is considered a manufacturer and must use one of the manufacturing codes (311110-339900).

Once the principal business activity is determined, entries must be made on Form 1120, Schedule K, lines 2a, 2b, and 2c, or on Form 1120-A, Part II, lines 1a, 1b, and 1c. For the business activity code number, enter the six digit code selected from the list below. On the next line (Form 1120, line 2b, or Form 1120-A, line 1b), enter a brief description of the company's business activity. Finally, enter a description of the principal product or service of the company on Form 1120, line 2c, or Form 1120-A, line 1c.

Agriculture, Forestry, Fishing and Hunting

Code

Crop Production
111100 Oilseed & Grain Farming
111210 Vegetable & Melon Farming (including potatoes & yams)
111300 Fruit & Tree Nut Farming
111400 Greenhouse, Nursery, & Floriculture Production
111900 Other Crop Farming (including tobacco, cotton, sugarcane, hay, peanut, sugar beet & all other crop farming)

Animal Production
112111 Beef Cattle Ranching & Farming
112112 Cattle Feedlots
112120 Dairy Cattle & Milk Production
112210 Hog & Pig Farming
112300 Poultry & Egg Production
112400 Sheep & Goat Farming
112510 Animal Aquaculture (including shellfish & finfish farms & hatcheries)
112900 Other Animal Production

Forestry and Logging
113110 Timber Tract Operations
113210 Forest Nurseries & Gathering of Forest Products
113310 Logging

Fishing, Hunting and Trapping
114110 Fishing
114210 Hunting & Trapping

Support Activities for Agriculture and Forestry
115110 Support Activities for Crop Production (including cotton ginning, soil preparation, planting, & cultivating)
115210 Support Activities for Animal Production
115310 Support Activities For Forestry

Mining
211110 Oil & Gas Extraction
212110 Coal Mining
212200 Metal Ore Mining
212310 Stone Mining & Quarrying
212320 Sand, Gravel, Clay, & Ceramic & Refractory Minerals Mining & Quarrying
212390 Other Nonmetallic Mineral Mining & Quarrying
213110 Support Activities for Mining

Utilities

Code
221100 Electric Power Generation, Transmission & Distribution
221210 Natural Gas Distribution
221300 Water, Sewage & Other Systems

Construction

Construction of Buildings
236110 Residential Building Construction
236200 Nonresidential Building Construction

Heavy and Civil Engineering Construction
237100 Utility System Construction
237210 Land Subdivision
237310 Highway, Street, & Bridge Construction
237990 Other Heavy & Civil Engineering Construction

Specialty Trade Contractors
238100 Foundation, Structure, & Building Exterior Contractors (including framing carpentry, masonry, glass, roofing, & siding)
238210 Electrical Contractors
238220 Plumbing, Heating, & Air-Conditioning Contractors
238290 Other Building Equipment Contractors
238300 Building Finishing Contractors (including drywall, insulation, painting, wallcovering, flooring, tile, & finish carpentry)
238900 Other Specialty Trade Contractors (including site preparation)

Manufacturing

Food Manufacturing
311110 Animal Food Mfg
311200 Grain & Oilseed Milling
311300 Sugar & Confectionery Product Mfg
311400 Fruit & Vegetable Preserving & Specialty Food Mfg
311500 Dairy Product Mfg
311610 Animal Slaughtering and Processing
311710 Seafood Product Preparation & Packaging
311800 Bakeries & Tortilla Mfg
311900 Other Food Mfg (including coffee, tea, flavorings & seasonings)

Code

Beverage and Tobacco Product Manufacturing
312110 Soft Drink & Ice Mfg
312120 Breweries
312130 Wineries
312140 Distilleries
312200 Tobacco Manufacturing

Textile Mills and Textile Product Mills
313000 Textile Mills
314000 Textile Product Mills

Apparel Manufacturing
315100 Apparel Knitting Mills
315210 Cut & Sew Apparel Contractors
315220 Men's & Boys' Cut & Sew Apparel Mfg
315230 Women's & Girls' Cut & Sew Apparel Mfg
315290 Other Cut & Sew Apparel Mfg
315990 Apparel Accessories & Other Apparel Mfg

Leather and Allied Product Manufacturing
316110 Leather & Hide Tanning & Finishing
316210 Footwear Mfg (including rubber & plastics)
316990 Other Leather & Allied Product Mfg

Wood Product Manufacturing
321110 Sawmills & Wood Preservation
321210 Veneer, Plywood, & Engineered Wood Product Mfg
321900 Other Wood Product Mfg

Paper Manufacturing
322100 Pulp, Paper, & Paperboard Mills
322200 Converted Paper Product Mfg

Printing and Related Support Activities
323100 Printing & Related Support Activities

Petroleum and Coal Products Manufacturing
324110 Petroleum Refineries (including integrated)
324120 Asphalt Paving, Roofing, & Saturated Materials Mfg
324190 Other Petroleum & Coal Products Mfg

Chemical Manufacturing
325100 Basic Chemical Mfg
325200 Resin, Synthetic Rubber, & Artificial & Synthetic Fibers & Filaments Mfg
325300 Pesticide, Fertilizer, & Other Agricultural Chemical Mfg
325410 Pharmaceutical & Medicine Mfg
325500 Paint, Coating, & Adhesive Mfg
325600 Soap, Cleaning Compound, & Toilet Preparation Mfg
325900 Other Chemical Product & Preparation Mfg

Plastics and Rubber Products Manufacturing
326100 Plastics Product Mfg
326200 Rubber Product Mfg

Nonmetallic Mineral Product Manufacturing
327100 Clay Product & Refractory Mfg
327210 Glass & Glass Product Mfg
327300 Cement & Concrete Product Mfg
327400 Lime & Gypsum Product Mfg
327900 Other Nonmetallic Mineral Product Mfg

Code

Primary Metal Manufacturing
331110 Iron & Steel Mills & Ferroalloy Mfg
331200 Steel Product Mfg from Purchased Steel
331310 Alumina & Aluminum Production & Processing
331400 Nonferrous Metal (except Aluminum) Production & Processing
331500 Foundries

Fabricated Metal Product Manufacturing
332110 Forging & Stamping
332210 Cutlery & Handtool Mfg
332300 Architectural & Structural Metals Mfg
332400 Boiler, Tank, & Shipping Container Mfg
332510 Hardware Mfg
332610 Spring & Wire Product Mfg
332700 Machine Shops; Turned Product; & Screw, Nut, & Bolt Mfg
332810 Coating, Engraving, Heat Treating, & Allied Activities
332900 Other Fabricated Metal Product Mfg

Machinery Manufacturing
333100 Agriculture, Construction, & Mining Machinery Mfg
333200 Industrial Machinery Mfg
333310 Commercial & Service Industry Machinery Mfg
333410 Ventilation, Heating, Air-Conditioning, & Commercial Refrigeration Equipment Mfg
333510 Metalworking Machinery Mfg
333610 Engine, Turbine & Power Transmission Equipment Mfg
333900 Other General Purpose Machinery Mfg

Computer and Electronic Product Manufacturing
334110 Computer & Peripheral Equipment Mfg
334200 Communications Equipment Mfg
334310 Audio & Video Equipment Mfg
334410 Semiconductor & Other Electronic Component Mfg
334500 Navigational, Measuring, Electromedical, & Control Instruments Mfg
334610 Manufacturing & Reproducing Magnetic & Optical Media

Electrical Equipment, Appliance, and Component Manufacturing
335100 Electric Lighting Equipment Mfg
335200 Household Appliance Mfg
335310 Electrical Equipment Mfg
335900 Other Electrical Equipment & Component Mfg

Transportation Equipment Manufacturing
336100 Motor Vehicle Mfg
336210 Motor Vehicle Body & Trailer Mfg
336300 Motor Vehicle Parts Mfg
336410 Aerospace Product & Parts Mfg
336510 Railroad Rolling Stock Mfg
336610 Ship & Boat Building
336990 Other Transportation Equipment Mfg

Furniture and Related Product Manufacturing
337000 Furniture & Related Product Manufacturing

Code

Miscellaneous Manufacturing
339110 Medical Equipment & Supplies Mfg
339900 Other Miscellaneous Manufacturing

Wholesale Trade

Merchant Wholesalers, Durable Goods

423100 Motor Vehicle & Motor Vehicle Parts & Supplies
423200 Furniture & Home Furnishings
423300 Lumber & Other Construction Materials
423400 Professional & Commercial Equipment & Supplies
423500 Metal & Mineral (except Petroleum)
423600 Electrical & Electronic Goods
423700 Hardware, & Plumbing & Heating Equipment & Supplies
423800 Machinery, Equipment, & Supplies
423910 Sporting & Recreational Goods & Supplies
423920 Toy & Hobby Goods & Supplies
423930 Recyclable Materials
423940 Jewelry, Watch, Precious Stone, & Precious Metals
423990 Other Miscellaneous Durable Goods

Merchant Wholesalers, Nondurable Goods

424100 Paper & Paper Products
424210 Drugs & Druggists' Sundries
424300 Apparel, Piece Goods, & Notions
424400 Grocery & Related Products
424500 Farm Product Raw Materials
424600 Chemical & Allied Products
424700 Petroleum & Petroleum Products
424800 Beer, Wine, & Distilled Alcoholic Beverages
424910 Farm Supplies
424920 Book, Periodical, & Newspapers
424930 Flower, Nursery Stock, & Florists' Supplies
424940 Tobacco & Tobacco Products
424950 Paint, Varnish, & Supplies
424990 Other Miscellaneous Nondurable Goods

Wholesale Electronic Markets and Agents and Brokers

425110 Business to Business Electronic Markets
425120 Wholesale Trade Agents & Brokers

Retail Trade

Motor Vehicle and Parts Dealers
441110 New Car Dealers
441120 Used Car Dealers
441210 Recreational Vehicle Dealers
441221 Motorcycle Dealers
441222 Boat Dealers
441229 All Other Motor Vehicle Dealers
441300 Automotive Parts, Accessories, & Tire Stores

Furniture and Home Furnishings Stores
442110 Furniture Stores
442210 Floor Covering Stores
442291 Window Treatment Stores
442299 All Other Home Furnishings Stores

Code

Electronics and Appliance Stores
443111 Household Appliance Stores
443112 Radio, Television, & Other Electronics Stores
443120 Computer & Software Stores
443130 Camera & Photographic Supplies Stores

Building Material and Garden Equipment and Supplies Dealers
444110 Home Centers
444120 Paint & Wallpaper Stores
444130 Hardware Stores
444190 Other Building Material Dealers
444200 Lawn & Garden Equipment & Supplies Stores

Food and Beverage Stores
445110 Supermarkets and Other Grocery (except Convenience) Stores
445120 Convenience Stores
445210 Meat Markets
445220 Fish & Seafood Markets
445230 Fruit & Vegetable Markets
445291 Baked Goods Stores
445292 Confectionery & Nut Stores
445299 All Other Specialty Food Stores
445310 Beer, Wine, & Liquor Stores

Health and Personal Care Stores
446110 Pharmacies & Drug Stores
446120 Cosmetics, Beauty Supplies, & Perfume Stores
446130 Optical Goods Stores
446190 Other Health & Personal Care Stores

Gasoline Stations
447100 Gasoline Stations (including convenience stores with gas)

Clothing and Clothing Accessories Stores
448110 Men's Clothing Stores
448120 Women's Clothing Stores
448130 Children's & Infants' Clothing Stores
448140 Family Clothing Stores
448150 Clothing Accessories Stores
448190 Other Clothing Stores
448210 Shoe Stores
448310 Jewelry Stores
448320 Luggage & Leather Goods Stores

Sporting Goods, Hobby, Book, and Music Stores
451110 Sporting Goods Stores
451120 Hobby, Toy, & Game Stores
451130 Sewing, Needlework, & Piece Goods Stores
451140 Musical Instrument & Supplies Stores
451211 Book Stores
451212 News Dealers & Newsstands
451220 Prerecorded Tape, Compact Disc, & Record Stores

General Merchandise Stores
452110 Department Stores
452900 Other General Merchandise Stores

Miscellaneous Store Retailers
453110 Florists
453210 Office Supplies & Stationery Stores
453220 Gift, Novelty, & Souvenir Stores
453310 Used Merchandise Stores
453910 Pet & Pet Supplies Stores
453920 Art Dealers
453930 Manufactured (Mobile) Home Dealers
453990 All Other Miscellaneous Store Retailers (including tobacco, candle, & trophy shops)

Code

Nonstore Retailers
454110 Electronic Shopping & Mail-Order Houses
454210 Vending Machine Operators
454311 Heating Oil Dealers
454312 Liquefied Petroleum Gas (Bottled Gas) Dealers
454319 Other Fuel Dealers
454390 Other Direct Selling Establishments (including door-to-door retailing, frozen food plan providers, party plan merchandisers, & coffee-break service providers)

Transportation and Warehousing

Air, Rail, and Water Transportation
481000 Air Transportation
482110 Rail Transportation
483000 Water Transportation

Truck Transportation
484110 General Freight Trucking, Local
484120 General Freight Trucking, Long-distance
484200 Specialized Freight Trucking

Transit and Ground Passenger Transportation
485110 Urban Transit Systems
485210 Interurban & Rural Bus Transportation
485310 Taxi Service
485320 Limousine Service
485410 School & Employee Bus Transportation
485510 Charter Bus Industry
485990 Other Transit & Ground Passenger Transportation

Pipeline Transportation
486000 Pipeline Transportation

Scenic & Sightseeing Transportation
487000 Scenic & Sightseeing Transportation

Support Activities for Transportation
488100 Support Activities for Air Transportation
488210 Support Activities for Rail Transportation
488300 Support Activities for Water Transportation
488410 Motor Vehicle Towing
488490 Other Support Activities for Road Transportation
488510 Freight Transportation Arrangement
488990 Other Support Activities for Transportation

Couriers and Messengers
492110 Couriers
492210 Local Messengers & Local Delivery

Warehousing and Storage
493100 Warehousing & Storage (except lessors of miniwarehouses & self-storage units)

Information

Publishing Industries (except Internet)
511110 Newspaper Publishers
511120 Periodical Publishers
511130 Book Publishers
511140 Directory & Mailing List Publishers
511190 Other Publishers
511210 Software Publishers

Motion Picture and Sound Recording Industries
512100 Motion Picture & Video Industries (except video rental)
512200 Sound Recording Industries

Code

Broadcasting (except Internet)
515100 Radio & Television Broadcasting
515210 Cable & Other Subscription Programming

Internet Publishing and Broadcasting
516110 Internet Publishing & Broadcasting

Telecommunications
517000 Telecommunications (including paging, cellular, satellite, cable & other program distribution, resellers, & other telecommunications)

Internet Service Providers, Web Search Portals, and Data Processing Services
518111 Internet Service Providers
518112 Web Search Portals
518210 Data Processing, Hosting, & Related Services

Other Information Services
519100 Other Information Services (including news syndicates & libraries)

Finance and Insurance

Depository Credit Intermediation
522110 Commercial Banking
522120 Savings Institutions
522130 Credit Unions
522190 Other Depository Credit Intermediation

Nondepository Credit Intermediation
522210 Credit Card Issuing
522220 Sales Financing
522291 Consumer Lending
522292 Real Estate Credit (including mortgage bankers & originators)
522293 International Trade Financing
522294 Secondary Market Financing
522298 All Other Nondepository Credit Intermediation

Activities Related to Credit Intermediation
522300 Activities Related to Credit Intermediation (including loan brokers, check clearing, & money transmitting)

Securities, Commodity Contracts, and Other Financial Investments and Related Activities
523110 Investment Banking & Securities Dealing
523120 Securities Brokerage
523130 Commodity Contracts Dealing
523140 Commodity Contracts Brokerage
523210 Securities & Commodity Exchanges
523900 Other Financial Investment Activities (including portfolio management & investment advice)

Insurance Carriers and Related Activities
524140 Direct Life, Health, & Medical Insurance & Reinsurance Carriers
524150 Direct Insurance & Reinsurance (except Life, Health & Medical) Carriers
524210 Insurance Agencies & Brokerages
524290 Other Insurance Related Activities (including third-party administration of insurance and pension funds)

Code

Funds, Trusts, and Other Financial Vehicles
525100 Insurance & Employee Benefit Funds
525910 Open-End Investment Funds (Form 1120-RIC)
525920 Trusts, Estates, & Agency Accounts
525930 Real Estate Investment Trusts (Form 1120-REIT)
525990 Other Financial Vehicles (including closed-end investment funds)

"Offices of Bank Holding Companies" and "Offices of Other Holding Companies" are located under **Management of Companies (Holding Companies)** below.

Real Estate and Rental and Leasing
Real Estate
531110 Lessors of Residential Buildings & Dwellings
531114 Cooperative Housing
531120 Lessors of Nonresidential Buildings (except Miniwarehouses)
531130 Lessors of Miniwarehouses & Self-Storage Units
531190 Lessors of Other Real Estate Property
531210 Offices of Real Estate Agents & Brokers
531310 Real Estate Property Managers
531320 Offices of Real Estate Appraisers
531390 Other Activities Related to Real Estate

Rental and Leasing Services
532100 Automotive Equipment Rental & Leasing
532210 Consumer Electronics & Appliances Rental
532220 Formal Wear & Costume Rental
532230 Video Tape & Disc Rental
532290 Other Consumer Goods Rental
532310 General Rental Centers
532400 Commercial & Industrial Machinery & Equipment Rental & Leasing

Lessors of Nonfinancial Intangible Assets (except copyrighted works)
533110 Lessors of Nonfinancial Intangible Assets (except copyrighted works)

Professional, Scientific, and Technical Services
Legal Services
541110 Offices of Lawyers
541190 Other Legal Services

Accounting, Tax Preparation, Bookkeeping, and Payroll Services
541211 Offices of Certified Public Accountants
541213 Tax Preparation Services
541214 Payroll Services
541219 Other Accounting Services

Architectural, Engineering, and Related Services
541310 Architectural Services
541320 Landscape Architecture Services
541330 Engineering Services
541340 Drafting Services
541350 Building Inspection Services
541360 Geophysical Surveying & Mapping Services
541370 Surveying & Mapping (except Geophysical) Services
541380 Testing Laboratories

Code

Specialized Design Services
541400 Specialized Design Services (including interior, industrial, graphic, & fashion design)

Computer Systems Design and Related Services
541511 Custom Computer Programming Services
541512 Computer Systems Design Services
541513 Computer Facilities Management Services
541519 Other Computer Related Services

Other Professional, Scientific, and Technical Services
541600 Management, Scientific, & Technical Consulting Services
541700 Scientific Research & Development Services
541800 Advertising & Related Services
541910 Marketing Research & Public Opinion Polling
541920 Photographic Services
541930 Translation & Interpretation Services
541940 Veterinary Services
541990 All Other Professional, Scientific, & Technical Services

Management of Companies (Holding Companies)
551111 Offices of Bank Holding Companies
551112 Offices of Other Holding Companies

Administrative and Support and Waste Management and Remediation Services
Administrative and Support Services
561110 Office Administrative Services
561210 Facilities Support Services
561300 Employment Services
561410 Document Preparation Services
561420 Telephone Call Centers
561430 Business Service Centers (including private mail centers & copy shops)
561440 Collection Agencies
561450 Credit Bureaus
561490 Other Business Support Services (including repossession services, court reporting, & stenotype services)
561500 Travel Arrangement & Reservation Services
561600 Investigation & Security Services
561710 Exterminating & Pest Control Services
561720 Janitorial Services
561730 Landscaping Services
561740 Carpet & Upholstery Cleaning Services
561790 Other Services to Buildings & Dwellings
561?00 Other Support Services (including packaging & labeling services, & convention & trade show organizers)

Waste Management and Remediation Services
562000 Waste Management & Remediation Services

Educational Services
611000 Educational Services (including schools, colleges, & universities)

Code

Health Care and Social Assistance
Offices of Physicians and Dentists
621111 Offices of Physicians (except mental health specialists)
621112 Offices of Physicians, Mental Health Specialists
621210 Offices of Dentists

Offices of Other Health Practitioners
621310 Offices of Chiropractors
621320 Offices of Optometrists
621330 Offices of Mental Health Practitioners (except Physicians)
621340 Offices of Physical, Occupational & Speech Therapists, & Audiologists
621391 Offices of Podiatrists
621399 Offices of All Other Miscellaneous Health Practitioners

Outpatient Care Centers
621410 Family Planning Centers
621420 Outpatient Mental Health & Substance Abuse Centers
621491 HMO Medical Centers
621492 Kidney Dialysis Centers
621493 Freestanding Ambulatory Surgical & Emergency Centers
621498 All Other Outpatient Care Centers

Medical and Diagnostic Laboratories
621510 Medical & Diagnostic Laboratories

Home Health Care Services
621610 Home Health Care Services

Other Ambulatory Health Care Services
621900 Other Ambulatory Health Care Services (including ambulance services & blood & organ banks)

Hospitals
622000 Hospitals

Nursing and Residential Care Facilities
623000 Nursing & Residential Care Facilities

Social Assistance
624100 Individual & Family Services
624200 Community Food & Housing, & Emergency & Other Relief Services
624310 Vocational Rehabilitation Services
624410 Child Day Care Services

Arts, Entertainment, and Recreation
Performing Arts, Spectator Sports, and Related Industries
711100 Performing Arts Companies
711210 Spectator Sports (including sports clubs & racetracks)
711300 Promoters of Performing Arts, Sports, & Similar Events
711410 Agents & Managers for Artists, Athletes, Entertainers, & Other Public Figures
711510 Independent Artists, Writers, & Performers

Museums, Historical Sites, and Similar Institutions
712100 Museums, Historical Sites, & Similar Institutions

Amusement, Gambling, and Recreation Industries
713100 Amusement Parks & Arcades
713200 Gambling Industries

Code

713900 Other Amusement & Recreation Industries (including golf courses, skiing facilities, marinas, fitness centers, & bowling centers)

Accommodation and Food Services
Accommodation
721110 Hotels (except Casino Hotels) & Motels
721120 Casino Hotels
721191 Bed & Breakfast Inns
721199 All Other Traveler Accommodation
721210 RV (Recreational Vehicle) Parks & Recreational Camps
721310 Rooming & Boarding Houses

Food Services and Drinking Places
722110 Full-Service Restaurants
722210 Limited-Service Eating Places
722300 Special Food Services (including food service contractors & caterers)
722410 Drinking Places (Alcoholic Beverages)

Other Services
Repair and Maintenance
811110 Automotive Mechanical & Electrical Repair & Maintenance
811120 Automotive Body, Paint, Interior, & Glass Repair
811190 Other Automotive Repair & Maintenance (including oil change & lubrication shops & car washes)
811210 Electronic & Precision Equipment Repair & Maintenance
811310 Commercial & Industrial Machinery & Equipment (except Automotive & Electronic) Repair & Maintenance
811410 Home & Garden Equipment & Appliance Repair & Maintenance
811420 Reupholstery & Furniture Repair
811430 Footwear & Leather Goods Repair
811490 Other Personal & Household Goods Repair & Maintenance

Personal and Laundry Services
812111 Barber Shops
812112 Beauty Salons
812113 Nail Salons
812190 Other Personal Care Services (including diet & weight reducing centers)
812210 Funeral Homes & Funeral Services
812220 Cemeteries & Crematories
812310 Coin-Operated Laundries & Drycleaners
812320 Drycleaning & Laundry Services (except Coin-Operated)
812330 Linen & Uniform Supply
812910 Pet Care (except Veterinary) Services
812920 Photofinishing
812930 Parking Lots & Garages
812990 All Other Personal Services

Religious, Grantmaking, Civic, Professional, and Similar Organizations
813000 Religious, Grantmaking, Civic, Professional, & Similar Organizations (including condominium and homeowners associations)

Index

■

Form **1120**			**U.S. Corporation Income Tax Return**			OMB No. 1545-0123
Department of the Treasury Internal Revenue Service			For calendar year 2002 or tax year beginning .... , 2002, ending .... , 20 .... ▶ Instructions are separate. See page 20 for Paperwork Reduction Act Notice.			**20**□□**02**

A Check if a:
1 Consolidated return (attach Form 851) □
2 Personal holding co. (attach Sch. PH) □
3 Personal service corp. (as defined in Regulations sec. 1.441-3(c)— see instructions) □

Use IRS label. Otherwise, print or type.

Name: Tentex Toys, Inc.
Number, street, and room or suite no. (If a P.O. box, see page 7 of instructions.): 36 Division Street
City or town, state, and ZIP code: Anytown, IL 60930

B Employer identification number

C Date incorporated: 3-1-79

D Total assets (see page 8 of instructions): $ 879,417

E Check applicable boxes: (1) □ Initial return (2) □ Final return (3) □ Name change (4) □ Address change

Income

1a	Gross receipts or sales 2,010,000	b Less returns and allowances 20,000	c Bal ▶ 1c 1,990,000
2	Cost of goods sold (Schedule A, line 8)		2 1,520,000
3	Gross profit. Subtract line 2 from line 1c		3 470,000
4	Dividends (Schedule C, line 19)		4 10,000
5	Interest		5 5,500
6	Gross rents		6
7	Gross royalties		7
8	Capital gain net income (attach Schedule D (Form 1120))		8
9	Net gain or (loss) from Form 4797, Part II, line 18 (attach Form 4797)		9
10	Other income (see page 9 of instructions—attach schedule)		10
11	**Total income.** Add lines 3 through 10	▶	11 485,500

Deductions (See instructions for limitations on deductions.)

12	Compensation of officers (Schedule E, line 4)		12 70,000
13	Salaries and wages (less employment credits)		13 38,000
14	Repairs and maintenance		14 800
15	Bad debts		15 1,600
16	Rents		16 9,200
17	Taxes and licenses		17 18,000
18	Interest		18 27,200
19	Charitable contributions (see page 11 of instructions for 10% limitation)		19 23,150
20	Depreciation (attach Form 4562)	20 17,600	
21	Less depreciation claimed on Schedule A and elsewhere on return	21a 12,400	21b 5,200
22	Depletion		22
23	Advertising		23 8,700
24	Pension, profit-sharing, etc., plans		24
25	Employee benefit programs		25
26	Other deductions (attach schedule)		26 78,300
27	**Total deductions.** Add lines 12 through 26	▶	27 277,150
28	Taxable income before net operating loss deduction and special deductions. Subtract line 27 from line 11		28 208,350
29	**Less:** a Net operating loss (NOL) deduction (see page 13 of instructions)	29a	
	b Special deductions (Schedule C, line 20)	29b 8,000	29c 8,000

Tax and Payments

30	**Taxable income.** Subtract line 29c from line 28		30 200,350
31	**Total tax** (Schedule J, line 11)		31 55,387
32	Payments: a 2001 overpayment credited to 2002	32a	
b	2002 estimated tax payments	32b 69,117	
c	Less 2002 refund applied for on Form 4466	32c ( ) d Bal ▶	32d 69,117
e	Tax deposited with Form 7004		32e
f	Credit for tax paid on undistributed capital gains (attach Form 2439)		32f
g	Credit for Federal tax on fuels (attach Form 4136). See instructions		32g ... 32h 69,117
33	Estimated tax penalty (see page 14 of instructions). Check if Form 2220 is attached ▶ □		33
34	**Tax due.** If line 32h is smaller than the total of lines 31 and 33, enter amount owed		34
35	**Overpayment.** If line 32h is larger than the total of lines 31 and 33, enter amount overpaid		35 13,730
36	Enter amount of line 35 you want: **Credited to 2003 estimated tax** ▶ 13,730 **Refunded** ▶		36

Sign Here
Under penalties of perjury, I declare that I have examined this return, including accompanying schedules and statements, and to the best of my knowledge and belief, it is true, correct, and complete. Declaration of preparer (other than taxpayer) is based on all information of which preparer has any knowledge.

▶ _James O. Barclay_ 3/7/xx ▶ _President_
Signature of officer   Date   Title

May the IRS discuss this return with the preparer shown below (see instructions)? □ Yes □ No

Paid Preparer's Use Only

Preparer's signature ▶		Date	Check if self-employed □	Preparer's SSN or PTIN
Firm's name (or yours if self-employed), address, and ZIP code ▶			EIN Phone no. ( )	

Cat. No. 11450Q

Form **1120** (2002)

Form 1120 (2002)   Page **2**

Schedule A   Cost of Goods Sold (see page 14 of instructions)

1	Inventory at beginning of year	1	126,000
2	Purchases	2	1,127,100
3	Cost of labor	3	402,000
4	Additional section 263A costs (attach schedule)	4	40,000
5	Other costs (attach schedule)	5	123,000
6	**Total.** Add lines 1 through 5	6	1,818,400
7	Inventory at end of year	7	298,400
8	**Cost of goods sold.** Subtract line 7 from line 6. Enter here and on line 2, page 1	8	1,520,000

9a Check all methods used for valuing closing inventory:

    (i) ☐ Cost as described in Regulations section 1.471-3

    (ii) ☐ Lower of cost or market as described in Regulations section 1.471-4

    (iii) ☐ Other (Specify method used and attach explanation.) ▶ ----------------------------

  b Check if there was a writedown of subnormal goods as described in Regulations section 1.471-2(c) . . . . ▶ ☐

  c Check if the LIFO inventory method was adopted this tax year for any goods (if checked, attach Form 970) . . . . . ▶ ☐

  d If the LIFO inventory method was used for this tax year, enter percentage (or amounts) of closing inventory computed under LIFO . . . . | 9d |

  e If property is produced or acquired for resale, do the rules of section 263A apply to the corporation? . . . . . ☑ Yes ☐ No

  f Was there any change in determining quantities, cost, or valuations between opening and closing inventory? If "Yes," attach explanation . . . . ☐ Yes ☑ No

Schedule C   Dividends and Special Deductions (see instructions beginning on page 15)

		(a) Dividends received	(b) %	(c) Special deductions (a) × (b)
1	Dividends from less-than-20%-owned domestic corporations that are subject to the 70% deduction (other than debt-financed stock)		70	
2	Dividends from 20%-or-more-owned domestic corporations that are subject to the 80% deduction (other than debt-financed stock)	10,000	80	8,000
3	Dividends on debt-financed stock of domestic and foreign corporations (section 246A)		see instructions	
4	Dividends on certain preferred stock of less-than-20%-owned public utilities		42	
5	Dividends on certain preferred stock of 20%-or-more-owned public utilities		48	
6	Dividends from less-than-20%-owned foreign corporations and certain FSCs that are subject to the 70% deduction		70	
7	Dividends from 20%-or-more-owned foreign corporations and certain FSCs that are subject to the 80% deduction		80	
8	Dividends from wholly owned foreign subsidiaries subject to the 100% deduction (section 245(b))		100	
9	**Total.** Add lines 1 through 8. See page 16 of instructions for limitation	/////	/////	8,000
10	Dividends from domestic corporations received by a small business investment company operating under the Small Business Investment Act of 1958		100	
11	Dividends from certain FSCs that are subject to the 100% deduction (section 245(c)(1))		100	
12	Dividends from affiliated group members subject to the 100% deduction (section 243(a)(3))		100	
13	Other dividends from foreign corporations not included on lines 3, 6, 7, 8, or 11			/////
14	Income from controlled foreign corporations under subpart F (attach Form(s) 5471)			/////
15	Foreign dividend gross-up (section 78)			/////
16	IC-DISC and former DISC dividends not included on lines 1, 2, or 3 (section 246(d))			/////
17	Other dividends			/////
18	Deduction for dividends paid on certain preferred stock of public utilities	/////		
19	**Total dividends.** Add lines 1 through 17. Enter here and on line 4, page 1 ▶	10,000	/////	/////
20	**Total special deductions.** Add lines 9, 10, 11, 12, and 18. Enter here and on line 29b, page 1 . . . . ▶			8,000

Schedule E   Compensation of Officers (see instructions for line 12, page 1, on page 10 of instructions)

Note: *Complete Schedule E only if total receipts (line 1a plus lines 4 through 10 on page 1) are $500,000 or more.*

	(a) Name of officer	(b) Social security number	(c) Percent of time devoted to business	(d) Common	(e) Preferred	(f) Amount of compensation
1	James O. Barclay	581-00-0936	100 %	45 %	%	55,000
			%	%	%	
	George M. Collins	447-00-2604	100 %	15 %	%	31,000
			%	%	%	
	Samuel Adams	401-00-2611	50 %	2 %	%	14,000
2	Total compensation of officers					100,000
3	Compensation of officers claimed on Schedule A and elsewhere on return					30,000
4	Subtract line 3 from line 2. Enter the result here and on line 12, page 1					70,000

Form **1120** (2002)

Form 1120 (2002)

Schedule J — Tax Computation (see page 17 of instructions)

1 Check if the corporation is a member of a controlled group (see sections 1561 and 1563) . . . . ▶ ☐

Important: Members of a controlled group, see instructions on page 17.

2a If the box on line 1 is checked, enter the corporation's share of the $50,000, $25,000, and $9,925,000 taxable income brackets (in that order):

(1) ☐ $_____ | **(2)** ☐ $_____ | **(3)** $_____

b Enter the corporation's share of: **(1)** Additional 5% tax (not more than $11,750) $_____

(2) Additional 3% tax (not more than $100,000) $_____

3 Income tax. Check if a qualified personal service corporation under section 448(d)(2) (see page 17) . ▶ ☐	**3**	
4 Alternative minimum tax (attach Form 4626)	**4**	61,387
5 Add lines 3 and 4	**5**	
6a Foreign tax credit (attach Form 1118) **6a**		
b Possessions tax credit (attach Form 5735) **6b**		
c Check: ☐ Nonconventional source fuel credit ☐ QEV credit (attach Form 8834) **6c**		
d General business credit. Check box(es) and indicate which forms are attached. ☐ Form 3800 ☑ Form(s) (specify) ▶ 8884 **6d** 6,000		
e Credit for prior year minimum tax (attach Form 8827) **6e**		
f Qualified zone academy bond credit (attach Form 8860) **6f**		
7 **Total credits.** Add lines 6a through 6f	**7**	6,000
8 Subtract line 7 from line 5	**8**	55,387
9 Personal holding company tax (attach Schedule PH (Form 1120)) . .	**9**	
10 Other taxes. Check if from: ☐ Form 4255 ☐ Form 8611 ☐ Form 8697 ☐ Form 8866 ☐ Other (attach schedule)	**10**	
11 **Total tax.** Add lines 8 through 10. Enter here and on line 31, page 1	**11**	55,387

Schedule K — Other Information (see page 19 of instructions)

	Yes	No
1 Check method of accounting: **a** ☐ Cash **b** ☐ Accrual **c** ☐ Other (specify) ▶		
2 See page 21 of the instructions and enter the:		
a Business activity code no. ▶ 3998		
b Business activity ▶ Manufacturing		
c Product or service ▶ Toys		
3 At the end of the tax year, did the corporation own, directly or indirectly, 50% or more of the voting stock of a domestic corporation? (For rules of attribution, see section 267(c).)		✓
If "Yes," attach a schedule showing: **(a)** name and employer identification number (EIN), **(b)** percentage owned, and **(c)** taxable income or (loss) before NOL and special deductions of such corporation for the tax year ending with or within your tax year.		
4 Is the corporation a subsidiary in an affiliated group or a parent-subsidiary controlled group?		✓
If "Yes," enter name and EIN of the parent corporation ▶		
5 At the end of the tax year, did any individual, partnership, corporation, estate, or trust own, directly or indirectly, 50% or more of the corporation's voting stock? (For rules of attribution, see section 267(c).) If "Yes," attach a schedule showing name and identifying number. (Do not include any information already entered in **4** above.) Enter percentage owned ▶		✓
6 During this tax year, did the corporation pay dividends (other than stock dividends and distributions in exchange for stock) in excess of the corporation's current and accumulated earnings and profits? (See sections 301 and 316.) . . .		✓
If "Yes," file **Form 5452,** Corporate Report of Nondividend Distributions.		
If this is a consolidated return, answer here for the parent corporation and on **Form 851,** Affiliations Schedule, for each subsidiary.		

	Yes	No
7 At any time during the tax year, did one foreign person own, directly or indirectly, at least 25% of **(a)** the total voting power of all classes of stock of the corporation entitled to vote or **(b)** the total value of all classes of stock of the corporation?		✓
If "Yes," enter: **(a)** Percentage owned ▶ and **(b)** Owner's country ▶		
c The corporation may have to file **Form 5472,** Information Return of a 25% Foreign-Owned U.S. Corporation or a Foreign Corporation Engaged in a U.S. Trade or Business. Enter number of Forms 5472 attached ▶		
8 Check this box if the corporation issued publicly offered debt instruments with original issue discount . . ▶ ☐		
If checked, the corporation may have to file **Form 8281,** Information Return for Publicly Offered Original Issue Discount Instruments.		
9 Enter the amount of tax-exempt interest received or accrued during the tax year ▶ $		
10 Enter the number of shareholders at the end of the tax year (if 75 or fewer) ▶		
11 If the corporation has an NOL for the tax year and is electing to forego the carryback period, check here ▶ ☐		
If the corporation is filing a consolidated return, the statement required by Regulations section 1.1502-21(b)(3)(i) or (ii) must be attached or the election will not be valid.		
12 Enter the available NOL carryover from prior tax years (Do not reduce it by any deduction on line 29a.) ▶ $		
13 Are the corporation's total receipts (line 1a plus lines 4 through 10 on page 1) for the tax year **and** its total assets at the end of the tax year less than $250,000?. . . .		✓
If "Yes," the corporation is not required to complete Schedules L, M-1, and M-2 on page 4. Instead, enter the total amount of cash distributions and the book value of property distributions (other than cash) made during the tax year. ▶ $		

Note: *If the corporation, at any time during the tax year, had assets or operated a business in a foreign country or U.S. possession, it may be required to attach **Schedule N (Form 1120),** Foreign Operations of U.S. Corporations, to this return. See Schedule N for details.*

Form **1120** (2002)

Form 1120 (2002)   Page **4**

Note: *The corporation is not required to complete Schedules L, M-1, and M-2 if Question 13 on Schedule K is answered "Yes."*

Schedule L — Balance Sheets per Books

Assets		Beginning of tax year		End of tax year	
		(a)	**(b)**	**(c)**	**(d)**
1 Cash			14,700		28,331
2a Trade notes and accounts receivable		98,400		103,700	
b Less allowance for bad debts		( )	98,400	( )	103,700
3 Inventories			126,000		298,400
4 U.S. government obligations					
5 Tax-exempt securities (see instructions)			100,000		120,000
6 Other current assets (attach schedule)			26,300		17,266
7 Loans to shareholders					
8 Mortgage and real estate loans					
9 Other investments (attach schedule)			100,000		80,000
10a Buildings and other depreciable assets		272,400		296,700	
b Less accumulated depreciation		(88,300)	184,100	(104,280)	192,420
11a Depletable assets					
b Less accumulated depletion		( )		( )	
12 Land (net of any amortization)			20,000		20,000
13a Intangible assets (amortizable only)					
b Less accumulated amortization		( )		( )	
14 Other assets (attach schedule)			14,800		19,300
15 Total assets			684,300		879,417
Liabilities and Shareholders' Equity					
16 Accounts payable			28,500		34,834
17 Mortgages, notes, bonds payable in less than 1 year			4,300		4,300
18 Other current liabilities (attach schedule)			6,800		7,400
19 Loans from shareholders					
20 Mortgages, notes, bonds payable in 1 year or more			176,700		264,100
21 Other liabilities (attach schedule)					
22 Capital stock: **a** Preferred stock					
b Common stock		200,000	200,000		200,000
23 Additional paid-in capital					
24 Retained earnings—Appropriated (attach schedule)			30,000		40,000
25 Retained earnings—Unappropriated			238,000		328,783
26 Adjustments to shareholders' equity (attach schedule)					
27 Less cost of treasury stock			( )		( )
28 Total liabilities and shareholders' equity			684,300		879,417

Schedule M-1 — Reconciliation of Income (Loss) per Books With Income per Return (see page 20 of instructions)

1 Net income (loss) per books	147,783	**7** Income recorded on books this year not included on this return (itemize):		
2 Federal income tax per books	55,387			
3 Excess of capital losses over capital gains	3,600	Tax-exempt interest $ 5,000		
4 Income subject to tax not recorded on books this year (itemize):		Insurance proceeds 9,500		
....		....		14,500
		8 Deductions on this return not charged against book income this year (itemize):		
5 Expenses recorded on books this year not deducted on this return (itemize):		**a** Depreciation . . . . $ 1,620		
a Depreciation . . . . $		**b** Charitable contributions $		
b Charitable contributions $ 850		....		
c Travel and entertainment $		....		1,620
See itemized statement attached (not shown) 16,850	17,700	**9** Add lines 7 and 8		16,120
6 Add lines 1 through 5	224,470	**10** Income (line 28, page 1)—line 6 less line 9		208,350

Schedule M-2 — Analysis of Unappropriated Retained Earnings per Books (Line 25, Schedule L)

1 Balance at beginning of year	238,000	**5** Distributions: **a** Cash		65,000
2 Net income (loss) per books	147,783	**b** Stock		
3 Other increases (itemize):		**c** Property		
Refund of 1998 income tax		**6** Other decreases (itemize): Reserve for contingencies		10,000
due to IRS examination	18,000	**7** Add lines 5 and 6		75,000
4 Add lines 1, 2, and 3	403,783	**8** Balance at end of year (line 4 less line 7)		328,783

Form **1120** (2002)

SCHEDULE D **(Form 1120)** Department of the Treasury Internal Revenue Service	**Capital Gains and Losses** ▶ Attach to Form 1120, 1120-A, 1120-F, 1120-FSC, 1120-H, 1120-IC-DISC, 1120-L, 1120-ND, 1120-PC, 1120-POL, 1120-REIT, 1120-RIC, 1120-SF, 990-C, or certain Forms 990-T.	OMB No. 1545-0123 2002

Name		Employer identification number

Part I   Short-Term Capital Gains and Losses—Assets Held One Year or Less

(a) Description of property (Example: 100 shares of Z Co.)	**(b)** Date acquired (mo., day, yr.)	**(c)** Date sold (mo., day, yr.)	**(d)** Sales price (see instructions)	**(e)** Cost or other basis (see instructions)	**(f)** Gain or (loss) (Subtract (e) from (d))
1					

2	Short-term capital gain from installment sales from Form 6252, line 26 or 37	**2**	
3	Short-term gain or (loss) from like-kind exchanges from Form 8824	**3**	
4	Unused capital loss carryover (attach computation)	**4**	( )
5	Net short-term capital gain or (loss). Combine lines 1 through 4	**5**	

Part II   Long-Term Capital Gains and Losses—Assets Held More Than One Year

6					

7	Enter gain from Form 4797, column (g), line 7 or 9	**7**	
8	Long-term capital gain from installment sales from Form 6252, line 26 or 37	**8**	
9	Long-term gain or (loss) from like-kind exchanges from Form 8824	**9**	
10	Capital gain distributions (see instructions)	**10**	
11	Net long-term capital gain or (loss). Combine lines 6 through 10	**11**	

Part III   Summary of Parts I and II

12	Enter excess of net short-term capital gain (line 5) over net long-term capital loss (line 11). . .	**12**	
13	Net capital gain. Enter excess of net long-term capital gain (line 11) over net short-term capital loss (line 5)	**13**	
14	Add lines 12 and 13. Enter here and on Form 1120, page 1, line 8, or the proper line on other returns	**14**	

Note: *If losses exceed gains, see **Capital losses** in the instructions on page 2.*

General Instructions

Section references are to the Internal Revenue Code unless otherwise noted.

Purpose of Schedule

Use Schedule D to report sales and exchanges of capital assets and gains on distributions to shareholders of appreciated capital assets.

Note: *For more information, see **Pub. 544**, Sales and Other Dispositions of Assets.*

Other Forms the Corporation May Have To File

Use **Form 4797,** Sales of Business Property, to report the following:

● The sale or exchange of:

1. Property used in a trade or business;

2. Depreciable and amortizable property;

3. Oil, gas, geothermal, or other mineral property; and

4. Section 126 property.

● The involuntary conversion (other than from casualty or theft) of property and capital assets held for business or profit.

● The disposition of noncapital assets other than inventory or property held primarily for sale to customers in the ordinary course of the corporation's trade or business.

● The section 291 adjustment to section 1250 property.

Use **Form 4684,** Casualties and Thefts, to report involuntary conversions of property due to casualty or theft.

Use **Form 6781,** Gains and Losses From Section 1256 Contracts and Straddles, to report gains and losses from section 1256 contracts and straddles.

Use **Form 8824,** Like-Kind Exchanges, if the corporation made one or more "like-kind" exchanges. A like-kind exchange occurs when the corporation exchanges business or investment property for property of a like kind. For exchanges of capital assets, include the gain or (loss) from Form 8824, if any, on line 3 or line 9.

For Paperwork Reduction Act Notice, see the Instructions for Forms 1120 and 1120-A.   Cat. No. 11460M   Schedule D (Form 1120) 2002

Capital Assets

Each item of property the corporation held (whether or not connected with its trade or business) is a capital asset **except** the following:

- Stock in trade or other property included in inventory or held mainly for sale to customers.

- Accounts or notes receivable acquired in the ordinary course of the trade or business for services rendered or from the sale of stock in trade or other property included in inventory or held mainly for sale to customers.

- Depreciable or real property used in the trade or business, even if it is fully depreciated.

- Certain copyrights; literary, musical, or artistic compositions; letters or memoranda; or similar property. See section 1221(a)(3).

- U.S. Government publications, including the Congressional Record, that the corporation received from the Government, other than by purchase at the normal sales price, or that the corporation got from another taxpayer who had received it in a similar way, if the corporation's basis is determined by reference to the previous owner's basis.

- Certain commodities derivative financial instruments held by a dealer. See section 1221(a)(6).

- Certain hedging transactions entered into in the normal course of the trade or business. See section 1221(a)(7).

- Supplies regularly used in the trade or business.

Capital losses. Capital losses are allowed only to the extent of capital gains. A net capital loss is carried back 3 years and forward 5 years as a short-term capital loss. Carry back a capital loss to the extent it does not increase or produce a net operating loss in the tax year to which it is carried. Foreign expropriation capital losses cannot be carried back, but are carried forward 10 years. A net capital loss of a regulated investment company (RIC) is carried forward 8 years.

Items for Special Treatment

Gain from installment sales. If the corporation sold property at a gain and it will receive a payment in a tax year after the year of sale, it generally must report the sale on the installment method unless it elects not to. However, the installment method may not be used to report sales of stock or securities traded on an established securities market.

Use **Form 6252,** Installment Sale Income, to report the sale on the installment method. Also use Form 6252 to report any payment received during the tax year from a sale made in an earlier year that was reported on the installment method. To elect out of the installment method, report the full amount of the gain on Schedule D for the year of the sale on a return filed by the due date (including extensions). If the original return was filed on time without making the election, the corporation may make the election on an amended return filed no later than 6 months after the original due date (excluding extensions). Write "Filed pursuant to section 301.9100-2" at the top of the amended return.

Rollover of gain from empowerment zones assets. If the corporation sold a qualifed empowerment zone asset held for more than 1 year, it may be able to elect to postpone part or all of the gain that would otherwise be included on Schedule D. If the corporation makes the election, the gain on the sale generally is recognized only to the extent, if any, that the amount realized on the sale exceeds the cost of qualified empowerment zone assets (replacement property) the corporation purchased during the 60-day period beginning on the date of the sale. The following rules apply.

- No portion of the cost of the replacement property may be taken into account to the extent the cost is taken into account to exclude gain on a different empowerment zone asset.

- The replacement property must qualify as an empowerment zone asset with respect to the same empowerment zone as the asset sold.

- The corporation must reduce the basis of the replacment property by the amount of postponed gain.

- This election does not apply to any gain **(a)** treated as ordinary income or **(b)** attributable to real property, or an intangible asset, which is not an integral part of an enterpise zone business.

- The District of Columbia enterprise zone is not treated as an empowerment zone for this purpose.

- The election is irrevocable without IRS consent.

See **Pub. 954,** Tax Incentives for Empowerment Zones and Other Distressed Communities, for the definition of empowerment zone and enterprise zone business. The corporation can find out if its business is located within an empowerment zone by using the RC/EZ/EC Address Locator at **http://hud.esri.com/locateservices/ezec.**

Qualified emplowerment zone assets are:

- Tangible property, if:

1. The corporation acquired the property after December 21, 2000,

2. The original use of the property in the empowermnet zone began with the corporation, and

3. Substantially all of the use of the property, during substantially all of the time that the corporation held it, was in the corporation's enterprise zone business; **and**

- Stock in a domestic corporation or a capital or profits interest in a domestic partnership, if:

1. The corporation acquired the stock or partnership interest after December 21, 2000, solely in exchange for cash, from the corporation at its original issue (directly or through an underwriter) or from the partnership;

2. The business was an enterprise zone business (or a new business being organized as an enterprise zone business) as of the time the corporation acquired the stock or partnership interest; and

3. The business qualified as an enterprise zone business during substantially all of the time during which the corporation held the stock or partnership interest.

How to report. Report the entire gain realized from the sale as the corporation otherwise would without regard to the election. On Schedule D, line 6, enter "Section 1397B Rollover" in column (a) and enter as a loss in column (f) the amount of gain included on Schedule D that the corporation is electing to postpone. If the corporation is reporting the sale directly on Schedule D, line 6, use the line directly below the line on which the sale is reported.

See section 1397B for more details.

Gain on distributions of appreciated property. Generally, gain (but not loss) is recognized on a nonliquidating distribution of appreciated property to the extent that the property's fair market value (FMV) exceeds its adjusted basis. See section 311.

Form 1120-A
Department of the Treasury
Internal Revenue Service

U.S. Corporation Short-Form Income Tax Return

For calendar year 2002 or tax year beginning................., 2002, ending................., 20.....
See separate instructions to make sure the corporation qualifies to file Form 1120-A.

OMB No. 1545-0890

2002

A Check this box if the corp. is a personal service corp. (as defined in Regulations section 1.441-3(c)—see instructions) ☐	Use IRS label. Other-wise, print or type.	Name **Rose Flower Shop, Inc.**	**B** Employer identification number
		Number, street, and room or suite no. (If a P.O. box, see page 7 of instructions.) **38 Superior Lane**	**C** Date incorporated **7-1-89**
		City or town, state, and ZIP code **Fair City, MD 20715**	**D** Total assets (see page 8 of instructions) $ 65,987

E Check applicable boxes: **(1)** ☐ Initial return **(2)** ☐ Name change **(3)** ☐ Address change
F Check method of accounting: **(1)** ☐ Cash **(2)** ☑ Accrual **(3)** ☐ Other (specify) ▶

Income

1a	Gross receipts or sales 248,000 **b** Less returns and allowances 7,500 **c** Balance ▶	**1c**	240,500
2	Cost of goods sold (see page 14 of instructions).	**2**	144,000
3	Gross profit. Subtract line 2 from line 1c	**3**	96,500
4	Domestic corporation dividends subject to the 70% deduction . . .	**4**	
5	Interest	**5**	
6	Gross rents	**6**	
7	Gross royalties	**7**	
8	Capital gain net income (attach Schedule D (Form 1120))	**8**	
9	Net gain or (loss) from Form 4797, Part II, line 18 (attach Form 4797)	**9**	
10	Other income (see page 9 of instructions).	**10**	
11	**Total income.** Add lines 3 through 10 . . . . ▶	**11**	97,442

Deductions
(See instructions for limitations on deductions.)

12	Compensation of officers (see page 10 of instructions).	**12**	23,000
13	Salaries and wages (less employment credits)	**13**	24,320
14	Repairs and maintenance	**14**	
15	Bad debts	**15**	
16	Rents	**16**	6,000
17	Taxes and licenses	**17**	3,320
18	Interest	**18**	1,340
19	Charitable contributions (see page 11 of instructions for 10% limitation) . .	**19**	1,820
20	Depreciation (attach Form 4562) **20**		
21	Less depreciation claimed elsewhere on return **21a**	**21b**	
22	Other deductions (attach schedule) . . . . . Advertising	**22**	3,000
23	**Total deductions.** Add lines 12 through 22 . . . . ▶	**23**	62,800
24	Taxable income before net operating loss deduction and special deductions. Subtract line 23 from line 11	**24**	34,642
25	Less: **a** Net operating loss deduction (see page 13 of instructions) **25a**		
	b Special deductions (see page 13 of instructions) **25b**	**25c**	

Tax and Payments

26	**Taxable income.** Subtract line 25c from line 24	**26**	34,642
27	**Total tax** (from page 2, Part I, line 6)	**27**	5,196
28	**Payments:**		
	a 2001 overpayment credited to 2002 **28a**		
	b 2002 estimated tax payments . **28b** 6,000		
	c Less 2002 refund applied for on Form 4466 **28c** ( ) Bal ▶ **28d** 6,000		
	e Tax deposited with Form 7004 . . . . . . **28e**		
	f Credit for tax paid on undistributed capital gains (attach Form 2439) **28f**		
	g Credit for Federal tax on fuels (attach Form 4136). See instructions . **28g**		
	h **Total payments.** Add lines 28d through 28g	**28h**	6,000
29	Estimated tax penalty (see page 14 of instructions). Check if Form 2220 is attached . . . ▶ ☐	**29**	
30	**Tax due.** If line 28h is smaller than the total of lines 27 and 29, enter amount owed	**30**	
31	**Overpayment.** If line 28h is larger than the total of lines 27 and 29, enter amount overpaid . . .	**31**	804
32	Enter amount of line 31 you want: **Credited to 2003 estimated tax** ▶	Refunded ▶ **32**	

Sign Here

Under penalties of perjury, I declare that I have examined this return, including accompanying schedules and statements, and to the best of my knowledge and belief, it is true, correct, and complete. Declaration of preparer (other than taxpayer) is based on all information of which preparer has any knowledge.

▶ *George Rose* | 2-15-XX | ▶ *President*
Signature of officer | Date | Title

May the IRS discuss this return with the preparer shown below (see instructions)? ☐ Yes ☐ No

Paid Preparer's Use Only

Preparer's signature ▶		Date	Check if self-employed ☐	Preparer's SSN or PTIN
Firm's name (or yours if self-employed), address, and ZIP code ▶		EIN	
		Phone no. ( )	

For Paperwork Reduction Act Notice, see page 20 of the instructions.   Cat. No. 11456E   Form **1120-A** (2002)

Form 1120-A (2002)   **Page 2**

Part I   Tax Computation (see page 17 of instructions)

1 Income tax. If the corporation is a qualified personal service corporation (see page 17), check here ▶ ☐	**1**	5,196
2a General business credit. Check box(es) and indicate which forms are attached.		
☐ Form 3800 ☐ Form(s) (specify) ▶	**2a**	
b Credit for prior year minimum tax (attach Form 8827)	**2b**	
3 **Total credits.** Add lines 2a and 2b	**3**	
4 Subtract line 3 from line 1	**4**	5,196
5 Other taxes. Check if from: ☐ Form 4255 ☐ Form 8611 ☐ Form 8697 ☐ Form 8866		
☐ Other (attach schedule)	**5**	
6 **Total tax.** Add lines 4 and 5. Enter here and on line 27, page 1	**6**	5,196

Part II   Other Information (see page 19 of instructions)

1 See page 21 and enter the:

  a Business activity code no. ▶ 5995

  b Business activity ▶ .... Flower shop

  c Product or service ▶ .... Flowers

2 At the end of the tax year, did any individual, partnership, estate, or trust own, directly or indirectly, 50% or more of the corporation's voting stock? (For rules of attribution, see section 267(c).) . Schedule not shown . . . ☑ Yes ☐ No
If "Yes," attach a schedule showing name and identifying number.

3 Enter the amount of tax-exempt interest received or accrued during the tax year . . . . . ▶ |$ –0–

4 Enter total amount of cash distributions and the book value of property distributions (other than cash) made during the tax year . . . . ▶ |$ –0–

5a If an amount is entered on line 2, page 1, enter from worksheet on page 14 instr.:

(1) Purchases	134,014
(2) Additional 263A costs (attach schedule)	
(3) Other costs (attach schedule) .	9,986

  b If property is produced or acquired for resale, do the rules of section 263A apply to the corporation? . . . . . ☐ Yes ☑ No

6 At any time during the 2002 calendar year, did the corporation have an interest in or a signature or other authority over a financial account (such as a bank account, securities account, or other financial account) in a foreign country? ☐ Yes ☑ No
If "Yes," the corporation may have to file Form TD F 90-22.1.
If "Yes," enter the name of the foreign country ▶ ....

7 Are the corporation's total receipts (line 1a plus lines 4 through 10 on page 1) for the tax year **and** its total assets at the end of the tax year less than $250,000? . . . . ☑ Yes ☐ No
If "Yes," the corporation is **not** required to complete Parts III and IV below.

Part III   Balance Sheets per Books

		(a) Beginning of tax year		(b) End of tax year	
Assets	**1** Cash				
	2a Trade notes and accounts receivable				
	b Less allowance for bad debts	(	)	(	)
	3 Inventories				
	4 U.S. government obligations				
	5 Tax-exempt securities (see instructions)				
	6 Other current assets (attach schedule)				
	7 Loans to shareholders				
	8 Mortgage and real estate loans				
	9a Depreciable, depletable, and intangible assets				
	b Less accumulated depreciation, depletion, and amortization	(	)	(	)
	10 Land (net of any amortization)				
	11 Other assets (attach schedule)				
	12 Total assets				
Liabilities and Shareholders' Equity	**13** Accounts payable				
	14 Other current liabilities (attach schedule)				
	15 Loans from shareholders				
	16 Mortgages, notes, bonds payable				
	17 Other liabilities (attach schedule)				
	18 Capital stock (preferred and common stock) . . .				
	19 Additional paid-in capital				
	20 Retained earnings				
	21 Adjustments to shareholders' equity (attach schedule) .				
	22 Less cost of treasury stock	(	)	(	)
	23 Total liabilities and shareholders' equity				

Part IV   Reconciliation of Income (Loss) per Books With Income per Return

1 Net income (loss) per books		**6** Income recorded on books this year not included on this return (itemize)..................	
2 Federal income tax per books			
3 Excess of capital losses over capital gains. .		**7** Deductions on this return not charged against book income this year (itemize).................	
4 Income subject to tax not recorded on books this year (itemize)			
5 Expenses recorded on books this year not deducted on this return (itemize)		**8** Income (line 24, page 1). Enter the sum of lines 1 through 5 less the sum of lines 6 and 7	

Form **1120-A** (2002)

2002

Department of the Treasury
Internal Revenue Service

Instructions for Form 1120S

U.S. Income Tax Return for an S Corporation

Section references are to the Internal Revenue Code unless otherwise noted.

Changes To Note

- If the corporation's total receipts (defined on page 29) for the tax year **and** its total assets at the end of the tax year are less than $250,000, it is not required to complete Schedules L and M-1.
- Additional guidance has been issued allowing qualifying small businesses to adopt or change to the cash method of accounting. For details, see **Schedule A—Cost of Goods Sold** on page 17.
- For tax years ending on or after December 31, 2001, if the corporation must make a section 481(a) adjustment because of an accounting period change, the adjustment period for a negative adjustment is now 1 year. For details, including special rules and exceptions, see Rev. Proc. 2002-19, 2002-13 I.R.B. 696. Also see **Change in Accounting Method** on page 4.
- As a result of changes to the North American Industry Classification System, some of the codes for Principal Business Activities have changed beginning in 2002. These changes have mainly occurred in the Construction, Wholesale Trade, and Information sectors. See pages 29 through 31 for the new applicable codes that should be entered in item E of page 1 of Form 1120S.
- The corporation must file a disclosure statement for each reportable tax shelter transaction in which it participated,

directly or indirectly, if the transaction is reasonably expected to affect any shareholder's Federal income tax liability. See **Tax shelter disclosure statement** on page 7 for more details.

Photographs of Missing Children

The Internal Revenue Service is a proud partner with the National Center for Missing and Exploited Children. Photographs of missing children selected by the Center may appear in instructions on pages that would otherwise be blank. You can help bring these children home by looking at the photographs and calling **1-800-THE-LOST** (1-800-843-5678) if you recognize a child.

Unresolved Tax Issues

If the corporation has attempted to deal with an IRS problem unsuccessfully, it should contact the Taxpayer Advocate. The Taxpayer Advocate independently represents the corporation's interests and concerns within the IRS by protecting its rights and resolving problems that have not been fixed through normal channels.

While Taxpayer Advocates cannot change the tax law or make a technical tax decision, they can clear up problems that resulted from previous contacts and ensure that the corporation's case is given a complete and impartial review.

The corporation's assigned personal advocate will listen to its point of view and will work with the corporation to address its concerns. The corporation can expect the advocate to provide:
- A "fresh look" at a new or on-going problem.
- Timely acknowledgment.
- The name and phone number of the individual assigned to its case.
- Updates on progress.
- Timeframes for action.
- Speedy resolution.
- Courteous service.

When contacting the Taxpayer Advocate, the corporation should provide the following information:
- The corporation's name, address, and employer identification number (EIN).
- The name and telephone number of an authorized contact person and the hours he or she can be reached.
- The type of tax return and year(s) involved.
- A detailed description of the problem.
- Previous attempts to solve the problem and the office that had been contacted.
- A description of the hardship the corporation is facing (if applicable).

Cat. No. 11515K

The corporation may contact a Taxpayer Advocate by calling a toll-free number, **1-877-777-4778**. Persons who have access to TTY/TDD equipment may call 1-800-829-4059 and ask for Taxpayer Advocate assistance. If the corporation prefers, it may call, write, or fax the Taxpayer Advocate office in its area. See **Pub. 1546**, The Taxpayer Advocate Service of the IRS, for a list of addresses and fax numbers.

How To Make a Contribution To Reduce the Public Debt

To make a contribution to reduce the public debt, send a check made payable to the "Bureau of the Public Debt" to Bureau of the Public Debt, Department G, P.O. Box 2188, Parkersburg, WV 26106-2188. Or, enclose a check with Form 1120S. Contributions to reduce the public debt are deductible, subject to the rules and limitations for charitable contributions.

How To Get Forms and Publications

Personal computer. You can access the IRS Web Site 24 hours a day, 7 days a week at **www.irs.gov** to:

- Order IRS products on-line.
- Download forms, instructions, and publications.
- See answers to frequently asked tax questions.
- Search publications on-line by topic or keyword.
- Send us comments or request help by e-mail.
- Sign up to receive local and national tax news by e-mail.

You can also reach us using file transfer protocol at **ftp.irs.gov**.

CD-ROM. Order **Pub. 1796**, Federal Tax Products on CD-ROM, and get:

- Current year forms, instructions, and publications.
- Prior year forms, instructions, and publications.
- Frequently requested tax forms that may be filled in electronically, printed out for submission, and saved for recordkeeping.
- The Internal Revenue Bulletin.

Buy the CD-ROM on the Internet at **www.irs.gov/cdorders** from the National Technical Information Service (NTIS) for $22 (no handling fee) or call **1-877-CDFORMS** (1-877-233-6767) toll free to buy the CD-ROM for $22 (plus a $5 handling fee).

By phone and in person. You can order forms and publications 24 hours a day, 7 days a week, by calling **1-800-TAX-FORM** (1-800-829-3676). You can also get most forms and publications at your local IRS office.

General Instructions

Purpose of Form

Form 1120S is used to report the income, deductions, gains, losses, etc., of a domestic corporation that has elected to be an S corporation by filing **Form 2553**, Election by a Small Business Corporation, and whose election is in effect for the tax year.

Who Must File

A corporation must file Form 1120S if **(a)** it elected to be an S corporation by filing Form 2553, **(b)** the IRS accepted the election, and **(c)** the election remains in effect. **Do not** file Form 1120S for any tax year before the year the election takes effect.

Termination of Election

Once the election is made, it stays in effect until it is terminated. If the election is terminated in a tax year beginning after 1996, the corporation (or a successor corporation) can make another election on Form 2553 only with IRS consent for any tax year before the 5th tax year after the first tax year in which the termination took effect. See Regulations section 1.1362-5 for more details.

An election terminates **automatically** in any of the following cases:

1. The corporation is no longer a small business corporation as defined in section 1361(b). The termination of an election in this manner is effective as of the day on which the corporation no longer meets the definition of a small business corporation. If the election terminates for this reason, attach to Form 1120S for the final year of the S corporation a statement notifying the IRS of the termination and the date it occurred.

2. The corporation, for each of three consecutive tax years, **(a)** has accumulated earnings and profits and **(b)** derives more than 25% of its gross receipts from passive investment income as defined in section 1362(d)(3)(C). The election terminates on the first day of the first tax year beginning after the third consecutive tax year. The corporation must pay a tax for each year it has excess net passive income. See the instructions for line 22a for details on how to figure the tax.

3. The election is revoked. An election may be revoked only with the consent of shareholders who, at the time the revocation is made, hold more than 50% of the number of issued and outstanding shares of stock (including non-voting stock). The revocation may specify an effective revocation date that is on or after the day the revocation is filed. If no date is specified, the revocation is effective at the start of a tax year if the revocation is made on or before the 15th day of the 3rd month of that tax year. If no date is specified and the revocation is made after the 15th day of the 3rd month of the tax year, the revocation is effective at the start of the next tax year.

To revoke the election, the corporation must file a statement with the service center where it filed its election to be an S corporation. In the statement, the corporation must notify the IRS that it is revoking its election to be an S corporation. The statement must be signed by each shareholder who consents to the revocation and contain the information required by Regulations section 1.1362-6(a)(3). A revocation may be rescinded before it takes effect. See Regulations section 1.1362-6(a)(4) for details.

For rules on allocating income and deductions between an S short year and a C short year and other special rules that apply when an election is terminated, see section 1362(e) and Regulations section 1.1362-3.

If an election was terminated under **1** or **2** above, and the corporation believes the termination was inadvertent, the corporation may request permission from the IRS to continue to be treated as an S corporation. See Regulations section 1.1362-4 for the specific requirements that must be met to qualify for inadvertent termination relief.

When To File

In general, file Form 1120S by the 15th day of the 3rd month following the date the corporation's tax year ended as shown at the top of Form 1120S. For calendar year corporations, the due date is March 17, 2003. If the due date falls on a Saturday, Sunday, or legal holiday, file on the next business day. A business day is any day that is not a Saturday, Sunday, or legal holiday.

If the S election was terminated during the tax year, file Form 1120S for the S short year by the due date (including extensions) of the C short year return.

Private Delivery Services

In addition to the United States mail, the corporation can use certain private delivery services designated by the IRS to meet the "timely mailing as timely filing/paying" rule for tax returns and payments. The most recent list of designated private delivery services was published by the IRS in September 2002. The list includes only the following:

- Airborne Express (Airborne): Overnight Air Express Service, Next Afternoon Service, Second Day Service.
- DHL Worldwide Express (DHL): DHL "Same Day" Service, DHL USA Overnight.
- Federal Express (FedEx): FedEx Priority Overnight, FedEx Standard Overnight, FedEx 2Day, FedEx International Priority, FedEx International First.
- United Parcel Service (UPS): UPS Next Day Air, UPS Next Day Air Saver, UPS 2nd Day Air, UPS 2nd Day Air A.M., UPS Worldwide Express Plus, UPS Worldwide Express.

The private delivery service can tell you how to get written proof of the mailing date.

-2-

Instructions for Form 1120S

Where To File

File your return at the applicable IRS address listed below.

If the corporation's principal business, office, or agency is located in:	And the total assets at the end of the tax year (Form 1120S, page 1, item E) are:	Use the following Internal Revenue Service Center address:
Connecticut, Delaware, District of Columbia, Illinois, Indiana, Kentucky, Maine, Maryland, Massachusetts, Michigan, New Hampshire, New Jersey, New York, North Carolina, Ohio, Pennsylvania, Rhode Island, South Carolina, Vermont, Virginia, West Virginia, Wisconsin	Less than $10 million	Cincinnati, OH 45999-0013
	$10 million or more	Ogden, UT 84201-0013
Alabama, Alaska, Arizona, Arkansas, California, Colorado, Florida, Georgia, Hawaii, Idaho, Iowa, Kansas, Louisiana, Minnesota, Mississippi, Missouri, Montana, Nebraska, Nevada, New Mexico, North Dakota, Oklahoma, Oregon, South Dakota, Tennessee, Texas, Utah, Washington, Wyoming	Any amount	Ogden, UT 84201-0013
A foreign country or U.S. possession	Any amount	Philadelphia, PA 19255-0013

Extension

Use **Form 7004,** Application for Automatic Extension of Time To File Corporation Income Tax Return, to request an automatic 6-month extension of time to file Form 1120S.

Period Covered

File the 2002 return for calendar year 2002 and fiscal years beginning in 2002 and ending in 2003. If the return is for a fiscal year or a short tax year, fill in the tax year space at the top of the form.

Note: *The 2002 Form 1120S may also be used if (a) the corporation has a tax year of less than 12 months that begins and ends in 2003 and (b) the 2003 Form 1120S is not available by the time the corporation is required to file its return. However, the corporation must show its 2003 tax year on the 2002 Form 1120S and incorporate any tax law changes that are effective for tax years beginning after December 31, 2002.*

Who Must Sign

The return must be signed and dated by the president, vice president, treasurer, assistant treasurer, chief accounting officer, or any other corporate officer (such as tax officer) authorized to sign. A receiver, trustee, or assignee must sign and date any return he or she is required to file on behalf of a corporation.

If an officer or employee of the corporation completes Form 1120S, the paid preparer's space should remain blank. In addition, anyone who prepares Form 1120S, but does not charge the corporation, should not complete that section. Generally, anyone who is paid to prepare the return must sign it and fill in the "Paid Preparer's Use Only" area.

The paid preparer **must** complete the required preparer information and:
• Sign it, by hand, in the space provided for the preparer's signature (signature stamps or labels are not acceptable).
• Give a copy of the return to the taxpayer.

Paid Preparer Authorization

If the corporation wants to allow the IRS to discuss its 2002 tax return with the paid preparer who signed it, check the "Yes" box in the signature area of the return. This authorization applies only to the individual whose signature appears in the "Paid Preparer's Use Only" section of the return. It does not apply to the firm, if any, shown in that section.

If the "Yes" box is checked, the corporation is authorizing the IRS to call the paid preparer to answer any questions that may arise during the processing of its return. The corporation is also authorizing the paid preparer to:
• Give the IRS any information that is missing from its return,
• Call the IRS for information about the processing of its return or the status of its refund or payment(s), and
• Respond to certain IRS notices that the corporation has shared with the preparer about math errors, offsets, and return preparation. The notices will not be sent to the preparer.

The corporation is not authorizing the paid preparer to receive any refund check, bind the corporation to anything (including any additional tax liability), or otherwise represent the corporation before the IRS. If the corporation wants to expand the paid preparer's authorization, see **Pub. 947,** Practice Before the IRS and Power of Attorney.

The authorization cannot be revoked. However, the authorization will automatically end no later than the due date (excluding extensions) for filing the 2002 tax return.

Accounting Methods

Figure ordinary income using the method of accounting regularly used in keeping the corporation's books and records. Generally, permissible methods include:
• Cash,
• Accrual, or
• Any other method authorized by the Internal Revenue Code.

In all cases, the method used must clearly reflect income. Unless the corporation is a qualifying taxpayer, it must use the accrual method for sales and purchases of inventory items. See **Schedule A—Cost of Goods Sold** on page 17 for details.

Generally, an S corporation may not use the cash method of accounting if the corporation is a tax shelter (as defined in section 448(d)(3)). See section 448 for details.

Under the accrual method, an amount is includible in income when:
• All the events have occurred that fix the right to receive the income, which is the earliest of the date (a) the required performance takes place, (b) payment is due, or (c) payment is received, and
• The amount can be determined with reasonable accuracy.

See Regulations section 1.451-1(a) for details.

Generally, an accrual basis taxpayer can deduct accrued expenses in the tax year in which:
• All events that determine liability have occurred,
• The amount of the liability can be figured with reasonable accuracy, and
• Economic performance takes place with respect to the expense. There are exceptions for certain items, including recurring expenses. See section 461(h) and the related regulations for the rules for determining when economic performance takes place.

Except for certain home construction contracts and other real property small construction contracts, long-term contracts must generally be accounted for using the percentage of completion method. For rules on long-term contracts, see section 460 and the underlying regulations.

Mark-to-Market Accounting Method

Dealers in securities must use the "mark-to-market" accounting method described in section 475. Under this method, any security that is inventory to the dealer must be included in inventory at its fair market value. Any security that is not inventory and that is held at the close of the tax year is treated as sold at its fair market value on the last business day of the tax year, and any gain or loss must be taken into account in determining gross income. The gain or loss taken into account is generally treated as ordinary gain or loss. For details, including

Instructions for Form 1120S -3-

exceptions, see section 475 and the related regulations.

Dealers in commodities and traders in securities and commodities may elect to use the mark-to-market accounting method. To make the election, the corporation must file a statement describing the election, the first tax year the election is to be effective, and, in the case of an election for traders in securities or commodities, the trade or business for which the election is made. Except for new taxpayers, the statement must be filed by the due date (not including extensions) of the income tax return for the tax year immediately **preceding** the election year and attached to that return, or, if applicable, to a request for an extension of time to file that return. For more details, see Rev. Proc. 99-17, 1999-1 C.B. 503, and sections 475(e) and (f).

Change in Accounting Method

Generally, the corporation must get IRS consent to change its method of accounting used to report taxable income (for income as a whole or for any material item). To do so, it must file **Form 3115,** Application for Change in Accounting Method. For more information, see **Pub. 538,** Accounting Periods and Methods. However, there are new procedures under which a corporation may obtain automatic consent to certain changes in accounting method. See Rev. Proc. 2002-9, 2002-3 I.R.B. 327, as modified by Rev. Proc. 2002-19 and Rev. Proc. 2002-54, 2002-35 I.R.B. 432.

Certain qualifying taxpayers or qualifying small business taxpayers (described on page 17) that want to use the cash method for an eligible trade or business may get an automatic consent to change their method of accounting. For details, see Rev. Proc. 2001-10, 2001-2 I.R.B. 272, Rev. Proc. 2002-28, 2002-18 I.R.B. 815, and Form 3115.

Section 481(a) adjustment. In changing its method of accounting, the corporation may also have to make an adjustment to prevent amounts of income or expense from being duplicated or omitted. This is called a section 481(a) adjustment, which is taken into account over a period of 4 tax years for a net positive adjustment and 1 tax year for a net negative adjustment. The corporation may elect to use a one year adjustment period for positive adjustments if the net section 481(a) adjustment for the change is less than $25,000. For more details on the section 481(a) adjustment, see Rev. Proc. 2002-19 and 2002-54. Include any net positive section 481(a) adjustment on page 1, line 5. If the net section 481(a) adjustment is negative, report it on page 1, line 19.

Accounting Periods

Generally, an S corporation may not change its accounting period to a tax year that is not a permitted year. A "permitted year" is a calendar year or any other accounting period for which the corporation can establish to the satisfaction of the IRS that there is a business purpose for the tax year.

To change an accounting period, see Rev. Proc. 2002-38, 2002-22 I.R.B. 1037, and **Form 1128,** Application To Adopt, Change, or Retain a Tax Year. Also see Pub. 538.

Election of a Tax Year Other Than a Required Year

Under the provisions of section 444, an S corporation may elect to have a tax year other than a permitted year, but only if the deferral period of the tax year is not longer than the shorter of 3 months or the deferral period of the tax year being changed. This election is made by filing **Form 8716,** Election To Have a Tax Year Other Than a Required Tax Year.

An S corporation may not make or continue an election under section 444 if it is a member of a tiered structure, other than a tiered structure that consists entirely of partnerships and S corporations that have the same tax year. For the S corporation to have a section 444 election in effect, it must make the payments required by section 7519 and file **Form 8752,** Required Payment or Refund Under Section 7519.

A section 444 election ends if an S corporation changes its accounting period to a calendar year or some other permitted year; it is penalized for willfully failing to comply with the requirements of section 7519; or its S election is terminated (unless it immediately becomes a personal service corporation). If the termination results in a short tax year, type or legibly print at the top of the first page of Form 1120S for the short tax year, "SECTION 444 ELECTION TERMINATED."

Rounding Off to Whole Dollars

You may round off cents to whole dollars on your return and accompanying schedules. To do so, drop amounts under 50 cents and increase amounts from 50 to 99 cents to the next higher dollar.

Recordkeeping

The corporation's records must be kept as long as they may be needed for the administration of any provision of the Internal Revenue Code. Usually, records that support an item of income, deduction, or credit on the corporation's return must be kept for 3 years from the date each shareholder's return is due or is filed, whichever is later. Keep records that verify the corporation's basis in property for as long as they are needed to figure the basis of the original or replacement property.

The corporation should also keep copies of any returns it has filed. They help in preparing future returns and in making computations when filing an amended return.

Depository Method of Tax Payment

The corporation must pay the tax due in full no later than the 15th day of the 3rd month after the end of the tax year. The

two methods of depositing corporate income taxes are discussed below.

Electronic Deposit Requirement

The corporation must make electronic deposits of **all** depository taxes (such as employment tax, excise tax, and corporate income tax) using the Electronic Federal Tax Payment System (EFTPS) in 2003 if:
• The total deposits of such taxes in 2001 were more than $200,000 or
• The corporation was required to use EFTPS in 2002.

If the corporation is required to use EFTPS and fails to do so, it may be subject to a 10% penalty. If the corporation is not required to use EFTPS, it may participate voluntarily. To enroll in or get more information about EFTPS, call 1-800-555-4477 or 1-800-945-8400. To enrol online, visit **www.eftps.gov.**

Depositing on time. For EFTPS deposits to be made timely, the corporation must initiate the transaction at least 1 business day before the date the deposit is due.

Deposits With Form 8109

If the corporation does not use EFTPS, deposit corporation income tax payments (and estimated tax payments) with **Form 8109,** Federal Tax Deposit Coupon. If you do not have a preprinted Form 8109, use Form 8109-B to make deposits. You can get this form **only** by calling 1-800-829-4933. Be sure to have your employer identification number (EIN) ready when you call.

Do not send deposits directly to an IRS office; otherwise, the corporation may have to pay a penalty. Mail or deliver the completed Form 8109 with the payment to an authorized depositary, i.e., a commercial bank or other financial institution authorized to accept Federal tax deposits.

Make checks or money orders payable to the depositary. To help ensure proper crediting, write the corporation's EIN, the tax period to which the deposit applies, and "Form 1120S" on the check or money order. Be sure to darken the "1120" box on the coupon. Records of these deposits will be sent to the IRS.

If the corporation prefers, it may mail the coupon and payment to: Financial Agent, Federal Tax Deposit Processing, P.O. Box 970030, St. Louis, MO 63197. Make the check or money order payable to "Financial Agent."

For more information on deposits, see the instructions in the coupon booklet (Form 8109) and **Pub. 583,** Starting a Business and Keeping Records.

Estimated Tax

Generally, the corporation must make estimated tax payments for the following taxes if the total of these taxes is $500 or more: **(a)** the tax on built-in gains, **(b)** the excess net passive income tax, and **(c)** the investment credit recapture tax.

The amount of estimated tax required to be paid annually is the smaller of **(a)** the total of the above taxes shown on the return for the tax year (or if no return is filed, the total of these taxes for the year)

-4-

Instructions for Form 1120S

or **(b)** the sum of *(i)* the investment credit recapture tax and the built-in gains tax shown on the return for the tax year (or if no return is filed, the total of these taxes for the year), and *(ii)* any excess net passive income tax shown on the corporation's return for the preceding tax year. If the preceding tax year was less than 12 months, the estimated tax must be determined under **(a).**

The estimated tax is generally payable in four equal installments. However, the corporation may be able to lower the amount of one or more installments by using the annualized income installment method or adjusted seasonal installment method under section 6655(e).

For a calendar year corporation, the payments are due for 2003 by April 15, June 16, September 15, and December 15. For a fiscal year corporation, they are due by the 15th day of the 4th, 6th, 9th, and 12th months of the fiscal year.

The corporation must make the payments using the depository method described on page 4.

Interest and Penalties

Interest
Interest is charged on taxes not paid by the due date, even if an extension of time to file is granted. Interest is also charged from the due date (including extensions) to the date of payment on the failure to file penalty, the accuracy-related penalty, and the fraud penalty. The interest charge is figured at a rate determined under section 6621.

Late Filing of Return
A corporation that does not file its tax return by the due date, including extensions, may have to pay a penalty of 5% a month, or part of a month, up to a maximum of 25%, for each month the return is not filed. The penalty is imposed on the net amount due. The minimum penalty for filing a return more than 60 days late is the smaller of the tax due or $100. The penalty will not be imposed if the corporation can show that the failure to file on time was due to reasonable cause. If the failure is due to reasonable cause, attach an explanation to the return.

Late Payment of Tax
A corporation that does not pay the tax when due generally may have to pay a penalty of ½ of 1% a month or part of a month, up to a maximum of 25%, for each month the tax is not paid. The penalty is imposed on the net amount due.

The penalty will not be imposed if the corporation can show that failure to pay on time was due to reasonable cause.

Failure To Furnish Information Timely
Section 6037(b) requires an S corporation to furnish to each shareholder a copy of the information shown on Schedule K-1 (Form 1120S) that is attached to Form 1120S. Provide Schedule K-1 to each shareholder on or before the day on which the corporation files Form 1120S.

For each failure to furnish Schedule K-1 to a shareholder when due and each failure to include on Schedule K-1 all the information required to be shown (or the inclusion of incorrect information), a $50 penalty may be imposed with regard to each Schedule K-1 for which a failure occurs. If the requirement to report correct information is intentionally disregarded, each $50 penalty is increased to $100 or, if greater, 10% of the aggregate amount of items required to be reported. See sections 6722 and 6724 for more information.

The penalty will not be imposed if the corporation can show that not furnishing information timely was due to reasonable cause and not due to willful neglect.

Trust Fund Recovery Penalty
This penalty may apply if certain excise, income, social security, and Medicare taxes that must be collected or withheld are not collected or withheld, or these taxes are not paid to the IRS. These taxes are generally reported on Forms 720, 941, 943, or 945. The trust fund recovery penalty may be imposed on all persons who are determined by the IRS to have been **responsible** for collecting, accounting for, and paying over these taxes, and who acted willfully in not doing so. The penalty is equal to the unpaid trust fund tax. See the instructions for Form 720, **Pub. 15 (Circular E)**, Employer's Tax Guide, or **Pub. 51 (Circular A)**, Agricultural Employer's Tax Guide, for more details, including the definition of responsible persons.

Other Forms, Returns, and Statements That May Be Required
● **Schedule N** (Form 1120), Foreign Operations of U.S. Corporations. The corporation may have to file this schedule if it had assets in or operated a business in a foreign country or a U.S. possession.
● **Forms W-2** and **W-3**, Wage and Tax Statement; and Transmittal of Wage and Tax Statements. Use these forms to report wages, tips, other compensation, withheld income taxes, and withheld social security/Medicare taxes for employees.
● **Form 720**, Quarterly Federal Excise Tax Return. Use Form 720 to report environmental taxes, communications and air transportation taxes, fuel taxes, luxury tax on passenger vehicles, manufacturers taxes, ship passenger tax, and certain other excise taxes.

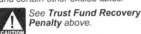 *See **Trust Fund Recovery Penalty** above.*

● **Form 926**, Return by a U.S. Transferor of Property to a Foreign Corporation. Use this form to report certain information required under section 6038B.
● **Form 940** or **Form 940-EZ**, Employer's Annual Federal Unemployment (FUTA) Tax Return. The corporation may be liable for FUTA tax and may have to file Form 940 or 940-EZ if it paid wages of $1,500 or more in any calendar quarter during the calendar year (or the preceding calendar year) or one or more employees

worked for the corporation for some part of a day in any 20 different weeks during the calendar year (or the preceding calendar year). A corporate officer who performs substantial services is considered an employee. Except as provided in section 3306(a), reasonable compensation for these services is subject to FUTA tax, no matter what the corporation calls the payments.
● **Form 941**, Employer's Quarterly Federal Tax Return. Employers must file this form quarterly to report income tax withheld on wages and employer and employee social security and Medicare taxes. A corporate officer who performs substantial services is considered an employee. Except as provided in sections 3121(a) and 3401(a), reasonable compensation for these services is subject to employer and employee social security and Medicare taxes and income tax withholding, no matter what the corporation calls the payments. Agricultural employers must file **Form 943**, Employer's Annual Tax Return for Agricultural Employees, instead of Form 941, to report income tax withheld and employer and employee social security and Medicare taxes on farmworkers.
● **Form 945**, Annual Return of Withheld Federal Income Tax. Use this form to report income tax withheld from nonpayroll payments, including pensions, annuities, IRAs, gambling winnings, and backup withholding.

 *See **Trust Fund Recovery Penalty** above.*

● **Form 966**, Corporate Dissolution or Liquidation.
● **Forms 1042** and **1042-S**, Annual Withholding Tax Return for U.S. Source Income of Foreign Persons; and Foreign Person's U.S. Source Income Subject to Withholding. Use these forms to report and transmit withheld tax on payments made to nonresident alien individuals, foreign partnerships, or foreign corporations to the extent such payments constitute gross income from sources within the United States (see sections 861 through 865). For more information, see sections 1441 and 1442, and **Pub. 515**, Withholding of Tax on Nonresident Aliens and Foreign Entities.
● **Form 1042-T**, Annual Summary and Transmittal of Forms 1042-S. Use Form 1042-T to transmit paper Forms 1042-S to the IRS.
● **Form 1096**, Annual Summary and Transmittal of U.S. Information Returns.
● **Form 1098**, Mortgage Interest Statement. Use this form to report the receipt from any individual of $600 or more of mortgage interest (including points) in the course of the corporation's trade or business.
● **Forms 1099-A, B, C, DIV, INT, LTC, MISC, MSA, OID, PATR, R,** and **S.** You may have to file these information returns to report acquisitions or abandonments of secured property; proceeds from broker and barter exchange transactions; cancellation of debt; certain dividends and distributions; interest payments; payments of long-term care and accelerated death benefits; miscellaneous

income payments; distributions from an Archer MSA or Medicare+Choice MSA; original issue discount; distributions from cooperatives to their patrons; distributions from pensions, annuities, retirement or profit-sharing plans, IRAs, insurance contracts, etc.; and proceeds from real estate transactions. Also use certain of these returns to report amounts that were received as a nominee on behalf of another person.

Use Form 1099-DIV to report actual dividends paid by the corporation. Only distributions from accumulated earnings and profits are classified as dividends. **Do not** issue Form 1099-DIV for dividends received by the corporation that are allocated to shareholders on line 4b of Schedule K-1.

For more information, see the Instructions for Forms 1099, 1098, 5498, and W-2G.

Note: *Every corporation must file Forms 1099-MISC if it makes payments of rents, commissions, or other fixed or determinable income (see section 6041) totaling $600 or more to any one person in the course of its trade or business during the calendar year.*

● **Form 3520,** Annual Return to Report Transactions With Foreign Trust and Receipt of Certain Foreign Gifts. The corporation may have to file this form if it:

1. Directly or indirectly transferred property or money to a foreign trust. For this purpose, any U.S. person who created a foreign trust is considered a transferor.

2. Is treated as the owner of any part of the assets of a foreign trust under the grantor trust rules.

3. Received a distribution from a foreign trust.

For more information, see the Instructions for Form 3520.

Note: *An owner of a foreign trust must ensure that the trust files an annual information return on* **Form 3520-A,** *Annual Information Return of Foreign Trust With a U.S. Owner.*

● **Form 5471,** Information Return of U.S. Persons With Respect to Certain Foreign Corporations. A corporation may have to file Form 5471 if any of the following apply:

1. It controls a foreign corporation.

2. It acquires, disposes of, or owns 5% or more in value of the outstanding stock of a foreign corporation.

3. It owns stock in a corporation that is a controlled foreign corporation for an uninterrupted period of 30 days or more during any tax year of the foreign corporation, and it owned that stock on the last day of that year.

● **Form 5713,** International Boycott Report. Every corporation that had operations in, or related to, a "boycotting" country, company, or national of a country must file Form 5713 to report those operations and figure the loss of certain tax benefits.

● **Form 8023,** Elections Under Section 338 for Corporations Making Qualified Stock Purchases. Corporations file this form to make elections under section 338 for a target corporation if the purchasing

corporation has made a qualified stock purchase.

● **Form 8264,** Application for Registration of a Tax Shelter. Tax shelter organizers must file Form 8264 to register tax shelters with the IRS for the purpose of receiving a tax shelter registration number.

● **Form 8271,** Investor Reporting of Tax Shelter Registration Number. Corporations that have acquired an interest in a tax shelter that is required to be registered use Form 8271 to report the tax shelter's registration number. Attach Form 8271 to any return on which a deduction, credit, loss, or other tax benefit attributable to a tax shelter is taken or any income attributable to a tax shelter is reported.

● **Form 8275,** Disclosure Statement. File Form 8275 to disclose items or positions, except those contrary to a regulation, that are not otherwise adequately disclosed on a tax return. The disclosure is made to avoid the parts of the accuracy-related penalty imposed for disregard of rules or substantial understatement of tax. Form 8275 is also used for disclosures relating to preparer penalties for understatements due to unrealistic positions or disregard of rules.

● **Form 8275-R,** Regulation Disclosure Statement, is used to disclose any item on a tax return for which a position has been taken that is contrary to Treasury regulations.

● **Form 8281,** Information Return for Publicly Offered Original Issue Discount Instruments. This form is used by issuers of publicly offered debt instruments having OID to provide the information required by section 1275(c).

● **Forms 8288** and **8288-A,** U.S. Withholding Tax Return for Dispositions by Foreign Persons of U.S. Real Property Interests; and Statement of Withholding on Dispositions by Foreign Persons of U.S. Real Property Interests. Use these forms to report and transmit withheld tax on the sale of U.S. real property by a foreign person. See section 1445 and the related regulations for additional information.

● **Form 8300,** Report of Cash Payments Over $10,000 Received in a Trade or Business. File this form to report the receipt of more than $10,000 in cash or foreign currency in one transaction (or a series of related transactions).

● **Form 8594,** Asset Acquisition Statement Under Section 1060. Corporations file this form to report the purchase or sale of a group of assets that constitute a trade or business if goodwill or going concern value could attach to the assets and if the buyer's basis is determined only by the amount paid for the assets.

● **Form 8697,** Interest Computation Under the Look-Back Method for Completed Long-Term Contracts. Certain S corporations that are not closely held may have to file Form 8697. Form 8697 is used to figure the interest due or to be refunded under the look-back method of section 460(b)(2) on certain long-term contracts that are accounted for under either the percentage of completion-capitalized cost method or the

percentage of completion method. Closely held corporations should see the instructions on page 25 for line 23, item 10, of Schedule K-1 for details on the Form 8697 information they must provide to their shareholders.

● **Form 8865,** Return of U.S. Person With Respect To Certain Foreign Partnerships. A corporation may have to file Form 8865 if it:

1. Controlled a foreign partnership (i.e., owned more than a 50% direct or indirect interest in the partnership).

2. Owned at least a 10% direct or indirect interest in a foreign partnership while U.S. persons controlled that partnership.

3. Had an acquisition, disposition, or change in proportional interest of a foreign partnership that:

a. Increased its direct interest to at least 10% or reduced its direct interest of at least 10% to less than 10%.

b. Changed its direct interest by at least a 10% interest.

4. Contributed property to a foreign partnership in exchange for a partnership interest if:

a. Immediately after the contribution, the corporation owned, directly or indirectly, at least a 10% interest in the foreign partnership; or

b. The fair market value of the property the corporation contributed to the foreign partnership in exchange for a partnership interest, when added to other contributions of property made to the foreign partnership during the preceding 12-month period, exceeds $100,000.

Also, the corporation may have to file Form 8865 to report certain dispositions by a foreign partnership of property it previously contributed to that foreign partnership if it was a partner at the time of the disposition.

For more details, including penalties for failing to file Form 8865, see Form 8865 and its separate instructions.

● **Form 8866,** Interest Computation Under the Look-Back Method for Property Depreciated Under the Income Forecast Method. Certain S corporations that are not closely held may have to file Form 8866. Form 8866 is used to figure the interest due or to be refunded under the look-back method of section 167(g)(2) for certain property placed in service after September 13, 1995, and depreciated under the income forecast method. Closely held corporations should see the instructions on page 26 for line 23, item 18, of Schedule K-1 for details on the Form 8866 information they must provide to their shareholders.

● **Form 8873,** Extraterritorial Income Exclusion. Use this form to report the amount of extraterritorial income excluded from the corporation's gross income for the tax year.

● **Form 8876,** Excise Tax on Structured Settlement Factoring Transactions. Use Form 8876 to report and pay the 40% excise tax imposed under section 5891.

● **Form 8883,** Asset Allocation Statement Under Section 338. Corporations use this form to report information about transactions involving a deemed sale of assets under section 338.

Instructions for Form 1120S

Statements

Tax shelter disclosure statement. For each reportable tax shelter transaction entered into **prior to January 1, 2003**, in which the corporation participated, directly or indirectly, it must attach a disclosure statement to its return for each tax year ending with or within the tax year of any shareholder whose Federal income tax liability is affected or reasonably expected to be affected by the corporation's participation in the transaction. In addition, for the first tax year a disclosure statement is attached to its return, the corporation must send a copy of the statement to the Internal Revenue Service, LM:PFTG:OTSA, Large & Mid-Size Business Division, 1111 Constitution Ave., N.W., Washington, DC 20224. If a transaction becomes a reportable transaction after the corporation files its return, it must attach the statement to the following year's return (whether or not any shareholder's tax liability is affected for that year). The corporation is considered to have indirectly participated if it participated as a partner in a partnership or if it knows or has reason to know that the tax benefits claimed were derived from a reportable transaction.

Disclosure is required for a reportable transaction that is a listed transaction. A transaction is a listed transaction if it is the same as or substantially similar to a transaction that the IRS has determined to be a tax avoidance transaction and has identified as a listed transaction by notice, regulation, or other published guidance. See Notice 2001-51, 2001-34 I.R.B. 190, for transactions identified by the IRS as listed transactions. The listed transactions identified in this notice will be updated in future published guidance.

See Temporary Regulations section 1.6011-4T for more details, including:

1. Definitions of reportable transaction, listed transaction, and substantially similar.

2. Form and content of the disclosure statement.

3. Filing requirements for the disclosure statement.

For reportable transactions entered into **after December 31, 2002**, use **Form 8886,** Reportable Transaction Disclosure Statement, to disclose information for each reportable transaction in which the corporation participated, directly or indirectly. Form 8886 must be filed for each tax year ending with or within the tax year of any shareholder whose Federal income tax liability is affected or reasonably expected to be affected by the corporation's participation in the transaction. The following are reportable transactions. Any transaction:

• The same as or substantially similar to tax avoidance transactions identified by the IRS.

• Offered under conditions of confidentiality.

• For which the corporation has contractual protection against disallowance of the tax benefits.

Instructions for Form 1120S

• Resulting in a loss of at least $5 million in any single year or $10 million in any combination of years.

• Resulting in a book-tax difference of more than $10 million on a gross basis.

• Resulting in a tax credit of more than $250,000, if the corporation held the asset generating the credit for less than 45 days.

See the Instructions for Form 8886 for more details.

Stock ownership in foreign corporations. If the corporation owned at least 5% in value of the outstanding stock of a foreign personal holding company, and the corporation was required to include in its gross income any undistributed foreign personal holding company income, attach the statement required by section 551(c).

Transfers to a corporation controlled by the transferor. If a person receives stock of a corporation in exchange for property, and no gain or loss is recognized under section 351, the transferor and transferee must each attach to their tax returns the information required by Regulations section 1.351-3.

Assembling the Return

To ensure that the corporation's tax return is correctly processed, attach all schedules and forms after page 4, Form 1120S, in the following order:

1. Schedule N (Form 1120).

2. Form 4136, Credit for Federal Tax Paid on Fuels.

3. Form 8050.

4. Additional schedules in alphabetical order.

5. Additional forms in numerical order.

To assist us in processing the return, **please complete every applicable entry space on Form 1120S and Schedule K-1.** If you attach statements, do not write "See attached" instead of completing the entry spaces on Form 1120S and Schedule K-1.

If you need more space on the forms or schedules, attach separate sheets and place them at the end of the return. Use the same size and format as on the printed forms. **But show the totals on the printed forms.** Be sure to put the corporation's name and EIN on each sheet.

Amended Return

To correct an error on a Form 1120S already filed, file an amended Form 1120S and check box F(5). If the amended return results in a change to income, or a change in the distribution of any income or other information provided any shareholder, an amended Schedule K-1 (Form 1120S) must also be filed with the amended Form 1120S and given to that shareholder. Be sure to check box D(2) on each Schedule K-1 to indicate that it is an amended Schedule K-1.

A change to the corporation's Federal return may affect its state return. This includes changes made as the result of an IRS examination of Form 1120S. For more information, contact the state tax agency for the state in which the corporation's return was filed.

Passive Activity Limitations

In general, section 469 limits the amount of losses, deductions, and credits that shareholders may claim from "passive activities." The passive activity limitations do not apply to the corporation. Instead, they apply to each shareholder's share of any income or loss and credit attributable to a passive activity. Because the treatment of each shareholder's share of corporate income or loss and credit depends upon the nature of the activity that generated it, the corporation must report income or loss and credits separately for each activity.

The instructions below (pages 7 through 11) and the instructions for Schedules K and K-1 (pages 18 through 26) explain the applicable passive activity limitation rules and specify the type of information the corporation must provide to its shareholders for each activity. If the corporation had more than one activity, it must report information for each activity on an attachment to Schedules K and K-1.

Generally, passive activities include **(a)** activities that involve the conduct of a trade or business in which the shareholder does not materially participate and **(b)** any rental activity (defined on page 8) even if the shareholder materially participates. For exceptions, see **Activities That Are Not Passive Activities** below. The level of each shareholder's participation in an activity must be determined by the shareholder.

The passive activity rules provide that losses and credits from passive activities can generally be applied only against income and tax from passive activities. Thus, passive losses and credits cannot be applied against income from salaries, wages, professional fees, or a business in which the shareholder materially participates; against "portfolio income" (defined on page 9); or against the tax related to any of these types of income.

Special rules require that net income from certain activities that would otherwise be treated as passive income must be recharacterized as nonpassive income for purposes of the passive activity limitations.

To allow each shareholder to apply the passive activity limitations at the individual level, the corporation must report income or loss and credits separately for each of the following: trade or business activities, rental real estate activities, rental activities other than rental real estate, and portfolio income.

Activities That Are Not Passive Activities

Passive activities do not include:

1. Trade or business activities in which the shareholder materially participated for the tax year.

2. Any rental real estate activity in which the shareholder materially participated if the shareholder met both of the following conditions for the tax year:

-7-

a. More than half of the personal services the shareholder performed in trades or businesses were performed in real property trades or businesses in which he or she materially participated, **and**

b. The shareholder performed more than 750 hours of services in real property trades or businesses in which he or she materially participated.

For purposes of this rule, each interest in rental real estate is a separate activity unless the shareholder elects to treat all interests in rental real estate as one activity.

If the shareholder is married filing jointly, either the shareholder or his or her spouse must separately meet both conditions **2a** and **b** above, without taking into account services performed by the other spouse.

A real property trade or business is any real property development, redevelopment, construction, reconstruction, acquisition, conversion, rental, operation, management, leasing, or brokerage trade or business. Services the shareholder performed as an employee are not treated as performed in a real property trade or business unless he or she owned more than 5% of the stock in the employer.

3. The rental of a dwelling unit used by a shareholder for personal purposes during the year for more than the **greater of** 14 days or 10% of the number of days that the residence was rented at fair rental value.

4. An activity of trading personal property for the account of owners of interests in the activity. For purposes of this rule, personal property means property that is actively traded, such as stocks, bonds, and other securities. See Temporary Regulations section 1.469-1T(e)(6).

Note: *The section 469(c)(3) exception for a working interest in oil and gas properties does not apply to an S corporation because state law generally limits the liability of shareholders.*

Trade or Business Activities

A trade or business activity is an activity (other than a rental activity or an activity treated as incidental to an activity of holding property for investment) that—

1. Involves the conduct of a trade or business (within the meaning of section 162),

2. Is conducted in anticipation of starting a trade or business, or

3. Involves research or experimental expenditures deductible under section 174 (or that would be if you chose to deduct rather than capitalize them).

If the shareholder does not materially participate in the activity, a trade or business activity of the corporation is a passive activity for the shareholder.

Each shareholder must determine if he or she materially participated in an activity. As a result, while the corporation's overall trade or business income (loss) is reported on page 1 of Form 1120S, the specific income and deductions from each separate trade or business activity must be reported on attachments to Form 1120S. Similarly, while each shareholder's allocable share of the corporation's overall trade or business income (loss) is reported on line 1 of Schedule K-1, each shareholder's allocable share of the income and deductions from each trade or business activity must be reported on attachments to each Schedule K-1. See **Passive Activity Reporting Requirements** on page 10 for more information.

Rental Activities

Generally, except as noted below, if the gross income from an activity consists of amounts paid principally for the use of real or personal tangible property held by the corporation, the activity is a rental activity.

There are several exceptions to this general rule. Under these exceptions, an activity involving the use of real or personal tangible property is **not** a rental activity if any of the following apply:
• The **average period of customer use** (defined below) for such property is 7 days or less.
• The average period of customer use for such property is 30 days or less and **significant personal services** (defined below) are provided by or on behalf of the corporation.
• **Extraordinary personal services** (defined below) are provided by or on behalf of the corporation.
• Rental of the property is treated as **incidental** to a nonrental activity of the corporation under Temporary Regulations section 1.469-1T(e)(3)(vi) and Regulations section 1.469-1(e)(3)(vi).
• The corporation customarily makes the property available during defined business hours for nonexclusive use by various customers.
• The corporation provides property for use in a nonrental activity of a partnership in its capacity as an owner of an interest in such partnership. Whether the corporation provides property used in an activity of a partnership in the corporation's capacity as an owner of an interest in the partnership is based on all the facts and circumstances.

In addition, a guaranteed payment described in section 707(c) is not income from a rental activity under any circumstances.

Average period of customer use. Figure the average period of customer use of property by dividing the total number of days in all rental periods by the number of rentals during the tax year. If the activity involves renting more than one class of property, multiply the average period of customer use of each class by the ratio of the gross rental income from that class to the activity's total gross rental income. The activity's average period of customer use equals the sum of these class-by-class average periods weighted by gross income. See Regulations section 1.469-1(e)(3)(iii).

Significant personal services. Personal services include only services performed by individuals. To determine if personal services are significant personal services, consider all of the relevant facts and circumstances. Relevant facts and circumstances include how often the services are provided, the type and amount of labor required to perform the services, and the value of the services in relation to the amount charged for the use of the property.

The following services are not considered in determining whether personal services are significant:
• Services necessary to permit the lawful use of the rental property.
• Services performed in connection with improvements or repairs to the rental property that extend the useful life of the property substantially beyond the average rental period.
• Services provided in connection with the use of any improved real property that are similar to those commonly provided in connection with long-term rentals of high-grade commercial or residential property. Examples include cleaning and maintenance of common areas, routine repairs, trash collection, elevator service, and security at entrances.

Extraordinary personal services. Services provided in connection with making rental property available for customer use are extraordinary personal services only if the services are performed by individuals and the customers' use of the rental property is incidental to their receipt of the services. For example, a patient's use of a hospital room generally is incidental to the care that the patient receives from the hospital's medical staff. Similarly, a student's use of a dormitory room in a boarding school is incidental to the personal services provided by the school's teaching staff.

Rental property incidental to a nonrental activity. An activity is not a rental activity if the rental of the property is incidental to a nonrental activity, such as the activity of holding property for investment, a trade or business activity, or the activity of dealing in property.

Rental of property is **incidental** to an **activity of holding property for investment** if both of the following apply:
• The main purpose for holding the property is to realize a gain from the appreciation of the property.
• The gross rental income from such property for the tax year is less than 2% of the smaller of the property's unadjusted basis or its fair market value.

Rental of property is **incidental** to a **trade or business activity** if all of the following apply:
• The corporation owns an interest in the trade or business at all times during the year.
• The rental property was mainly used in the trade or business activity during the tax year or during at least 2 of the 5 preceding tax years.
• The gross rental income from the property is less than 2% of the smaller of the property's unadjusted basis or its fair market value.

The sale or exchange of property that is also rented during the tax year (where the gain or loss is recognized) is treated as incidental to the activity of dealing in property if, at the time of the sale or

Instructions for Form 1120S

exchange, the property was held primarily for sale to customers in the ordinary course of the corporation's trade or business.

See Temporary Regulations section 1.469-1T(e)(3) and Regulations section 1.469-1(e)(3) for more information on the definition of rental activities for purposes of the passive activity limitations.

Reporting of rental activities. In reporting the corporation's income or losses and credits from rental activities, the corporation must separately report **(a)** rental real estate activities and **(b)** rental activities other than rental real estate activities.

Shareholders who actively participate in a rental real estate activity may be able to deduct part or all of their rental real estate losses (and the deduction equivalent of rental real estate credits) against income (or tax) from nonpassive activities. Generally, the combined amount of rental real estate losses and the deduction equivalent of rental real estate credits from all sources (including rental real estate activities not held through the corporation) that may be claimed is limited to $25,000.

Report rental real estate activity income (loss) on **Form 8825,** Rental Real Estate Income and Expenses of a Partnership or an S Corporation, and on line 2 of Schedules K and K-1, rather than on page 1 of Form 1120S. Report credits related to rental real estate activities on lines 12c and 12d and low-income housing credits on line 12b of Schedules K and K-1.

Report income (loss) from rental activities other than rental real estate on line 3 and credits related to rental activities other than rental real estate on line 12e of Schedules K and K-1.

Portfolio Income

Generally, portfolio income includes all gross income, other than income derived in the ordinary course of a trade or business, that is attributable to interest; dividends; royalties; income from a real estate investment trust, a regulated investment company, a real estate mortgage investment conduit, a common trust fund, a controlled foreign corporation, a qualified electing fund, or a cooperative; income from the disposition of property that produces income of a type defined as portfolio income; and income from the disposition of property held for investment. See **Self-Charged Interest** below for an exception.

Solely for purposes of the preceding paragraph, gross income derived in the ordinary course of a trade or business includes **(and portfolio income, therefore, does not include)** only the following types of income:
• Interest income on loans and investments made in the ordinary course of a trade or business of lending money.
• Interest on accounts receivable arising from the performance of services or the sale of property in the ordinary course of a trade or business of performing such services or selling such property, but only if credit is customarily offered to customers of the business.

• Income from investments made in the ordinary course of a trade or business of furnishing insurance or annuity contracts or reinsuring risks underwritten by insurance companies.
• Income or gain derived in the ordinary course of an activity of trading or dealing in any property if such activity constitutes a trade or business (unless the dealer held the property for investment at any time before such income or gain is recognized).
• Royalties derived by the taxpayer in the ordinary course of a trade or business of licensing intangible property.
• Amounts included in the gross income of a patron of a cooperative by reason of any payment or allocation to the patron based on patronage occurring with respect to a trade or business of the patron.
• Other income identified by the IRS as income derived by the taxpayer in the ordinary course of a trade or business.

See Temporary Regulations section 1.469-2T(c)(3) for more information on portfolio income.

Report portfolio income on line 4 of Schedules K and K-1, rather than on page 1 of Form 1120S.

Report deductions related to portfolio income on line 9 of Schedules K and K-1.

Self-Charged Interest

Certain "self-charged" interest income and expense may be treated as passive activity gross income and passive activity deductions if the loan proceeds are used in a passive activity. Generally, self-charged interest income and expense result from loans to and from the corporation and its shareholders. It also includes loans between the corporation and another S corporation or partnership if each owner in the borrowing entity has the same proportional ownership interest in the lending entity. See Regulations section 1.469-7 for details.

Grouping Activities

Generally, one or more trade or business activities or rental activities may be treated as a single activity if the activities make up an appropriate economic unit for measurement of gain or loss under the passive activity rules. Whether activities make up an appropriate economic unit depends on all the relevant facts and circumstances. The factors given the greatest weight in determining whether activities make up an appropriate economic unit are—
1. Similarities and differences in types of trades or businesses,
2. The extent of common control,
3. The extent of common ownership,
4. Geographical location, and
5. Reliance between or among the activities.

Example. The corporation has a significant ownership interest in a bakery and a movie theater in Baltimore and in a bakery and a movie theater in Philadelphia. Depending on the relevant facts and circumstances, there may be more than one reasonable method for grouping the corporation's activities. For

instance, the following groupings may or may not be permissible:
• A single activity,
• A movie theater activity and a bakery activity,
• A Baltimore activity and a Philadelphia activity, or
• Four separate activities.

Once the corporation chooses a grouping under these rules, it must continue using that grouping in later tax years unless a material change in the facts and circumstances makes it clearly inappropriate.

The IRS may regroup the corporation's activities if the corporation's grouping fails to reflect one or more appropriate economic units and one of the primary purposes for the grouping is to avoid the passive activity limitations.

Limitation on grouping certain activities. The following activities may not be grouped together:

1. A rental activity with a trade or business activity unless the activities being grouped together make up an appropriate economic unit, and

a. The rental activity is insubstantial relative to the trade or business activity or vice versa, or

b. Each owner of the trade or business activity has the same proportionate ownership interest in the rental activity. If so, the portion of the rental activity involving the rental of property to be used in the trade or business activity may be grouped with the trade or business activity.

2. An activity involving the rental of real property with an activity involving the rental of personal property (except for personal property provided in connection with real property), or vice versa.

3. Any activity with another activity in a different type of business and in which the corporation holds an interest as a limited partner or as a limited entrepreneur (as defined in section 464(e)(2)) if that other activity engages in holding, producing, or distributing motion picture films or videotapes; farming; leasing section 1245 property; or exploring for or exploiting oil and gas resources or geothermal deposits.

Activities conducted through partnerships. Once a partnership determines its activities under these rules, the corporation as a partner may use these rules to group those activities with:
• Each other,
• Activities conducted directly by the corporation, or
• Activities conducted through other partnerships.

The corporation may not treat as separate activities those activities grouped together by the partnership.

Recharacterization of Passive Income

Under Temporary Regulations section 1.469-2T(f) and Regulations section 1.469-2(f), net passive income from certain passive activities must be treated as nonpassive income. Net passive income is the excess of an activity's passive activity gross income over its passive activity deductions (current year deductions and prior year unallowed losses).

Income from the following six sources is subject to recharacterization. Note that any net passive income recharacterized as nonpassive income is treated as investment income for purposes of figuring investment interest expense limitations if it is from **(a)** an activity of renting substantially nondepreciable property from an equity-financed lending activity or **(b)** an activity related to an interest in a pass-through entity that licenses intangible property.

1. Significant participation passive activities. A significant participation passive activity is any trade or business activity in which the shareholder both participates for more than 100 hours during the tax year and does not materially participate. Because each shareholder must determine his or her level of participation, the corporation will not be able to identify significant participation passive activities.

2. Certain nondepreciable rental property activities. Net passive income from a rental activity is nonpassive income if less than 30% of the unadjusted basis of the property used or held for use by customers in the activity is subject to depreciation under section 167.

3. Passive equity-financed lending activities. If the corporation has net income from a passive equity-financed lending activity, the smaller of the net passive income or equity-financed interest income from the activity is nonpassive income.

Note: *The amount of income from the activities in items **1** through **3** above that any shareholder will be required to recharacterize as nonpassive income may be limited under Temporary Regulations section 1.469-2T(f)(8). Because the corporation will not have information regarding all of a shareholder's activities, it must identify all corporate activities meeting the definitions in items **2** and **3** as activities that may be subject to recharacterization.*

4. Rental activities incidental to a development activity. Net rental activity income is the excess of passive activity gross income from renting or disposing of property over passive activity deductions (current year deductions and prior year unallowed losses) that are reasonably allocable to the rented property. Net rental activity income is nonpassive income for a shareholder if all of the following apply:

• The corporation recognizes gain from the sale, exchange, or other disposition of the rental property during the tax year.

• The use of the item of property in the rental activity started less than 12 months before the date of disposition. The use of an item of rental property begins on the first day on which **(a)** the corporation owns an interest in the property, **(b)** substantially all of the property is either rented or held out for rent and ready to be rented, and **(c)** no significant value-enhancing services remain to be performed.

• The shareholder materially participated or significantly participated for any tax year in an activity that involved the performing of services to enhance the value of the property (or any other item of property, if the basis of the property disposed of is determined in whole or in part by reference to the basis of that item of property).

Because the corporation cannot determine a shareholder's level of participation, the corporation must identify net income from property described above (without regard to the shareholder's level of participation) as income that may be subject to recharacterization.

5. Activities involving property rented to a nonpassive activity. If a taxpayer rents property to a trade or business activity in which the taxpayer materially participates, the taxpayer's net rental activity income (defined in item 4) from the property is nonpassive income.

6. Acquisition of an interest in a pass-through entity that licenses intangible property. Generally, net royalty income from intangible property is nonpassive income if the taxpayer acquired an interest in the pass-through entity after it created the intangible property or performed substantial services or incurred substantial costs in developing or marketing the intangible property.

Net royalty income is the excess of passive activity gross income from licensing or transferring any right in intangible property over passive activity deductions (current year deductions and prior year unallowed losses) that are reasonably allocable to the intangible property.

See Temporary Regulations section 1.469-2T(f)(7)(iii) for exceptions to this rule.

Passive Activity Reporting Requirements

To allow shareholders to correctly apply the passive activity loss and credit limitation rules, any corporation that carries on more than one activity must:

1. Provide an attachment for each activity conducted through the corporation that identifies the type of activity conducted (trade or business, rental real estate, rental activity other than rental real estate, or investment).

2. On the attachment for each activity, provide a schedule, using the same line numbers as shown on Schedule K-1, detailing the net income (loss), credits, and all items required to be separately stated under section 1366(a)(1) from each trade or business activity, from each rental real estate activity, from each rental activity other than a rental real estate activity, and from investments.

3. Identify the net income (loss) and the shareholder's share of corporation interest expense from each activity of renting a dwelling unit that any shareholder uses for personal purposes during the year for more than the greater of 14 days or 10% of the number of days that the residence is rented at fair rental value.

4. Identify the net income (loss) and the shareholder's share of interest expense from each activity of trading personal property conducted through the corporation.

5. For any gain (loss) from the disposition of an interest in an activity or of an interest in property used in an activity (including dispositions before 1987 from which gain is being recognized after 1986):

a. Identify the activity in which the property was used at the time of disposition;

b. If the property was used in more than one activity during the 12 months preceding the disposition, identify the activities in which the property was used and the adjusted basis allocated to each activity; and

c. For gains only, if the property was substantially appreciated at the time of the disposition and the applicable holding period specified in Regulations section 1.469-2(c)(2)(iii)(A) was not satisfied, identify the amount of the nonpassive gain and indicate whether or not the gain is investment income under Regulations section 1.469-2(c)(2)(iii)(F).

6. Identify the shareholder's share of the corporation's self-charged interest income or expense (see **Self-Charged Interest** on page 9).

a. Loans between a shareholder and the corporation. Identify the lending or borrowing shareholder's share of the self-charged interest income or expense. If the shareholder made the loan to the corporation, also identify the activity in which the loan proceeds were used. If the proceeds were used in more than one activity, allocate the interest to each activity based on the amount of the proceeds used in each activity.

b. Loans between the corporation and another S corporation or partnership. If the corporation's shareholders have the same proportional ownership interest in the corporation and the other S corporation or partnership, identify each shareholder's share of the interest income or expense from the loan. If the corporation was the borrower, also identify the activity in which the loan proceeds were used. If the proceeds were used in more than one activity, allocate the interest to each activity based on the amount of the proceeds used in each activity.

7. Specify the amount of gross portfolio income, the interest expense properly allocable to portfolio income, and expenses other than interest expense that are clearly and directly allocable to portfolio income.

8. Identify the ratable portion of any section 481 adjustment (whether a net positive or a net negative adjustment) allocable to each corporate activity.

9. Identify any gross income from sources specifically excluded from passive activity gross income, including:

a. Income from intangible property, if the shareholder is an individual whose personal efforts significantly contributed to the creation of the property;

b. Income from state, local, or foreign income tax refunds; and

Instructions for Form 1120S

c. Income from a covenant not to compete, if the shareholder is an individual who contributed the covenant to the corporation.

10. Identify any deductions that are not passive activity deductions.

11. If the corporation makes a full or partial disposition of its interest in another entity, identify the gain (loss) allocable to each activity conducted through the entity, and the gain allocable to a passive activity that would have been recharacterized as nonpassive gain had the corporation disposed of its interest in property used in the activity (because the property was substantially appreciated at the time of the disposition, and the gain represented more than 10% of the shareholder's total gain from the disposition).

12. Identify the following items that may be subject to the recharacterization rules under Temporary Regulations section 1.469-2T(f) and Regulations section 1.469-2(f):

a. Net income from an activity of renting substantially nondepreciable property;

b. The smaller of equity-financed interest income or net passive income from an equity-financed lending activity;

c. Net rental activity income from property developed (by the shareholder or the corporation), rented, and sold within 12 months after the rental of the property commenced;

d. Net rental activity income from the rental of property by the corporation to a trade or business activity in which the shareholder had an interest (either directly or indirectly); and

e. Net royalty income from intangible property if the shareholder acquired the shareholder's interest in the corporation after the corporation created the intangible property or performed substantial services or incurred substantial costs in developing or marketing the intangible property.

13. Identify separately the credits from each activity conducted by or through the corporation.

Extraterritorial Income Exclusion

The corporation may exclude extraterritorial income to the extent of qualifying foreign trade income. For details and to figure the amount of the exclusion, see Form 8873 and its separate instructions. The corporation must report the extraterritorial income exclusion on its return as follows:

1. If the corporation met the foreign economic process requirements explained in the Instructions for Form 8873, it may report the exclusion as a non-separately stated item on whichever of the following lines apply to that activity:
- Form 1120S, page 1, line 19;
- Form 8825, line 15; or
- Form 1120S, Schedule K, line 3b.

In addition, the corporation must report as an item of information on Schedule K-1, line 23, the shareholder's pro rata share of foreign trading gross receipts from Form 8873, line 15.

2. If the foreign trading gross receipts of the corporation for the tax year are $5 million or less and the corporation did not meet the foreign economic process requirements, it may not report the extraterritorial income exclusion as a non-separately stated item on its return. Instead, it must report the following separately-stated items to the shareholders on Schedule K-1, line 23:

- The shareholder's pro rata share of foreign trading gross receipts from Form 8873, line 15.
- The shareholder's pro rata share of the extraterritorial income exclusion from Form 8873, line 55, and identify the activity to which the exclusion relates.

Note: *Upon request of a shareholder, the corporation should furnish a copy of the corporation's Form 8873 if that shareholder has a reduction for international boycott operations, illegal bribes, kickbacks, etc.*

Specific Instructions

General Information

Name, Address, and Employer Identification Number

Use the label that was mailed to the corporation. Cross out any errors and print the correct information on the label.

Name. If the corporation did not receive a label, print or type the corporation's true name (as set forth in the corporate charter or other legal document creating it).

Address. Include the suite, room, or other unit number after the street address. If a preaddressed label is used, include the information on the label. If the Post Office does not deliver to the street address and the corporation has a P.O. box, show the box number instead of the street address.

Employer identification number (EIN). Show the correct EIN in item C on page 1 of Form 1120S.

Item B—Business Code No.

See the **Codes for Principal Business Activity** on pages 29 through 31 of these instructions.

Item E—Total Assets

Enter the corporation's total assets at the end of the tax year, as determined by the accounting method regularly used in maintaining the corporation's books and records. If there were no assets at the end of the tax year, enter "0." If the S election terminated during the tax year, see the instructions for Schedule L on page 26 for special rules that may apply when figuring the corporation's year-end assets.

Item F—Initial Return, Final Return, Name Change, Address Change, and Amended Return

If this is the corporation's first return, check box F(1).

If the corporation has ceased to exist, check box F(2). Also check box D(1) on

-11-

each Schedule K-1 to indicate that it is a final Schedule K-1.

If the corporation changed its name since it last filed a return, check box F(3). Generally, a corporation cannot change its name unless it amended its articles of incorporation and files the amendment with the state in which it is incorporated.

Indicate a change in address by checking box F(4). If a change in address occurs after the return is filed, use **Form 8822,** Change of Address, to notify the IRS of the new address.

If this amends a previously filed return, check box F(5). If Schedules K-1 are also being amended, check box D(2) on each Schedule K-1.

Income

 *Report only trade or business activity income or loss on lines 1a through 6. **Do not report rental activity income or portfolio income or loss on these lines.** (See **Passive Activity Limitations** beginning on page 7 for definitions of rental income and portfolio income.) Rental activity income and portfolio income are reported on Schedules K and K-1 (rental real estate activities are also reported on Form 8825).*

Tax-exempt income. Do not include any tax-exempt income on lines 1 through 5. A corporation that receives any exempt income other than interest, or holds any property or engages in an activity that produces exempt income, reports this income on line 18 of Schedules K and K-1.

Report tax-exempt interest income, including exempt-interest dividends received as a shareholder in a mutual fund or other regulated investment company, on line 17 of Schedules K and K-1.

See **Deductions** beginning on page 12 for information on how to report expenses related to tax-exempt income.

Cancelled debt exclusion. If the S corporation has had debt discharged resulting from a title 11 bankruptcy proceeding, or while insolvent, see **Form 982,** Reduction of Tax Attributes Due to Discharge of Indebtedness, and **Pub. 908,** Bankruptcy Tax Guide.

Line 1—Gross Receipts or Sales

Enter gross receipts or sales from all trade or business operations except those you report on lines 4 and 5. In general, advance payments are reported in the year of receipt. To report income from long-term contracts, see section 460. For special rules for reporting certain advance payments for goods and long-term contracts, see Regulations section 1.451-5. For permissible methods for reporting certain advance payments for services by an accrual method corporation, see Rev. Proc. 71-21,1971-2 C.B. 549.

Installment sales. Generally, the installment method cannot be used for dealer dispositions of property. A "dealer disposition" is any disposition of **(a)**

personal property by a person who regularly sells or otherwise disposes of property of the same type on the installment plan or **(b)** real property held for sale to customers in the ordinary course of the taxpayer's trade or business.

Exception. These restrictions on using the installment method do not apply to dispositions of property used or produced in a farming business or sales of timeshares and residential lots for which the corporation elects to pay interest under section 453(l)(3).

Enter on line 1a the gross profit on collections from installment sales for any of the following:
• Dealer dispositions of property before March 1, 1986.
• Dispositions of property used or produced in the trade or business of farming.
• Certain dispositions of timeshares and residential lots reported under the installment method.

Attach a schedule showing the following information for the current and the 3 preceding years:
• Gross sales.
• Cost of goods sold.
• Gross profits.
• Percentage of gross profits to gross sales.
• Amount collected.
• Gross profit on the amount collected.

Line 2—Cost of Goods Sold

See the instructions for Schedule A on page 17.

Line 4—Net Gain (Loss) From Form 4797

 Include only ordinary gains or losses from the sale, exchange, or involuntary conversion of assets used in a trade or business activity. Ordinary gains or losses from the sale, exchange, or involuntary conversions of assets used in rental activities are reported separately on Schedule K as part of the net income (loss) from the rental activity in which the property was used.

A corporation that is a partner in a partnership must include on **Form 4797,** Sales of Business Property, its share of ordinary gains (losses) from sales, exchanges, or involuntary or compulsory conversions (other than casualties or thefts) of the partnership's trade or business assets.

Do not include any recapture of the section 179 expense deduction. See the instructions on page 25 for Schedule K-1, line 23, item 3, and the Instructions for Form 4797 for more information.

Line 5—Other Income (Loss)

Enter on line 5 trade or business income (loss) that is not included on lines 1a

through 4. Examples of such income include:
• Interest income derived in the ordinary course of the corporation's trade or business, such as interest charged on receivable balances.
• Recoveries of bad debts deducted in earlier years under the specific charge-off method.
• Taxable income from insurance proceeds.
• The amount of credit figured on **Form 6478,** Credit for Alcohol Used as Fuel.

The corporation must also include in other income the:
• Recapture amount under section 280F if the business use of listed property drops to 50% or less. To figure the recapture amount, the corporation must complete Part IV of Form 4797.
• Recapture of any deduction previously taken under section 179A. The S corporation may have to recapture part or all of the benefit of any allowable deduction for qualified clean-fuel vehicle property (or clean-fuel vehicle refueling property), if the property ceases to qualify for the deduction within 3 years after the date it was placed in service. See **Pub. 535,** Business Expenses, for details on how to figure the recapture.

If "other income" consists of only one item, identify it by showing the account caption in parentheses on line 5. A separate schedule need not be attached to the return in this case.

Do not net any expense item (such as interest) with a similar income item. Report all trade or business expenses on lines 7 through 19.

Do not include items requiring separate computations by shareholders that must be reported on Schedules K and K-1. See the instructions for Schedules K and K-1 beginning on page 18.

Ordinary Income (Loss) From a Partnership, Estate, or Trust

Enter the ordinary trade or business income (loss) from a partnership shown on Schedule K-1 (Form 1065), from an estate or trust shown on Schedule K-1 (Form 1041), or from a foreign partnership, estate, or trust. Show the partnership's, estate's, or trust's name, address, and EIN (if any) on a separate statement attached to this return. If the amount entered is from more than one source, identify the amount from each source.

Do not include portfolio income or rental activity income (loss) from a partnership, estate, or trust on this line. Instead, report these amounts on the applicable lines of Schedules K and K-1, or on line 20a of Form 8825 if the amount is from a rental real estate activity.

Ordinary income or loss from a partnership that is a publicly traded

partnership is not reported on this line. Instead, report the amount separately on line 6 of Schedules K and K-1.

Treat shares of other items separately reported on Schedule K-1 issued by the other entity as if the items were realized or incurred by the S corporation.

If there is a loss from a partnership, the amount of the loss that may be claimed is subject to the at-risk and basis limitations as appropriate.

If the tax year of the S corporation does not coincide with the tax year of the partnership, estate, or trust, include the ordinary income (loss) from the other entity in the tax year in which the other entity's tax year ends.

Deductions

 *Report **only** trade or business activity expenses on lines 7 through 19.*

Do not report rental activity expenses or deductions allocable to portfolio income on these lines. Rental activity expenses are separately reported on Form 8825 or line 3 of Schedules K and K-1. Deductions allocable to portfolio income are separately reported on line 9 of Schedules K and K-1. See **Passive Activity Limitations** beginning on page 7 for more information on rental activities and portfolio income.

Do not report any nondeductible amounts (such as expenses connected with the production of tax-exempt income) on lines 7 through 19. Instead, report nondeductible expenses on line 19 of Schedules K and K-1. If an expense is connected with both taxable income and nontaxable income, allocate a reasonable part of the expense to each kind of income.

Limitations on Deductions

Section 263A uniform capitalization rules. The uniform capitalization rules of section 263A require corporations to capitalize or include in inventory costs certain costs incurred in connection with:
• The production of real and tangible personal property held in inventory or held for sale in the ordinary course of business.
• Real property or personal property (tangible and intangible) acquired for resale.
• The production of real property and tangible personal property by a corporation for use in its trade or business or in an activity engaged in for profit.

The costs required to be capitalized under section 263A are not deductible until the property to which the costs relate is sold, used, or otherwise disposed of by the corporation.

Exceptions. Section 263A **does not** apply to:
• Personal property acquired for resale if the taxpayer's average annual gross receipts for the 3 prior tax years are $10 million or less.
• Timber.
• Most property produced under a long-term contract.
• Certain property produced in a farming business. See below.

The corporation must report the following costs separately to the shareholders for purposes of determinations under section 59(e):
• Research and experimental costs under section 174.
• Intangible drilling costs for oil, gas, and geothermal property.
• Mining exploration and development costs.
• Inventory of a corporation that accounts for inventories in the same manner as materials and supplies that are not incidental. See **Cost of Goods Sold** on page 17.

Tangible personal property produced by a corporation includes a film, sound recording, video tape, book, or similar property.

Corporations subject to the rules are required to capitalize not only direct costs but an allocable portion of most indirect costs (including taxes) that benefit the assets produced or acquired for resale or are incurred by reason of the performance of production or resale activities.

For inventory, some of the *indirect costs* that must be capitalized are:
• Administration expenses.
• Taxes.
• Depreciation.
• Insurance.
• Compensation paid to officers attributable to services.
• Rework labor.
• Contributions to pension, stock bonus, and certain profit-sharing, annuity, or deferred compensation plans.

Regulations section 1.263A-1(e)(3) specifies other indirect costs that relate to production or resale activities that must be capitalized and those that may be currently deducted.

Interest expense paid or incurred during the production period of designated property must be capitalized and is governed by special rules. For more details, see Regulations sections 1.263A-8 through 1.263A-15.

For more details on the uniform capitalization rules, see Regulations sections 1.263A-1 through 1.263A-3.

Special rules for certain corporations engaged in farming. For S corporations not required to use the accrual method of accounting, the rules of section 263A **do not** apply to expenses of raising any—
• Animal or
• Plant that has a preproductive period of 2 years or less.

Shareholders of S corporations not required to use the accrual method of accounting may elect to currently deduct the preproductive period expenses of certain plants that have a preproductive period of more than 2 years. Because

each shareholder makes the election to deduct these expenses, the corporation should not capitalize them. Instead, the corporation should report the expenses separately on line 21 of Schedule K and each shareholder's pro rata share on line 23 of Schedule K-1.

See sections 263A(d) and (e) and Regulations section 1.263A-4 for definitions and other details.

Transactions between related taxpayers. Generally, an accrual basis S corporation may deduct business expenses and interest owed to a related party (including any shareholder) **only** in the tax year of the corporation that includes the day on which the payment is includible in the income of the related party. See section 267 for details.

Section 291 limitations. If the S corporation was a C corporation for any of the 3 immediately preceding years, the corporation may be required to adjust deductions allowed to the corporation for depletion of iron ore and coal, and the amortizable basis of pollution control facilities. See section 291 to determine the amount of the adjustment.

Business start-up expenses. Business start-up expenses must be capitalized. An election may be made to amortize them over a period of not less than 60 months. See section 195 and Regulations section 1.195-1.

Reducing certain expenses for which credits are allowable. For each credit listed below, the corporation must reduce the otherwise allowable deductions for expenses used to figure the credit by the amount of the current year credit.

1. The work opportunity credit,
2. The welfare-to-work credit,
3. The credit for increasing research activities,
4. The enhanced oil recovery credit,
5. The disabled access credit,
6. The empowerment zone and renewable community employment credit,
7. The Indian employment credit,
8. The credit for employer social security and Medicare taxes paid on certain employee tips,
9. The orphan drug credit, and
10. The New York Liberty Zone business employment credit.

If the corporation has any of these credits, be sure to figure each current year credit before figuring the deductions for expenses on which the credit is based.

Line 7—Compensation of Officers and Line 8—Salaries and Wages

Enter on line 7 the total compensation of all officers paid or incurred in the trade or business activities of the corporation. Enter on line 8 the amount of salaries and wages paid or incurred to employees (other than officers) during the tax year in the trade or business activities of the corporation.

Reduce the amounts on lines 7 and 8 by any applicable employment credits from:
• **Form 5884,** Work Opportunity Credit,
• **Form 8861,** Welfare-to-Work Credit,

• **Form 8844,** Empowerment Zone and Renewable Community Employment Credit,
• **Form 8845,** Indian Employment Credit, and
• **Form 8884,** New York Liberty Zone Business Employment Credit.

See the instructions for these forms for more information.

Include fringe benefit expenditures made on behalf of officers and employees owning more than 2% of the corporation's stock. Also report these fringe benefits as wages in box 1 of Form W-2. Do not include amounts paid or incurred for fringe benefits of officers and employees owning 2% or less of the corporation's stock. These amounts are reported on line 18, page 1, of Form 1120S. See the instructions for that line for information on the types of expenditures that are treated as fringe benefits and for the stock ownership rules.

Report amounts paid for health insurance coverage for a more than 2% shareholder (including that shareholder's spouse and dependents) as an information item in box 14 of that shareholder's Form W-2. For 2002, a more than 2% shareholder may be allowed to deduct up to 70% of such amounts on Form 1040, line 30.

Do not include amounts reported elsewhere on the return, such as salaries and wages included in cost of goods sold, elective contributions to a section 401(k) cash or deferred arrangement, or amounts contributed under a salary reduction SEP agreement or a SIMPLE IRA plan.

If a shareholder or a member of the family of one or more shareholders of the corporation renders services or furnishes capital to the corporation for which reasonable compensation is not paid, the IRS may make adjustments in the items taken into account by such individuals and the value of such services or capital. See section 1366(e).

Line 9—Repairs and Maintenance

Enter the costs of incidental repairs and maintenance, such as labor and supplies, that do not add to the value of the property or appreciably prolong its life, but only to the extent that such costs relate to a trade or business activity and are not claimed elsewhere on the return. New buildings, machinery, or permanent improvements that increase the value of the property are not deductible. They are chargeable to capital accounts and may be depreciated or amortized.

Line 10—Bad Debts

Enter the total debts that became worthless in whole or in part during the year, but only to the extent such debts relate to a trade or business activity. Report deductible nonbusiness bad debts as a short-term capital loss on Schedule D (Form 1120S).

 Cash method taxpayers cannot take a bad debt deduction unless the amount was previously included in income.

Line 11—Rents

If the corporation rented or leased a vehicle, enter the total annual rent or lease expense paid or incurred in the trade or business activities of the corporation. Also complete Part V of **Form 4562**, Depreciation and Amortization. If the corporation leased a vehicle for a term of 30 days or more, the deduction for vehicle lease expense may have to be reduced by an amount called the **inclusion amount.** The corporation may have an inclusion amount if—

The lease term began:	And the vehicle's fair market value on the first day of the lease exceeded:
After 12/31/98	$15,500
After 12/31/96 but before 1/1/99	$15,800
After 12/31/94 but before 1/1/97	$15,500
After 12/31/93 but before 1/1/95	$14,600

If the lease term began before January 1, 1994, see **Pub. 463,** Travel, Entertainment, Gift, and Car Expenses, to find out if the corporation has an inclusion amount.

See Pub. 463 for instructions on figuring the inclusion amount.

Line 12—Taxes and Licenses

Enter taxes and licenses paid or incurred in the trade or business activities of the corporation, if not reflected in cost of goods sold. Federal import duties and Federal excise and stamp taxes are deductible only if paid or incurred in carrying on the trade or business of the corporation.

Do not deduct the following taxes on line 12:
- State and local sales taxes paid or incurred in connection with the acquisition or disposition of business property. These taxes must be added to the cost of the property, or in the case of a disposition, subtracted from the amount realized.
- Taxes assessed against local benefits that increase the value of the property assessed, such as for paving, etc.
- Federal income taxes (except for the portion of built-in gains tax allocable to ordinary income), or taxes reported elsewhere on the return.
- Section 901 foreign taxes. Report these taxes separately on line 15g, Schedule K.
- Taxes allocable to a rental activity. Taxes allocable to a rental real estate activity are reported on Form 8825. Taxes allocable to a rental activity other than a rental real estate activity are reported on line 3b of Schedule K.
- Taxes allocable to portfolio income. Report these taxes separately on line 9 of Schedules K and K-1.
- Taxes paid or incurred for the production or collection of income, or for the management, conservation, or maintenance of property held to produce income. Report these taxes separately on line 10 of Schedules K and K-1.

See section 263A(a) for information on capitalization of allocable costs (including taxes) for any property.

Line 13—Interest

Include on line 13 only interest incurred in the trade or business activities of the corporation that is not claimed elsewhere on the return. **Do not** include interest expense:
- On debt used to purchase rental property or debt used in a rental activity. Interest allocable to a rental real estate activity is reported on Form 8825 and is used in arriving at net income (loss) from rental real estate activities on line 2 of Schedules K and K-1. Interest allocable to a rental activity other than a rental real estate activity is included on line 3b of Schedule K and is used in arriving at net income (loss) from a rental activity (other than a rental real estate activity). This net amount is reported on line 3c of Schedule K and line 3 of Schedule K-1.
- Clearly and directly allocable to portfolio or investment income. This interest expense is reported separately on line 11a of Schedule K.
- On debt proceeds allocated to distributions made to shareholders during the tax year. Instead, report such interest on line 10 of Schedules K and K-1. To determine the amount to allocate to distributions to shareholders, see Notice 89-35, 1989-1 C.B. 675.
- On debt required to be allocated to the production of designated property. Interest allocable to designated property produced by an S corporation for its own use or for sale must instead be capitalized. The corporation must also capitalize any interest on debt allocable to an asset used to produce designated property. A shareholder may have to capitalize interest that the shareholder incurs during the tax year for the production expenditures of the S corporation. Similarly, interest incurred by an S corporation may have to be capitalized by a shareholder for the shareholder's own production expenditures. The information required by the shareholder to properly capitalize interest for this purpose must be provided by the corporation on an attachment for line 23 of Schedule K-1. See section 263A(f) and Regulations sections 1.263A-8 through 1.263A-15 for additional information, including the definition of "designated property."

Special rules apply to:
- Allocating interest expense among activities so that the limitations on passive activity losses, investment interest, and personal interest can be properly figured. Generally, interest expense is allocated in the same manner as debt is allocated. Debt is allocated by tracing disbursements of the debt proceeds to specific expenditures. Temporary Regulations section 1.163-8T gives rules for tracing debt proceeds to expenditures.
- Prepaid interest, which generally can only be deducted over the period to which the prepayment applies. See section 461(g) for details.
- Limit the interest deduction if the corporation is a policyholder or beneficiary with respect to a life insurance, endowment, or annuity contract issued after June 8, 1997. For details, see section 264(f). Attach a statement showing the computation of the deduction.

Line 14—Depreciation

Enter on line 14a only the depreciation claimed on assets used in a trade or business activity. See the Instructions for Form 4562 or **Pub. 946,** How To Depreciate Property, to figure the amount of depreciation to enter on this line. Complete and attach Form 4562 only if the corporation placed property in service during the tax year or claims depreciation on any car or other listed property.

Do not include any section 179 expense deduction on this line. This amount is not deductible by the corporation. Instead, it is passed through to the shareholders on line 8 of Schedule K-1.

Line 15—Depletion

If the corporation claims a deduction for timber depletion, complete and attach **Form T,** Forest Activities Schedules.

 Do not deduct depletion for oil and gas properties. Each shareholder figures depletion on these properties under section 613A(c)(11). See the instructions on page 25 for Schedule K-1, line 23, item 2, for information on oil and gas depletion that must be supplied to the shareholders by the corporation.

Line 17—Pension, Profit-Sharing, etc., Plans

Enter the deductible contributions not claimed elsewhere on the return made by the corporation for its employees under a qualified pension, profit-sharing, annuity, or simplified employee pension (SEP) or SIMPLE plan, and under any other deferred compensation plan.

If the corporation contributes to an individual retirement arrangement (IRA) for employees, include the contribution in salaries and wages on page 1, line 8, or Schedule A, line 3, and not on line 17.

Employers who maintain a pension, profit-sharing, or other funded deferred compensation plan, whether or not qualified under the Internal Revenue Code and whether or not a deduction is claimed for the current tax year, generally must file the applicable form listed below.
- **Form 5500,** Annual Return/Report of Employee Benefit Plan. File this form for a plan that is not a one-participant plan (see below).
- **Form 5500-EZ,** Annual Return of One-Participant (Owners and Their Spouses) Retirement Plan. File this form for a plan that only covers the owner (or the owner and his or her spouse) but only if the owner (or the owner and his or her spouse) owns the entire business.

There are penalties for failure to file these forms on time and for overstating the pension plan deduction.

Line 18—Employee Benefit Programs

Enter amounts for fringe benefits paid or incurred on behalf of employees owning 2% or less of the corporation's stock. These fringe benefits include **(a)** employer contributions to certain accident and health plans, **(b)** the cost of up to

Instructions for Form 1120S

$50,000 of group-term life insurance on an employee's life, and (c) meals and lodging furnished for the employer's convenience.

Do not deduct amounts that are an incidental part of a pension, profit-sharing, etc., plan included on line 17 or amounts reported elsewhere on the return.

Report amounts paid on behalf of more than 2% shareholders on line 7 or 8, whichever applies. A shareholder is considered to own more than 2% of the corporation's stock if that person owns on any day during the tax year more than 2% of the outstanding stock of the corporation or stock possessing more than 2% of the combined voting power of all stock of the corporation. See section 318 for attribution rules.

Line 19—Other Deductions

Attach your own schedule listing by type and amount all allowable deductions related to a trade or business activity **only** for which there is no separate line on page 1 of Form 1120S. Enter the total on this line. Examples of other deductions include:
- Amortization (except as noted below)— see the Instructions for Form 4562 for more information. Complete and attach Form 4562 if the corporation is claiming amortization of costs that began during the tax year.
- Insurance premiums.
- Legal and professional fees.
- Supplies used and consumed in the business.
- Utilities.

Also, see **Special Rules** below for limits on certain other deductions.

Do not deduct on line 19:
- Items that must be reported separately on Schedules K and K-1.
- Qualified expenditures to which an election under section 59(e) may apply. See the instructions on page 24 for lines 16a and 16b of Schedule K-1 for details on treatment of these items.
- Amortization of reforestation expenditures under section 194. The corporation can elect to amortize up to $10,000 of qualified reforestation expenditures paid or incurred during the tax year. However, the amortization is not deducted by the corporation but the amortizable basis is instead separately allocated among the shareholders. See the instructions on page 26 for Schedule K-1, line 23, item 19 and Pub. 535 for more details.
- Fines or penalties paid to a government for violating any law. Report these expenses on Schedule K, line 19.
- Expenses allocable to tax-exempt income. Report these expenses on Schedule K, line 19.
- Net operating losses as provided by section 172 or the special deductions in sections 241 through 249 (except the election to amortize organizational expenditures under section 248). These deductions cannot be claimed by an S corporation.

Note: Shareholders are allowed, subject to limitations, to deduct from gross income the corporation's net operating loss. See section 1366.

Special Rules

Commercial revitalization deduction. If the corporation constructs, purchases, or substantially rehabilitates a qualified building in a renewal community, it may qualify for a deduction of either (a) 50% of qualified capital expenditures in the year the building is placed in service or (b) amortization of 100% of the qualified capital expenditures over a 120-month period beginning with the month the building is placed in service. If the corporation elects to amortize these expenditures, complete and attach Form 4562. To qualify, the building must be nonresidential (as defined in section 168(e)(2)) and placed in service by the corporation. The corporation must be the original user of the building unless it is substantially rehabilitated. The amount of the qualified expenditures cannot exceed the lesser of $10 million or the amount allocated to the building by the commercial revitalization agency of the state in which the building is located. Any remaining expenditures are depreciated over the regular depreciation recovery period. See **Pub. 954,** Tax Incentives for Empowerment Zones and Other Distressed Communities, and section 1400I for details.

Rental real estate. The corporation cannot deduct commercial revitalization expenditures for a building placed in service as rental real estate. Instead, the commercial revitalization deduction for rental real estate is reported separately to shareholders; see line 23, item 22, of Schedule K-1.

Travel, meals, and entertainment. Subject to limitations and restrictions discussed below, a corporation can deduct ordinary and necessary travel, meals, and entertainment expenses paid or incurred in its trade or business. Special rules apply to deductions for gifts, skybox rentals, luxury water travel, convention expenses, and entertainment tickets. See section 274 and Pub. 463 for more details.

Travel. The corporation cannot deduct travel expenses of any individual accompanying a corporate officer or employee, including a spouse or dependent of the officer or employee, unless:
- That individual is an employee of the corporation, and
- His or her travel is for a bona fide business purpose and would otherwise be deductible by that individual.

Meals and entertainment. Generally, the corporation can deduct only 50% of the amount otherwise allowable for meals and entertainment expenses. In addition (subject to exceptions under section 274(k)(2)):
- Meals must not be lavish or extravagant,
- A bona fide business discussion must occur during, immediately before, or immediately after the meal; and
- An employee of the corporation must be present at the meal.

See section 274(n)(3) for a special rule that applies to expenses for meals consumed by individuals subject to the

hours of service limits of the Department of Transportation.

Membership dues. The corporation may deduct amounts paid or incurred for membership dues in civic or public service organizations, professional organizations (such as bar and medical associations), business leagues, trade associations, chambers of commerce, boards of trade, and real estate boards. However, no deduction is allowed if a principal purpose of the organization is to entertain, or provide entertainment facilities for, members or their guests. In addition, corporations may not deduct membership dues in any club organized for business, pleasure, recreation, or other social purpose. This includes country clubs, golf and athletic clubs, airline and hotel clubs, and clubs operated to provide meals under conditions favorable to business discussion.

Entertainment facilities. The corporation cannot deduct an expense paid or incurred for a facility (such as a yacht or hunting lodge) used for an activity usually considered entertainment, amusement, or recreation.

Note: *The corporation may be able to deduct otherwise nondeductible meals, travel, and entertainment expenses if the amounts are treated as compensation and reported on Form W-2 for an employee or on Form 1099-MISC for an independent contractor.*

Lobbying expenses. Do not deduct amounts paid or incurred to participate in, or intervene in any political campaign on behalf of a candidate for public office, or to influence the general public regarding legislative matters, elections, or referendums. In addition, corporations generally cannot deduct expenses paid or incurred to influence Federal or state legislation, or to influence the actions or positions of certain Federal executive branch officials. However, certain in-house lobbying expenditures that do not exceed $2,000 are deductible. See section 162(e) for more details.

Clean-fuel vehicles and certain refueling property. A deduction is allowed for part of the cost of qualified clean-fuel vehicle property and qualified clean-fuel vehicle refueling property placed in service during the tax year. For more details, see section 179A and Pub. 535.

Certain corporations engaged in farming. Section 464(f) limits the deduction for certain expenditures of S corporations engaged in farming that use the cash method of accounting, and whose prepaid farm supplies are more than 50% of other deductible farming expenses. Prepaid farm supplies include expenses for feed, seed, fertilizer, and similar farm supplies not used or consumed during the year. They also include the cost of poultry that would be allowable as a deduction in a later tax year if the corporation were to (a) capitalize the cost of poultry bought for use in its farm business and deduct it ratably over the lesser of 12 months or the useful life of the poultry and (b) deduct the cost of poultry bought for

Instructions for Form 1120S

resale in the year it sells or otherwise disposes of it. If the limit applies, the corporation can deduct prepaid farm supplies that do not exceed 50% of its other deductible farm expenses in the year of payment. The excess is deductible only in the year the corporation uses or consumes the supplies (other than poultry, which is deductible as explained above). For exceptions and more details on these rules, see **Pub. 225,** Farmer's Tax Guide.

Line 21—Ordinary Income (Loss)

Enter this income or loss on line 1 of Schedule K. Line 21 income is not used in figuring the tax on line 22a or 22b. See the instructions for line 22a for figuring taxable income for purposes of line 22a or 22b tax.

Tax and Payments

Line 22a—Excess Net Passive Income Tax

If the corporation has always been an S corporation, the excess net passive income tax does not apply.

If the corporation has accumulated earnings and profits (E&P) at the close of its tax year, has passive investment income for the tax year that is in excess of 25% of gross receipts, **and** has taxable income at year-end, the corporation must pay a tax on the excess net passive income. Complete lines 1 through 3 and line 9 of the worksheet below to make this determination. If line 2 is greater than line 3 and the corporation has taxable income (see instructions for line 9 of worksheet), it must pay the tax. Complete a separate schedule using the format of lines 1 through 11 of the worksheet below to figure the tax. Enter the tax on line 22a, page 1, Form 1120S, and attach the computation schedule to Form 1120S.

Reduce each item of passive income passed through to shareholders by its portion of tax on line 22a. See section 1366(f)(3).

Line 22b—Tax From Schedule D (Form 1120S)

Enter the built-in gains tax from line 22 of Part III of Schedule D. See the instructions for Part III of Schedule D to

determine if the corporation is liable for the tax.

Line 22c

Include in the total for line 22c the following:

Investment credit recapture tax. The corporation is liable for investment credit recapture attributable to credits allowed for tax years for which the corporation was not an S corporation. Figure the corporation's investment credit recapture tax by completing **Form 4255,** Recapture of Investment Credit.

To the left of the line 22c total, enter the amount of recapture tax and "Tax From Form 4255." Attach Form 4255 to Form 1120S.

LIFO recapture tax. The corporation may be liable for the additional tax due to LIFO recapture under Regulations section 1.1363-2 if—
• The corporation used the LIFO inventory pricing method for its last tax year as a C corporation, or
• A C corporation transferred LIFO inventory to the corporation in a nonrecognition transaction in which those assets were transferred basis property.

The additional tax due to LIFO recapture is figured for the corporation's last tax year as a C corporation or for the tax year of the transfer, whichever applies. See the Instructions for Forms 1120 and 1120-A to figure the tax. The tax is paid in four equal installments. The C corporation must pay the first installment by the due date (not including extensions) of Form 1120 for the corporation's last tax year as a C corporation or for the tax year of the transfer, whichever applies. The S corporation must pay each of the remaining installments by the due date (not including extensions) of Form 1120S for the 3 succeeding tax years. Include this year's installment in the total amount to be entered on line 22c. To the left of the total on line 22c, enter the installment amount and "LIFO tax."

Interest due under the look-back method for completed long-term contracts. If the corporation owes interest, attach **Form 8697,** Interest Computation Under the Look-Back Method for Completed Long-Term Contracts. To the left of the total on line 22c, enter the amount owed and "From Form 8697."

Interest due under the look-back method for property depreciated under the income forecast method. If the corporation owes interest, attach **Form 8866,** Interest Computation Under the Look-Back Method for Property Depreciated Under the Income Forecast Method. To the left of the total on line 22c, enter the amount owed and "From Form 8866."

Line 23d

If the S corporation is a beneficiary of a trust and the trust makes a section 643(g) election to credit its estimated tax payments to its beneficiaries, include the corporation's share of the payment (reported to the corporation on Schedule K-1 (Form 1041)) in the total amount entered on line 23d. Also, to the left of line 23d, enter "T" and the amount of the payment.

Line 24—Estimated Tax Penalty

A corporation that fails to make estimated tax payments when due may be subject to an underpayment penalty for the period of underpayment. Use **Form 2220,** Underpayment of Estimated Tax by Corporations, to see if the corporation owes a penalty and to figure the amount of the penalty. If you attach Form 2220 to Form 1120S, be sure to check the box on line 24 and enter the amount of any penalty on this line.

Line 27

If the corporation wants its refund directly deposited into its account at any U.S. bank or other financial institution instead of having a check sent to the corporation, complete Form 8050 and attach it to the corporation's return. However, the corporation cannot have its refund from an amended return directly deposited.

Worksheet for Line 22a

1. Enter gross receipts for the tax year (see section 1362(d)(3)(B) for gross receipts from the sale of capital assets)* . . . . _____
2. Enter passive investment income as defined in section 1362(d)(3)(C)* . _____
3. Enter 25% of line 1 (If line 2 is less than line 3, stop here. You are not liable for this tax.) . . . . _____

4. Excess passive investment income— Subtract line 3 from line 2 . . _____
5. Enter deductions directly connected with the production of income on line 2 (see section 1375(b)(2))* . . _____
6. Net passive income—Subtract line 5 from line 2 . . . . _____
7. Divide amount on line 4 by amount on line 2 . . . . _____ %

8. Excess net passive income—Multiply line 6 by line 7 . . . . _____
9. Enter taxable income (see instructions for taxable income below) . . _____
10. Enter smaller of line 8 or line 9 . . _____
11. Excess net passive income tax—Enter 35% of line 10. Enter here and on line 22a, page 1, Form 1120S . . . _____

*Income and deductions on lines 1, 2, and 5 are from total operations for the tax year. This includes applicable income and expenses from page 1, Form 1120S, as well as those reported separately on Schedule K. See section 1375(b)(4) for an exception regarding lines 2 and 5.

Line 9 of Worksheet—Taxable income

Line 9 taxable income is defined in Regulations section 1.1374-1(d). Figure this income by completing lines 1 through 28 of **Form 1120,** U.S. Corporation Income Tax Return. Include the Form 1120 computation with the worksheet computation you attach to Form 1120S. You do not have to attach the schedules, etc., called for on Form 1120. However, you may want to complete certain Form 1120 schedules, such as Schedule D (Form 1120) if you have capital gains or losses.

Instructions for Form 1120S

Schedule A—Cost of Goods Sold

Generally, inventories are required at the beginning and end of each tax year if the production, purchase, or sale of merchandise is an income-producing factor. See Regulations section 1.471-1.

However, if the corporation is a qualifying taxpayer or a qualifying small business taxpayer, it may adopt or change its accounting method to account for inventoriable items in the same manner as materials and supplies that are not incidental.

A **qualifying taxpayer** is a taxpayer **(a)** whose average annual gross receipts for the 3 prior tax years are $1 million or less and **(b)** whose business is not a tax shelter (as defined in section 448(d)(3)).

A **qualifying small business taxpayer (a)** whose average annual gross receipts for the 3 prior tax years are more than $1 million but not more than $10 million, **(b)** whose business is not a tax shelter (as defined in section 448(d)(3)), and **(c)** whose principal business activity is not an ineligible activity as explained in Rev. Proc. 2002-28.

Under this accounting method, inventory costs for raw materials purchased for use in producing finished goods and merchandise purchased for resale are deductible in the year the finished goods or merchandise are sold (but not before the year the corporation paid for the raw materials or merchandise if it is also using the cash method). For additional information on this method of accounting for inventoriable items, see Rev. Proc. 2001-10 if you are a qualifying taxpayer or Rev. Proc. 2002-28 if you are a qualifying small business taxpayer.

Enter amounts paid for all raw materials and merchandise during the tax year on line 2. The amount the corporation can deduct for the tax year is figured on line 8.

Section 263A Uniform Capitalization Rules

The uniform capitalization rules of section 263A are discussed under **Limitations on Deductions** on page 12. See those instructions before completing Schedule A.

Line 1—Inventory at Beginning of Year

If the corporation is changing its method of accounting for the current tax year to no longer account for inventories, it must refigure last year's closing inventory using the new method of accounting and enter the result on line 1. If there is a difference between last year's closing inventory and the refigured amount, attach an explanation and take it into account when figuring the corporation's section 481(a) adjustment (explained on page 4).

Line 4—Additional Section 263A Costs

An entry is required on this line only for corporations that have elected a simplified method of accounting.

Instructions for Form 1120S

For corporations that have elected the simplified production method, additional section 263A costs are generally those costs, other than interest, that were not capitalized under the corporation's method of accounting immediately prior to the effective date of section 263A that are required to be capitalized under section 263A. For new corporations, additional section 263A costs are the costs, other than interest, that must be capitalized under section 263A, but which the corporation would not have been required to capitalize if it had existed before the effective date of section 263A. For more details, see Regulations section 1.263A-2(b).

For corporations that have elected the simplified resale method, additional section 263A costs are generally those costs incurred with respect to the following categories:
• Off-site storage or warehousing;
• Purchasing;
• Handling, such as processing, assembly, repackaging, and transporting; and
• General and administrative costs (mixed service costs).

For more details, see Regulations section 1.263A-3(d).

Enter on line 4 the balance of section 263A costs paid or incurred during the tax year not includable on lines 2, 3, and 5.

Line 5—Other Costs

Enter on line 5 any other inventoriable costs paid or incurred during the tax year not entered on lines 2 through 4.

Line 7—Inventory at End of Year

See Regulations sections 1.263A-1 through 1.263A-3 for details on figuring the costs to be included in ending inventory.

If the corporation accounts for inventories in the same manner as materials and supplies that are not incidental, enter on line 7 the portion of its raw materials and merchandise purchased for resale that are included on line 6 and were not sold during the year. See Rev. Proc. 2001-10 and Rev. Proc. 2002-28 for more information.

Lines 9a Through 9e—Inventory Valuation Methods

Inventories can be valued at:
• Cost.
• Cost or market value (whichever is lower).
• Any other method approved by the IRS that conforms to the requirements of the applicable regulations.

However, the corporation is required to use cost if it chooses to account for inventory items in the same manner as materials and supplies that are not incidental.

Corporations that account for inventories in the same manner as materials and supplies that are not incidental may currently deduct expenditures for direct labor and all indirect costs that would otherwise be included in inventory costs.

The average cost (rolling average) method of valuing inventories generally does not conform to the requirements of the regulations. See Rev. Rul. 71-234, 1971-1 C.B. 148.

Corporations that use erroneous valuation methods must change to a method permitted for Federal income tax purposes. To make this change, use Form 3115.

On line 9a, check the method(s) used for valuing inventories. Under "lower of cost or market," *market* (for normal goods) means the current bid price prevailing on the inventory valuation date for the particular merchandise in the volume usually purchased by the taxpayer. For a manufacturer, market applies to the basic elements of cost—raw materials, labor, and burden. If section 263A applies to the taxpayer, the basic elements of cost must reflect the current bid price of all direct costs and all indirect costs properly allocable to goods on hand at the inventory date.

Inventory may be valued below cost when the merchandise is unsalable at normal prices or unusable in the normal way because the goods are "subnormal" due to damage, imperfections, shop wear, etc., within the meaning of Regulations section 1.471-2(c). These goods may be valued at a current bona fide selling price minus direct cost of disposition (but not less than scrap value) if such a price can be established.

If this is the first year the last-in, first-out (LIFO) inventory method was either adopted or extended to inventory goods not previously valued under the LIFO method provided in section 472, attach **Form 970,** Application To Use LIFO Inventory Method, or a statement with the information required by Form 970. Also check the LIFO box on line 9c. On line 9d, enter the amount or the percent of total closing inventories covered under section 472. Estimates are acceptable.

If the corporation has changed or extended its inventory method to LIFO and has had to "write up" its opening inventory to cost in the year of election, report the effect of this write-up as income (line 5, page 1) proportionately over a 3-year period that begins with the tax year of the election (section 472(d)).

See Pub. 538 for more information on inventory valuation methods.

Schedule B—Other Information

Be sure to answer the questions and provide other information in items 1 through 8.

Line 7

Complete line 7 if the corporation **(a)** was a C corporation before it elected to be an S corporation **or** the corporation acquired an asset with a basis determined by reference to its basis (or the basis of any other property) in the hands of a C corporation and **(b)** has net unrealized built-in gain (defined below) in excess of the net recognized built-in gain from prior years.

The corporation is liable for section 1374 tax if **(a)** and **(b)** above apply and it has a net recognized built-in gain (section 1374(d)(2)) for its tax year.

The corporation's net unrealized built-in gain is the amount, if any, by which the fair market value of the assets of the corporation at the beginning of its first S corporation year (or as of the date the assets were acquired, for any asset with a basis determined by reference to its basis (or the basis of any other property) in the hands of a C corporation) exceeds the aggregate adjusted basis of such assets at that time.

Enter on line 7 the corporation's net unrealized built-in gain reduced by the net recognized built-in gain for prior years. See sections 1374(c)(2) and (d)(1).

Line 8

Check the box on line 8 if the corporation was a C corporation in a prior year and has accumulated earnings and profits (E&P) at the close of its 2002 tax year. For details on figuring accumulated E&P, see section 312. If the corporation has accumulated E&P, it may be liable for tax imposed on excess net passive income. See the instructions for line 22a, page 1, of Form 1120S for details on this tax.

General Instructions for Schedules K and K-1— Shareholders' Shares of Income, Credits, Deductions, etc.

Purpose of Schedules

The corporation is liable for taxes on lines 22a, 22b, and 22c, page 1, Form 1120S. Shareholders are liable for income tax on their shares of the corporation's income (reduced by any taxes paid by the corporation on income) and must include their share of the income on their tax return whether or not it is distributed to them. Unlike most partnership income, S corporation income is **not** self-employment income and is not subject to self-employment tax.

Schedule K is a summary schedule of all the shareholders' shares of the corporation's income, deductions, credits, etc. Schedule K-1 shows each shareholder's separate share. Attach a copy of each shareholder's Schedule K-1 to the Form 1120S filed with the IRS. Keep a copy as a part of the corporation's records, and give each shareholder a separate copy.

The total pro rata share items (column (b)) of all Schedules K-1 should equal the amount reported on the same line of Schedule K. Lines 1 through 20 of Schedule K correspond to lines 1 through 20 of Schedule K-1. Other lines do not correspond, but instructions explain the differences.

Be sure to give each shareholder a copy of the Shareholder's Instructions for Schedule K-1 (Form 1120S). These instructions are available separately from Schedule K-1 at most IRS offices.

Note: *Instructions that apply only to line items reported on Schedule K-1 may be prepared and given to each shareholder instead of the instructions printed by the IRS.*

Substitute Forms

The corporation **does not** need IRS approval to use a substitute Schedule K-1 if it is an exact copy of the IRS schedule, **or** if it contains only those lines the taxpayer is required to use, and the lines have the same numbers and titles and are in the same order as on the IRS Schedule K-1. In either case, the substitute schedule must include the OMB number and either **(a)** the Shareholder's Instructions for Schedule K-1 (Form 1120S) or **(b)** instructions that apply to the items reported on Schedule K-1 (Form 1120S).

The corporation must request IRS approval to use other substitute Schedules K-1. To request approval, write to Internal Revenue Service, Attention: Substitute Forms Program Coordinator, W:CAR:MP:FP:S:SP, 1111 Constitution Avenue, NW, Washington, DC 20224.

The corporation may be subject to a penalty if it files a substitute Schedule K-1 that does not conform to the specifications of Rev. Proc. 2001-45, 2001-37 I.R.B. 227.

Shareholder's Pro Rata Share Items

General Rule

Items of income, loss, deductions, etc., are allocated to a shareholder on a daily basis, according to the number of shares of stock held by the shareholder on each day during the tax year of the corporation. See the instructions for item A.

A shareholder who disposes of stock is treated as the shareholder for the day of disposition. A shareholder who dies is treated as the shareholder for the day of the shareholder's death.

Special Rules

Termination of shareholder's interest. If a shareholder terminates his or her interest in a corporation during the tax year, the corporation, with the consent of all affected shareholders (including the one whose interest is terminated), may elect to allocate income and expenses, etc., as if the corporation's tax year consisted of 2 separate tax years, the first of which ends on the date of the shareholder's termination.

To make the election, the corporation must attach a statement to a timely filed original or amended Form 1120S for the tax year for which the election is made. In the statement, the corporation must state that it is electing under section 1377(a)(2) and Regulations section 1.1377-1(b) to treat the tax year as if it consisted of 2 separate tax years. The statement must also explain how the shareholder's entire interest was terminated (e.g., sale or gift), and state that the corporation and each affected shareholder consent to the corporation making the election. A corporate officer must sign the statement under penalties of perjury on behalf of the

corporation. A single statement may be filed for all terminating elections made for the tax year. If the election is made, write "Section 1377(a)(2) Election Made" at the top of each affected shareholder's Schedule K-1.

For more details on the election, see Regulations section 1.1377-1(b).

Qualifying dispositions. If a qualifying disposition takes place during the tax year, the corporation may make an irrevocable election to allocate income and expenses, etc., as if the corporation's tax year consisted of 2 tax years, the first of which ends on the close of the day on which the qualifying disposition occurs. A qualifying disposition is:

   1. A disposition by a shareholder of at least 20% of the corporation's outstanding stock in one or more transactions in any 30-day period during the tax year,

   2. A redemption treated as an exchange under section 302(a) or 303(a) of at least 20% of the corporation's outstanding stock in one or more transactions in any 30-day period during the tax year, or

   3. An issuance of stock that equals at least 25% of the previously outstanding stock to one or more new shareholders in any 30-day period during the tax year.

To make the election, the corporation must attach a statement to a timely filed original or amended Form 1120S for the tax year for which the election is made. In the statement, the corporation must state that it is electing under Regulations section 1.1368-1(g)(2)(i) to treat the tax year as if it consisted of separate tax years. The statement must also give the facts relating to the qualifying disposition (e.g., sale, gift, stock issuance, or redemption), and state that each shareholder who held stock in the corporation during the tax year consents to the election. A corporate officer must sign the statement under penalties of perjury on behalf of the corporation. A single election statement may be filed for all elections made under this special rule for the tax year.

For more details on the election, see Regulations section 1.1368-1(g)(2).

Specific Instructions (Schedule K Only)

Enter the total amount for each applicable line item on Schedule K.

Specific Instructions (Schedule K-1 Only)

General Information

On each Schedule K-1, complete the date spaces at the top; enter the names, addresses, and identifying numbers of the shareholder and corporation; complete items A through D; and enter the shareholder's pro rata share of each item. **Schedule K-1 must be prepared and given to each shareholder on or before the day on which Form 1120S is filed.**

Note: *Space has been provided on line 23 (Supplemental Information) of*

Instructions for Form 1120S

Schedule K-1 for the corporation to provide additional information to shareholders. This space, if sufficient, should be used in place of any attached schedules required for any lines on Schedule K-1, or other amounts not shown on lines 1 through 22 of Schedule K-1. Please be sure to identify the applicable line number next to the information entered below line 23.

Special Reporting Requirements for Corporations With Multiple Activities

If items of income, loss, deduction, or credit from more than one activity (determined for purposes of the passive activity loss and credit limitations) are reported on lines 1, 2, or 3 of Schedule K-1, the corporation must provide information for each activity to its shareholders. See **Passive Activity Reporting Requirements** on page 10 for details on the reporting requirements.

Special Reporting Requirements for At-Risk Activities

If the corporation is involved in one or more at-risk activities for which a loss is reported on Schedule K-1, the corporation must report information separately for each at-risk activity. See section 465(c) for a definition of at-risk activities.

For each at-risk activity, the following information must be provided on an attachment to Schedule K-1:

1. A statement that the information is a breakdown of at-risk activity loss amounts.

2. The identity of the at-risk activity; the loss amount for the activity; other income and deductions; and other information that relates to the activity.

Specific Items

Item A

If there was no change in shareholders or in the relative interest in stock the shareholders owned during the tax year, enter the percentage of total stock owned by each shareholder during the tax year. For example, if shareholders X and Y each owned 50% for the entire tax year, enter 50% in item A for each shareholder. Each shareholder's pro rata share items (lines 1 through 20 of Schedule K-1) are figured by multiplying the Schedule K amount on the corresponding line of Schedule K by the percentage in item A.

If there was a change in shareholders or in the relative interest in stock the shareholders owned during the tax year, each shareholder's percentage of ownership is weighted for the number of days in the tax year that stock was owned. For example, A and B each held 50% for half the tax year and A, B, and C held 40%, 40%, and 20%, respectively, for the remaining half of the tax year. The percentage of ownership for the year for A, B, and C is figured as follows and is then entered in item A.

	a	b	c (a × b)	
	% of total stock owned	% of tax year held	% of ownership for the year	
A	50 40	50 50	25 +20	45
B	50 40	50 50	25 +20	45
C	20	50	10	10
Total	. . . .			100%

If there was a change in shareholders or in the relative interest in stock the shareholders owned during the tax year, each shareholder's pro rata share items generally are figured by multiplying the Schedule K amount by the percentage in item A. However, if a shareholder terminated his or her entire interest in the corporation during the year or a qualifying disposition took place, the corporation may elect to allocate income and expenses, etc., as if the tax year consisted of 2 tax years, the first of which ends on the day of the termination or qualifying disposition. See **Special Rules** on page 18 for more details. Each shareholder's pro rata share items are figured separately for each period on a daily basis, based on the percentage of stock held by the shareholder on each day.

Item B

Enter the Internal Revenue Service Center address where the Form 1120S, to which a copy of this K-1 was attached, was or will be filed.

Item C

If the corporation is a registration-required tax shelter or has invested in a registration-required tax shelter, it must enter its tax shelter registration number in item C. Also, a corporation that has invested in a registration-required shelter must furnish a copy of its Form 8271 to its shareholders. See Form 8271 for more details.

Specific Instructions (Schedules K and K-1, Except as Noted)

Income (Loss)

Reminder: Before entering income items on Schedule K or K-1, be sure to reduce the items of income for the following:

1. Built-in gains tax (Schedule D, Part III, line 22). Each recognized built-in gain item (within the meaning of section 1374(d)(3)) is reduced by its proportionate share of the built-in gains tax.

2. Excess net passive income tax (line 22a, page 1, Form 1120S). Each item of passive investment income (within the meaning of section 1362(d)(3)(C)) is reduced by its proportionate share of the net passive income tax.

Line 1—Ordinary Income (Loss) From Trade or Business Activities

Enter the amount from line 21, page 1. Enter the income or loss without reference to **(a)** shareholders' basis in the stock of the corporation and in any indebtedness of the corporation to the shareholders (section 1366(d)), **(b)** shareholders' at-risk limitations, and **(c)** shareholders' passive activity limitations. These limitations, if applicable, are determined at the shareholder level.

If the corporation is involved in more than one trade or business activity, see **Passive Activity Reporting Requirements** on page 10 for details on the information to be reported for each activity. If an at-risk activity loss is reported on line 1, see **Special Reporting Requirements for At-Risk Activities** on this page.

Line 2—Net Income (Loss) From Rental Real Estate Activities

Enter the net income or loss from rental real estate activities of the corporation from **Form 8825,** Rental Real Estate Income and Expenses of a Partnership or an S Corporation. Each Form 8825 has space for reporting the income and expenses of up to eight properties.

If the corporation has income or loss from more than one rental real estate activity reported on line 2, see **Passive Activity Reporting Requirements** on page 10 for details on the information to be reported for each activity. If an at-risk activity loss is reported on line 2, see **Special Reporting Requirements for At-Risk Activities** on this page.

Line 3—Income and Expenses of Other Rental Activities

Enter on lines 3a and 3b of Schedule K (line 3 of Schedule K-1) the income and expenses of rental activities other than those reported on Form 8825. If the corporation has more than one rental activity reported on line 3, see **Passive Activity Reporting Requirements** on page 10 for details on the information to be reported for each activity. If an at-risk activity loss is reported on line 3, see **Special Reporting Requirements for At-Risk Activities** on this page. Also see **Rental Activities** on page 8 for a definition and other details on other rental activities.

Lines 4a Through 4f—Portfolio Income (Loss)

Enter portfolio income (loss) on lines 4a through 4f. See **Portfolio Income** on page 9 for the definition of portfolio income. Do not reduce portfolio income by deductions allocated to it. Report such deductions (other than interest expense) on line 9 of Schedules K and K-1. Interest expense allocable to portfolio income is generally investment interest expense and is reported on line 11a of Schedules K and K-1.

Lines 4a and 4b. Enter only taxable interest and ordinary dividends that are portfolio income. Interest income derived in the ordinary course of the corporation's trade or business, such as interest charged on receivable balances, is

Instructions for Form 1120S

reported on line 5, page 1, Form 1120S. See Temporary Regulations section 1.469-2T(c)(3).

Lines 4d, 4e(1), 4e(2), and 4e(3). Enter on line 4d the gain or loss that is portfolio income (loss) from Schedule D (Form 1120S), line 6. Enter on line 4e(1) the gain or loss that is portfolio income (loss) from Schedule D (Form 1120S), line 14. Enter on line 4e(2) the gain or loss that is portfolio income (loss) from Schedule D (Form 1120S), line 13. Enter on line 4e(3) the gains (not losses) from the disposition of assets (excluding property that could qualify for section 1202 gain) held more than 5 years that is portfolio income included on Schedule D (Form 1120S), line 14.

If any gain or loss from lines 6, 13, and 14 of Schedule D is not portfolio income (e.g., gain or loss from the disposition of nondepreciable personal property used in a trade or business), do not report this income or loss on lines 4d and 4e(1) through 4e(3). Instead, report it on line 6 of Schedules K and K-1.

Line 4f. Enter any other portfolio income not reported on lines 4a through 4e.

If the corporation holds a residual interest in a REMIC, report on an attachment for line 4f each shareholder's share of taxable income (net loss) from the REMIC (line 1b of Schedule Q (Form 1066)); excess inclusion (line 2c of Schedule Q (Form 1066)); and section 212 expenses (line 3b of Schedule Q (Form 1066)). Because Schedule Q (Form 1066) is a quarterly statement, the corporation must follow the Schedule Q (Form 1066) Instructions for Residual Interest Holder to figure the amounts to report to shareholders for the corporation's tax year.

Line 5—Net Section 1231 Gain (Loss) (Other Than Due to Casualty or Theft)

Enter the net section 1231 gain (loss) (excluding net gain from involuntary conversions due to casualty or theft) from Form 4797, line 7. If the corporation had a gain from any section 1231 property held more than 5 years, show the total of all such gains on an attachment to Schedule K-1; do not include any gain attributable to straight-line depreciation from section 1250 property. Indicate on the statement that this amount should be included in the shareholder's computation of qualified 5-year gain only if the amount on the shareholder's Form 4797, line 7, is more than zero.

Report net gain or loss from involuntary conversions due to casualty or theft on line 6.

If the corporation is involved in more than one trade or business or rental activity, see **Passive Activity Reporting Requirements** on page 10 for details on the information to be reported for each activity. If an at-risk activity loss is reported on line 5, see **Special Reporting Requirements for At-Risk Activities** on page 19.

Line 6—Other Income (Loss)

Enter any other item of income or loss not included on lines 1 through 5. Items to be reported on line 6 include:
• Recoveries of tax benefit items (section 111).
• Gambling gains and losses (section 165(d)).
• Gains from the disposition of an interest in oil, gas, geothermal, or other mineral properties (section 1254).
• Net gain (loss) from involuntary conversions due to casualty or theft. The amount for this item is shown on **Form 4684**, Casualties and Thefts, line 38a or 38b.
• Any net gain or loss from section 1256 contracts from **Form 6781**, Gains and Losses From Section 1256 Contracts and Straddles.
• Gain from the sale or exchange of qualified small business stock (as defined in the Instructions for Schedule D) that is eligible for the 50% section 1202 exclusion. To be eligible for the section 1202 exclusion, the stock must have been held by the corporation for more than 5 years. Corporate shareholders are not eligible for the section 1202 exclusion. Additional limitations apply at the shareholder level. Report each shareholder's share of section 1202 gain on Schedule K-1. Each shareholder will determine if he or she qualifies for the section 1202 exclusion. Report on an attachment to Schedule K-1 for each sale or exchange the name of the qualified small business that issued the stock, the shareholder's share of the corporation's adjusted basis and sales price of the stock, and the dates the stock was bought and sold.
• Gain eligible for section 1045 rollover (replacement stock purchased by the corporation). Include only gain from the sale or exchange of qualified small business stock (as defined in the Instructions for Schedule D) that was deferred by the corporation under section 1045 and reported on Schedule D. See the Instructions for Schedule D for more details. Corporate shareholders are not eligible for the section 1045 rollover. Additional limitations apply at the shareholder level. Report each shareholder's share of the gain eligible for section 1045 rollover on Schedule K-1. Each shareholder will determine if he or she qualifies for the rollover. Report on an attachment to Schedule K-1 for each sale or exchange the name of the qualified small business that issued the stock, the shareholder's share of the corporation's adjusted basis and sales price of the stock, and the dates the stock was bought and sold.
• Gain eligible for section 1045 rollover (replacement stock not purchased by the corporation). Include only gain from the sale or exchange of qualified small business stock (as defined in the Instructions for Schedule D) the corporation held for more than 6 months but that **was not** deferred by the corporation under section 1045. See the Instructions for Schedule D for more details. A shareholder (other than a corporation) may be eligible to defer his or her pro rata share of this gain under

section 1045 if he or she purchases other qualified small business stock during the 60-day period that began on the date the stock was sold by the corporation. Additional limitations apply at the shareholder level. Report on an attachment to Schedule K-1 for each sale or exchange the name of the qualified small business that issued the stock, the shareholder's share of the corporation's adjusted basis and sales price of the stock, and the dates the stock was bought and sold.
• If the corporation had a gain from the disposition of non-depreciable personal property used in a trade or business held more than 5 years, show the total of all such gains on an attachment to Schedule K-1. Indicate on the statement that the shareholder should include this amount on line 5 of the worksheet for line 29 of Schedule D (Form 1040). If the income or loss is attributable to more than one activity, report the income or loss amount separately for each activity on an attachment to Schedule K-1 and identify the activity to which the income or loss relates.

If the corporation is involved in more than one trade or business or rental activity, see **Passive Activity Reporting Requirements** on page 10 for details on the information to be reported for each activity. If an at-risk activity loss is reported on line 6, see **Special Reporting Requirements for At-Risk Activities** on page 19.

Deductions

Line 7—Charitable Contributions

Enter the amount of charitable contributions paid during the tax year. On an attachment to Schedules K and K-1, show separately the dollar amount of contributions subject to each of the 50%, 30%, and 20% of adjusted gross income limits. For additional information, see **Pub. 526**, Charitable Contributions.

 An accrual basis S corporation may not elect to treat a contribution as having been paid in the tax year the board of directors authorizes the payment if the contribution is not actually paid until the next tax year.

Generally, no deduction is allowed for any contribution of $250 or more unless the corporation obtains a written acknowledgment from the charitable organization that shows the amount of cash contributed, describes any property contributed, and gives an estimate of the value of any goods or services provided in return for the contribution. The acknowledgment must be obtained by the due date (including extensions) of the corporation's return, or if earlier, the date the corporation files its return. Do not attach the acknowledgment to the tax return, but keep it with the corporation's records. These rules apply in addition to the filing requirements for Form 8283 described on page 21.

Certain contributions made to an organization conducting lobbying activities are not deductible. See section 170(f)(9) for more details.

Instructions for Form 1120S

If the corporation contributes property other than cash and the deduction claimed for such property exceeds $500, complete **Form 8283**, Noncash Charitable Contributions, and attach it to Form 1120S. The corporation must give a copy of its Form 8283 to every shareholder if the deduction for any item or group of similar items of contributed property exceeds $5,000, even if the amount allocated to any shareholder is $5,000 or less.

If the deduction for an item or group of similar items of contributed property is $5,000 or less, the corporation must report each shareholder's pro rata share of the amount of noncash contributions to enable individual shareholders to complete their own Forms 8283. See the Instructions for Form 8283 for more information.

If the corporation made a qualified conservation contribution under section 170(h), also include the fair market value of the underlying property before and after the donation, as well as the type of legal interest contributed, and describe the conservation purpose furthered by the donation. Give a copy of this information to each shareholder.

Line 8—Section 179 Expense Deduction

An S corporation may elect to expense part of the cost of certain tangible property that the corporation purchased during the tax year for use in its trade or business or certain rental activities. See the Instructions for Form 4562 for more information.

Complete Part I of Form 4562 to figure the corporation's section 179 expense deduction. The corporation does not claim the deduction itself, but instead passes it through to the shareholders. Attach Form 4562 to Form 1120S and show the total section 179 expense deduction on Schedule K, line 8. Report each individual shareholder's pro rata share on Schedule K-1, line 8. Do not complete line 8 of Schedule K-1 for any shareholder that is an estate or trust.

If the corporation is an enterprise zone business, also report on an attachment to Schedules K and K-1 the cost of section 179 property placed in service during the year that is qualified zone property.

See the instructions for line 23 of Schedule K-1, item 3, for any recapture of a section 179 amount.

Line 9—Deductions Related to Portfolio Income (Loss)

Enter on line 9 the deductions clearly and directly allocable to portfolio income (other than interest expense). Interest expense related to portfolio income is investment interest expense and is reported on line 11a of Schedules K and K-1. Generally, the line 9 expenses are section 212 expenses and are subject to section 212 limitations at the shareholder level.

Note: *No deduction is allowed under section 212 for expenses allocable to a convention, seminar, or similar meeting. Because these expenses are not deductible by shareholders, the corporation does not report these expenses on line 9 or line 10. The expenses are nondeductible and are reported as such on line 19 of Schedules K and K-1.*

Line 10—Other Deductions

Enter any other deductions not included on lines 7, 8, 9, and 15g. On an attachment, identify the deduction and amount, and if the corporation has more than one activity, the activity to which the deduction relates.

Examples of items to be reported on an attachment to line 10 include:
● Amounts (other than investment interest required to be reported on line 11a of Schedules K and K-1) paid by the corporation that would be allowed as itemized deductions on a shareholder's income tax return if they were paid directly by a shareholder for the same purpose. These amounts include, but are not limited to, expenses under section 212 for the production of income other than from the corporation's trade or business.
● Any penalty on early withdrawal of savings not reported on line 9 because the corporation withdrew funds from its time savings deposit before its maturity.
● Soil and water conservation expenditures (section 175).
● Expenditures paid or incurred for the removal of architectural and transportation barriers to the elderly and disabled that the corporation has elected to treat as a current expense. See section 190.
● Contributions to a capital construction fund.
● Interest expense allocated to debt-financed distributions. See Notice 89-35, 1989-1 C.B. 675, for more information.
● If there was a gain (loss) from a casualty or theft to property not used in a trade or business or for income-producing purposes, provide each shareholder with the needed information to complete Form 4684.

Investment Interest

Lines 11a and 11b must be completed for all shareholders.

Line 11a—Investment Interest Expense

Include on this line the interest properly allocable to debt on property held for investment purposes. Property held for investment includes property that produces income (unless derived in the ordinary course of a trade or business) from interest, dividends, annuities, or royalties; and gains from the disposition of property that produces those types of income or is held for investment.

Investment interest expense **does not** include interest expense allocable to a passive activity.

Report investment interest expense only on line 11a of Schedules K and K-1.

The amount on line 11a will be deducted by individual shareholders on Schedule A (Form 1040), line 13, after applying the investment interest expense limitations of section 163(d).

For more information, see **Form 4952**, Investment Interest Expense Deduction.

Lines 11b(1) and 11b(2)— Investment Income and Expenses

Enter on line 11b(1) only the investment income included on lines 4a, b, c, and f of Schedule K-1. Do not include other portfolio gains or losses on this line.

Enter on line 11b(2) only the investment expense included on line 9 of Schedule K-1.

If there are other items of investment income or expense included in the amounts that are required to be passed through separately to the shareholders on Schedule K-1, such as net short-term capital gain or loss, net long-term capital gain or loss, and other portfolio gains or losses, give each shareholder a schedule identifying these amounts.

Investment income includes gross income from property held for investment, the excess of net gain attributable to the disposition of property held for investment over net capital gain from the disposition of property held for investment, and any net capital gain from the disposition of property held for investment that each shareholder elects to include in investment income under section 163(d)(4)(B)(iii). Generally, investment income and investment expenses do not include any income or expenses from a passive activity. See Regulations section 1.469-2(f)(10) for exceptions.

Property subject to a net lease is not treated as investment property because it is subject to the passive loss rules. Do not reduce investment income by losses from passive activities.

Investment expenses are deductible expenses (other than interest) directly connected with the production of investment income. See the Instructions for Form 4952 for more information on investment income and expenses.

Credits

Note: *If the corporation has credits from more than one trade or business activity on line 12a or 13, or from more than one rental activity on line 12b, 12c, 12d, or 12e, it must report separately on an attachment to Schedule K-1, the amount of each credit and provide any other applicable activity information listed in* **Passive Activity Reporting Requirements** *on page 10. However,* **do not** *attach* **Form 3800**, *General Business Credit, to Form 1120S.*

Line 12a—Credit for Alcohol Used as Fuel

Enter on line 12a of Schedule K the credit for alcohol used as fuel attributable to trade or business activities. Enter on line 12d or 12e the credit for alcohol used as fuel attributable to rental activities. Figure the credit on **Form 6478**, Credit for Alcohol Used as Fuel, and attach it to Form 1120S. The credit must be included in income on page 1, line 5, of Form 1120S. See section 40(f) for an election the corporation can make to have the credit not apply.

Instructions for Form 1120S   -21-

Enter each shareholder's share of the credit for alcohol used as fuel on line 12a, 12d, or 12e of Schedule K-1.

If this credit includes the small ethanol producer credit, identify on a statement attached to each Schedule K-1 **(a)** the amount of the small producer credit included in the total credit allocated to the shareholder, **(b)** the number of gallons of qualified ethanol fuel production allocated to the shareholder, and **(c)** the shareholder's pro rata share, in gallons, of the corporation's productive capacity for alcohol.

Line 12b—Low-Income Housing Credit

Section 42 provides for a credit that may be claimed by owners of low-income residential rental buildings. If shareholders are eligible to claim the low-income housing credit, complete the applicable parts of **Form 8586,** Low-Income Housing Credit, and attach it to Form 1120S. Enter the credit figured by the corporation on Form 8586, and any low-income housing credit received from other entities in which the corporation is allowed to invest, on the applicable line as explained below. The corporation must also complete and attach **Form 8609,** Low-Income Housing Credit Allocation Certification, and **Schedule A (Form 8609),** Annual Statement, to Form 1120S. See the Instructions for Form 8586 and Form 8609 for information on completing these forms.

Line 12b(1). If the corporation invested in a partnership to which the provisions of section 42(j)(5) apply, report on line 12b(1) the credit the partnership reported to the corporation on line 12a(1) of Schedule K-1 (Form 1065).

Line 12b(2). Report on line 12b(2) any low-income housing credit not reported on line 12b(1). This includes any credit from a partnership reported to the corporation on line 12a(2) of Schedule K-1 (Form 1065).

Note: *If part or all of the credit reported on line 12b(1) or 12b(2) is attributable to additions to qualified basis of property placed in service before 1990, report on an attachment to Schedules K and K-1 the amount of the credit on each line that is attributable to property placed in service* **(a)** *before 1990 and* **(b)** *after 1989.*

Line 12c—Qualified Rehabilitation Expenditures Related to Rental Real Estate Activities

Enter total qualified rehabilitation expenditures related to rental real estate activities of the corporation. For line 12c of Schedule K, complete the applicable lines of **Form 3468,** Investment Credit, that apply to qualified rehabilitation expenditures for property related to rental real estate activities of the corporation for which income or loss is reported on line 2 of Schedule K. See Form 3468 for details on qualified rehabilitation expenditures. Attach Form 3468 to Form 1120S.

For line 12c of Schedule K-1, enter each shareholder's pro rata share of the expenditures. On the dotted line to the left of the entry space for line 12c, enter the

line number of Form 3468 on which the shareholder should report the expenditures. If there is more than one type of expenditure, or the expenditures are from more than one line 2 activity, report this information separately for each expenditure or activity on an attachment to Schedules K and K-1.

Note: *Qualified rehabilitation expenditures **not** related to rental real estate activities must be listed separately on line 23 of Schedule K-1.*

Line 12d—Credits (Other Than Credits Shown on Lines 12b and 12c) Related to Rental Real Estate Activities

Enter on line 12d any other credit (other than credits on lines 12b and 12c) related to rental real estate activities. On the dotted line to the left of the entry space for line 12d, identify the type of credit. If there is more than one type of credit or the credit is from more than one line 2 activity, report this information separately for each credit or activity on an attachment to Schedules K and K-1. These credits may include any type of credit listed in the instructions for line 13.

Line 12e—Credits Related to Other Rental Activities

Enter on line 12e any credit related to other rental activities for which income or loss is reported on line 3 of Schedules K and K-1. On the dotted line to the left of the entry space for line 12e, identify the type of credit. If there is more than one type of credit or the credit is from more than one line 3 activity, report this information separately for each credit or activity on an attachment to Schedules K and K-1. These credits may include any type of credit listed in the instructions for line 13.

Line 13—Other Credits

Enter on line 13 any other credit, except credits or expenditures shown or listed for lines 12a through 12e of Schedules K and K-1 or the credit for Federal tax paid on fuels (which is reported on line 23c of page 1). On the dotted line to the left of the entry space for line 13, identify the type of credit. If there is more than one type of credit or the credit is from more than one activity, report this information separately for each credit or activity on an attachment to Schedules K and K-1.

The credits to be reported on line 13 and other required attachments follow.
• Credit for backup withholding on dividends, interest, or patronage dividends.
• Nonconventional source fuel credit. Figure this credit on a separate schedule and attach it to Form 1120S. See section 29 for rules on figuring the credit.
• Qualified electric vehicle credit (Form 8834).
• Unused investment credit from cooperatives. If the corporation is a member of a cooperative that passes an unused investment credit through to its members, the credit is in turn passed through to the corporation's shareholders.
• Work opportunity credit (Form 5884).
• Welfare-to-work credit (Form 8861).

• Credit for increasing research activities (Form 6765).
• Enhanced oil recovery credit (Form 8830).
• Disabled access credit (Form 8826).
• Renewable electricity production credit (Form 8835).
• Empowerment zone and renewable community employment credit (Form 8844).
• Indian employment credit (Form 8845).
• Credit for employer social security and Medicare taxes paid on certain employee tips (Form 8846).
• Orphan drug credit (Form 8820).
• New markets credit (Form 8874).
• Credit for contributions to selected community development corporations (Form 8847).
• Credit for small employer pension start-up costs (Form 8881).
• Credit for employer-provided child care facilities and services (Form 8882).
• New York Liberty Zone business employee credit (Form 8884).
• Qualified zone academy bond credit (Form 8860).
• General credits from an electing large partnership.

See the instructions on page 25 for line 21 (Schedule K) and line 23 (Schedule K-1) to report expenditures qualifying for the **(a)** rehabilitation credit not related to rental real estate activities, **(b)** energy credit, or **(c)** reforestation credit.

Adjustments and Tax Preference Items

Lines 14a through 14e must be completed for all shareholders.

Enter items of income and deductions that are adjustments or tax preference items for the alternative minimum tax (AMT). See **Form 6251,** Alternative Minimum Tax—Individuals, or Schedule I of **Form 1041,** U.S. Income Tax Return for Estates and Trusts, to determine the amounts to enter and for other information.

Do not include as a tax preference item any qualified expenditures to which an election under section 59(e) may apply. Because these expenditures are subject to an election by each shareholder, the corporation cannot figure the amount of any tax preference related to them. Instead, the corporation must pass through to each shareholder on lines 16a and 16b of Schedule K-1 the information needed to figure the deduction.

Line 14a—Depreciation Adjustment on Property Placed in Service After 1986

Figure the adjustment for line 14a based only on tangible property placed in service after 1986 (and tangible property placed in service after July 31, 1986, and before 1987 for which the corporation elected to use the general depreciation system). **Do not** make an adjustment for motion picture films, videotapes, sound recordings, certain public utility property (as defined in section 168(f)(2)), property depreciated under the unit-of-production method (or any other method not

Instructions for Form 1120S

expressed in a term of years), or qualified Indian reservation property.

For property placed in service **before 1999**, refigure depreciation for the AMT as follows (using the same convention used for the regular tax):
• For section 1250 property (generally, residential rental and nonresidential real property), use the straight line method over 40 years.
• For tangible property (other than section 1250 property) depreciated using the straight line method for the regular tax, use the straight line method over the property's class life. Use 12 years if the property has no class life.
• For any other tangible property, use the 150% declining balance method, switching to the straight line method the first tax year it gives a larger deduction, over the property's AMT class life. Use 12 years if the property has no class life.

Note: *See Pub. 946 for a table of class lives.*

For property placed in service **after 1998**, refigure depreciation for the AMT **only** for property depreciated for the regular tax using the 200% declining balance method. For the AMT, use the 150% declining balance method, switching to the straight line method the first tax year it gives a larger deduction, and the same convention and recovery period used for the regular tax.

Figure the adjustment by subtracting the AMT deduction for depreciation from the regular tax deduction and enter the result on line 14a. If the AMT deduction is more than the regular tax deduction, enter the difference as a negative amount. Depreciation capitalized to inventory must also be refigured using the AMT rules. Include on this line the current year adjustment to income, if any, resulting from the difference.

Line 14b—Adjusted Gain or Loss

If the corporation disposed of any tangible property placed in service after 1986 (or after July 31, 1986, if an election was made to use the General Depreciation System), or if it disposed of a certified pollution control facility placed in service after 1986, refigure the gain or loss from the disposition using the adjusted basis for the AMT. The property's adjusted basis for the AMT is its cost or other basis minus all depreciation or amortization deductions allowed or allowable for the AMT during the current tax year and previous tax years. Enter on this line the difference between the regular tax gain (loss) and the AMT gain (loss). If the AMT gain is less than the regular tax gain, **or** the AMT loss is more than the regular tax loss, **or** there is an AMT loss and a regular tax gain, enter the difference as a negative amount.

If any part of the adjustment is allocable to net short-term capital gain (loss), net long-term capital gain (loss), or net section 1231 gain (loss), attach a schedule that identifies the amount of the adjustment allocable to each type of gain or loss. For a net long-term capital gain (loss), also identify the amount of the adjustment that is 28% rate gain (loss). For a net section 1231 gain (loss), also

identify the amount of adjustment that is unrecaptured section 1250 gain.

No schedule is required if the adjustment is allocable solely to ordinary gain (loss).

Line 14c—Depletion (Other Than Oil and Gas)

Do not include any depletion on oil and gas wells. The shareholders must figure their depletion deductions and preference items separately under section 613A.

Refigure the depletion deduction under section 611 for mines, wells (other than oil and gas wells), and other natural deposits for the AMT. Percentage depletion is limited to 50% of the taxable income from the property as figured under section 613(a), using only income and deductions for the AMT. Also, the deduction is limited to the property's adjusted basis at the end of the year, as refigured for the AMT. Figure this limit separately for each property. When refiguring the property's adjusted basis, take into account any AMT adjustments made this year or in previous years that affect basis (other than the current year's depletion).

Enter the difference between the regular tax and AMT deduction. If the AMT deduction is greater, enter the difference as a negative amount.

Lines 14d(1) and 14d(2)

Generally, the amounts to be entered on these lines are only the income and deductions for oil, gas, and geothermal properties that are used to figure the amount on line 21, page 1, Form 1120S.

If there are any items of income or deductions for oil, gas, and geothermal properties included in the amounts that are required to be passed through separately to the shareholders on Schedule K-1, give each shareholder a schedule that shows, for the line on which the income or deduction is included, the amount of income or deductions included in the total amount for that line. Do not include any of these direct pass-through amounts on line 14d(1) or 14d(2). The shareholder is told in the Shareholder's Instructions for Schedule K-1 (Form 1120S) to adjust the amounts on lines 14d(1) and 14d(2) for any other income or deductions from oil, gas, or geothermal properties included on lines 2 through 10 and 23 of Schedule K-1 in order to determine the total income and deductions from oil, gas, and geothermal properties for the corporation.

Figure the amounts for lines 14d(1) and 14d(2) separately for oil and gas properties that are not geothermal deposits and for all properties that are geothermal deposits.

Give the shareholders a schedule that shows the separate amounts included in the computation of the amounts on lines 14d(1) and 14d(2).

Line 14d(1)—Gross income from oil, gas, and geothermal properties. Enter the total amount of gross income (within the meaning of section 613(a)) from all oil, gas, and geothermal properties received or accrued during the

tax year and included on page 1, Form 1120S.

Line 14d(2)—Deductions allocable to oil, gas, and geothermal properties. Enter the amount of any deductions allowed for the AMT that are allocable to oil, gas, and geothermal properties.

Line 14e—Other Adjustments and Tax Preference Items

Attach a schedule that shows each shareholder's share of other items not shown on lines 14a through 14d(2) that are adjustments or tax preference items or that the shareholder needs to complete Form 6251 or Schedule I of Form 1041. See these forms and their instructions to determine the amount to enter. Other adjustments or tax preference items include the following:
• Accelerated depreciation of real property under pre-1987 rules.
• Accelerated depreciation of leased personal property under pre-1987 rules.
• Long-term contracts entered into after February 28, 1986. Except for certain home construction contracts, the taxable income from these contracts must be figured using the percentage of completion method of accounting for the AMT.
• Losses from tax shelter farm activities. No loss from any tax shelter farm activity is allowed for the AMT.

Foreign Taxes

Lines 15a through 15h must be completed if the corporation has foreign income, deductions, or losses, or has paid or accrued foreign taxes. See **Pub. 514**, Foreign Tax Credit for Individuals, for more information.

Line 15a—Name of Foreign Country or U.S. Possession

Enter the name of the foreign country or U.S. possession from which the corporation had income or to which the corporation paid or accrued taxes. If the corporation had income from, or paid or accrued taxes to, **more than one** foreign country or U.S. possession, enter **"See attached"** and attach a schedule for each country for lines 15a through 15h.

Line 15b—Gross Income From All Sources

Enter the corporation's gross income from all sources, including all U.S. and foreign source income.

Line 15c—Gross Income Sourced at Shareholder Level

Enter the total gross income of the corporation that is required to be sourced at the shareholder level. This includes income from the sale of most personal property other than inventory, depreciable property, and certain intangible property. See Pub. 514 and section 865 for details. Attach a schedule showing the following information:
• The amount of this gross income (without regard to its source) in each category identified in the instructions for line 15d, including each of the listed categories.
• Specifically identify gains on the sale of personal property other than inventory,

depreciable property, and certain intangible property on which a foreign tax of 10% or more was paid or accrued. Also list losses on the sale of such property if the foreign country would have imposed a 10% or higher tax had the sale resulted in a gain. See **Sales or Exchanges of Certain Personal Property** in Pub. 514 and section 865.

• Specify foreign source capital gains or losses within each separate limitation category. Also separately identify foreign source gains or losses within each separate limitation category that are 28% rate gains and losses, unrecaptured section 1250 gains, and qualified 5-year gains.

Line 15d—Foreign Gross Income Sourced at Corporate Level

Separately report gross income from sources outside the United States by category of income as follows. See Pub. 514 for information on the categories of income.

Line 15d(1). Passive foreign source income.

Line 15d(2). Attach a schedule showing the amount of foreign source income included in each of the following listed categories of income:
• Financial services income;
• High withholding tax interest;
• Shipping income;
• Dividends from each noncontrolled section 902 corporation;
• Dividends from a domestic international sales corporation (DISC) or a former DISC;
• Distributions from a foreign sales corporation (FSC) or a former FSC;
• Section 901(j) income; and
• Certain income re-sourced by treaty.

Line 15d(3). General limitation foreign source income (all other foreign source income).

Line 15e—Deductions Allocated and Apportioned at Shareholder Level

Enter on line 15e(1) the corporation's total interest expense (including interest equivalents under Temporary Regulations section 1.861-9T(b)). Do not include interest directly allocable under Temporary Regulations section 1.861-10T to income from a specific property. This type of interest is allocated and apportioned at the corporate level and is included on lines 15f(1) through (3). On line 15e(2), enter the total of all other deductions or losses that are required to be allocated at the shareholder level. For example, include on line 15e(2) research and experimental expenditures (see Regulations section 1.861-17(f)).

Line 15f—Deductions Allocated and Apportioned at Corporate Level to Foreign Source Income

Separately report corporate deductions that are apportioned at the corporate level to (1) passive foreign source income, (2) each of the listed foreign categories of income, and (3) general limitation foreign source income (see the instructions for

line 15d). See Pub. 514 for more information.

Line 15g—Total Foreign Taxes

Enter in U.S. dollars the total foreign taxes (described in section 901 or section 903) that were paid or accrued by the corporation (according to its method of accounting for such taxes). Translate these amounts into U.S. dollars by using the applicable exchange rate (see Pub. 514).

Attach a schedule reporting the following information:

1. The total amount of foreign taxes (including foreign taxes on income sourced at the shareholder level) relating to each category of income (see instructions for line 15d).

2. The dates on which the taxes were paid or accrued, the exchange rates used, and the amounts in both foreign currency and U.S. dollars, for:
• Taxes withheld at source on interest.
• Taxes withheld at source on dividends.
• Taxes withheld at source on rents and royalties.
• Other foreign taxes paid or accrued.

Line 15h—Reduction in Taxes Available for Credit

Enter the total reductions in taxes available for credit. Attach a schedule showing the reductions for:
• Taxes on foreign mineral income (section 901(e)).
• Taxes on foreign oil and gas extraction income (section 907(a)).
• Taxes attributable to boycott operations (section 908).
• Failure to timely file (or furnish all of the information required on) Forms 5471 and 8865.
• Any other items (specify).

Other

Lines 16a and 16b—Section 59(e)(2) Expenditures

Generally, section 59(e) allows each shareholder to make an election to deduct the shareholder's pro rata share of the corporation's otherwise deductible qualified expenditures ratably over 10 years (3 years for circulation expenditures), beginning with the tax year in which the expenditures were made (or for intangible drilling and development costs, over the 60-month period beginning with the month in which such costs were paid or incurred). The term "qualified expenditures" includes only the following types of expenditures paid or incurred during the tax year:
• Circulation expenditures.
• Research and experimental expenditures.
• Intangible drilling and development costs.
• Mining exploration and development costs.

If a shareholder makes the election, the above items are not treated as tax preference items.

Because the shareholders are generally allowed to make this election, the corporation cannot deduct these amounts or include them as adjustments or tax preference items on Schedule K-1. Instead, on lines 16a and 16b of Schedule K-1, the corporation passes through the information the shareholders need to figure their separate deductions.

On line 16a, enter the type of expenditures claimed on line 16b. Enter on line 16b the qualified expenditures paid or incurred during the tax year to which an election under section 59(e) may apply. Enter this amount for all shareholders whether or not any shareholder makes an election under section 59(e). If the expenditures are for intangible drilling and development costs, enter the month in which the expenditures were paid or incurred (after the type of expenditures on line 16a). If there is more than one type of expenditure included in the total shown on line 16b (or intangible drilling and development costs were paid or incurred for more than 1 month), report this information separately for each type of expenditure (or month) on an attachment to Schedules K and K-1.

Line 17—Tax-Exempt Interest Income

Enter on line 17 tax-exempt interest income, including any exempt-interest dividends received from a mutual fund or other regulated investment company. This information must be reported by individuals on line 8b of Form 1040. Generally, the basis of the shareholder's stock is increased by the amount shown on this line under section 1367(a)(1)(A).

Line 18—Other Tax-Exempt Income

Enter on line 18 all income of the corporation exempt from tax other than tax-exempt interest (e.g., life insurance proceeds). Generally, the basis of the shareholder's stock is increased by the amount shown on this line under section 1367(a)(1)(A).

Line 19—Nondeductible Expenses

Enter on line 19 nondeductible expenses paid or incurred by the corporation. Do not include separately stated deductions shown elsewhere on Schedules K and K-1, capital expenditures, or items for which the deduction is deferred to a later tax year. Generally, the basis of the shareholder's stock is decreased by the amount shown on this line under section 1367(a)(2)(D).

Line 20

Enter total distributions made to each shareholder other than dividends reported on line 22 of Schedule K. Noncash distributions of appreciated property are valued at fair market value. See **Distributions** on page 27 for the ordering rules on distributions.

Line 21 (Schedule K Only)

Attach a statement to Schedule K to report the corporation's total income, expenditures, or other information for items 1 through 21 of the line 23 (Schedule K-1 Only) instruction below.

Line 22 (Schedule K Only)

Enter total dividends paid to shareholders from accumulated earnings and profits. Report these dividends to shareholders on Form 1099-DIV. Do not report them on Schedule K-1.

Lines 22a and 22b (Schedule K-1 Only)—Recapture of Low-Income Housing Credit

If recapture of part or all of the low-income housing credit is required because **(a)** prior year qualified basis of a building decreased or **(b)** the corporation disposed of a building or part of its interest in a building, see **Form 8611,** Recapture of Low-Income Housing Credit. The instructions for Form 8611 indicate when Form 8611 is completed by the corporation and what information is provided to shareholders when recapture is required.

Note: *If a shareholder's ownership interest in a building decreased because of a transaction at the shareholder level, the corporation must provide the necessary information to the shareholder to enable the shareholder to figure the recapture.*

If the corporation filed **Form 8693,** Low-Income Housing Credit Disposition Bond, to avoid recapture of the low-income housing credit, no entry should be made on line 22 of Schedule K-1.

See Form 8586, Form 8611, and section 42 for more information.

Supplemental Information

Line 23 (Schedule K-1 Only)

Enter in the line 23 Supplemental Information space of Schedule K-1, or on an attached schedule if more space is needed, each shareholder's share of any information asked for on lines 1 through 22 that is required to be reported in detail, and items **1** through **24** below. Please identify the applicable line number next to the information entered in the Supplemental Information space. Show income or gains as a positive number. Show losses in parentheses.

1. Taxes paid on undistributed capital gains by a regulated investment company or a real estate investment trust (REIT). As a shareholder of a regulated investment company or a REIT, the corporation will receive notice on **Form 2439,** Notice to Shareholder of Undistributed Long-Term Capital Gains, of the amount of tax paid on undistributed capital gains.

2. Gross income and other information relating to oil and gas well properties that are reported to shareholders to allow them to figure the depletion deduction for oil and gas well properties. See section 613A(c)(11) for details.

The corporation cannot deduct depletion on oil and gas wells. Each shareholder must determine the allowable amount to report on his or her return. See Pub. 535 for more information.

3. Recapture of section 179 expense deduction. For property placed in service after 1986, the section 179 deduction is recaptured at any time the business use of property drops to 50% or less. Enter the amount originally passed through and the corporation's tax year in which it was passed through. Inform the shareholder if the recapture amount was caused by the disposition of the section 179 property. See section 179(d)(10) for more information. Do not include this amount on line 4 or 5, page 1, Form 1120S.

4. Recapture of certain mining exploration expenditures (section 617).

5. Any information or statements the corporation is required to furnish to shareholders to allow them to comply with requirements under section 6111 (registration of tax shelters) or section 6662(d)(2)(B)(ii) (regarding adequate disclosure of items that may cause an understatement of income tax).

6. If the corporation is involved in farming or fishing activities, report the gross income from these activities to shareholders.

7. Any information needed by a shareholder to compute the interest due under section 453(l)(3). If the corporation elected to report the dispositions of certain timeshares and residential lots on the installment method, each shareholder's tax liability must be increased by the shareholder's pro rata share of the interest on tax attributable to the installment payments received during the tax year.

8. Any information needed by a shareholder to compute the interest due under section 453A(c). If an obligation arising from the disposition of property to which section 453A applies is outstanding at the close of the year, each shareholder's tax liability must be increased by the tax due under section 453A(c) on the shareholder's pro rata share of the tax deferred under the installment method.

9. Any information needed by a shareholder to properly capitalize interest as required by section 263A(f). See **Section 263A uniform capitalization rules** on page 12 for more information.

10. If the corporation is a closely held S corporation (defined in section 460(b)) and it entered into any long-term contracts after February 28, 1986, that are accounted for under either the percentage of completion-capitalized cost method or the percentage of completion method, it must attach a schedule to Form 1120S showing the information required in items (a) and (b) of the instructions for lines 1 and 3 of Part II for **Form 8697,** Interest Computation Under the Look-Back Method for Completed Long-Term Contracts. It must also report the amounts for Part II, lines 1 and 3, to its shareholders. See the Instructions for Form 8697 for more information.

11. Expenditures qualifying for the **(a)** rehabilitation credit not related to rental real estate activities, **(b)** energy credit, or

(c) reforestation credit. Complete and attach Form 3468 to Form 1120S. See Form 3468 and related instructions for information on eligible property and the lines on Form 3468 to complete. Do not include that part of the cost of the property the corporation has elected to expense under section 179. Attach to each Schedule K-1 a separate schedule in a format similar to that shown on Form 3468 detailing each shareholder's pro rata share of qualified expenditures. Also indicate the lines of Form 3468 on which the shareholders should report these amounts.

12. Recapture of investment credit. Complete and attach **Form 4255,** Recapture of Investment Credit, when investment credit property is disposed of, or it no longer qualifies for the credit, before the end of the recapture period or the useful life applicable to the property. State the type of property at the top of Form 4255, and complete lines 2, 4, and 5, whether or not any shareholder is subject to recapture of the credit. Attach to each Schedule K-1 a separate schedule providing the information the corporation is required to show on Form 4255, but list only the shareholder's pro rata share of the cost of the property subject to recapture. Also indicate the lines of Form 4255 on which the shareholders should report these amounts.

The corporation itself is liable for investment credit recapture in certain cases. See the instructions for line 22c, page 1, Form 1120S, for details.

13. Any information needed by a shareholder to compute the recapture of the qualified electric vehicle credit. See Pub. 535 for more information.

14. Recapture of new markets credit (see Form 8874).

15. Any information a shareholder may need to figure recapture of the Indian employment credit. Generally, if the corporation terminates a qualified employee less than 1 year after the date of initial employment, any Indian employment credit allowed for a prior tax year by reason of wages paid or incurred to that employee must be recaptured. For details, see section 45A(d).

16. Nonqualified withdrawals by the corporation from a capital construction fund.

17. Unrecaptured section 1250 gain. Figure this amount for each section 1250 property in Part III of Form 4797 (except property for which gain is reported using the installment method on Form 6252) for which you had an entry in Part I of Form 4797 by subtracting line 26g of Form 4797 from the **smaller** of line 22 or line 24 of Form 4797. Figure the total of these amounts for all section 1250 properties. Generally, the result is the corporation's unrecaptured section 1250 gain. However, if the corporation is reporting gain on the installment method for a section 1250 property held more than 1 year, see the next paragraph to figure the unrecaptured section 1250 gain on that property allocable to this tax year. Report each shareholder's pro rata share of the total amount as "Unrecaptured section 1250 gain."

The total unrecaptured section 1250 gain for an installment sale of section 1250 property held more than 1 year is figured in a manner similar to that used in the preceding paragraph. However, the total unrecaptured section 1250 gain must be allocated to the installment payments received from the sale. To do so, the corporation generally must treat the gain allocable to each installment payment as unrecaptured section 1250 gain until all such gain has been used in full. Figure the unrecaptured section 1250 gain for installment payments received during the tax year as the **smaller** of **(a)** the amount from line 26 or line 37 of Form 6252 (whichever applies) or **(b)** the total unrecaptured section 1250 gain for the sale reduced by all gain reported in prior years (excluding section 1250 ordinary income recapture). However, if the corporation chose not to treat all of the gain from payments received after May 6, 1997, and before August 24, 1999, as unrecaptured section 1250 gain, use only the amount the corporation chose to treat as unrecaptured section 1250 gain for those payments to reduce the total unrecaptured section 1250 gain remaining to be reported for the sale.

If the corporation received a Schedule K-1 or Form 1099-DIV from an estate, a trust, a REIT, or a mutual fund reporting "unrecaptured section 1250 gain," **do not** add it to the corporation's own unrecaptured section 1250 gain. Instead, report it as a separate amount. For example, if the corporation received a Form 1099-DIV from a REIT with unrecaptured section 1250 gain, report it as "Unrecaptured section 1250 gain from a REIT."

Also report as a separate amount any gain from the sale or exchange of an interest in a partnership attributable to unrecaptured section 1250 gain. See Regulations section 1.1(h)-1 and attach a statement required under Regulations section 1.1(h)-1(e).

18. If the corporation is a closely held S corporation (defined in section 460(b)(4)) and it depreciated certain property placed in service after September 13, 1995, under the income forecast method, it must attach to Form 1120S the information specified in the instructions for Form 8866, line 2, for the 3rd and 10th tax years beginning after the tax year the property was placed in service. It must also report the line 2 amounts to its shareholders. See the Instructions for Form 8866 for more details.

19. Amortization of reforestation expenditures. Report the amortizable basis and year in which the amortization began for the current year and the 7 preceding years. For limits that may apply, see section 194 and Pub. 535.

20. Any information needed by a shareholder to figure the interest due under section 1260(b). If any portion of a constructive ownership transaction was open in any prior year, each shareholder's tax liability must be increased by the shareholder's pro rata share of interest due on any deferral of gain recognition. See section 1260(b) for

details, including how to figure the interest.

21. Any information needed by a shareholder to figure the extraterritorial income exclusion. See **Extraterritorial Income Exclusion** on page 11 for more information.

22. Commercial revitalization deduction from rental real estate activities. See **Line 19—Other Deductions** for the **Special Rules** that apply to the deduction.

23. If the corporation participates in a reportable tax shelter transaction, attach a copy of the corporation's tax shelter disclosure statement to Schedule K-1 or provide the information each shareholder will need to complete a tax shelter disclosure statement for the transaction. See **Tax shelter disclosure statement** on page 7 for more information.

If the corporation enters into a transaction defined in section 988(c)(1) (relating to foreign currency transactions) after December 31, 2002, and any shareholder's pro rata share of the loss is at least $50,000, provide those shareholders with the information they will need to complete Form 8886. Unless the corporation's loss from this transaction is at least $5 million in a single tax year or $10 million in any combination of tax years, the corporation is not required to file Form 8886.

24. Any other information the shareholders need to prepare their tax returns.

Note: *Schedules L and M-1 are not required to be completed if the corporation answered "Yes" to question 9 of Schedule B.*

Schedule L—Balance Sheets per Books

The balance sheets should agree with the corporation's books and records. Include certificates of deposit as cash on line 1 of Schedule L.

If the S election terminated during the tax year, the year-end balance sheet generally should agree with the books and records at the end of the C short year. However, if the corporation elected under section 1362(e)(3) to have items assigned to each short year under normal tax accounting rules, the year-end balance sheet should agree with the books and records at the end of the S short year.

Line 5—Tax-Exempt Securities
Include on this line—

1. State and local government obligations, the interest on which is excludible from gross income under section 103(a), and

2. Stock in a mutual fund or other regulated investment company that distributed exempt-interest dividends during the tax year of the corporation.

Line 24—Retained Earnings
If the corporation maintains separate accounts for appropriated and unappropriated retained earnings, it may

want to continue such accounting for purposes of preparing its financial balance sheet. Also, if the corporation converts to C corporation status in a subsequent year, it will be required to report its appropriated and unappropriated retained earnings on separate lines of Schedule L of Form 1120.

Line 25—Adjustments to Shareholders' Equity
Some examples of adjustments to report on this line include:
- Unrealized gains and losses on securities held "available for sale."
- Foreign currency translation adjustments.
- The excess of additional pension liability over unrecognized prior service cost.
- Guarantees of employee stock (ESOP) debt.
- Compensation related to employee stock award plans.

If the total adjustment to be entered is a negative amount, enter the amount in parentheses.

Schedule M-1— Reconciliation of Income (Loss) per Books With Income (Loss) per Return

Line 3b—Travel and Entertainment
Include on this line the part of the cost of meals and entertainment not allowed under section 274(n); expenses for the use of an entertainment facility; the part of business gifts over $25; expenses of an individual allocable to conventions on cruise ships over $2,000; employee achievement awards over $400; the part of the cost of entertainment tickets that exceeds face value (also subject to 50% disallowance); the part of the cost of skyboxes that exceeds the face value of nonluxury box seat tickets; the part of the cost of luxury water travel not allowed under section 274(m); expenses for travel as a form of education; nondeductible club dues; and other travel and entertainment expenses not allowed as a deduction.

Schedule M-2—Analysis of Accumulated Adjustments Account, Other Adjustments Account, and Shareholders' Undistributed Taxable Income Previously Taxed

Column (a)—Accumulated Adjustments Account
The accumulated adjustments account (AAA) is an account of the S corporation that generally reflects the accumulated

undistributed net income of the corporation for the corporation's post-1982 years. S corporations with accumulated E&P must maintain the AAA to determine the tax effect of distributions during S years and the post-termination transition period. An S corporation without accumulated E&P does not need to maintain the AAA in order to determine the tax effect of distributions. Nevertheless, if an S corporation without accumulated E&P engages in certain transactions to which section 381(a) applies, such as a merger into an S corporation with accumulated E&P, the S corporation must be able to calculate its AAA at the time of the merger for purposes of determining the tax effect of post-merger distributions. Therefore, it is recommended that the AAA be maintained by all S corporations.

On the first day of the corporation's first tax year as an S corporation, the balance of the AAA is zero. At the end of the tax year, adjust the AAA for the items for the tax year as explained below and in the order listed.

1. Increase the AAA by income (other than tax-exempt income) and the excess of the deduction for depletion over the basis of the property subject to depletion (unless the property is an oil and gas property the basis of which has been allocated to shareholders).

2. Generally, decrease the AAA by deductible losses and expenses, nondeductible expenses (other than expenses related to tax-exempt income and Federal taxes attributable to a C corporation tax year), and the sum of the shareholders' deductions for depletion for any oil or gas property held by the corporation as described in section 1367(a)(2)(E). However, if the total decreases under **2** exceeds the total increases under **1** above, the excess is a "net negative adjustment." If the corporation has a net negative adjustment, **do not** take it into account under **2**. Instead, take it into account only under **4** below.

3. Decrease AAA (but not below zero) by property distributions (other than dividend distributions from accumulated E&P), unless the corporation elects to reduce accumulated E&P first. See **Distributions** below for definitions and other details.

4. Decrease AAA by any net negative adjustment. For adjustments to the AAA for redemptions, reorganizations, and corporate separations, see Regulations section 1.1368-2(d).

Note: *The AAA may have a negative balance at year end. See section 1368(e).*

Column (b)—Other Adjustments Account

The other adjustments account is adjusted for tax-exempt income (and related expenses) and Federal taxes attributable to a C corporation tax year. After these adjustments are made, the account is reduced for any distributions made during the year. See **Distributions** below.

Column (c)—Shareholders' Undistributed Taxable Income Previously Taxed

The shareholders' undistributed taxable income previously taxed account, also called previously taxed income (PTI), is maintained only if the corporation had a balance in this account at the start of its 2002 tax year. If there is a beginning balance for the 2002 tax year, no adjustments are made to the account except to reduce the account for distributions made under section 1375(d) (as in effect before the enactment of the Subchapter S Revision Act of 1982). See **Distributions** below for the order of distributions from the account.

Each shareholder's right to nontaxable distributions from PTI is personal and cannot be transferred to another person. The corporation is required to keep records of each shareholder's net share of PTI.

Distributions

General rule. Unless the corporation makes one of the elections described below, property distributions (including cash) are applied in the following order to reduce accounts of the S corporation that are used to figure the tax effect of distributions made by the corporation to its shareholders:

1. Reduce the AAA determined without regard to any net negative adjustment for the tax year (but not below zero). If distributions during the tax year exceed the AAA at the close of the tax year determined without regard to any net negative adjustment for the tax year, the AAA is allocated pro rata to each distribution made during the tax year. See section 1368(c).

2. Reduce shareholders' PTI account for any section 1375(d) (as in effect before 1983) distributions. A distribution from the PTI account is tax free to the extent of a shareholder's basis in his or her stock in the corporation.

3. Reduce accumulated E&P. Generally, the S corporation has accumulated E&P only if it has not distributed E&P accumulated in prior years when the S corporation was a C corporation (section 1361(a)(2)). See section 312 for information on E&P. The only adjustments that can be made to the accumulated E&P of an S corporation are **(a)** reductions for dividend distributions; **(b)** adjustments for redemptions, liquidations, reorganizations, etc.; and **(c)** reductions for investment credit recapture tax for which the corporation is liable. See sections 1371(c) and (d)(3).

4. Reduce the other adjustments account.

5. Reduce any remaining shareholders' equity accounts.

Elections relating to source of distributions. The corporation may modify the above ordering rules by making one or more of the following elections:

1. *Election to distribute accumulated E&P first.* If the corporation has accumulated E&P and wants to distribute this E&P before

making distributions from the AAA, it may elect to do so with the consent of all its affected shareholders (section 1368(e)(3)(B)). This election is irrevocable and applies only for the tax year for which it is made. For details on making the election, see **Statement regarding elections** below.

2. *Election to make a deemed dividend.* If the corporation wants to distribute all or part of its accumulated E&P through a deemed dividend, it may elect to do so with the consent of all its affected shareholders (section 1368(e)(3)(B)). Under this election, the corporation will be treated as also having made the election to distribute accumulated E&P first. The amount of the deemed dividend cannot exceed the accumulated E&P at the end of the tax year, reduced by any actual distributions of accumulated E&P made during the tax year. A deemed dividend is treated as if it were a pro rata distribution of money to the shareholders, received by the shareholders, and immediately contributed back to the corporation, all on the last day of the tax year. This election is irrevocable and applies only for the tax year for which it is made. For details on making the election, see **Statement regarding elections** below.

3. *Election to forego PTI.* If the corporation wants to forego distributions of PTI, it may elect to do so with the consent of all its affected shareholders (section 1368(e)(3)(B)). Under this election, paragraph 2 under the **General rule** above does not apply to any distribution made during the tax year. This election is irrevocable and applies only for the tax year for which it is made. For details on making the election, see **Statement regarding elections** below.

Statement regarding elections. To make any of the above elections, the corporation must attach a statement to a timely filed original or amended Form 1120S for the tax year for which the election is made. In the statement, the corporation must identify the election it is making and must state that each shareholder consents to the election. A corporate officer must sign the statement under penalties of perjury on behalf of the corporation. The statement of election to make a deemed dividend must include the amount of the deemed dividend distributed to each shareholder.

Example

The following example shows how the Schedule M-2 accounts are adjusted for items of income (loss), deductions, and distributions reported on Form 1120S. In this example, the corporation has no PTI or accumulated E&P.

Items per return are:

1. Page 1, line 21 income—$10,000
2. Schedule K, line 2 loss—($3,000)
3. Schedule K, line 4a income—$4,000
4. Schedule K, line 4b income—$16,000
5. Schedule K, line 7 deduction—$24,000
6. Schedule K, line 10 deduction—$3,000

Instructions for Form 1120S

-27-

7. Schedule K, line 13 work opportunity credit—$6,000

8. Schedule K, line 17 tax-exempt interest—$5,000

9. Schedule K, line 19 nondeductible expenses—$6,000 (reduction in salaries and wages for work opportunity credit), and

10. Schedule K, line 20 distributions—$65,000.

Based on return items 1 through 10 and starting balances of zero, the columns for the AAA and the other adjustments account are completed as shown in the Schedule M-2 Worksheet below.

For the AAA, the worksheet line 3—$20,000 amount is the total of the Schedule K, lines 4a and 4b income of $4,000 and $16,000. The worksheet line 5—$36,000 amount is the total of the Schedule K, line 2 loss of ($3,000), line 7 deduction of $24,000, line 10 deduction of $3,000, and the line 19 nondeductible expenses of $6,000. The worksheet line 7 is zero. The AAA at the end of the tax year (figured without regard to distributions and the net negative adjustment of $6,000) is zero, and distributions cannot reduce the AAA below zero.

For the other adjustments account, the worksheet line 3 amount is the Schedule K, line 17, tax-exempt interest income of $5,000. The worksheet line 7 amount is $5,000, reducing the other adjustments account to zero. The remaining $60,000 of distributions are not entered on Schedule M-2.

Schedule M-2 **Worksheet**

		(a) Accumulated adjustments account	(b) Other adjustments account	(c) Shareholders' undistributed taxable income previously taxed
1	Balance at beginning of tax year . . .	-0-	-0-	
2	Ordinary income from page 1, line 21 .	10,000		
3	Other additions	20,000	5,000	
4	Loss from page 1, line 21	( )		
5	Other reductions	(36,000)	( )	
6	Combine lines 1 through 5	(6,000)	5,000	
7	Distributions other than dividend distributions	-0-	5,000	
8	Balance at end of tax year. Subtract line 7 from line 6	(6,000)	-0-	

Paperwork Reduction Act Notice. We ask for the information on this form to carry out the Internal Revenue laws of the United States. You are required to give us the information. We need it to ensure that you are complying with these laws and to allow us to figure and collect the right amount of tax.

You are not required to provide the information requested on a form that is subject to the Paperwork Reduction Act unless the form displays a valid OMB control number. Books or records relating to a form or its instructions must be retained as long as their contents may become material in the administration of any Internal Revenue law. Generally, tax returns and return information are confidential, as required by section 6103.

The time needed to complete and file this form and related schedules will vary depending on individual circumstances. The estimated average times are:

Form	Recordkeeping	Learning about the law or the form	Preparing the form	Copying, assembling, and sending the form to the IRS
1120S	64 hr., 5 min.	23 hr., 55 min.	45 hr., 33 min.	5 hr., 37 min.
Sch. D (1120S)	7 hr., 10 min.	4 hr., 25 min.	9 hr., 23 min.	1 hr., 23 min.
Sch. K-1 (1120S)	16 hr., 30 min.	10 hr., 36 min.	15 hr., 4 min.	1 hr., 4 min.

If you have comments concerning the accuracy of these time estimates or suggestions for making these forms simpler, we would be happy to hear from you. You can write to the Tax Forms Committee, Western Area Distribution Center, Rancho Cordova, CA 95743-0001. **Do not** send the tax form to this address. Instead, see **Where To File** on page 3.

Codes for Principal Business Activity

This list of principal business activities and their associated codes is designed to classify an enterprise by the type of activity in which it is engaged to facilitate the administration of the Internal Revenue Code. These principal business activity codes are based on the North American Industry Classification System.

Using the list of activities and codes below, determine from which activity the company derives the largest percentage of its "total receipts." Total receipts is defined as the sum of gross receipts or sales (page 1, line 1a); all other income (page 1, lines 4 and 5); income reported on Schedule K, lines 3a, 4a, 4b, and 4c; income or net gain reported on Schedule K, lines 4d, 4e(1), 4f, 5, and 6; and income or net gain reported on Form 8825, lines 2, 19, and 20a. If the company purchases raw materials and supplies them to a subcontractor to produce the finished product, but retains title to the product, the company is considered a manufacturer and must use one of the manufacturing codes (311110-339900).

Once the principal business activity is determined, enter the six-digit code from the list below on page 1, item B. Also enter a brief description of the business activity on page 2, Schedule B, line 2(a) and the principal product or service of the business on line 2(b).

Agriculture, Forestry, Fishing and Hunting

Code

Crop Production
111100	Oilseed & Grain Farming
111210	Vegetable & Melon Farming (including potatoes & yams)
111300	Fruit & Tree Nut Farming
111400	Greenhouse, Nursery, & Floriculture Production
111900	Other Crop Farming (including tobacco, cotton, sugarcane, hay, peanut, sugar beet & all other crop farming)

Animal Production
112111	Beef Cattle Ranching & Farming
112112	Cattle Feedlots
112120	Dairy Cattle & Milk Production
112210	Hog & Pig Farming
112300	Poultry & Egg Production
112400	Sheep & Goat Farming
112510	Animal Aquaculture (including shellfish & finfish farms & hatcheries)
112900	Other Animal Production

Forestry and Logging
113110	Timber Tract Operations
113210	Forest Nurseries & Gathering of Forest Products
113310	Logging

Fishing, Hunting and Trapping
114110	Fishing
114210	Hunting & Trapping

Support Activities for Agriculture and Forestry
115110	Support Activities for Crop Production (including cotton ginning, soil preparation, planting, & cultivating)
115210	Support Activities for Animal Production
115310	Support Activities For Forestry

Mining
211110	Oil & Gas Extraction
212110	Coal Mining
212200	Metal Ore Mining
212310	Stone Mining & Quarrying
212320	Sand, Gravel, Clay, & Ceramic & Refractory Minerals Mining & Quarrying
212390	Other Nonmetallic Mineral Mining & Quarrying
213110	Support Activities for Mining

Utilities
221100	Electric Power Generation, Transmission & Distribution
221210	Natural Gas Distribution
221300	Water, Sewage & Other Systems

Construction

Code

Construction of Buildings
236110	Residential Building Construction
236200	Nonresidential Building Construction

Heavy and Civil Engineering Construction
237100	Utility System Construction
237210	Land Subdivision
237310	Highway, Street, & Bridge Construction
237990	Other Heavy & Civil Engineering Construction

Specialty Trade Contractors
238100	Foundation, Structure, & Building Exterior Contractors (including framing carpentry, masonry, glass, roofing, & siding)
238210	Electrical Contractors
238220	Plumbing, Heating, & Air-Conditioning Contractors
238290	Other Building Equipment Contractors
238300	Building Finishing Contractors (including drywall, insulation, painting, wallcovering, flooring, tile, & finish carpentry)
238900	Other Specialty Trade Contractors (including site preparation)

Manufacturing

Food Manufacturing
311110	Animal Food Mfg
311200	Grain & Oilseed Milling
311300	Sugar & Confectionery Product Mfg
311400	Fruit & Vegetable Preserving & Specialty Food Mfg
311500	Dairy Product Mfg
311610	Animal Slaughtering and Processing
311710	Seafood Product Preparation & Packaging
311800	Bakeries & Tortilla Mfg
311900	Other Food Mfg (including coffee, tea, flavorings & seasonings)

Code

Beverage and Tobacco Product Manufacturing
312110	Soft Drink & Ice Mfg
312120	Breweries
312130	Wineries
312140	Distilleries
312200	Tobacco Manufacturing

Textile Mills and Textile Product Mills
313000	Textile Mills
314000	Textile Product Mills

Apparel Manufacturing
315100	Apparel Knitting Mills
315210	Cut & Sew Apparel Contractors
315220	Men's & Boys' Cut & Sew Apparel Mfg
315230	Women's & Girls' Cut & Sew Apparel Mfg
315290	Other Cut & Sew Apparel Mfg
315990	Apparel Accessories & Other Apparel Mfg

Leather and Allied Product Manufacturing
316110	Leather & Hide Tanning & Finishing
316210	Footwear Mfg (including rubber & plastics)
316990	Other Leather & Allied Product Mfg

Wood Product Manufacturing
321110	Sawmills & Wood Preservation
321210	Veneer, Plywood, & Engineered Wood Product Mfg
321900	Other Wood Product Mfg

Paper Manufacturing
322100	Pulp, Paper, & Paperboard Mills
322200	Converted Paper Product Mfg

Printing and Related Support Activities
323100	Printing & Related Support Activities

Petroleum and Coal Products Manufacturing
324110	Petroleum Refineries (including integrated)
324120	Asphalt Paving, Roofing, & Saturated Materials Mfg
324190	Other Petroleum & Coal Products Mfg

Chemical Manufacturing
325100	Basic Chemical Mfg
325200	Resin, Synthetic Rubber, & Artificial & Synthetic Fibers & Filaments Mfg
325300	Pesticide, Fertilizer, & Other Agricultural Chemical Mfg
325410	Pharmaceutical & Medicine Mfg
325500	Paint, Coating, & Adhesive Mfg
325600	Soap, Cleaning Compound, & Toilet Preparation Mfg
325900	Other Chemical Product & Preparation Mfg

Plastics and Rubber Products Manufacturing
326100	Plastics Product Mfg
326200	Rubber Product Mfg

Nonmetallic Mineral Product Manufacturing
327100	Clay Product & Refractory Mfg
327210	Glass & Glass Product Mfg
327300	Cement & Concrete Product Mfg
327400	Lime & Gypsum Product Mfg
327900	Other Nonmetallic Mineral Product Mfg

Code

Primary Metal Manufacturing
331110	Iron & Steel Mills & Ferroalloy Mfg
331200	Steel Product Mfg from Purchased Steel
331310	Alumina & Aluminum Production & Processing
331400	Nonferrous Metal (except Aluminum) Production & Processing
331500	Foundries

Fabricated Metal Product Manufacturing
332110	Forging & Stamping
332210	Cutlery & Handtool Mfg
332300	Architectural & Structural Metals Mfg
332400	Boiler, Tank, & Shipping Container Mfg
332510	Hardware Mfg
332610	Spring & Wire Product Mfg
332700	Machine Shops; Turned Product; & Screw, Nut, & Bolt Mfg
332810	Coating, Engraving, Heat Treating, & Allied Activities
332900	Other Fabricated Metal Product Mfg

Machinery Manufacturing
333100	Agriculture, Construction, & Mining Machinery Mfg
333200	Industrial Machinery Mfg
333310	Commercial & Service Industry Machinery Mfg
333410	Ventilation, Heating, Air-Conditioning, & Commercial Refrigeration Equipment Mfg
333510	Metalworking Machinery Mfg
333610	Engine, Turbine & Power Transmission Equipment Mfg
333900	Other General Purpose Machinery Mfg

Computer and Electronic Product Manufacturing
334110	Computer & Peripheral Equipment Mfg
334200	Communications Equipment Mfg
334310	Audio & Video Equipment Mfg
334410	Semiconductor & Other Electronic Component Mfg
334500	Navigational, Measuring, Electromedical, & Control Instruments Mfg
334610	Manufacturing & Reproducing Magnetic & Optical Media

Electrical Equipment, Appliance, and Component Manufacturing
335100	Electric Lighting Equipment Mfg
335200	Household Appliance Mfg
335310	Electrical Equipment Mfg
335900	Other Electrical Equipment & Component Mfg

Transportation Equipment Manufacturing
336100	Motor Vehicle Mfg
336210	Motor Vehicle Body & Trailer Mfg
336300	Motor Vehicle Parts Mfg
336410	Aerospace Product & Parts Mfg
336510	Railroad Rolling Stock Mfg
336610	Ship & Boat Building
336990	Other Transportation Equipment Mfg

Furniture and Related Product Manufacturing
337000	Furniture & Related Product Manufacturing

Code

Miscellaneous Manufacturing
339110 Medical Equipment & Supplies Mfg
339900 Other Miscellaneous Manufacturing

Wholesale Trade

Merchant Wholesalers, Durable Goods
423100 Motor Vehicle & Motor Vehicle Parts & Supplies
423200 Furniture & Home Furnishings
423300 Lumber & Other Construction Materials
423400 Professional & Commercial Equipment & Supplies
423500 Metal & Mineral (except Petroleum)
423600 Electrical & Electronic Goods
423700 Hardware, & Plumbing & Heating Equipment & Supplies
423800 Machinery, Equipment, & Supplies
423910 Sporting & Recreational Goods & Supplies
423920 Toy & Hobby Goods & Supplies
423930 Recyclable Materials
423940 Jewelry, Watch, Precious Stone, & Precious Metals
423990 Other Miscellaneous Durable Goods

Merchant Wholesalers, Nondurable Goods
424100 Paper & Paper Products
424210 Drugs & Druggists' Sundries
424300 Apparel, Piece Goods, & Notions
424400 Grocery & Related Products
424500 Farm Product Raw Materials
424600 Chemical & Allied Products
424700 Petroleum & Petroleum Products
424800 Beer, Wine, & Distilled Alcoholic Beverages
424910 Farm Supplies
424920 Book, Periodical, & Newspapers
424930 Flower, Nursery Stock, & Florists' Supplies
424940 Tobacco & Tobacco Products
424950 Paint, Varnish, & Supplies
424990 Other Miscellaneous Nondurable Goods

Wholesale Electronic Markets and Agents and Brokers
425110 Business to Business Electronic Markets
425120 Wholesale Trade Agents & Brokers

Retail Trade

Motor Vehicle and Parts Dealers
441110 New Car Dealers
441120 Used Car Dealers
441210 Recreational Vehicle Dealers
441221 Motorcycle Dealers
441222 Boat Dealers
441229 All Other Motor Vehicle Dealers
441300 Automotive Parts, Accessories, & Tire Stores

Furniture and Home Furnishings Stores
442110 Furniture Stores
442210 Floor Covering Stores
442291 Window Treatment Stores
442299 All Other Home Furnishings Stores

Code

Electronics and Appliance Stores
443111 Household Appliance Stores
443112 Radio, Television, & Other Electronics Stores
443120 Computer & Software Stores
443130 Camera & Photographic Supplies Stores

Building Material and Garden Equipment and Supplies Dealers
444110 Home Centers
444120 Paint & Wallpaper Stores
444130 Hardware Stores
444190 Other Building Material Dealers
444200 Lawn & Garden Equipment & Supplies Stores

Food and Beverage Stores
445110 Supermarkets and Other Grocery (except Convenience) Stores
445120 Convenience Stores
445210 Meat Markets
445220 Fish & Seafood Markets
445230 Fruit & Vegetable Markets
445291 Baked Goods Stores
445292 Confectionery & Nut Stores
445299 All Other Specialty Food Stores
445310 Beer, Wine, & Liquor Stores

Health and Personal Care Stores
446110 Pharmacies & Drug Stores
446120 Cosmetics, Beauty Supplies, & Perfume Stores
446130 Optical Goods Stores
446190 Other Health & Personal Care Stores

Gasoline Stations
447100 Gasoline Stations (including convenience stores with gas)

Clothing and Clothing Accessories Stores
448110 Men's Clothing Stores
448120 Women's Clothing Stores
448130 Children's & Infants' Clothing Stores
448140 Family Clothing Stores
448150 Clothing Accessories Stores
448190 Other Clothing Stores
448210 Shoe Stores
448310 Jewelry Stores
448320 Luggage & Leather Goods Stores

Sporting Goods, Hobby, Book, and Music Stores
451110 Sporting Goods Stores
451120 Hobby, Toy, & Game Stores
451130 Sewing, Needlework, & Piece Goods Stores
451140 Musical Instrument & Supplies Stores
451211 Book Stores
451212 News Dealers & Newsstands
451220 Prerecorded Tape, Compact Disc, & Record Stores

General Merchandise Stores
452110 Department Stores
452900 Other General Merchandise Stores

Miscellaneous Store Retailers
453110 Florists
453210 Office Supplies & Stationery Stores
453220 Gift, Novelty, & Souvenir Stores
453310 Used Merchandise Stores
453910 Pet & Pet Supplies Stores
453920 Art Dealers
453930 Manufactured (Mobile) Home Dealers
453990 All Other Miscellaneous Store Retailers (including tobacco, candle, & trophy shops)

Code

Nonstore Retailers
454110 Electronic Shopping & Mail-Order Houses
454210 Vending Machine Operators
454311 Heating Oil Dealers
454312 Liquefied Petroleum Gas (Bottled Gas) Dealers
454319 Other Fuel Dealers
454390 Other Direct Selling Establishments (including door-to-door retailing, frozen food plan providers, party plan merchandisers, & coffee-break service providers)

Transportation and Warehousing

Air, Rail, and Water Transportation
481000 Air Transportation
482110 Rail Transportation
483000 Water Transportation

Truck Transportation
484110 General Freight Trucking, Local
484120 General Freight Trucking, Long-distance
484200 Specialized Freight Trucking

Transit and Ground Passenger Transportation
485110 Urban Transit Systems
485210 Interurban & Rural Bus Transportation
485310 Taxi Service
485320 Limousine Service
485410 School & Employee Bus Transportation
485510 Charter Bus Industry
485990 Other Transit & Ground Passenger Transportation

Pipeline Transportation
486000 Pipeline Transportation

Scenic & Sightseeing Transportation
487000 Scenic & Sightseeing Transportation

Support Activities for Transportation
488100 Support Activities for Air Transportation
488210 Support Activities for Rail Transportation
488300 Support Activities for Water Transportation
488410 Motor Vehicle Towing
488490 Other Support Activities for Road Transportation
488510 Freight Transportation Arrangement
488990 Other Support Activities for Transportation

Couriers and Messengers
492110 Couriers
492210 Local Messengers & Local Delivery

Warehousing and Storage
493100 Warehousing & Storage (except lessors of miniwarehouses & self-storage units)

Information

Publishing Industries (except Internet)
511110 Newspaper Publishers
511120 Periodical Publishers
511130 Book Publishers
511140 Directory & Mailing List Publishers
511190 Other Publishers
511210 Software Publishers

Motion Picture and Sound Recording Industries
512100 Motion Picture & Video Industries (except video rental)
512200 Sound Recording Industries

Code

Broadcasting (except Internet)
515100 Radio & Television Broadcasting
515210 Cable & Other Subscription Programming

Internet Publishing and Broadcasting
516110 Internet Publishing & Broadcasting

Telecommunications
517000 Telecommunications (including paging, cellular, satellite, cable & other program distribution, resellers, & other telecommunications)

Internet Service Providers, Web Search Portals, and Data Processing Services
518111 Internet Service Providers
518112 Web Search Portals
518210 Data Processing, Hosting, & Related Services

Other Information Services
519100 Other Information Services (including news syndicates & libraries)

Finance and Insurance

Depository Credit Intermediation
522110 Commercial Banking
522120 Savings Institutions
522130 Credit Unions
522190 Other Depository Credit Intermediation

Nondepository Credit Intermediation
522210 Credit Card Issuing
522220 Sales Financing
522291 Consumer Lending
522292 Real Estate Credit (including mortgage bankers & originators)
522293 International Trade Financing
522294 Secondary Market Financing
522298 All Other Nondepository Credit Intermediation

Activities Related to Credit Intermediation
522300 Activities Related to Credit Intermediation (including loan brokers, check clearing, & money transmitting)

Securities, Commodity Contracts, and Other Financial Investments and Related Activities
523110 Investment Banking & Securities Dealing
523120 Securities Brokerage
523130 Commodity Contracts Dealing
523140 Commodity Contracts Brokerage
523210 Securities & Commodity Exchanges
523900 Other Financial Investment Activities (including portfolio management & investment advice)

Insurance Carriers and Related Activities
524140 Direct Life, Health, & Medical Insurance & Reinsurance Carriers
524150 Direct Insurance & Reinsurance (except Life, Health & Medical) Carriers
524210 Insurance Agencies & Brokerages
524290 Other Insurance Related Activities (including third-party administration of insurance and pension funds)

Instructions for Form 1120S

Code

Funds, Trusts, and Other Financial Vehicles
Real Estate
525100 Insurance & Employee Benefit Funds
525910 Open-End Investment Funds (Form 1120-RIC)
525920 Trusts, Estates, & Agency Accounts
525930 Real Estate Investment Trusts (Form 1120-REIT)
525990 Other Financial Vehicles (including closed-end investment funds)

"Offices of Bank Holding Companies" and "Offices of Other Holding Companies" are located under **Management of Companies (Holding Companies)** below.

Real Estate and Rental and Leasing
531110 Lessors of Residential Buildings & Dwellings
531114 Cooperative Housing
531120 Lessors of Nonresidential Buildings (except Miniwarehouses)
531130 Lessors of Miniwarehouses & Self-Storage Units
531190 Lessors of Other Real Estate Property
531210 Offices of Real Estate Agents & Brokers
531310 Real Estate Property Managers
531320 Offices of Real Estate Appraisers
531390 Other Activities Related to Real Estate

Rental and Leasing Services
532100 Automotive Equipment Rental & Leasing
532210 Consumer Electronics & Appliances Rental
532220 Formal Wear & Costume Rental
532230 Video Tape & Disc Rental
532290 Other Consumer Goods Rental
532310 General Rental Centers
532400 Commercial & Industrial Machinery & Equipment Rental & Leasing

Lessors of Nonfinancial Intangible Assets (except copyrighted works)
533110 Lessors of Nonfinancial Intangible Assets (except copyrighted works)

Professional, Scientific, and Technical Services
Legal Services
541110 Offices of Lawyers
541190 Other Legal Services

Accounting, Tax Preparation, Bookkeeping, and Payroll Services
541211 Offices of Certified Public Accountants
541213 Tax Preparation Services
541214 Payroll Services
541219 Other Accounting Services

Architectural, Engineering, and Related Services
541310 Architectural Services
541320 Landscape Architecture Services
541330 Engineering Services
541340 Drafting Services
541350 Building Inspection Services
541360 Geophysical Surveying & Mapping Services
541370 Surveying & Mapping (except Geophysical) Services
541380 Testing Laboratories

Code

Specialized Design Services
541400 Specialized Design Services (including interior, industrial, graphic, & fashion design)
Computer Systems Design and Related Services
541511 Custom Computer Programming Services
541512 Computer Systems Design Services
541513 Computer Facilities Management Services
541519 Other Computer Related Services

Other Professional, Scientific, and Technical Services
541600 Management, Scientific, & Technical Consulting Services
541700 Scientific Research & Development Services
541800 Advertising & Related Services
541910 Marketing Research & Public Opinion Polling
541920 Photographic Services
541930 Translation & Interpretation Services
541940 Veterinary Services
541990 All Other Professional, Scientific, & Technical Services

Management of Companies (Holding Companies)
551111 Offices of Bank Holding Companies
551112 Offices of Other Holding Companies

Administrative and Support and Waste Management and Remediation Services
Administrative and Support Services
561110 Office Administrative Services
561210 Facilities Support Services
561300 Employment Services
561410 Document Preparation Services
561420 Telephone Call Centers
561430 Business Service Centers (including private mail centers & copy shops)
561440 Collection Agencies
561450 Credit Bureaus
561490 Other Business Support Services (including repossession services, court reporting, & stenotype services)
561500 Travel Arrangement & Reservation Services
561600 Investigation & Security Services
561710 Exterminating & Pest Control Services
561720 Janitorial Services
561730 Landscaping Services
561740 Carpet & Upholstery Cleaning Services
561790 Other Services to Buildings & Dwellings
561900 Other Support Services (including packaging & labeling services, & convention & trade show organizers)

Waste Management and Remediation Services
562000 Waste Management & Remediation Services

Educational Services
611000 Educational Services (including schools, colleges, & universities)

Code

Health Care and Social Assistance
Offices of Physicians and Dentists
621111 Offices of Physicians (except mental health specialists)
621112 Offices of Physicians, Mental Health Specialists
621210 Offices of Dentists

Offices of Other Health Practitioners
621310 Offices of Chiropractors
621320 Offices of Optometrists
621330 Offices of Mental Health Practitioners (except Physicians)
621340 Offices of Physical, Occupational & Speech Therapists, & Audiologists
621391 Offices of Podiatrists
621399 Offices of All Other Miscellaneous Health Practitioners

Outpatient Care Centers
621410 Family Planning Centers
621420 Outpatient Mental Health & Substance Abuse Centers
621491 HMO Medical Centers
621492 Kidney Dialysis Centers
621493 Freestanding Ambulatory Surgical & Emergency Centers
621498 All Other Outpatient Care Centers

Medical and Diagnostic Laboratories
621510 Medical & Diagnostic Laboratories

Home Health Care Services
621610 Home Health Care Services

Other Ambulatory Health Care Services
621900 Other Ambulatory Health Care Services (including ambulance services & blood & organ banks)

Hospitals
622000 Hospitals

Nursing and Residential Care Facilities
623000 Nursing & Residential Care Facilities

Social Assistance
624100 Individual & Family Services
624200 Community Food & Housing, & Emergency & Other Relief Services
624310 Vocational Rehabilitation Services
624410 Child Day Care Services

Arts, Entertainment, and Recreation
Performing Arts, Spectator Sports, and Related Industries
711100 Performing Arts Companies
711210 Spectator Sports (including sports clubs & racetracks)
711300 Promoters of Performing Arts, Sports, & Similar Events
711410 Agents & Managers for Artists, Athletes, Entertainers, & Other Public Figures
711510 Independent Artists, Writers, & Performers

Museums, Historical Sites, and Similar Institutions
712100 Museums, Historical Sites, & Similar Institutions

Amusement, Gambling, and Recreation Industries
713100 Amusement Parks & Arcades
713200 Gambling Industries

Code

713900 Other Amusement & Recreation Industries (including golf courses, skiing facilities, marinas, fitness centers, & bowling centers)

Accommodation and Food Services
Accommodation
721110 Hotels (except Casino Hotels) & Motels
721120 Casino Hotels
721191 Bed & Breakfast Inns
721199 All Other Traveler Accommodation
721210 RV (Recreational Vehicle) Parks & Recreational Camps
721310 Rooming & Boarding Houses

Food Services and Drinking Places
722110 Full-Service Restaurants
722210 Limited-Service Eating Places
722300 Special Food Services (including food service contractors & caterers)
722410 Drinking Places (Alcoholic Beverages)

Other Services
Repair and Maintenance
811110 Automotive Mechanical & Electrical Repair & Maintenance
811120 Automotive Body, Paint, Interior, & Glass Repair
811190 Other Automotive Repair & Maintenance (including oil change & lubrication shops & car washes)
811210 Electronic & Precision Equipment Repair & Maintenance
811310 Commercial & Industrial Machinery & Equipment (except Automotive & Electronic) Repair & Maintenance
811410 Home & Garden Equipment & Appliance Repair & Maintenance
811420 Reupholstery & Furniture Repair
811430 Footwear & Leather Goods Repair
811490 Other Personal & Household Goods Repair & Maintenance

Personal and Laundry Services
812111 Barber Shops
812112 Beauty Salons
812113 Nail Salons
812190 Other Personal Care Services (including diet & weight reducing centers)
812210 Funeral Homes & Funeral Services
812220 Cemeteries & Crematories
812310 Coin-Operated Laundries & Drycleaners
812320 Drycleaning & Laundry Services (except Coin-Operated)
812330 Linen & Uniform Supply
812910 Pet Care (except Veterinary) Services
812920 Photofinishing
812930 Parking Lots & Garages
812990 All Other Personal Services

Religious, Grantmaking, Civic, Professional, and Similar Organizations
813000 Religious, Grantmaking, Civic, Professional, & Similiar Organizations (including condominium and homeowners associations)

Index

Form **1120S**	**U.S. Income Tax Return for an S Corporation**	OMB No. 1545-0130

Department of the Treasury
Internal Revenue Service

▶ Do not file this form unless the corporation has timely filed Form 2553 to elect to be an S corporation.
▶ See separate instructions.

2002

For calendar year 2002, or tax year beginning , 2002, and ending , 20

A Effective date of election as an S corporation: 12-1-98

Use IRS label. Otherwise, print or type.

Name: StratoTech, Inc.

Number, street, and room or suite no. (If a P.O. box, see page 11 of the instructions.): 482 Winston Street

City or town, state, and ZIP code: Metro City, OH 43705

B Business code no. (see pages 29–31): 5008

C Employer identification number: 10:4487965

D Date incorporated: 3-1-75

E Total assets (see page 11): $ 771,334

F Check applicable boxes: (1) ☒ Initial return (2) ☐ Final return (3) ☐ Name change (4) ☐ Address change (5) ☐ Amended return

G Enter number of shareholders in the corporation at end of the tax year ▶ 6

Caution: Include only trade or business income and expenses on lines 1a through 21. See page 11 of the instructions for more information.

Income

1a	Gross receipts or sales 1,545,700	**b** Less returns and allowances 21,000	**c** Bal ▶ **1c** 1,524,700
2	Cost of goods sold (Schedule A, line 8)	**2**	954,700
3	Gross profit. Subtract line 2 from line 1c	**3**	570,000
4	Net gain (loss) from Form 4797, Part II, line 18 (attach Form 4797)	**4**	
5	Other income (loss) (attach schedule)	**5**	
6	**Total income (loss).** Combine lines 3 through 5 ▶	**6**	570,000

Deductions (see page 12 of the instructions for limitations)

7	Compensation of officers	**7**	170,000
8	Salaries and wages (less employment credits)	**8**	138,000
9	Repairs and maintenance	**9**	800
10	Bad debts	**10**	1,600
11	Rents	**11**	9,200
12	Taxes and licenses	**12**	15,000
13	Interest	**13**	14,200
14a	Depreciation (if required, attach Form 4562) **14a** 15,200		
b	Depreciation claimed on Schedule A and elsewhere on return **14b**		
c	Subtract line 14b from line 14a	**14c**	15,200
15	Depletion (**Do not deduct oil and gas depletion.**)	**15**	
16	Advertising	**16**	8,700
17	Pension, profit-sharing, etc., plans	**17**	
18	Employee benefit programs	**18**	
19	Other deductions (attach schedule)	**19**	78,300
20	**Total deductions.** Add the amounts shown in the far right column for lines 7 through 19 ▶	**20**	451,000
21	Ordinary income (loss) from trade or business activities. Subtract line 20 from line 6	**21**	119,000

Tax and Payments

22	**Tax: a** Excess net passive income tax (attach schedule) **22a**		
	b Tax from Schedule D (Form 1120S) **22b**		
	c Add lines 22a and 22b (see page 16 of the instructions for additional taxes)	**22c**	
23	**Payments: a** 2002 estimated tax payments and amount applied from 2001 return **23a**		
	b Tax deposited with Form 7004 **23b**		
	c Credit for Federal tax paid on fuels (attach Form 4136) **23c**		
	d Add lines 23a through 23c	**23d**	
24	Estimated tax penalty. Check if Form 2220 is attached ▶ ☐	**24**	
25	**Tax due.** If the total of lines 22c and 24 is larger than line 23d, enter amount owed. See page 4 of the instructions for depository method of payment ▶	**25**	
26	**Overpayment.** If line 23d is larger than the total of lines 22c and 24, enter amount overpaid ▶	**26**	
27	Enter amount of line 26 you want: **Credited to 2003 estimated tax ▶** Refunded ▶	**27**	

Sign Here

Under penalties of perjury, I declare that I have examined this return, including accompanying schedules and statements, and to the best of my knowledge and belief, it is true, correct, and complete. Declaration of preparer (other than taxpayer) is based on all information of which preparer has any knowledge.

John H. Green | 3-10-XX | President

Signature of officer | Date | Title

May the IRS discuss this return with the preparer shown below (see instructions)? ☐ Yes ☐ No

Paid Preparer's Use Only

Preparer's signature		Date	Check if self-employed ☐	Preparer's SSN or PTIN
Firm's name (or yours if self-employed), address, and ZIP code			EIN	
			Phone no. ( )	

For Paperwork Reduction Act Notice, see the separate instructions. Cat. No. 11510H Form **1120S** (2002)

Form 1120S (2002)   Page **2**

Schedule A   Cost of Goods Sold (see page 17 of the instructions)

1	Inventory at beginning of year	**1** 126,000
2	Purchases	**2** 1,127,100
3	Cost of labor	**3**
4	Additional section 263A costs *(attach schedule)*	**4**
5	Other costs *(attach schedule)*	**5**
6	**Total.** Add lines 1 through 5	**6** 1,253,100
7	Inventory at end of year	**7** 298,400
8	**Cost of goods sold.** Subtract line 7 from line 6. Enter here and on page 1, line 2	**8** 954,700

9a Check all methods used for valuing closing inventory: (i) ☐ Cost as described in Regulations section 1.471-3

     (ii) ☐ Lower of cost or market as described in Regulations section 1.471-4

     (iii) ☐ Other (specify method used and attach explanation) ▶ ....

  b Check if there was a writedown of "subnormal" goods as described in Regulations section 1.471-2(c) . . . . . . ▶ ☐

  c Check if the LIFO inventory method was adopted this tax year for any goods *(if checked, attach Form 970)* . . . . . ▶ ☐

  d If the LIFO inventory method was used for this tax year, enter percentage (or amounts) of closing
     inventory computed under LIFO **9d**

  e Do the rules of section 263A (for property produced or acquired for resale) apply to the corporation? . . . . ☐ Yes ☑ No

  f Was there any change in determining quantities, cost, or valuations between opening and closing inventory? . . ☐ Yes ☑ No
     If "Yes," attach explanation.

Schedule B   Other Information

		Yes	No
1	Check method of accounting: **(a)** ☐ Cash **(b)** ☑ Accrual **(c)** ☐ Other (specify) ▶..........................		
2	Refer to the list on pages 29 through 31 of the instructions and state the corporation's principal:		
	(a) Business activity ▶ ..5008 Distributor................ **(b)** Product or service ▶ ..heavy equipment..........		
3	Did the corporation at the end of the tax year own, directly or indirectly, 50% or more of the voting stock of a domestic corporation? (For rules of attribution, see section 267(c).) If "Yes," attach a schedule showing: **(a)** name, address, and employer identification number and **(b)** percentage owned		✓
4	Was the corporation a member of a controlled group subject to the provisions of section 1561?		✓
5	Check this box if the corporation has filed or is required to file **Form 8264,** Application for Registration of a Tax Shelter ▶ ☐		
6	Check this box if the corporation issued publicly offered debt instruments with original issue discount . . ▶ ☐		
	If so, the corporation may have to file **Form 8281,** Information Return for Publicly Offered Original Issue Discount Instruments.		
7	If the corporation: **(a)** was a C corporation before it elected to be an S corporation **or** the corporation acquired an asset with a basis determined by reference to its basis (or the basis of any other property) in the hands of a C corporation **and (b)** has net unrealized built-in gain (defined in section 1374(d)(1)) in excess of the net recognized built-in gain from prior years, enter the net unrealized built-in gain reduced by net recognized built-in gain from prior years (see page 17 of the instructions) . . . . ▶ $		
8	Check this box if the corporation had accumulated earnings and profits at the close of the tax year (see page 18 of the instructions) . . . . ▶ ☐		
9	Are the corporation's total receipts (see page 29 of the instructions) for the tax year **and** total assets at the end of the tax year less than $250,000? If "Yes," the corporation is not required to complete Schedules L and M-1.		✓

Note: *If the corporation had assets or operated a business in a foreign country or U.S. possession, it may be required to attach* **Schedule N (Form 1120),** *Foreign Operations of U.S. Corporations, to this return. See Schedule N for details.*

Schedule K   Shareholders' Shares of Income, Credits, Deductions, etc.

	(a) Pro rata share items		(b) Total amount
1	Ordinary income (loss) from trade or business activities (page 1, line 21)	**1**	119,000
2	Net income (loss) from rental real estate activities *(attach Form 8825)*	**2**	
3a	Gross income from other rental activities	**3a**		
b	Expenses from other rental activities *(attach schedule)* .	**3b**		
c	Net income (loss) from other rental activities. Subtract line 3b from line 3a	**3c**	
4	Portfolio income (loss):		
a	Interest income	**4a**	4,000
b	Ordinary dividends	**4b**	16,000
c	Royalty income	**4c**	
d	Net short-term capital gain (loss) *(attach Schedule D (Form 1120S))*.	**4d**	
e	**(1)** Net long-term capital gain (loss) *(attach Schedule D (Form 1120S))*.	**4e(1)**	
	(2) 28% rate gain (loss) ▶ .... **(3)** Qualified 5-year gain ▶..................		
f	Other portfolio income (loss) *(attach schedule)*.	**4f**	
5	Net section 1231 gain (loss) (other than due to casualty or theft) *(attach Form 4797)* . .	**5**	
6	Other income (loss) *(attach schedule)*	**6**	

(left margin, vertical text: Income (Loss))

Form **1120S** (2002)

Form 1120S (2002)   Page **3**

Schedule K	Shareholders' Shares of Income, Credits, Deductions, etc. *(continued)*		
	(a) Pro rata share items		**(b)** Total amount

Deductions

7	Charitable contributions *(attach schedule)*	**7**	24,000
8	Section 179 expense deduction *(attach Form 4562)*	**8**	
9	Deductions related to portfolio income (loss) (itemize)	**9**	
10	Other deductions *(attach schedule)*	**10**	

Investment Interest

11a	Interest expense on investment debts	**11a**	3,000
b (1)	Investment income included on lines 4a, 4b, 4c, and 4f above	**11b(1)**	20,000
(2)	Investment expenses included on line 9 above	**11b(2)**	

Credits

12a	Credit for alcohol used as a fuel *(attach Form 6478)*	**12a**	
b	Low-income housing credit:		
(1)	From partnerships to which section 42(j)(5) applies	**12b(1)**	
(2)	Other than on line 12b(1)	**12b(2)**	
c	Qualified rehabilitation expenditures related to rental real estate activities *(attach Form 3468)*	**12c**	
d	Credits (other than credits shown on lines 12b and 12c) related to rental real estate activities	**12d**	
e	Credits related to other rental activities	**12e**	
13	Other credits	**13**	6,000

Adjustments and Tax Preference Items

14a	Depreciation adjustment on property placed in service after 1986	**14a**	
b	Adjusted gain or loss	**14b**	
c	Depletion (other than oil and gas)	**14c**	
d (1)	Gross income from oil, gas, or geothermal properties	**14d(1)**	
(2)	Deductions allocable to oil, gas, or geothermal properties	**14d(2)**	
e	Other adjustments and tax preference items *(attach schedule)*	**14e**	

Foreign Taxes

15a	Name of foreign country or U.S. possession ▶		
b	Gross income from all sources	**15b**	
c	Gross income sourced at shareholder level	**15c**	
d	Foreign gross income sourced at corporate level:		
(1)	Passive	**15d(1)**	
(2)	Listed categories *(attach schedule)*	**15d(2)**	
(3)	General limitation	**15d(3)**	
e	Deductions allocated and apportioned at shareholder level:		
(1)	Interest expense	**15e(1)**	
(2)	Other	**15e(2)**	
f	Deductions allocated and apportioned at corporate level to foreign source income:		
(1)	Passive	**15f(1)**	
(2)	Listed categories *(attach schedule)*	**15f(2)**	
(3)	General limitation	**15f(3)**	
g	Total foreign taxes (check one): ▶ ☐ Paid ☐ Accrued	**15g**	
h	Reduction in taxes available for credit *(attach schedule)*	**15h**	

Other

16	Section 59(e)(2) expenditures: **a** Type ▶ .... **b** Amount ▶	**16b**	
17	Tax-exempt interest income	**17**	8,000
18	Other tax-exempt income	**18**	
19	Nondeductible expenses	**19**	16,350
20	Total property distributions (including cash) other than dividends reported on line 22 below	**20**	65,000
21	Other items and amounts required to be reported separately to shareholders *(attach schedule)*		
22	Total dividend distributions paid from accumulated earnings and profits	**22**	
23	**Income (loss).** (Required only if Schedule M-1 must be completed.) Combine lines 1 through 6 in column (b). From the result, subtract the sum of lines 7 through 11a, 15g, and 16b	**23**	112,000

Form **1120S** (2002)

Form 1120S (2002)   Page **4**

Note: The corporation is not required to complete Schedules L and M-1 if question 9 of Schedule B is answered "Yes."

Schedule L — Balance Sheets per Books

Assets	Beginning of tax year (a)	(b)	End of tax year (c)	(d)
1 Cash		14,700		14,514
2a Trade notes and accounts receivable	98,400		33,700	
b Less allowance for bad debts		98,400		33,700
3 Inventories		126,000		298,400
4 U.S. Government obligations				
5 Tax-exempt securities		100,000		100,000
6 Other current assets (attach schedule)		26,300		26,300
7 Loans to shareholders				
8 Mortgage and real estate loans				
9 Other investments (attach schedule)		100,000		100,000
10a Buildings and other depreciable assets	204,700			
b Less accumulated depreciation	36,000	168,700		189,120
11a Depletable assets				
b Less accumulated depletion				
12 Land (net of any amortization)		20,000		20,000
13a Intangible assets (amortizable only)				
b Less accumulated amortization				
14 Other assets (attach schedule)		14,800		19,300
15 Total assets		668,900		771,334
Liabilities and Shareholders' Equity				
16 Accounts payable		28,500		34,834
17 Mortgages, notes, bonds payable in less than 1 year		4,300		4,300
18 Other current liabilities (attach schedule)		6,800		7,400
19 Loans from shareholders				
20 Mortgages, notes, bonds payable in 1 year or more		161,300		215,530
21 Other liabilities (attach schedule)				
22 Capital stock		2,000		2,000
23 Additional paid-in capital		198,000		198,000
24 Retained earnings		268,000		309,270
25 Adjustments to shareholders' equity (attach schedule)				
26 Less cost of treasury stock		( )		(771,334)
27 Total liabilities and shareholders' equity		668,900		

Schedule M-1 — Reconciliation of Income (Loss) per Books With Income (Loss) per Return

1 Net income (loss) per books	106,270	5 Income recorded on books this year not included on Schedule K, lines 1 through 6 (itemize):	
2 Income included on Schedule K, lines 1 through 6, not recorded on books this year (itemize):		a Tax-exempt interest $ 5,000	5,000
	0		
3 Expenses recorded on books this year not included on Schedule K, lines 1 through 11a, 15g, and 16b (itemize):		6 Deductions included on Schedule K, lines 1 through 11a, 15g, and 16b, not charged against book income this year (itemize):	
a Depreciation $		a Depreciation $ 5,620	
b Travel and entertainment $			5,620
	16,350	7 Add lines 5 and 6	10,620
4 Add lines 1 through 3	122,620	8 Income (loss) (Schedule K, line 23). Line 4 less line 7	112,000

Schedule M-2 — Analysis of Accumulated Adjustments Account, Other Adjustments Account, and Shareholders' Undistributed Taxable Income Previously Taxed (see page 26 of the instructions)

	(a) Accumulated adjustments account	(b) Other adjustments account	(c) Shareholders' undistributed taxable income previously taxed
1 Balance at beginning of tax year	0	0	
2 Ordinary income from page 1, line 21	119,000		
3 Other additions	20,000	5,000	
4 Loss from page 1, line 21	(0)		
5 Other reductions	(42,500)	(850)	
6 Combine lines 1 through 5	96,500	4,150	
7 Distributions other than dividend distributions	65,000	0	
8 Balance at end of tax year. Subtract line 7 from line 6	31,500	4,150	

Form **1120S** (2002)

SCHEDULE D **(Form 1120S)** Department of the Treasury Internal Revenue Service	**Capital Gains and Losses and Built-In Gains** ▶ Attach to Form 1120S. ▶ See separate instructions.	OMB No. 1545-0130 20**02**

Name | Employer identification number

Part I   Short-Term Capital Gains and Losses—Assets Held One Year or Less

(a) Description of property (Example, 100 shares of "Z" Co.)	**(b)** Date acquired (mo., day, yr.)	**(c)** Date sold (mo., day, yr.)	**(d)** Sales price	**(e)** Cost or other basis (see instructions)	**(f)** Gain or (loss) ((d) minus (e))	
1						

2	Short-term capital gain from installment sales from Form 6252, line 26 or 37	**2**	
3	Short-term capital gain or (loss) from like-kind exchanges from Form 8824 .	**3**	
4	Combine lines 1 through 3 in column (f)	**4**	
5	Tax on short-term capital gain included on line 22 below	**5**	( )
6	**Net short-term capital gain or (loss).** Combine lines 4 and 5. Enter here and on Form 1120S, Schedule K, line 4d or 6	**6**	

Part II   Long-Term Capital Gains and Losses—Assets Held More Than One Year

(a) Description of property (Example, 100 shares of "Z" Co.)	**(b)** Date acquired (mo., day, yr.)	**(c)** Date sold (mo., day, yr.)	**(d)** Sales price	**(e)** Cost or other basis (see instructions)	**(f)** Gain or (loss) ((d) minus (e))	**(g)** 28% rate gain or (loss) * (see instr. below)
7						

8	Long-term capital gain from installment sales from Form 6252, line 26 or 37 .	**8**	
9	Long-term capital gain or (loss) from like-kind exchanges from Form 8824 .	**9**	
10	Capital gain distributions	**10**	
11	Combine lines 7 through 10 in column (f)	**11**	
12	Tax on long-term capital gain included on line 22 below.	**12**	( ) ( )
13	Combine lines 7 through 12 in column (g). Enter here and on Form 1120S, Schedule K, line 4e(2) or 6.	**13**	
14	**Net long-term capital gain or (loss).** Combine lines 11 and 12 in column (f). Enter here and on Form 1120S, Schedule K, line 4e(1) or 6	**14**	

*28% rate gain or (loss) includes **all** "collectibles gains and losses" (as defined in the instructions).

Part III   Built-In Gains Tax (See instructions **before** completing this part.)

15	Excess of recognized built-in gains over recognized built-in losses (attach computation schedule)	**15**	
16	Taxable income (attach computation schedule)	**16**	
17	Net recognized built-in gain. Enter the smallest of line 15, line 16, or line 7 of Schedule B . . .	**17**	
18	Section 1374(b)(2) deduction	**18**	
19	Subtract line 18 from line 17. If zero or less, enter -0- here and on line 22.	**19**	
20	Enter 35% of line 19	**20**	
21	Business credit and minimum tax credit carryforwards under section 1374(b)(3) from C corporation years	**21**	
22	**Tax.** Subtract line 21 from line 20 (if zero or less, enter -0-). Enter here and on Form 1120S, page 1, line 22b	**22**	

For Paperwork Reduction Act Notice, see the Instructions for Form 1120S.   Cat. No. 11516V   Schedule D (Form 1120S) 2002

20**02**

Department of the Treasury
Internal Revenue Service

Instructions for Schedule D (Form 1120S)

Capital Gains and Losses and Built-In Gains

Section references are to the Internal Revenue Code unless otherwise noted.

General Instructions

Purpose of Schedule

Schedule D is used by all S corporations to report:
● Sales or exchanges of capital assets.
● Gains on distributions to shareholders of appreciated capital assets (referred to here as distributions).
● Nonbusiness bad debts.
● Net recognized built-in gain as defined in section 1374(d)(2). The built-in gains tax is figured in Part III of Schedule D.

Note: *The capital gains tax under section 1374 (prior to its amendment by the Tax Reform Act of 1986) no longer applies. See Regulations section 1.1374-8(d), Example 1.*

Other Forms The Corporation May Have To File

Use **Form 4797**, Sales of Business Property, to report:
● Sales, exchanges, and distributions of property used in a trade or business.
● Sales, exchanges, and distributions of depreciable and amortizable property.
● Sales or other dispositions of securities or commodities held in connection with a trading business, if the corporation made a mark-to-market election (see page 4 of the Instructions for Form 1120S).
● Involuntary conversions (other than from casualties or thefts).
● The disposition of noncapital assets (other than inventory or property held primarily for sale to customers in the ordinary course of a trade or business).
   Use **Form 4684**, Casualties and Thefts, to report involuntary conversions of property due to casualty or theft.

Use **Form 6781**, Gains and Losses From Section 1256 Contracts and Straddles, to report gains and losses from section 1256 contracts and straddles.

Use **Form 8824**, Like-Kind Exchanges, if the corporation made one or more like-kind exchange. A "like-kind exchange" occurs when business or investment property is exchanged for property of a like kind. For exchanges of capital assets, enter the gain or loss from Form 8824, if any, on line 3 or line 9 in column (f), and in column (g) if required.

Capital Asset

Each item of property the corporation held (whether or not connected with its trade or business) is a capital asset **except:**
● Stock in trade or other property included in inventory or held mainly for sale to customers.
● Accounts or notes receivable acquired in the ordinary course of the trade or business for services rendered or from the sale of stock in trade or other property held mainly for sale to customers.
● Depreciable or real property used in the trade or business, even if it is fully depreciated.
● Certain copyrights; literary, musical, or artistic compositions; letters or memorandums; or similar property. See section 1221(a)(3).
● U.S. Government publications, including the Congressional Record, that the corporation received from the Government, other than by purchase at the normal sales price, or that the corporation got from another taxpayer who had received it in a similar way, if the corporation's basis is determined by reference to the previous owner.
● Certain commodities derivative financial instruments held by a dealer. See section 1221(a)(6).

● Certain hedging transactions entered into in the normal course of the trade or business. See section 1221(a)(7).
● Supplies regularly used in the trade or business.

Items for Special Treatment

Note: *For more information, see **Pub. 544**, Sales and Other Dispositions of Assets.*

Loss from a sale or exchange between the corporation and a related person. Except for distributions in complete liquidation of a corporation, no loss is allowed from the sale or exchange of property between the corporation and certain related persons. See section 267 for details.

Loss from a wash sale. The corporation cannot deduct a loss from a wash sale of stock or securities (including contracts or options to acquire or sell stock or securities) unless the corporation is a dealer in stock or securities and the loss was sustained in a transaction made in the ordinary course of the corporation's trade or business. A wash sale occurs if the corporation acquires (by purchase or exchange), or has a contract or option to acquire, substantially identical stock or securities within 30 days before or after the date of the sale or exchange. See section 1091 for more information.

Gain on distribution of appreciated property. Generally, gain (but not loss) is recognized on a nonliquidating distribution of appreciated property to the extent that the property's fair market value exceeds its adjusted basis. See section 311 for details.

Gain or loss on distribution of property in complete liquidation. Generally, gain or loss is recognized by a corporation upon the liquidating distribution of property as if it had sold the property at its fair market value.

Cat. No. 64419L

See section 336 for details and exceptions.

Gain or loss on certain short-term Federal, state, and municipal obligations. Such obligations are treated as capital assets in determining gain or loss. On any gain realized, a portion is treated as ordinary income and the balance is considered as a short-term capital gain. See section 1271.

Gain from installment sales. If the corporation sold property at a gain and it will receive a payment in a tax year after the year of sale, it generally must report the sale on the installment method unless it elects not to. However, the installment method may not be used to report sales of stock or securities traded on an established securities market.

Use **Form 6252**, Installment Sale Income, to report the sale on the installment method. Also use Form 6252 to report any payment received during the tax year from a sale made in an earlier year that was reported on the installment method. To elect out of the installment method, report the full amount of the gain on Schedule D for the year of the sale on a return filed by the due date (including extensions). If the original return was filed on time, the corporation may make the election on an amended return filed no later than 6 months after the original due date (excluding extensions). Write "Filed pursuant to section 301.9100-2" at the top of the amended return.

Gain or loss on an option to buy or sell property. See sections 1032 and 1234 for the rules that apply to a purchaser or grantor of an option or a securities futures contract (as defined in section 1234B). For details, **Pub. 550**, Investment Income and Expenses.

Gain or loss from a short sale of property. Report the gain or loss to the extent that the property used to close the short sale is considered a capital asset in the hands of the taxpayer.

Loss from securities that are capital assets that become worthless during the year. Except for securities held by a bank, treat the loss as a capital loss as of the last day of the tax year. See section 582 for the rules on the treatment of securities held by a bank.

Nonrecognition of gain on sale of stock to an employee stock ownership plan (ESOP) or an eligible cooperative. See section 1042 and Temporary Regulations section

1.1042-1T for rules under which a taxpayer may elect not to recognize gain from the sale of certain stock to an ESOP or an eligible cooperative.

Disposition of market discount bonds. See section 1276 for rules on the disposition of any market discount bonds.

Capital gain distributions. Report the **total** amount of capital gain distributions as long-term capital gain on line 10, column (f), regardless of how long the corporation held the investment. Enter on line 10, column (g), the 28% rate gain portion of your total capital gain distributions.

Nonbusiness bad debts. A nonbusiness bad debt must be treated as a short-term capital loss and can be deducted only in the year the debt becomes totally worthless. For each bad debt, enter the name of the debtor and "schedule attached" in column (a) of line 1 and the amount of the bad debt as a loss in column (f). Also attach a statement of facts to support each bad debt deduction.

Real estate subdivided for sale. Certain lots or parcels that are part of a tract of real estate subdivided for sale may be treated as capital assets. See section 1237.

Sale of a partnership interest. A sale or other disposition of an interest in a partnership owning unrealized receivables or inventory items may result in ordinary gain or loss. See **Pub. 541**, Partnerships, for more details.

Special rules for traders in securities. Traders in securities are engaged in the **business** of buying and selling securities for their own account. To be engaged in a business as a trader in securities the corporation:
• Must seek to **profit from daily market movements** in the prices of securities and not from dividends, interest, or capital appreciation.
• Must be involved in a trading activity that is **substantial**.
• Must carry on the activity with **continuity** and **regularity**.

The following facts and circumstances should be considered in determining if a corporation's activity is a business:
• Typical holding periods for securities bought and sold.
• The frequency and dollar amount of the corporation's trades during the year.
• The extent to which the activity is pursued to produce income for a livelihood.

• The amount of time devoted to the activity.

Like an investor, a trader must report each sale of securities (taking into account commissions and any other costs of acquiring or disposing of the securities) on Schedule D or on an attached statement containing all the same information for each sale in a similar format. However, if a trader made the mark-to-market election (see page 4 of the Instructions for Form 1120S), each transaction is reported in Part II of Form 4797 instead of Schedule D.

The limitation on investment interest expense that applies to investors does not apply to interest paid or incurred in a trading business. A trader reports interest expense and other expenses (excluding commissions and other costs of acquiring and disposing of securities) from a trading business on page 1 of Form 1120S.

A trader also may hold securities for investment. The rules for investors generally will apply to those securities. Allocate interest and other expenses between a trading business and investment securities. Investment interest expense is reported on line 11a of Schedules K and K-1.

Certain constructive ownership transactions. Gain in excess of the gain the corporation would have recognized if it had held a financial asset directly during the term of a derivative contract must be treated as ordinary income. See section 1260 for details.

Constructive sale treatment for certain appreciated positions. Generally, the corporation must recognize gain (but not loss) on the date it enters into a constructive sale of any appreciated interest in stock, a partnership interest, or certain debt instruments as if the position were disposed of at fair market value on that date.

The corporation is treated as making a constructive sale of an appreciated position if it (or a related person, in some cases) does **one** of the following:
• Enters into a short sale of the same or substantially identical property (i.e., a "short sale against the box").
• Enters into an offsetting notional principal contract relating to the same or substantially identical property.
• Enters into a futures or forward contract to deliver the same or substantially identical property.

Instructions for Schedule D (Form 1120S)

- Acquires the same or substantially identical property (if the appreciated position is a short sale, offsetting notional principal contract, or a futures or forward contract).

   Exception. Generally, constructive sale treatment **does not** apply if:
- The transaction was closed before the end of the 30th day after the end of the year in which it was entered into,
- The appreciated position to which the transaction relates was held throughout the 60-day period starting on the date the transaction was closed, **and**
- At no time during that 60-day period was the corporation's risk of loss reduced by holding certain other positions.

   For details and other exceptions to these rules, see Pub. 550.

Rollover of gain from qualified stock. If the corporation sold qualified small business stock (defined below) that it held for more than 6 months, it may postpone gain if it purchased other qualified small business stock during the 60-day period that began on the date of the sale. The corporation must recognize gain to the extent the sale proceeds exceed the cost of the replacement stock. Reduce the basis of the replacement stock by any postponed gain.

   If the corporation chooses to postpone gain, report the entire gain realized on the sale on line 1 or 7. Directly below the line on which the corporation reported the gain, enter in column (a) "Section 1045 Rollover" and enter as a (loss) in column (f) the amount of the postponed gain.

   ⚠️ **CAUTION** *The corporation also must separately state the amount of the gain rolled over on qualified stock under section 1045 on Form 1120S, Schedule K, line 6, because each shareholder must determine if he or she qualifies for the rollover at the shareholder level. Also, the corporation must include on Schedule D, line 1 or 7 (and on Form 1120S, Schedule K, line 6), any gain that could qualify for the section 1045 rollover at the shareholder level instead of the corporate level (because a shareholder was entitled to purchase replacement stock). If the corporation had a gain on qualified stock that could qualify for the 50% exclusion under section 1202, report that gain on Schedule D, line 7 (and on Form 1120S, Schedule K, line 6).*

   To be **qualified small business stock**, the stock must meet **all** of the following tests:
- It must be stock in a C corporation.
- It must have been originally issued after August 10, 1993.
- As of the date the stock was issued, the C corporation was a qualified small business. A qualified small business is a domestic C corporation with total gross assets of $50 million or less **(a)** at all times after August 9, 1993, and before the stock was issued, and **(b)** immediately after the stock was issued. Gross assets include those of any predecessor of the corporation. All corporations that are members of the same parent-subsidiary controlled group are treated as one corporation.
- The corporation must have acquired the stock at its original issue (either directly or through an underwriter), either in exchange for money or other property or as pay for services (other than as an underwriter) to the corporation. In certain cases, the corporation may meet the test if it acquired the stock from another person who met this test (such as by gift or inheritance) or through a conversion or exchange of qualified small business stock held by the corporation.
- During substantially all the time the corporation held the stock:

   1. The issuer was a C corporation,

   2. At least 80% of the value of the issuer's assets were used in the active conduct of one or more qualified businesses (defined below), and

   3. The issuing corporation **was not** a foreign corporation, DISC, former DISC, corporation that has made (or that has a subsidiary that has made) a section 936 election, regulated investment company, real estate investment trust, REMIC, FASIT, or cooperative.

Note: *A specialized small business investment company (SSBIC) is treated as having met test 2 above.*

   A **qualified business** is any business **other than** the following:
- One involving services performed in the fields of health, law, engineering, architecture, accounting, actuarial science, performing arts, consulting, athletics, financial services, or brokerage services.
- One whose principal asset is the reputation or skill of one or more employees.
- Any banking, insurance, financing, leasing, investing, or similar business.

- Any farming business (including the raising or harvesting of trees).
- Any business involving the production of products for which percentage depletion can be claimed.
- Any business of operating a hotel, motel, restaurant, or similar business.

Rollover of gain from empowerment zone assets. If the corporation sold a qualified empowerment zone asset it held for than one year, it may be able to elect to postpone part or all of the gain. For details, see **Pub. 954,** Tax Incentives for Empowerment Zones and Other Distressed Communities, and section 1397B.

Specific Instructions

Parts I and II

Generally, report sales or exchanges (including like-kind exchanges) even if there is no gain or loss. In Part I, report the sale, exchange, or distribution of capital assets held 1 year or less. In Part II, report the sale, exchange, or distribution of capital assets held more than 1 year. Use the trade dates for the dates of acquisition and sale of stocks and bonds traded on an exchange or over-the-counter market.

Column (b)—Date acquired. The acquisition date for an asset the corporation held on January 1, 2001, for which it made an election to recognize any gain on a deemed sale is the date of the deemed sale.

Column (e)—Cost or other basis. In determining gain or loss, the basis of property is generally its cost (see section 1012 and related regulations). Special rules for determining basis are provided in sections in subchapters C, K, O, and P of the Code. These rules may apply to the corporation on the receipt of certain distributions with respect to stock (section 301), liquidation of another corporation (334), transfer to another corporation (358), transfer from a shareholder or reorganization (362), bequest (1014), contribution or gift (1015), tax-free exchange (1031), involuntary conversion (1033), certain asset acquisitions (1060), or wash sale of stock (1091). Attach an explanation if you use a basis other than actual cash cost of the property.

   If the corporation is allowed a charitable contribution deduction because it sold property to a charitable organization, figure the adjusted basis for determining gain from the sale by dividing the amount realized by the fair market value and multiplying that result by the adjusted basis.

If the corporation elected to recognize gain on an asset held on January 1, 2001, its basis in the asset is its closing market price or fair market value, whichever applies, on the date of the deemed sale, whether the deemed sale resulted in a gain or unallowed loss.

See section 852(f) for the treatment of certain load charges incurred in acquiring stock in a mutual fund with a reinvestment right.

Before making an entry in column (e), increase the cost or other basis by any expense of sale, such as broker's fees, commissions, option premiums, and state and local transfer taxes, unless the net sales price was reported in column (d).

Column (f)—Gain or (loss). Make a separate entry in this column for each transaction reported on lines 1 and 7 and any other line(s) that apply to the corporation. For lines 1 and 7, subtract the amount in column (e) from the amount in column (d). Enter negative amounts in parentheses.

Column (g)—28% rate gain or (loss). Enter the amount, if any, from Part II, column (f), that is from collectibles gains and losses. A **collectibles gain or loss** is any long-term gain or deductible long-term loss from the sale or exchange of a collectible that is a capital asset.

Collectibles include works of art, rugs, antiques, metals (such as gold, silver, and platinum bullion), gems, stamps, coins, alcoholic beverages, and certain other tangible property.

Also include gain (but not loss) from the sale or exchange of an interest in a partnership or trust held more than 1 year and attributable to unrealized appreciation of collectibles. For details, see Regulations section 1.1(h)-1. Also, attach the statement required under Regulations section 1.1(h)-1(e).

Part III—Built-In Gains Tax

Section 1374 provides for a tax on built-in gains, **without regard to when S corporation status was elected**, if the corporation acquired an asset with a basis determined by reference to its

basis (or the basis of any other property) in the hands of a C corporation.

Line 15. Enter the amount that would be the taxable income of the corporation for the tax year if only recognized built-in gains (including any carryover of gain under section 1374(d)(2)(B)) and recognized built-in losses were taken into account.

Section 1374(d)(3) defines a **recognized built-in gain** as any gain recognized during the recognition period (the 10-year period beginning on the first day of the first tax year for which the corporation is an S corporation, or beginning the date the asset was acquired by the S corporation, for an asset with a basis determined by reference to its basis (or the basis of any other property) in the hands of a C corporation) on the sale or distribution (disposition) of any asset, except to the extent the corporation establishes that—
- The asset was not held by the corporation as of the beginning of the first tax year the corporation was an S corporation (except this does not apply to an asset acquired by the S corporation with a basis determined by reference to its basis (or the basis of any other property) in the hands of a C corporation), or
- The gain exceeds the excess of the fair market value of the asset as of the start of the first tax year (or as of the date the asset was acquired by the S corporation, for an asset with a basis determined by reference to its basis (or the basis of any other property) in the hands of a C corporation) over the adjusted basis of the asset at that time.

Certain transactions involving the disposal of timber, coal, or domestic iron ore under section 631 are not subject to the built-in gains tax. For details, see Rev. Rul. 2001-50, 2001-43 I.R.B. 343.

Section 1374(d)(4) defines a **recognized built-in loss** as any loss recognized during the recognition period (stated above) on the disposition of any asset to the extent the corporation establishes that—
- The asset was held by the corporation as of the beginning of the first tax year the corporation was an S corporation (except that this does not apply to an asset acquired by the S corporation with a basis determined by

reference to its basis (or the basis of any other property) in the hands of a C corporation), and
- The loss does not exceed the excess of the adjusted basis of the asset as of the beginning of the first tax year (or as of the date the asset was acquired by the S corporation, for an asset with a basis determined by reference to its basis (or the basis of any other property) in the hands of a C corporation), over the fair market value of the asset as of that time.

The corporation must show on an attachment its total net recognized built-in gain and list separately any capital gain or loss and ordinary gain or loss.

Line 16. Figure taxable income by completing lines 1 through 28 of Form 1120. Follow the instructions for Form 1120. Enter the amount from line 28 of Form 1120 on line 16 of Schedule D. Attach to Schedule D the Form 1120 computation or other worksheet used to figure taxable income.

Note: *Taxable income is defined in section 1375(b)(1)(B) and is generally figured in the same manner as taxable income for line 9 of the worksheet for line 22a of Form 1120S (see page 16 of the Instructions for Form 1120S).*

Line 17. If for any tax year the amount on line 15 exceeds the taxable income on line 16, the excess is treated as a recognized built-in gain in the succeeding tax year. This carryover provision applies only in the case of an S corporation that made its election to be an S corporation after March 30, 1988. See section 1374(d)(2)(B).

Line 18. Enter the section 1374(b)(2) deduction. Generally, this is any net operating loss carryforward or capital loss carryforward (to the extent of net capital gain included in recognized built-in gain for the tax year) arising in tax years for which the corporation was a C corporation. See section 1374(b)(2) for details.

Line 22. The built-in gains tax is treated as a loss sustained by the corporation during the same tax year. Deduct the tax attributable to:
- Ordinary gain as a deduction for taxes on Form 1120S, line 12.
- Short-term capital gain as short-term capital loss on Schedule D, line 5.
- Long-term capital gain as long-term capital loss on Schedule D, line 12.

Instructions for Schedule D (Form 1120S)

Form **941**
(Rev. January 2002)
Department of the Treasury
Internal Revenue Service

Employer's Quarterly Federal Tax Return

▶ See separate instructions revised January 2002 for information on completing this return.

Please type or print.

OMB No. 1545-0029

Enter state code for state in which deposits were made **only** if different from state in address to the right ▶ (see page 2 of instructions).

Name (as distinguished from trade name)	Date quarter ended
Trade name, if any Peter Cone	Employer identification number
Address (number and street)	City, state, and ZIP code
	362 Main Street Pine Town VA 23000	

T	
FF	
FD	
FP	
I	
T	

If address is different from prior return, check here ▶

IRS Use

1 1 1 1 1 1 1 1 1 1   2   3 3 3 3 3 3 3   4 4 4   5 5 5
6   7   8 8 8 8 8 8 8   9 9 9 9 9   10 10 10 10 10 10 10 10 10 10

If you do not have to file returns in the future, check here ▶ ☐ and enter date final wages paid ▶
If you are a seasonal employer, see **Seasonal employers** on page 1 of the instructions and check here ▶ ☐

1	Number of employees in the pay period that includes March 12th . ▶	**1**		
2	Total wages and tips, plus other compensation	**2**	19,500	00
3	Total income tax withheld from wages, tips, and sick pay	**3**	1,872	00
4	Adjustment of withheld income tax for preceding quarters of calendar year	**4**		
5	Adjusted total of income tax withheld (line 3 as adjusted by line 4—see instructions) . . .	**5**	1,872	00

6	Taxable social security wages	**6a**	19,500	× 12.4% (.124) =	**6b**	2,418	00
	Taxable social security tips	**6c**		× 12.4% (.124) =	**6d**		
7	Taxable Medicare wages and tips . . .	**7a**	19,500	× 2.9% (.029) =	**7b**	565	50

8	Total social security and Medicare taxes (add lines 6b, 6d, and 7b). Check here if wages are not subject to social security and/or Medicare tax . . . . ▶ ☐	**8**	2,983	50
9	Adjustment of social security and Medicare taxes (see instructions for required explanation) Sick Pay $ _____ ± Fractions of Cents $ _____ ± Other $ _____ =	**9**		
10	Adjusted total of social security and Medicare taxes (line 8 as adjusted by line 9—see instructions)	**10**	2,983	50
11	**Total taxes** (add lines 5 and 10)	**11**	4,855	50
12	Advance earned income credit (EIC) payments made to employees	**12**		
13	Net taxes (subtract line 12 from line 11). **If $2,500 or more, this must equal line 17, column (d) below (or line D of Schedule B (Form 941))**	**13**	4,855	50
14	Total deposits for quarter, including overpayment applied from a prior quarter	**14**	4,855	50
15	**Balance due** (subtract line 14 from line 13). See instructions	**15**		

16 **Overpayment.** If line 14 is more than line 13, enter excess here ▶ $ _____
and check if to be: ☐ Applied to next return **or** ☐ Refunded.

- **All filers:** If line 13 is less than $2,500, you need not complete line 17 or Schedule B (Form 941).
- **Semiweekly schedule depositors:** Complete Schedule B (Form 941) and check here . . . . ▶ ☐
- **Monthly schedule depositors:** Complete line 17, columns (a) through (d), and check here. . . . . . . ▶ ☐

17	Monthly Summary of Federal Tax Liability. Do not complete if you were a semiweekly schedule depositor.			
	(a) First month liability	**(b)** Second month liability	**(c)** Third month liability	**(d)** Total liability for quarter
	1,494.00	1,867.50	1,494.00	4,855.50

Third Party Designee

Do you want to allow another person to discuss this return with the IRS (see separate instructions)? ☐ **Yes.** Complete the following. ☐ **No**

Designee's name ▶ _____   Phone no. ▶ ( )   Personal identification number (PIN) ▶ ☐☐☐☐☐

Sign Here

Under penalties of perjury, I declare that I have examined this return, including accompanying schedules and statements, and to the best of my knowledge and belief, it is true, correct, and complete.

Signature ▶ *Peter Cone*   Print Your Name and Title ▶ PETER CONE, Owner   Date ▶ 2/5/XX

For Privacy Act and Paperwork Reduction Act Notice, see back of Payment Voucher.   Cat. No. 17001Z   Form **941** (Rev. 1-2002)

Form 941 (Rev. 1-2002)

Where to file. In the list below, find the state where your legal residence, principal place of business, office, or agency is located. Send your return to the **Internal Revenue Service** at the address listed for your location. No street address is needed. **Note:** *Where you file depends on whether or not you are including a payment.*

Exception for exempt organizations and government entities. If you are filing Form 941 for an exempt organization or government entity (Federal, state, local, or Indian tribal government), use the following addresses, regardless of your location:

Return without payment: Ogden, UT 84201-0046
Return with payment: P.O. Box 660264 Dallas, TX 75266-0264

YOUR LOCATION	RETURN WITHOUT A PAYMENT	RETURN WITH PAYMENT
Connecticut, Delaware, District of Columbia, Illinois, Indiana, Kentucky, Maine, Maryland, Massachusetts, Michigan, New Hampshire, New Jersey, New York, North Carolina, Ohio, Pennsylvania, Rhode Island, South Carolina, Vermont, Virginia, West Virginia, Wisconsin	Cincinnati, OH 45999-0005	P.O. Box 105703 Atlanta, GA 30348-5703
Alabama, Alaska, Arizona, Arkansas, California, Colorado, Florida, Georgia, Hawaii, Idaho, Iowa, Kansas, Louisiana, Minnesota, Mississippi, Missouri, Montana, Nebraska, Nevada, New Mexico, North Dakota, Oklahoma, Oregon, South Dakota, Tennessee, Texas, Utah, Washington, Wyoming	Ogden, UT 84201-0005	P.O. Box 660264 Dallas, TX 75266-0264
No legal residence or principal place of business in any state	Philadelphia, PA 19255-0005	P.O. Box 80106 Cincinnati, OH 45280-0006

SCHEDULE K-1
(Form 1120S)

Department of the Treasury
Internal Revenue Service

Shareholder's Share of Income, Credits, Deductions, etc.

▶ See separate instructions.

For calendar year 2002 or tax year
beginning   , 2002, and ending   , 20

OMB No. 1545-0130

2002

Shareholder's identifying number ▶	Corporation's identifying number ▶
Shareholder's name, address, and ZIP code	Corporation's name, address, and ZIP code
John H. Green 4340 Holmes Parkway Metro City, OH 43704	Strato Tech, Inc. 482 Winston Street Metro City, OH 43705

A Shareholder's percentage of stock ownership for tax year (see instructions for Schedule K-1) . . . . ▶   45   %

B Internal Revenue Service Center where corporation filed its return ▶   Cincinnati, OH

C Tax shelter registration number (see instructions for Schedule K-1) . . . . ▶

D Check applicable boxes: **(1)** ☐ Final K-1   **(2)** ☐ Amended K-1

		(a) Pro rata share items		(b) Amount	(c) Form 1040 filers enter the amount in column (b) on:
Income (Loss)	**1**	Ordinary income (loss) from trade or business activities . . .	**1**	53,550	See page 4 of the Shareholder's Instructions for Schedule K-1 (Form 1120S).
	2	Net income (loss) from rental real estate activities	**2**		
	3	Net income (loss) from other rental activities	**3**		
	4	Portfolio income (loss):			
	a	Interest	**4a**	1,800	Sch. B, Part I, line 1
	b	Ordinary dividends	**4b**	7,200	Sch. B, Part II, line 5
	c	Royalties	**4c**		Sch. E, Part I, line 4
	d	Net short-term capital gain (loss)	**4d**		Sch. D, line 5, col. (f)
	e	**(1)** Net long-term capital gain (loss)	**4e(1)**		Sch. D, line 12, col. (f)
		(2) 28% rate gain (loss)	**4e(2)**		Sch. D, line 12, col. (g)
		(3) Qualified 5-year gain	**4e(3)**		Line 5 of worksheet for Sch. D, line 29
	f	Other portfolio income (loss) *(attach schedule)*	**4f**		(Enter on applicable line of your return.)
	5	Net section 1231 gain (loss) (other than due to casualty or theft)	**5**		See Shareholder's Instructions for Schedule K-1 (Form 1120S).
	6	Other income (loss) *(attach schedule)*	**6**		(Enter on applicable line of your return.)
Deductions	**7**	Charitable contributions *(attach schedule)*	**7**	10,800	Sch. A, line 15 or 16
	8	Section 179 expense deduction	**8**		See pages 5 and 6 of the Shareholder's Instructions for Schedule K-1 (Form 1120S).
	9	Deductions related to portfolio income (loss) *(attach schedule)* .	**9**		
	10	Other deductions *(attach schedule)*	**10**		
Investment Interest	**11a**	Interest expense on investment debts	**11a**	1,350	Form 4952, line 1
	b	**(1)** Investment income included on lines 4a, 4b, 4c, and 4f above	**11b(1)**	9,000	See Shareholder's Instructions for Schedule K-1 (Form 1120S).
		(2) Investment expenses included on line 9 above	**11b(2)**		
Credits	**12a**	Credit for alcohol used as fuel	**12a**		Form 6478, line 10
	b	Low-income housing credit:			
		(1) From section 42(j)(5) partnerships	**12b(1)**		Form 8586, line 5
		(2) Other than on line 12b(1)	**12b(2)**		
	c	Qualified rehabilitation expenditures related to rental real estate activities	**12c**		
	d	Credits (other than credits shown on lines 12b and 12c) related to rental real estate activities	**12d**		See pages 6 and 7 of the Shareholder's Instructions for Schedule K-1 (Form 1120S).
	e	Credits related to other rental activities	**12e**		
	13	Other credits	**13**	2,700	

For Paperwork Reduction Act Notice, see the Instructions for Form 1120S.   Cat. No. 11520D   **Schedule K-1 (Form 1120S) 2002**

Schedule K-1 (Form 1120S) 2002   Page **2**

		(a) Pro rata share items		(b) Amount	(c) Form 1040 filers enter the amount in column (b) on:
Adjustments and Tax Preference Items	**14a**	Depreciation adjustment on property placed in service after 1986	14a		See page 7 of the Shareholder's Instructions for Schedule K-1 (Form 1120S) and Instructions for Form 6251
	b	Adjusted gain or loss	14b		
	c	Depletion (other than oil and gas)	14c		
	d	(1) Gross income from oil, gas, or geothermal properties	14d(1)		
		(2) Deductions allocable to oil, gas, or geothermal properties	14d(2)		
	e	Other adjustments and tax preference items *(attach schedule)*	14e		
Foreign Taxes	**15a**	Name of foreign country or U.S. possession ▶			
	b	Gross income from all sources	15b		
	c	Gross income sourced at shareholder level	15c		
	d	Foreign gross income sourced at corporate level:			
		(1) Passive	15d(1)		
		(2) Listed categories *(attach schedule)*	15d(2)		
		(3) General limitation	15d(3)		
	e	Deductions allocated and apportioned at shareholder level:			Form 1116, Part I
		(1) Interest expense	15e(1)		
		(2) Other	15e(2)		
	f	Deductions allocated and apportioned at corporate level to foreign source income:			
		(1) Passive	15f(1)		
		(2) Listed categories *(attach schedule)*	15f(2)		
		(3) General limitation	15f(3)		
	g	Total foreign taxes (check one): ▶ ☐ Paid ☐ Accrued	15g		Form 1116, Part II
	h	Reduction in taxes available for credit *(attach schedule)*	15h		See Instructions for Form 1116
Other	**16**	Section 59(e)(2) expenditures: a Type ▶			See Shareholder's Instructions for Schedule K-1 (Form 1120S).
	b	Amount	16b		
	17	Tax-exempt interest income	17	2,250	Form 1040, line 8b
	18	Other tax-exempt income	18		
	19	Nondeductible expenses	19	7,358	See page 7 of the Shareholder's Instructions for Schedule K-1 (Form 1120S).
	20	Property distributions (including cash) other than dividend distributions reported to you on Form 1099-DIV	20	29,250	
	21	Amount of loan repayments for "Loans From Shareholders"	21		
	22	Recapture of low-income housing credit:			
		a From section 42(j)(5) partnerships	22a		Form 8611, line 8
		b Other than on line 22a	22b		

23   Supplemental information required to be reported separately to each shareholder *(attach additional schedules if more space is needed)*:

Supplemental Information

                                                                      Schedule K-1 (Form 1120S) 2002

Department of the Treasury
Internal Revenue Service

2002

Shareholder's Instructions for Schedule K-1 (Form 1120S)

Shareholder's Share of Income, Credits, Deductions, etc.
(For Shareholder's Use Only)

Section references are to the Internal Revenue Code unless otherwise noted.

General Instructions

Purpose of Schedule K-1

The corporation uses Schedule K-1 (Form 1120S) to report your pro rata share of the corporation's income (reduced by any tax the corporation paid on the income), credits, deductions, etc. **Please keep it for your records. Do not file it with your tax return.** The corporation has filed a copy with the IRS.

Although the corporation may have to pay a built-in gains tax and an excess net passive income tax, you, the shareholder, are liable for income tax on your share of the corporation's income, whether or not distributed, and you must include your share on your tax return if a return is required. **Your distributive share of S corporation income is not self-employment income and it is not subject to self-employment tax.**

You should use these instructions to help you report the items shown on Schedule K-1 on your tax return.

Where *"(attach schedule)"* appears next to a line on Schedule K-1, it means the information for these lines (if applicable) will be shown in the "Supplemental Information" space below line 23 of Schedule K-1. If additional space was needed, the corporation will have attached a statement to Schedule K-1 to show the information for the line item.

The notation "(see instructions for Schedule K-1)" in items A and C at the top of Schedule K-1 is directed to the corporation. You, as a shareholder, should disregard these notations.

Schedule K-1 does not show the amount of actual **dividend** distributions the corporation made to you. The corporation must report to you such amounts totaling $10 or more for the calendar year on **Form 1099-DIV,** Dividends and Distributions. You report actual dividend distributions on Form 1040, line 9.

Basis of Your Stock

You are responsible for maintaining records to show the computation of the basis of your stock in the corporation. Schedule K-1 provides information to help you make the computation at the end of each corporate

tax year. The basis of your stock (generally, its cost) is adjusted as follows and, except as noted, in the order listed. In addition, basis may be adjusted under other provisions of the Internal Revenue Code.

1. Basis is increased by **(a)** all income (including tax-exempt income) reported on Schedule K-1 and **(b)** the excess of the deduction for depletion (other than oil and gas depletion) over the basis of the property subject to depletion.

 You must report the taxable income on your return (if you are required to file one) for it to increase your basis.

 *Basis is **not** increased by income from discharge of your indebtedness in the S corporation.*

2. Basis is decreased by property distributions (including cash) made by the corporation (excluding dividend distributions reported on Form 1099-DIV and distributions in excess of basis) reported on Schedule K-1, line 20.

3. Basis is decreased by **(a)** nondeductible expenses and **(b)** the depletion deduction for any oil and gas property held by the corporation, but only to the extent your pro rata share of the property's adjusted basis exceeds that deduction.

4. Basis is decreased by all deductible losses and deductions reported on Schedule K-1.

You may elect to decrease your basis under **4** above prior to decreasing your basis under **3** above. If you make this election, any amount described under **3** that exceeds the basis of your stock and debt owed to you by the corporation is treated as an amount described under **3** for the following tax year. To make the election, attach a statement to your timely filed original or amended return that states you agree to the carryover rule of Regulations section 1.1367-1(f) and the name of the S corporation to which the rule applies. Once made, the election applies to the year for which it is made and all future tax years for that S corporation, unless the IRS agrees to revoke your election.

The basis of each share of stock is increased or decreased (but not below zero) based on its pro rata share of the above adjustments. If the total decreases in basis

attributable to a share exceed that share's basis, the excess reduces (but not below zero) the remaining bases of all other shares of stock in proportion to the remaining basis of each of those shares.

Inconsistent Treatment of Items

Generally, you must report subchapter S items shown on your Schedule K-1 (and any attached schedules) the same way that the corporation treated the items on its return.

If the treatment on your original or amended return is inconsistent with the corporation's treatment, or if the corporation has not filed a return, you must file **Form 8082,** Notice of Inconsistent Treatment or Administrative Adjustment Request (AAR), with your original or amended return to identify and explain any inconsistency (or to note that a corporate return has not been filed).

If you are required to file Form 8082, but fail to do so, you may be subject to the accuracy-related penalty. This penalty is in addition to any tax that results from making your amount or treatment of the item consistent with that shown on the corporation's return. Any deficiency that results from making the amounts consistent may be assessed immediately.

Errors

If you believe the corporation has made an error on your Schedule K-1, notify the corporation and ask for a corrected Schedule K-1. **Do not** change any items on your copy. Be sure that the corporation sends a copy of the corrected Schedule K-1 to the IRS. If you are unable to reach agreement with the corporation regarding the inconsistency, you must file Form 8082.

International Boycotts

Every corporation that had operations in, or related to, a boycotting country, company, or national of a country, must file **Form 5713,** International Boycott Report.

If the corporation cooperated with an international boycott, it must give you a copy of its Form 5713. You must file your own Form 5713 to report the activities of the corporation and any other boycott operations that you may have. You may lose certain tax benefits if the corporation participated in, or cooperated with, an

Cat. No. 11521O

international boycott. See Form 5713 and the instructions for more information.

Elections

Generally, the corporation decides how to figure taxable income from its operations. For example, it chooses the accounting method and depreciation methods it will use.

However, certain elections are made by you separately on your income tax return and not by the corporation. These elections are made under:
- Section 59(e) (deduction of certain qualified expenditures ratably over the period of time specified in that section—see the instructions for lines 16a and 16b);
- Section 617 (deduction and recapture of certain mining exploration expenditures); and
- Section 901 (foreign tax credit).

Additional Information

For more information on the treatment of S corporation income, credits, deductions, etc., see **Pub. 535,** Business Expenses; **Pub. 550,** Investment Income and Expenses; and **Pub. 925,** Passive Activity and At-Risk Rules.

To get forms and publications, see the instructions for your tax return.

Limitations on Losses, Deductions, and Credits

Aggregate Losses and Deductions Limited to Basis of Stock and Debt

Generally, the deduction for your share of aggregate losses and deductions reported on Schedule K-1 is limited to the basis of your stock (determined with regard to distributions received during the tax year) and debt owed to you by the corporation. The basis of your stock is figured at year-end. See **Basis of Your Stock** on page 1. The basis of loans to the corporation is the balance the corporation now owes you, less any reduction for losses in a prior year. See the instructions for line 21. Any loss not allowed for the tax year because of this limitation is available for indefinite carryover, limited to the basis of your stock and debt, in each subsequent tax year. See section 1366(d) for details.

At-Risk Limitations

Generally, you will have to complete **Form 6198,** At-Risk Limitations, to figure your allowable loss, if you have:

1. A loss or other deduction from any activity carried on by the corporation as a trade or business or for the production of income, and

2. Amounts in the activity for which you are not at risk.

The at-risk rules generally limit the amount of loss (including loss on the disposition of assets) and other deductions (such as the section 179 expense deduction) that you can claim to the amount you could actually lose in the activity. However, if you acquired your stock before 1987, the at-risk rules do not apply to losses from an activity of holding real property placed in service before 1987 by the corporation. The activity of holding mineral property does not qualify for this exception.

Generally, you are not at risk for amounts such as the following:
- The basis of your stock in the corporation or basis of your loans to the corporation if the cash or other property used to purchase the stock or make the loans was from a source **(a)** covered by nonrecourse indebtedness (except for certain qualified nonrecourse financing, as defined in section 465(b)(6)); **(b)** protected against loss by a guarantee, stop-loss agreement, or other similar arrangement; or **(c)** that is covered by indebtedness from a person who has an interest in the activity or from a related person to a person (except you) having such an interest, other than a creditor.
- Any cash or property contributed to a corporate activity, or your interest in the corporate activity, that is **(a)** covered by nonrecourse indebtedness (except for certain qualified nonrecourse financing, as defined in section 465(b)(6)); **(b)** protected against loss by a guarantee, stop-loss agreement, or other similar arrangement; or **(c)** that is covered by indebtedness from a person who has an interest in such activity or from a related person to a person (except you) having such an interest, other than a creditor.

Any loss from a section 465 activity not allowed for this tax year will be treated as a deduction allocable to the activity in the next tax year.

To help you complete Form 6198, the corporation should specify on an attachment to Schedule K-1 your share of the total pre-1976 losses from a section 465(c)(1) activity (i.e., films or video tapes, and leasing section 1245, farm, or oil and gas property) for which there existed a corresponding amount of nonrecourse liability at the end of the year in which the losses occurred. Also, you should get a separate statement of income, expenses, etc., for each activity from the corporation.

Passive Activity Limitations

Section 469 provides rules that limit the deduction of certain losses and credits. The rules apply to shareholders who—
- Are individuals, estates, or trusts and
- Have a passive activity loss or credit for the year.

Generally, passive activities **include:**

1. Trade or business activities in which you **did not** materially participate and

2. Activities that meet the definition of rental activities under Temporary Regulations section 1.469-1T(e)(3) and Regulations section 1.469-1(e)(3).

Passive activities **do not** include:

1. Trade or business activities in which you materially participated.

2. Rental real estate activities in which you materially participated if you were a "real estate professional" for the tax year. You were a **real estate professional** only if you met both of the following conditions:

a. More than half of the personal services you performed in trades or businesses were performed in real property trades or businesses in which you materially participated **and**

b. You performed more than 750 hours of services in real property trades or businesses in which you materially participated.

For purposes of this rule, each interest in rental real estate is a separate activity, unless you elect to treat all interests in rental real estate as one activity. For details on making this election, see the Instructions for Schedule E (Form 1040).

If you are married filing jointly, either you or your spouse must separately meet both of the above conditions, without taking into account services performed by the other spouse.

A real property trade or business is any real property development, redevelopment, construction, reconstruction, acquisition, conversion, rental, operation, management, leasing, or brokerage trade or business. Services you performed as an employee are not treated as performed in a real property trade or business unless you owned more than 5% of the stock (or more than 5% of the capital or profits interest) in the employer.

3. The rental of a dwelling unit any shareholder used for personal purposes during the year for more than the **greater of** 14 days or 10% of the number of days that the residence was rented at fair rental value.

4. Activities of trading personal property for the account of owners of interests in the activities.

The corporation will identify separately each activity that may be passive to you. If the corporation had more than one activity, it will report information in the line 23 Supplemental Information space, or attach a statement if more space is needed, that **(a)** identifies each activity (trade or business activity, rental real estate activity, rental activity other than rental real estate, etc.); **(b)** specifies the income (loss), deductions, and credits from each activity; and **(c)** provides other details you may need to determine if an activity loss or credit is subject to the passive activity limitations.

If you determine that you have a passive activity loss or credit, get **Form 8582,** Passive Activity Loss Limitations, to figure your allowable passive losses, and **Form 8582-CR,** Passive Activity Credit Limitations, to figure your allowable passive credit. See the instructions for these forms for more information.

Material participation. You must determine if you materially participated **(a)** in each trade or business activity held through the corporation and **(b),** if you were a real estate professional (defined above), in each rental real estate activity held through the corporation. **All determinations of material participation are made based on your participation during the corporation's tax year.**

Material participation standards for shareholders who are individuals are listed below. Special rules apply to certain retired or disabled farmers and to the surviving spouses of farmers. See the Instructions for Form 8582 for details.

Individuals. If you are an individual, you are considered to materially participate in a trade or business activity only if one or more of the following apply:

1. You participated in the activity for more than 500 hours during the tax year.

2. Your participation in the activity for the tax year constituted substantially all of

-2-

Instructions for Schedule K-1 (Form 1120S)

the participation in the activity of all individuals (including individuals who are not owners of interests in the activity).

3. You participated in the activity for more than 100 hours during the tax year, and your participation in the activity for the tax year was not less than the participation in the activity of any other individual (including individuals who were not owners of interests in the activity) for the tax year.

4. The activity was a significant participation activity for the tax year, and your aggregate participation in all significant participation activities (including those outside the corporation) during the tax year exceeded 500 hours. A **significant participation activity** is any trade or business activity in which you participated for more than 100 hours during the year and in which you did not materially participate under any of the material participation tests (other than this test 4).

5. You materially participated in the activity for any 5 tax years (whether or not consecutive) during the 10 tax years that immediately precede the tax year.

6. The activity was a personal service activity and you materially participated in the activity for any 3 tax years (whether or not consecutive) preceding the tax year. A **personal service activity** involves the performance of personal services in the fields of health, law, engineering, architecture, accounting, actuarial science, performing arts, consulting, or any other trade or business, in which capital is not a material income-producing factor.

7. Based on all of the facts and circumstances, you participated in the activity on a regular, continuous, and substantial basis during the tax year.

Work counted toward material participation. Generally, any work that you or your spouse does in connection with an activity held through an S corporation (in which you own stock at the time the work is done) is counted toward material participation. However, work in connection with an activity is not counted toward material participation if either of the following applies:

1. The work is not the type of work that owners of the activity would usually do and one of the principal purposes of the work that you or your spouse does is to avoid any passive loss or credit limitations.

2. You do the work in your capacity as an investor and you are not directly involved in the day-to-day operations of the activity. Examples of work done as an investor that would not count toward material participation include:

a. Studying and reviewing financial statements or reports on operations of the activity,

b. Preparing or compiling summaries or analyses of the finances or operations of the activity, and

c. Monitoring the finances or operations of the activity in a nonmanagerial capacity.

Effect of determination. If you determine that you **(a)** materially participated in a trade or business activity of the corporation or **(b)** were a real estate professional (defined on page 2), in a rental real estate activity of the corporation, report

the income (loss), deductions, and credits from that activity as indicated in either column (c) of Schedule K-1 or the instructions for your tax return.

If you determine that you **did not** materially participate in a trade or business activity of the corporation, or you have income (loss), deductions, or credits from a rental activity of the corporation (other than a rental real estate activity in which you materially participated, if you were a real estate professional), the amounts from that activity are passive. Report passive income (losses), deductions, and credits as follows:

1. If you have an overall gain (the excess of income over deductions and losses, including any prior year unallowed loss) from a passive activity, report the income, deductions, and losses from the activity as indicated on Schedule K-1 or in these instructions.

2. If you have an overall loss (the excess of deductions and losses, including any prior year unallowed loss, over income) or credits from a passive activity, you must report the income, deductions, losses, and credits from **all** passive activities using the Instructions for Form 8582 or Form 8582-CR, to see if your deductions, losses, and credits are limited under the passive activity rules.

Special allowance for a rental real estate activity. If you **actively participated** in a rental real estate activity, you may be able to deduct up to $25,000 of the loss from the activity from nonpassive income. This special allowance is an exception to the general rule disallowing losses in excess of income from passive activities. The special allowance is not available if you were married, are filing a separate return for the year, and did not live apart from your spouse at all times during the year.

Only individuals and qualifying estates can actively participate in a rental real estate activity. Estates (other than qualifying estates) and trusts cannot actively participate.

You are not considered to actively participate in a rental real estate activity if, at any time during the tax year, your interest (including your spouse's interest) in the activity was less than 10% (by value) of all interests in the activity.

Active participation is a less stringent requirement than material participation. You may be treated as actively participating if you participated, for example, in making management decisions or arranging for others to provide services (such as repairs) in a significant and bona fide sense.

Management decisions that can count as active participation include approving new tenants, deciding on rental terms, approving capital or repair expenditures, and other similar decisions.

An estate is a qualifying estate if the decedent would have satisfied the active participation requirement for the activity for the tax year the decedent died. A qualifying estate is treated as actively participating for tax years ending less than 2 years after the date of the decedent's death.

Modified adjusted gross income limitation. The maximum special allowance that single individuals and married individuals filing a joint return can qualify for is $25,000. The maximum is $12,500 for married individuals who file separate returns and who lived apart at all times during the year. The maximum special allowance for which an estate can qualify is $25,000 reduced by the special allowance for which the surviving spouse qualifies.

If your modified adjusted gross income (defined below) is $100,000 or less ($50,000 or less if married filing separately), your loss is deductible up to the amount of the maximum special allowance referred to in the preceding paragraph. If your modified adjusted gross income is more than $100,000 (more than $50,000 if married filing separately), the special allowance is limited to 50% of the difference between $150,000 ($75,000 if married filing separately) and your modified adjusted gross income. When modified adjusted gross income is $150,000 or more ($75,000 or more if married filing separately), there is no special allowance.

Modified adjusted gross income is your adjusted gross income figured without taking into account:

● Any passive activity loss.
● Any rental real estate loss allowed under section 469(c)(7) to real estate professionals (as defined on page 2).
● Any taxable social security or equivalent railroad retirement benefits.
● Any deductible contributions to an IRA or certain other qualified retirement plans under section 219.
● The student loan interest deduction.
● The tuition and fees deduction.
● The deduction for one-half of self-employment taxes.
● The exclusion from income of interest from Series EE or I U.S. Savings Bonds used to pay higher education expenses.
● The exclusion of amounts received under an employer's adoption assistance program.

Commercial revitalization deduction. The special $25,000 allowance for the commercial revitalization deduction from rental real estate activities is not subject to the active participation rules or modified adjusted gross income limits discussed above. See item 23 of the Supplemental Information instructions on page 8.

Special rules for certain other activities. If you have net income (loss), deductions, or credits from any activity to which special rules apply, the corporation will identify the activity and all amounts relating to it on Schedule K-1 or on an attachment.

If you have net income subject to recharacterization under Temporary Regulations section 1.469-2T(f) and Regulations section 1.469-2(f), report such amounts according to the Instructions for Form 8582.

If you have net income (loss), deductions, or credits from either of the following activities, treat such amounts as nonpassive and report them as instructed in column (c) of Schedule K-1 or in these instructions:

1. The rental of a dwelling unit any shareholder used for personal purposes during the year for more than the greater of 14 days or 10% of the number of days that the residence was rented at fair rental value.

2. Trading personal property for the account of owners of interests in the activity.

Self-charged interest. The corporation will report any "self-charged" interest income or expense that resulted from loans between you and the corporation (or between the corporation and other S corporation or partnership in which you have an interest). If there was more than one activity, the corporation will provide a statement allocating the interest income or expense with respect to each activity. The self-charged interest rules do not apply to your interest in the S corporation if the corporation made an election under Regulations section 1.469-7(g) to avoid the application of these rules. See the Instructions for Form 8582 for more information.

Specific Instructions

Item C

If the corporation is a registration-required tax shelter or has invested in a registration-required tax shelter, it should have completed Item C. If you claim or report any income, loss, deduction, or credit from a tax shelter, you are required to attach **Form 8271,** Investor Reporting of Tax Shelter Registration Number, to your tax return. If the corporation has invested in a tax shelter, it is required to give you a copy of its Form 8271 with your Schedule K-1. Use this information to complete your Form 8271.

If the corporation itself is a registration-required tax shelter, use the information on Schedule K-1 (name of corporation, corporation identifying number, and tax shelter registration number) to complete your Form 8271.

Lines 1 Through 23

The amounts on lines 1 through 23 show your pro rata share of ordinary income, loss, deductions, credits, and other information from all corporate activities. These amounts do not take into account limitations on losses, credits, or other items that may have to be adjusted because of:

1. The adjusted basis of your stock and debt in the corporation,

2. The at-risk limitations,

3. The passive activity limitations, or

4. Any other limitations that must be taken into account at the shareholder level in figuring taxable income (e.g., the section 179 expense limitation).

The limitations of **1, 2,** and **3** are discussed above, and the limitations for **4** are discussed throughout these instructions and in other referenced forms and instructions.

If you are an individual, and your pro rata share items are not affected by any of the limitations, report the amounts shown in column (b) of Schedule K-1 as indicated in column (c). If any of the limitations apply, adjust the column (b) amounts for the limitations before you enter the amounts on

your return. When applicable, the passive activity limitations on losses are applied after the limitations on losses for a shareholder's basis in stock and debt and the shareholder's at-risk amount.

Note: *The line number references in column (c) are to forms in use for tax years beginning in 2002. If you are a calendar year shareholder in a fiscal year 2002–2003 corporation, enter these amounts on the corresponding lines of the tax form in use for 2003.*

 If you have losses, deductions, credits, etc., from a prior year that were not deductible or usable because of certain limitations, such as the basis rules or the at-risk limitations, take them into account in determining your income, loss, etc., for this year. However, except for passive activity losses and credits, do not combine the prior-year amounts with any amounts shown on this Schedule K-1 to get a net figure to report on your return. Instead, report the amounts on your return on a year-by-year basis.

Income (Loss)

Line 1—Ordinary Income (Loss) From Trade or Business Activities

The amount reported on line 1 is your share of the ordinary income (loss) from trade or business activities of the corporation. Generally, where you report this amount on Form 1040 depends on whether the amount is from an activity that is a passive activity to you. If you are an individual shareholder, find your situation below and report your line 1 income (loss) as instructed after applying the basis and at-risk limitations on losses.

1. Report line 1 income (loss) from trade or business activities in which you materially participated on Schedule E (Form 1040), Part II, column (i) or (k).

2. Report line 1 income (loss) from trade or business activities in which you did not materially participate, as follows:

a. If income is reported on line 1, report the income on Schedule E, Part II, column (h).

b. If a loss is reported on line 1, follow the Instructions for Form 8582 to determine how much of the loss can be reported on Schedule E, Part II, column (g).

Line 2—Net Income (Loss) From Rental Real Estate Activities

Generally, the income (loss) reported on line 2 is a passive activity amount for all shareholders. However, the income (loss) on line 2 is not from a passive activity if you were a real estate professional (defined on page 2) and you materially participated in the activity.

If you are filing a 2002 Form 1040, use the following instructions to determine where to enter a line 2 amount:

1. If you have a loss from a passive activity on line 2 and you meet **all** of the following conditions, enter the loss on Schedule E (Form 1040), Part II, column (g):

a. You actively participated in the corporate rental real estate activities. (See **Special allowance for a rental real estate activity** on page 3.)

b. Rental real estate activities with active participation were your only passive activities.

c. You have no prior year unallowed losses from these activities.

d. Your total loss from the rental real estate activities was not more than $25,000 (not more than $12,500 if married filing separately and you lived apart from your spouse all year).

e. If you are a married person filing separately, you lived apart from your spouse all year.

f. You have no current or prior year unallowed credits from a passive activity.

g. Your modified adjusted gross income was not more than $100,000 (not more than $50,000 if married filing separately and you lived apart from your spouse all year).

2. If you have a loss from a passive activity on line 2 and you **do not** meet all of the conditions in **1** above, follow the Instructions for Form 8582 to determine how much of the loss can be reported on Schedule E (Form 1040), Part II, column (g).

3. If you were a real estate professional and you materially participated in the activity, report line 2 income (loss) on Schedule E, Part II, column (i) or (k).

4. If you have income from a passive activity on line 2, enter the income on Schedule E, Part II, column (h).

Line 3—Net Income (Loss) From Other Rental Activities

The amount on line 3 is a passive activity amount for all shareholders. Report the income or loss as follows:

1. If line 3 is a loss, report the loss using the Instructions for Form 8582.

2. If income is reported on line 3, report the income on Schedule E (Form 1040), Part II, column (h).

Lines 4a Through 4f—Portfolio Income (Loss)

Portfolio income or loss is not subject to the passive activity limitations. Portfolio income includes income not derived in the ordinary course of a trade or business from interest, ordinary dividends, annuities, or royalties, and gain or loss on the sale of property that produces such income or is held for investment.

Column (c) of Schedule K-1 tells shareholders where to report this income on Form 1040 and related schedules.

Line 4f of Schedule K-1 is used to report income other than that reported on lines 4a through 4e. The type and the amount of income reported on line 4f will be listed in the line 23 Supplemental Information space of Schedule K-1.

If the corporation held a residual interest in a real estate mortgage investment conduit (REMIC), it will report on line 4f your share of REMIC taxable income or (net loss) that you report on Schedule E (Form 1040), Part IV, column (d). It will also report your share of any "excess inclusion" that you report on Schedule E, Part IV, column (c), and your share of section 212 expenses that you report on Schedule E, Part IV, column (e). If you itemize your deductions on Schedule A (Form 1040), you may also deduct these section 212 expenses as a miscellaneous

-4-

Instructions for Schedule K-1 (Form 1120S)

itemized deduction subject to the 2% limit on Schedule A, line 22.

Line 5—Net Section 1231 Gain (Loss) (Other Than Due to Casualty or Theft)

Net section 1231 gain or loss is reported on line 5. Any amount of gain from section 1231 property held more than 5 years will be indicated on an attachment to Schedule K-1. Include this amount in your computation of qualified 5-year gain **only** if the amount on line 7 of your **Form 4797**, Sales of Business Property, is more than zero. The corporation will also identify in the line 23 Supplemental Information space the activity to which the amount on line 5 relates.

The amount on line 5 is generally a passive activity amount if it is from a:
• Rental activity **or**
• Trade or business activity in which you did not materially participate.

However, an amount on line 5 from a rental real estate activity is not from a passive activity if you were a real estate professional (defined on page 2) and you materially participated in the activity.

If the amount on line 5 is either **(a)** a loss that is **not** from a passive activity or **(b)** a gain, report it on Form 4797, line 2, column (g). **Do not** complete columns (b) through (f) on line 2. Instead, write "From Schedule K-1 (Form 1120S)" across these columns.

If the amount on line 5 is a loss from a passive activity, see **Passive Loss Limitations** in the Instructions for Form 4797. You may need to refigure line 5 using the Instructions for Form 8582 to determine the amount to enter on Form 4797.

Line 6—Other Income (Loss)

Amounts on this line are other items of income, gain, or loss not included on lines 1 through 5. The corporation should give you a description and the amount of your share for each of these items.

Report loss items that are passive activity amounts to you using the Instructions for Form 8582.

Report income or gain items that are passive activity amounts to you as instructed below.

The instructions below also tell you where to report line 6 items if such items are **not** passive activity amounts.

Line 6 items include the following:
• Income from recoveries of tax benefit items. A tax benefit item is an amount you deducted in a prior tax year that reduced your income tax. Report this amount on Form 1040, line 21, to the extent it reduced your tax.
• Gambling gains and losses.

1. If the corporation was not engaged in the trade or business of gambling:

a. Report gambling winnings on Form 1040, line 21.

b. Deduct gambling losses to the extent of winnings on Schedule A, line 27.

2. If the corporation was engaged in the trade or business of gambling:

a. Report gambling winnings in Part II of Schedule E.

b. Deduct gambling losses to the extent of winnings in Part II of Schedule E.

• Net gain (loss) from involuntary conversions due to casualty or theft. The corporation will give you a schedule that shows the amounts to be reported on **Form 4684,** Casualties and Thefts, line 34, columns (b)(i), (b)(ii), and (c).
• Net short-term capital gain or loss, net long-term capital gain or loss, and the 28% rate gain or loss from Schedule D (Form 1120S) that is **not** portfolio income (e.g., gain or loss from the disposition of nondepreciable personal property used in a trade or business activity of the corporation). Report total net short-term gain or loss on Schedule D (Form 1040), line 5; total long-term capital gain or loss on Schedule D (Form 1040), line 12, column (f); and the 28% rate gain or loss on Schedule D (Form 1040), line 12, column (g). Any amount of long-term capital gain from such property held more than 5 years will be indicated on an attachment to Schedule K-1. Include this amount on line 5 of the worksheet for line 29 of Schedule D (Form 1040).
• Any net gain or loss from section 1256 contracts. Report this amount on line 1 of **Form 6781,** Gains and Losses From Section 1256 Contracts and Straddles.
• Gain from the sale or exchange of qualified small business stock (as defined in the Instructions for Schedule D) that is eligible for the 50% section 1202 exclusion. The corporation should also give you the name of the corporation that issued the stock, your share of the corporation's adjusted basis and sales price of the stock, and the dates the stock was bought and sold. Corporate shareholders are not eligible for the section 1202 exclusion. The following additional limitations apply at the shareholder level:

1. You must have held an interest in the corporation when the corporation acquired the qualified small business stock and at all times thereafter until the corporation disposed of the qualified small business stock.

2. Your pro rata share of the eligible section 1202 gain cannot exceed the amount that would have been allocated to you based on your interest in the corporation at the time the stock was acquired.

See the Instructions for Schedule D (Form 1040) for details on how to report the gain and the amount of the allowable exclusion.

• Gain eligible for section 1045 rollover (replacement stock purchased by the corporation). The corporation should also give you the name of the corporation that issued the stock, your share of the corporation's adjusted basis and sales price of the stock, and the dates the stock was bought and sold. Corporate shareholders are not eligible for the section 1045 rollover. To qualify for the section 1045 rollover:

1. You must have held an interest in the corporation during the entire period in which the corporation held the qualified small business stock (more than 6 months prior to the sale), and

2. Your pro rata share of the gain eligible for the section 1045 rollover cannot exceed the amount that would have been allocated to you based on your interest in

the corporation at the time the stock was acquired.

See the Instructions for Schedule D (Form 1040) for details on how to report the gain and the amount of the allowable postponed gain.
• Gain eligible for section 1045 rollover (replacement stock not purchased by the corporation). The corporation should also give you the name of the corporation that issued the stock, your share of the corporation's adjusted basis and sales price of the stock, and the dates the stock was bought and sold. Corporate shareholders are not eligible for the section 1045 rollover. To qualify for the section 1045 rollover:

1. You must have held an interest in the corporation during the entire period in which the corporation held the qualified small business stock (more than 6 months prior to the sale).

2. Your pro rata share of the gain eligible for the section 1045 rollover cannot exceed the amount that would have been allocated to you based on your interest in the corporation at the time the stock was acquired, and

3. You must purchase other qualified small business stock (as defined in the Instructions for Schedule D (Form 1040)) during the 60-day period that began on the date the stock was sold by the corporation.

See the Instructions for Schedule D (Form 1040) for details on how to report the gain and the amount of the allowable postponed gain.

Deductions

Line 7—Charitable Contributions

The corporation will give you a schedule that shows the amount of contributions subject to the 50%, 30%, and 20% limitations. For more details, see the instructions for Schedule A (Form 1040).

If property other than cash is contributed, and the claimed deduction for one item or group of similar items of property exceeds $5,000, the corporation is required to give you a copy of **Form 8283,** Noncash Charitable Contributions, and you must attach it to your tax return. **Do not** deduct the amount shown on Form 8283. It is the corporation's contribution. You should deduct the amount shown on Schedule K-1, line 7.

If the corporation provides you with information that the contribution was property other than cash and does not give you a Form 8283, see the Instructions for Form 8283 for filing requirements. A Form 8283 does not have to be filed unless the total claimed deduction of all contributed items of property exceeds $500.

Charitable contribution deductions are not taken into account in figuring your passive activity loss for the year. Do not enter them on Form 8582.

Line 8—Section 179 Expense Deduction

The corporation will identify your share of the section 179 expense deduction and the activity associated with it. Use Part I of **Form 4562,** Depreciation and Amortization, to figure your allowable section 179 expense deduction from all sources. If the section

179 expense deduction is from a passive activity, see the Instructions for Form 8582.

Line 9—Deductions Related to Portfolio Income (Loss)

Amounts on line 9 are deductions that are clearly and directly allocable to portfolio income reported on lines 4a through 4f (other than investment interest expense and section 212 expenses from a REMIC). Generally, you should enter line 9 amounts on Schedule A (Form 1040), line 22. See the instructions for Schedule A, lines 22 and 27, for more information.

These deductions are not taken into account in figuring your passive activity loss for the year. Do not enter them on Form 8582.

Line 10—Other Deductions

Amounts on this line are other deductions not included on lines 7, 8, 9, 15g, and 16a, such as:
- Itemized deductions that Form 1040 filers enter on Schedule A (Form 1040).

Note: *If there was a gain (loss) from a casualty or theft to property **not** used in a trade or business or for income-producing purposes, you will be notified by the corporation. You will have to complete your own Form 4684.*
- Any penalty on early withdrawal of savings.
- Soil and water conservation expenditures. See section 175 for limitations on the amount you are allowed to deduct.
- Expenditures for the removal of architectural and transportation barriers to the elderly and disabled that the corporation elected to treat as a current expense. The deductions are limited by section 190(c) to $15,000 per year from all sources.
- Interest expense allocated to debt-financed distributions. The manner in which you report such interest expense depends on your use of the distributed debt proceeds. See Notice 89-35, 1989-1 C.B. 675, for details.
- Contributions to a capital construction fund (CCF). The deduction for a CCF investment is not taken on Schedule E (Form 1040). Instead, you subtract the deduction from the amount that would normally be entered as taxable income on line 41 (Form 1040). In the margin to the left of line 41, write "CCF" and the amount of the deduction.

If the corporation has more than one corporate activity (line 1, 2, or 3 of Schedule K-1), it will identify the activity to which the expenses relate.

The corporation should also give you a description and your share of each of the expense items. Associate any passive activity deduction included on line 10 with the line 1, 2, or 3 activity to which it relates and report the deduction using the Instructions for Form 8582 (or only on Schedule E (Form 1040), if applicable).

Investment Interest

If the corporation paid or accrued interest on debts properly allocable to investment property, the amount of interest you are allowed to deduct may be limited.

For more information on the special provisions that apply to investment interest

expense, see **Form 4952,** Investment Interest Expense Deduction, and **Pub. 550,** Investment Income and Expenses.

Line 11a—Interest Expense on Investment Debts

Enter this amount on Form 4952, line 1, along with investment interest expense from Schedule K-1, line 10, if any, and from other sources to determine how much of your total investment interest is deductible.

Lines 11b(1) and (2)—Investment Income and Investment Expenses

Use the amounts on these lines to determine the amounts to enter in Part II of Form 4952.

 The amounts shown on lines 11b(1) and 11b(2) include only investment income and expenses reported on lines 4a, 4b, 4c, 4f, and 9 of this Schedule K-1. If applicable, the corporation will have listed in the line 23 Supplemental Information space any other items of investment income and expenses reported elsewhere on this Schedule K-1. Be sure to take these amounts into account, along with the amounts on lines 11b(1) and 11b(2) and your investment income and expenses from other sources, when figuring the amounts to enter in Part II of Form 4952.

Credits

 If you have credits that are passive activity credits to you, you must complete Form 8582-CR in addition to the credit forms identified below. See the Instructions for Form 8582-CR for more information.

*Also, if you are entitled to claim more than one listed general business credit (investment credit, work opportunity credit, welfare-to-work credit, credit for alcohol used as fuel, research credit, low-income housing credit, enhanced oil recovery credit, disabled access credit, renewable electricity production credit, Indian employment credit, credit for employer social security and Medicare taxes paid on certain employee tips, orphan drug credit, new markets credit, credit for small employer pension plan startup costs, credit for employer-provided child care facilities and services, and credit for contributions to selected community development corporations), you must complete **Form 3800,** General Business Credit, in addition to the credit forms identified. If you have more than one credit, see the Instructions for Form 3800.*

Line 12a—Credit for Alcohol Used as Fuel

Your share of the corporation's credit for alcohol used as fuel from all trade or business activities is reported on line 12a. Enter this credit on **Form 6478,** Credit for Alcohol Used as Fuel, to determine your allowed credit for the year.

Line 12b—Low-Income Housing Credit

Your share of the corporation's low-income housing credit is shown on lines 12b(1) and 12b(2). Your allowable credit is entered on **Form 8586,** Low-Income Housing Credit, to determine your allowed credit for the year.

If the corporation invested in a partnership to which the provisions of section 42(j)(5) apply, it will report separately on line 12b(1) your share of the credit it received from the partnership.

Your share of all other low-income housing credits of the corporation is reported on line 12b(2). You must keep a separate record of the amount of low-income housing credit from these lines so that you will be able to correctly figure any recapture of the credit that may result from the disposition of all or part of your stock in the corporation. For more information, see the instructions for **Form 8611,** Recapture of Low-Income Housing Credit.

Line 12c—Qualified Rehabilitation Expenditures Related to Rental Real Estate Activities

The corporation should identify your share of rehabilitation expenditures from each rental real estate activity. Enter the expenditures on the appropriate line of **Form 3468,** Investment Credit, to figure your allowable credit.

Line 12d—Credits (Other Than Credits Shown on Lines 12b and 12c) Related to Rental Real Estate Activities

The corporation will identify the type of credit and any other information you need to figure credits from rental real estate activities (other than the low-income housing credit and qualified rehabilitation expenditures).

Line 12e—Credits Related to Other Rental Activities

If applicable, your share of any credit from other rental activities will be reported on line 12e. Income or loss from these activities is reported on line 3 of Schedule K-1. If more than one credit is involved, the credits will be listed separately, each credit identified as a line 12e credit, and the activity to which the credit relates will be identified. This information will be shown on the line 23 Supplemental Information space. The credit may be limited by the passive activity limitations.

Line 13—Other Credits

If applicable, your pro rata share of any other credit (other than on lines 12a through 12e) will be shown on line 13. If more than one credit is reported, the credits will be shown and identified in the line 23 Supplemental Information space. Expenditures qualifying for the **(a)** rehabilitation credit from other than rental real estate activities, **(b)** energy credit, or **(c)** reforestation credit will be reported to you on line 23.

Line 13 credits include the following:
- Credit for backup withholding on dividends, interest income, and other types of income. Include the amount the corporation reports to you in the total that you enter on line 62, page 2, Form 1040.
- Nonconventional source fuel credit. Enter this credit on a schedule you prepare yourself to determine the allowed credit to take on your tax return. See section 29 for rules on how to figure the credit.

-6-

- Qualified electric vehicle credit (Form 8834).
- Unused investment credit from cooperatives. Enter this credit on Form 3468 to figure your allowable investment credit.
- Work opportunity credit (Form 5884).
- Welfare-to-work credit (Form 8861).
- Credit for increasing research activities (Form 6765).
- Enhanced oil recovery credit (Form 8830).
- Disabled access credit (Form 8826).
- Renewable electricity production credit (Form 8835).
- Empowerment zone and renewable community employment credit (Form 8844).
- Indian employment credit (Form 8845).
- Credit for employer social security and Medicare taxes paid on certain employee tips (Form 8846).
- Orphan drug credit (Form 8820).
- Credit for contributions to selected community development corporations (Form 8847).
- New markets credit (Form 8874).
- Credit for small employer pension plan startup costs (Form 8881).
- Credit for employer-provided child care facilities and services (Form 8882).
- New York liberty zone business employee credit (Form 8884).
- General credits from an electing large partnership. Report these credits on Form 3800, line 1r.
- Qualified zone academy bond credit (Form 8860).

Adjustments and Tax Preference Items

Use the information reported on lines 14a through 14e (as well as adjustments and tax preference items from other sources) to prepare your **Form 6251,** Alternative Minimum Tax—Individuals, or Schedule I of **Form 1041,** U.S. Income Tax Return for Estates and Trusts.

Lines 14d(1) and 14d(2)—Gross Income From, and Deductions Allocable to, Oil, Gas, and Geothermal Properties

The amounts reported on these lines include only the gross income from, and deductions allocable to, oil, gas, and geothermal properties included on line 1 of Schedule K-1. The corporation should have reported separately any income from or deductions allocable to such properties that are included on lines 2 through 10. This separate information is reported in the line 23 Supplemental Information space. Use the amounts reported on lines 14d(1) and 14d(2) and any amounts reported separately to help you determine the net amount to enter on line 14e of Form 6251.

Line 14e—Other Adjustments and Tax Preference Items

Enter the line 14e adjustments and tax preference items shown in the line 23 Supplemental Information space, with other items from other sources, on the applicable lines of Form 6251.

Foreign Taxes

Use the information on lines 15a through 15h and attached schedules, to figure your foreign tax credit. For more information, see

Form 1116, Foreign Tax Credit (Individual, Estate, Trust, or Nonresident Alien Individual), and its instructions.

Other

Lines 16a and 16b—Section 59(e)(2) Expenditures

The corporation will show on line 16a the type of qualified expenditures to which an election under section 59(e) may apply. It will identify the amount of the expenditures on line 16b. If there is more than one type of expenditure, the amount of each type will be listed on an attachment.

Generally, section 59(e) allows each shareholder to elect to deduct certain expenses ratably over the number of years in the applicable period rather than deduct the full amount in the current year. Under the election, you may deduct circulation expenditures ratably over a 3-year period. Research and experimental expenditures and mining exploration and development costs qualify for a writeoff period of 10 years. Intangible drilling and development costs may be deducted over a 60-month period, beginning with the month in which such costs were paid or incurred.

If you make this election, these items are not treated as adjustments or tax preference items for purposes of the alternative minimum tax. Make the election on Form 4562.

Because each shareholder decides whether to make the election under section 59(e), the corporation cannot provide you with the amount of the adjustment or tax preference item related to the expenses listed on line 16a. You must decide both how to claim the expenses on your return and how to figure the resulting adjustment or tax preference item.

Line 17—Tax-Exempt Interest Income

You must report on your return, as an item of information, your share of the tax-exempt interest received or accrued by the corporation during the year. Individual shareholders must include this amount on Form 1040, line 8b. Generally, you must increase the basis of your stock by this amount.

Line 18—Other Tax-Exempt Income

Generally, you must increase the basis of your stock by the amount shown on line 18, but do not include it in income on your tax return.

Line 19—Nondeductible Expenses

The nondeductible expenses paid or incurred by the corporation are not deductible on your tax return. Generally, you must decrease the basis of your stock by this amount.

Line 20

Reduce the basis of your stock (as explained on page 1) by the distributions on line 20. If these distributions exceed the basis of your stock, the excess is treated as gain from the sale or exchange of property and is reported on Schedule D (Form 1040).

Line 21

If the line 21 payments are made on a loan with a reduced basis, the repayments must be allocated in part to a return of your basis in the loan and in part to the receipt of income. See Regulations section 1.1367-2 for information on reduction in basis of a loan and restoration in basis of a loan with a reduced basis. See Rev. Rul. 64-162, 1964-1 (Part 1) C.B. 304 and Rev. Rul. 68-537, 1968-2 C.B. 372, for other information.

Lines 22a and 22b—Recapture of Low-Income Housing Credit

The corporation will report separately on line 22a your share of any recapture of a low-income housing credit from its investment in partnerships to which the provisions of section 42(j)(5) apply. All other recapture of low-income housing credits will be reported on line 22b. You must keep a separate record of recapture from line 22a and 22b so that you will be able to correctly figure any credit recapture that may result from the disposition of all or part of your corporate stock. Use the line 22a and 22b amounts to figure the low-income housing credit recapture on Form 8611. See the instructions for Form 8611 and section 42(j) for additional information.

Supplemental Information

Line 23

If applicable, the corporation should have listed in line 23, Supplemental Information, or on an attached statement to Schedule K-1, your distributive share of the following:

1. Taxes paid on undistributed capital gains by a regulated investment company or real estate investment trust. Form 1040 filers, enter your share of these taxes on line 68 of Form 1040, check the box for Form 2439, and add the words "Form 1120S." Also reduce the basis of your stock by this tax.

2. Gross income from the property, share of production for the tax year, etc., needed to figure your depletion deduction for oil and gas wells. The corporation should also allocate to you a proportionate share of the adjusted basis of each corporate oil or gas property. See Pub. 535 on how to figure your depletion deduction. Also, reduce the basis of your stock by the amount of this deduction to the extent the deduction does not exceed your share of the adjusted basis of the property.

3. Recapture of the section 179 expense deduction. If the recapture was caused by a disposition of the property, include the amount on Form 4797, line 17. The recapture amount is limited to the amount you deducted in earlier years.

4. Recapture of certain mining exploration expenditures (section 617).

5. Any information or statements you need to comply with section 6111 (registration of tax shelters) or 6662(d)(2)(B)(ii) (regarding adequate disclosure of items that may cause an understatement of income tax).

6. Gross farming and fishing income. If you are an individual shareholder, enter this income, as an item of information, on Schedule E (Form 1040), Part V, line 41. **Do**

not report this income elsewhere on Form 1040.

For a shareholder that is an estate or trust, report this income to the beneficiaries, as an item of information, on Schedule K-1 (Form 1041). **Do not** report it elsewhere on Form 1041.

7. Any information you need to figure the interest due under section 453(l)(3). If the corporation elected to report the dispositions of certain timeshares and residential lots on the installment method, your tax liability must be increased by the interest on tax attributable to your pro rata share of the installment payments received by the corporation during its tax year. If applicable, use the information provided by the corporation to figure your interest. Include the interest on Form 1040, line 61. Also write "453(l)(3)" and the amount of the interest on the dotted line to the left of line 61.

8. Any information you need to figure the interest due under section 453A(c) with respect to certain installment sales of property. If you are an individual, report the interest on Form 1040, line 61. Write "453A(c)" and the amount of the interest on the dotted line to the left of line 61. See the instructions for **Form 6252,** Installment Sale Income, for more information. Also see section 453A(c) for details on making the computation.

9. Capitalization of interest under section 263A(f). To the extent certain production or construction expenditures of the corporation are made from proceeds associated with debt you incur as an owner-shareholder, you must capitalize the interest on this debt. If applicable, use the information on expenditures the corporation gives to you to determine the amount of interest you must capitalize. See Regulations sections 1.263A-8 through 1.263A-15 for more information.

10. Any information you need to figure the interest due or to be refunded under the look-back method of section 460(b)(2) on certain long-term contracts. Use **Form 8697,** Interest Computation Under the Look-Back Method for Completed Long-Term Contracts, to report any such interest.

11. Your share of expenditures qualifying for the **(a)** rehabilitation credit from other than rental real estate activities, **(b)** energy credit, or **(c)** reforestation credit. Enter the expenditures on the appropriate line of Form 3468 to figure your allowable credit.

12. Investment credit properties subject to recapture. Any information you need to figure your recapture tax on **Form 4255,** Recapture of Investment Credit. See the Form 3468 on which you took the original credit for other information you need to complete Form 4255.

You may also need Form 4255 if you disposed of more than one-third of your stock in the corporation.

13. Preproductive period farm expenses. You may elect to deduct these expenses

currently or capitalize them under section 263A. See **Pub. 225,** Farmer's Tax Guide, and Regulations section 1.263A-4 for more information.

14. Any information you need to figure the recapture of the new markets credit (see Form 8874).

15. Any information you need to figure recapture of the qualified electric vehicle credit. See Pub. 535 for details, including how to figure the recapture.

16. Any information you need to figure your recapture of the Indian employment credit. Generally, if the corporation terminated a qualified employee less than 1 year after the date of initial employment, any Indian employment credit allowed for a prior tax year by reason of wages paid or incurred to that employee must be recaptured. For details, see section 45A(d).

17. Nonqualified withdrawals by the corporation from a capital construction fund (CCF). These withdrawals are taxed separately from your other gross income at the highest marginal ordinary income or capital gain tax rate. Attach a statement to your Federal income tax return to show your computation of both the tax and interest for a nonqualified withdrawal. Include the tax and interest on Form 1040, line 61. To the left of line 61, write the amount of tax and interest and "CCF."

18. Unrecaptured section 1250 gain. Generally, report this amount on line 5 of the **Unrecaptured Section 1250 Gain Worksheet** in the Schedule D (Form 1040) instructions. However, for an amount passed through from an estate, trust, real estate investment trust, or regulated investment company, report it on line 11 of that worksheet. Report on line 10 of that worksheet any gain from the corporation's sale or exchange of a partnership interest that is attributable to unrecaptured section 1250 gain.

19. Any information you need to figure the interest due or to be refunded under the look-back method of section 167(g)(2) for certain property placed in service after September 13, 1995, and depreciated under the income forecast method. Use **Form 8866,** Interest Computation Under the Look-Back Method for Property Depreciated Under the Income Forecast Method, to report any such interest.

20. Amortizable basis of reforestation expenditures and the year paid or incurred. To figure your allowable amortization, including limits that may apply, see section 194 and Pub. 535. Follow the Instructions for Form 8582 to report amortization allocable to a passive activity. Report amortization from a trade or business activity in which you materially participated on a separate line in Part II, column (i), of Schedule E (Form 1040).

21. Any information you need to figure the interest due under section 1260(b). If the corporation had gain from certain constructive ownership transactions, your

tax liability must be increased by the interest charge on any deferral of gain recognition under section 1260(b). If you are an individual, report the interest on Form 1040, line 61. Write "1260(b)" and the amount of the interest on the dotted line to the left of line 61. See section 1260(b) for details, including how to figure the interest.

22. Extraterritorial income exclusion:

• *Corporation did not claim the exclusion.* If the corporation reports your pro rata share of foreign trading gross receipts and the extraterritorial income exclusion, the corporation was not entitled to claim the exclusion because it did not meet the foreign economic process requirements. You may still qualify for your pro rata share of this exclusion if the corporation's foreign trading gross receipts for the tax year were $5 million or less. To qualify for this exclusion, your foreign trading gross receipts from all sources for the tax year also must have been $5 million or less. If you qualify for the exclusion, report the exclusion amount in accordance with the instructions on page 4 for line 1, 2, or 3, whichever applies. See **Form 8873,** Extraterritorial Income Exclusion, for more information.

• *Corporation claimed the exclusion.* If the corporation reports your pro rata share of foreign trading gross receipts but not the amount of the extraterritorial income exclusion, the corporation met the foreign economic process requirements and claimed the exclusion when figuring your pro rata share of corporate income. You also may need to know the amount of your pro rata share of foreign trading gross receipts from this corporation to determine if you met the $5 million or less exception discussed above for purposes of qualifying for an extraterritorial income exclusion from other sources.

Note: *Upon request, the corporation should furnish you a copy of the corporation's Form 8873 if there is a reduction for international boycott operations, illegal bribes, kickbacks, etc.*

23. The amount of commercial revitalization deduction from rental real estate activities. Follow the instructions for Form 8582 to determine how much of this deduction can be reported on Schedule E, Part II, column (g).

24. A disclosure statement for each reportable tax shelter transaction the corporation participates in. As a shareholder in the corporation, you are an indirect participant in the tax shelter transactions entered into by the corporation. You are required to file a tax shelter disclosure statement for each of these transactions with your income tax return. See the Instructions for Schedule E (Form 1040) for more information.

25. Any other information you may need to file with your individual tax return that is not shown elsewhere on Schedule K-1.

THE X CORPORATION EXHIBIT: STOCK LEDGER

NAME OF STOCKHOLDER	ADDRESS OF STOCKHOLDER	DATE BECAME OWNER	CERTIFICATES ISSUED		FROM WHOM SHARES WERE TRANSFERRED (If Original Issue Enter As Such)	
			CERTIF. NOS.	NO. OF SHARES		
Arlo Anders	100 Division St. Anytown, IL 60930	2/10/96	1	100		
Susan Boyle	300 W. Main St. Orange, MD 20904	2/10/96	2	100		
Carla Babson	488 Winston St. Metro City, OH 43705	2/11/96	3	200		

AMOUNT PAID THEREON	DATE OF TRANSFER OF SHARES	TO WHOM SHARES ARE TRANSFERRED	CERTIFICATES SURRENDERED		NUMBER OF SHARES HELD (BALANCE)	VALUE OF STOCK TRANSFER TAX STAMP AFFIXED
			CERTIF. NOS.	NO. OF SHARES		
$10,000						$100
$10,000						$100
$20,000						$200

Blank Legal Forms

T he five legal forms in this appendix have been left blank and can be removed for your use. The first four forms have been reprinted with permission from: *Corporate Practice Handbook*, published by New York State Bar Association, One Elk Street, Albany, New York 12207.

FORM 1

CERTIFICATE OF INCORPORATION
OF
[CORPORATION]
UNDER SECTION _____ OF THE
BUSINESS CORPORATION LAW

I, [NAME OF INCORPORATOR], being of the age of eighteen years or over, for the purpose of forming a corporation pursuant to Section _____ of the Business Corporation Law of _____ , do hereby certify:

1. The name of the corporation is [NAME OF CORPORATION].

2. The purposes for which it is formed are:

To purchase, receive, take by grant, gift, devise, bequest or otherwise, lease or otherwise acquire, own, hold, improve, employ, use and otherwise deal in and with real or personal property, or any interest therein, wherever situated; and

To have and to exercise all rights and powers that are now or may hereafter be granted to a corporation by law.

The foregoing shall be construed as objects, purposes and powers, and the enumeration thereof shall not be held to limit or restrict in any manner the powers now or hereafter conferred on this corporation by the laws of the State of _____ . The objects and powers specified herein shall, except as otherwise expressed, be in no way limited or restricted by reference to or inference from the terms of any other clause or paragraph of these articles. The objects, purposes, and powers specified in each of the clauses or paragraphs of this Certificate of Incorporation shall be regarded as independent objects, purposes, or powers.

3. The office of the corporation is to be located in the City of _____ , County of _____ , State of _____ .

4. The aggregate number of shares of stock which the corporation shall have the authority to issue is _____ (_____) shares of Common Stock, each of which shall have a par value of _____ Dollars ($ _____) per share.

5. The Secretary of State is designated as the agent of the corporation upon whom process against the corporation may be served. The post office address to which the Secretary of State shall mail a copy of any process against the corporation served upon him is: _____

_____ .

6. The name and address of the registered agent which is to be the agent of the corporation upon whom process against it may be served are:

_____

_____ .

IN WITNESS WHEREOF, I have made and signed this certificate this _____ day of _____ , 19_____ , and I affirm the statements contained herein as true under penalties of perjury.

_____
[Name and Home or Business Address of Incorporator]

FORM OF NOTARIZATION

STATE OF _____)

                          : ss.:

COUNTY OF _____)

    On this _____ day of _____ , 19 _____ , before me personally came [NAME OF INCORPORATOR], to me personally known, who, being by me duly sworn, did depose and say that (s)he resides at [HOME ADDRESS OF INCORPORATOR]; that (s)he is the individual who executed the within instrument; and that (s)he signed [his] [her] name thereto.

                                  _____

                                        Notary Public

FORM 2

SAMPLE BY-LAWS

ARTICLE I

OFFICES

Section 1. The office of the Corporation shall be located in the City of
_____ , in the County of _____ , in the State of _____ .

Section 2. The Corporation may also have offices at such other places both
within and without the State of _____ as the board of directors may
from time to time determine or the business of the Corporation may require.

ARTICLE II

ANNUAL MEETINGS OF SHAREHOLDERS

Section 1. All meetings of shareholders for the election of directors shall be
held in such City, County and State and at such time and place as may be fixed
from time to time by the board of directors and set forth in the notice of such
meeting.

Section 2. Annual meetings of shareholders shall be held on the third
Friday in _____ of each year if not a legal holiday, and if a legal holiday, then
on the next business day following at which they shall elect by a plurality vote
a board of directors, and transact such other business as may properly be
brought before the meeting.

Section 3. Written or printed notice of the annual meeting stating the place,
date and hour of the meeting shall be delivered not less than ten nor more than
fifty days before the date of the meeting, either personally or by mail, by or at
the direction of the president, the secretary, or the officer or persons calling
the meeting, to each shareholder of record entitled to vote at such meeting.

ARTICLE III

SPECIAL MEETINGS OF SHAREHOLDERS

Section 1. Special meetings of shareholders may be held at such time and place within or without the State of _____ as shall be stated in the notice of the meeting or in a duly executed waiver of notice thereof.

Section 2. Special meetings of shareholders, for any purpose or purposes, unless otherwise prescribed by statute or by the certificate of incorporation, may be called by the president, the board of directors, or the holders of not less than a majority of all the shares entitled to vote at the meeting.

Section 3. Written or printed notice of a special meeting stating the place, date and hour of the meeting and the purpose or purposes for which the meeting is called shall be delivered not less than ten nor more than fifty days before the date of the meeting, either personally or by mail, by, or at the direction of, the president, the board or, if the special meeting is called by holders of not less than a majority of all the shares entitled to vote at the special meeting, the secretary, to each shareholder of record entitled to vote at such meeting. The notice should also indicate that it is being issued by, or at the direction of, the person calling the meeting.

Section 4. The business transacted at any special meeting of shareholders shall be limited to the purposes stated in the notice.

ARTICLE IV

QUORUM AND VOTING OF STOCK

Section 1. The holders of a majority of the shares of stock issued and outstanding and entitled to vote, represented in person or by proxy, shall constitute a quorum at all meetings of the shareholders for the transaction of business except as otherwise provided by statute or by the certificate of incorporation. If, however, such quorum shall not be present or represented by proxy shall have power to adjourn the meeting from time to time, without notice other than announcement at the meeting, until a quorum shall be present or represented. At such adjourned meeting at which a quorum shall be present or represented, any business may be transacted which might have been transacted at the meeting as originally notified.

Section 2. If a quorum is present, the affirmative vote of a majority of the shares of stock represented at the meeting shall be the act of the shareholders, unless the vote of a greater or lesser number of shares of stock is required by law or the certificate of incorporation.

Section 3. Each outstanding share of stock having voting power shall be entitled to one vote on each matter submitted to vote at a meeting of shareholders. A shareholder may vote either in person or by proxy executed in writing by the shareholder or by his duly authorized attorney-in-fact.

Section 4. The board of directors in advance of any shareholders' meeting may appoint one or more inspectors to act at the meeting or any adjournment thereof. If inspectors are not so appointed, the person presiding at a shareholders' meeting may, and, on the request of any shareholder entitled to vote thereat, shall, appoint one or more inspectors. In case any person appointed as inspector fails to appear or act, the vacancy may be filled by the board in advance of the meeting or at the meeting by the person presiding thereat. Each inspector, before entering upon the discharge of his duties, shall take and sign an oath faithfully to execute the duties of inspector at such meeting with strict impartiality and according to the best of his ability.

Section 5. Whenever shareholders are required or permitted to take any action by vote, such action may be taken without a meeting on written consent, setting forth the action so taken, signed by the holders of all outstanding shares entitled to vote thereon.

ARTICLE V

DIRECTORS

Section 1. The number of directors shall be _____ (_____), which number may be increased or decreased by amendment of these by-laws. Each director shall be at least eighteen years of age. The directors need not be residents of the State of _____ nor shareholders of the Corporation. The directors, other than the first board of directors, shall be elected at the annual meeting of the shareholders, except as hereinafter provided, and each director elected shall serve until the next succeeding annual meeting or until his successor shall have been elected and qualified. The first board of directors shall hold office until the first meeting of shareholders.

Section 2. Any or all of the directors may be removed, with or without cause, at any time by the vote of the shareholders at a special meeting called for that purpose.

Any director may be removed for cause by the action of the directors at a special meeting called for that purpose.

Section 3. Unless otherwise provided in the certificate of incorporation, newly created directorships resulting from an increase in the board of directors and all vacancies occurring in the board of directors, including vacancies caused by removal without cause, may be filled by the affirmative vote of a majority of the board of directors; however, if the number of directors then in office is less than a quorum, then such newly created directorships and vacancies may be filled by a vote of a majority of the directors then in office. A director elected to fill a vacancy shall hold office until the next meeting of shareholders at which election of directors is the regular order of business, and until his successor shall have been elected and qualified. A director elected to fill a newly created directorship shall serve until the next succeeding annual meeting of shareholders and until his successor shall have been elected and qualified.

Section 4. The business affairs of the Corporation shall be managed by its board of directors, which may exercise all such powers of the Corporation and do all such lawful acts and things as are not by statute or by the certificate of incorporation or by these by-laws directed or required to be exercised or done by the shareholders.

Section 5. The directors may keep the books of the Corporation, except such as are required by law to be kept within the State of, at such place or places as they may from time to time determine.

Section 6. The board of directors, by the affirmative vote of a majority of the directors then in office, and irrespective of any personal interest of any of its members, shall have authority to establish reasonable compensation of all directors for services to the Corporation as directors, officers or otherwise.

ARTICLE VI

MEETINGS OF THE BOARD OF DIRECTORS

Section 1. Meetings of the board of directors, regular or special, may be held either within or without the State of _____ .

Section 2. The first meeting of each newly elected board of directors shall be held at such time and place as shall be fixed by the vote of the shareholders at the annual meeting and no notice of such meeting shall be necessary to the newly elected directors in order legally to constitute the meeting, provided a quorum shall be present, or it may convene at such place and time as shall be fixed by the consent in writing of all the directors.

Section 3. Regular meetings of the board of directors may be held upon such notice, or without notice, and at such time and at such place as shall from time to time be determined by the board of directors.

Section 4. Special meetings of the board of directors may be called by the chairman of the board of directors or by the president or by any two directors at any time. Notice of any special meeting shall be mailed to each director addressed to him at his residence or usual place of business at least two days before the day on which the meeting is to be held, or if sent to him at such place by telegraph or cable, or delivered personally or by telephone, not later than the day before the day on which the meeting is to be held.

Section 5. Notice of a meeting need not be given to any director who submits a signed waiver of notice whether before or after the meeting, or who attends the meeting without protesting, prior thereto or at its commencement, the lack of notice. Neither the business to be transacted at, nor the purpose of, any regular or special meeting of the board of directors need be specified in the notice or waiver of notice of such meeting.

Section 6. A majority of the directors shall constitute a quorum for the transaction of business unless a greater or lesser number is required by law or by the certificate of incorporation. The vote of a majority of the directors present at any meeting at which a quorum is present shall be the act of the board of directors, unless the vote of a greater number is required by law or by the certificate of incorporation. If a quorum shall not be present at any meeting of directors, the directors present may adjourn the meeting from time to time, without notice other than announcement at the meeting, until a quorum shall be present.

Section 7. Unless the certificate of incorporation provides otherwise, any action required or permitted to be taken at a meeting of the directors or a committee thereof may be taken without a meeting if a consent in writing to the adoption of a resolution authorizing the action so taken shall be signed by all of the directors entitled to vote with respect to the subject matter thereof.

Section 8. Unless otherwise restricted by the certificate of incorporation or these by-laws, members of the board of directors, or any committee designated by the board of directors, may participate in a meeting of the board of directors, or any committee, by means of conference telephone or similar communications equipment by means of which all persons participating in the meeting can hear each other, and such participation in a meeting shall constitute presence in person at the meeting.

ARTICLE VII

EXECUTIVE COMMITTEE

Section 1. The board of directors, by resolution adopted by a majority of the entire board, may designate, from among its members, an executive committee and other committees, each consisting of three or more directors, and each of which, to the extent provided in the resolution, shall have all the authority of the board, except as otherwise required by law. Vacancies in the membership of the committee shall be filled by the board of directors at a regular or special meeting of the board of directors.

Section 2. Any member of a committee may resign at any time. Such resignation shall be made in writing and shall take effect at the time specified therein, or, if no time be specified, at the time of its receipt by the president or secretary. The acceptance of a resignation shall not be necessary to make it effective unless so specified therein.

Section 3. A majority of the members of a committee shall constitute a quorum. The act of a majority of the members of a committee present at any meeting at which a quorum is present shall be the act of such committee. The members of a committee shall act only as a committee, and the individual members thereof shall have no powers as such.

Section 4. Each committee shall keep a record of its acts and proceedings, and shall report the same to the board of directors when and as required by the board of directors.

Section 5. A committee may hold its meetings at the principal office of the Corporation, or at any other place which a majority of the committee may at any time agree upon. Each committee may make such rules as it may deem expedient for the regulation and carrying on of its meetings and proceedings. Unless otherwise ordered by the executive committee, any notice of a meeting of such committee may be given by the secretary or by the chairman of the committee and shall be sufficiently given if mailed to each member at his residence or usual place of business at least two days before the day on which the meeting is to be held or if sent to him at such place by telegraph or cable, or delivered personally or by telephone, not later than 24 hours prior to the time at which the meeting is to be held.

Section 6. The members of any committee shall be entitled to such compensation as may be allowed them by resolution of the board of directors.

ARTICLE VIII

NOTICES

Section 1. Whenever, by law or by the provisions of the certificate of incorporation or of these by-laws, notice is required to be given to any director or shareholder, it shall not be construed to mean personal notice, but such notice may be given in writing, by mail, addressed to such director or shareholder, at his address as it appears on the records of the Corporation, with postage thereon prepaid, and such notice shall be deemed to be given at the time when the same shall be deposited in the United States mail. Notice to directors may also be given by telegram.

Section 2. Whenever any notice of a meeting is required to be given by law or by the provisions of the certificate of incorporation or these by-laws, a waiver thereof in writing signed by the person or persons entitled to such notice, whether before or after the time stated therein, shall be deemed equivalent to the giving of such notice.

ARTICLE IX

OFFICERS

Section 1. The officers of the Corporation shall be chosen by the board of directors and shall be a president, a vice president, a secretary and a treasurer, and such other officers, as may be appointed in accordance with the provisions of Section 3 of this Article IX. The board of directors in its discretion may also elect a chairman of the board of directors. The board of directors may also choose one or more additional vice presidents, and one or more assistant secretaries and assistant treasurers.

Section 2. The board of directors at its first meeting after each annual meeting of shareholders shall choose a president, a vice president, a secretary and a treasurer, none of whom need be a member of the board.

Any two or more offices may be held by the same person, except the offices of president and secretary. When all the issued and outstanding stock of the Corporation is owned by one person, such person may hold all or any combination of offices.

Section 3. The board of directors may appoint such other officers and agents as it shall deem necessary who shall hold their offices for such terms and shall exercise such powers and perform such duties as shall be determined from time to time by the board of directors.

Section 4. The salaries of all officers and agents of the Corporation shall be fixed by the board of directors.

Section 5. The officers of the Corporation shall hold office until their successors are chosen and qualify. Any officer elected or appointed by the board of directors may be removed at any time by the affirmative vote of a majority of the board of directors. Any vacancy occurring in any office of the Corporation shall be filled by the board of directors.

CHAIRMAN OF THE BOARD OF DIRECTORS

Section 6. The chairman of the board of directors shall be a director and shall preside at all meetings of the board of directors at which he shall be present and shall have such power and perform such duties as may from time to time be assigned to him by the board of directors.

THE PRESIDENT

Section 7. The president shall be the chief executive officer of the Corporation, shall preside at all meetings of the shareholders and, in the absence of the chairman of the board of directors, shall have general and active management of the business of the Corporation and shall see that all orders and resolutions of the board of directors are carried into effect.

He shall have the power to call special meetings of the stockholders or of the board of directors or of the executive committee at any time.

Section 8. He shall execute bonds, mortgages and other contracts requiring a seal under the seal of the Corporation, except where required or permitted by law to be otherwise signed and executed and except where the signing and execution thereof shall be expressly delegated by the board of directors to some other officer or agent of the Corporation.

THE VICE PRESIDENTS

Section 9. The vice president or, if there shall be more than one, the vice presidents in the order determined by the board of directors shall, in the absence or disability of the president, perform the duties and exercise the powers of the president and shall perform such other duties and have such other powers as the board of directors may from time to time prescribe.

THE SECRETARY AND ASSISTANT SECRETARIES

Section 10. The secretary shall attend all meetings of the board of directors and all meetings of the shareholders and record all the proceedings of the meetings of the Corporation and of the board of directors in a book to be kept for that purpose and shall perform like duties for the standing committees when required. He shall give, or cause to be given, notice of all meetings of the shareholders and special meetings of the board of directors, and shall perform such other duties as may be prescribed by the board of directors or the president, under whose supervision he shall be. He shall have custody of the corporate seal of the Corporation, if any, and he shall have authority to affix the same to any instrument requiring it and, when so affixed, it may be attested by his signature. The board of directors may give general authority to any other officer to affix the seal of the Corporation and to attest the affixing by his signature.

Section 11. The assistant secretary or, if there be more than one, the assistant secretaries in the order determined by the board of directors shall, in the absence or disability of the secretary, perform the duties and exercise the powers of the secretary and shall perform such other duties and have such other powers as the board of directors may from time to time prescribe.

THE TREASURER AND ASSISTANT TREASURERS

Section 12. The treasurer shall have the custody of the corporate funds and securities and shall keep full and accurate accounts of receipts and disbursements in books belonging to the Corporation and shall deposit all moneys and other valuable effects in the name and to the credit of the Corporation in such depositories as may be designated by the board of directors.

Section 13. He shall disburse the funds of the Corporation as may be ordered by the board of directors, taking proper vouchers for such disbursements, and shall render to the president and the board of directors at its regular meetings, or when the board of directors so requires, an account of all his transactions as treasurer and of the financial condition of the Corporation.

Section 14. If required by the board of directors, he shall give the Corporation a bond in such sum and with such surety or sureties as shall be satisfactory to the board of directors for the faithful performance of the duties of his office and for the restoration to the Corporation, in case of his death, resignation, retirement or removal from office, of all books, papers, vouchers, money and other property of whatever kind in his possession or under his control belonging to the Corporation.

Section 15. The assistant treasurer or, if there shall be more than one, the assistant treasurers in the order determined by the board of directors shall, in the absence or disability of the treasurer, perform the duties and exercise the powers of the treasurer and shall perform such other duties and have such other powers as the board of directors may from time to time prescribe.

ARTICLE X

CERTIFICATES FOR SHARES

Section 1. The shares of the Corporation shall be represented by certificates signed by the chairman or the president or a vice president and the sec-

retary or an assistant secretary or the treasurer or an assistant treasurer of the Corporation and may be sealed with the seal of the Corporation or a facsimile thereof.

When the Corporation is authorized to issue more than one class of shares, there shall be set forth upon the face or back of the certificate, or the certificate shall have a statement, that the Corporation will furnish to any shareholder upon request and without charge, a full statement of the designation, relative rights, preferences and limitations of the shares of each class of stock which the Corporation is authorized to issue.

Section 2. The signatures of the officers of the Corporation upon a certificate may be facsimiles if the certificate is countersigned by a transfer agent or registered by a registrar other than the Corporation itself or an employee of the Corporation. In case any officer who has signed or whose facsimile signature has been placed upon a certificate shall have ceased to be such officer before such certificate is issued, it may be issued by the Corporation with the same effect as if he were such officer at the date of issue.

LOST CERTIFICATES

Section 3. The board of directors may direct a new certificate to be issued in place of any certificate theretofore issued by the Corporation alleged to have been lost or destroyed. When authorizing such issue of a new certificate, the board of directors, in its discretion and as a condition precedent to the issuance thereof, may prescribe such terms and conditions as it deems expedient, and may require such indemnities as it deems adequate, to protect the Corporation from any claim that may be made against it with respect to any such certificate alleged to have been lost or destroyed.

TRANSFER OF SHARES

Section 4. Upon surrender to the Corporation or the transfer agent of the Corporation of a certificate representing shares duly endorsed or accompanied by proper evidence of succession, assignment or authority to transfer, a new certificate shall be issued to the person entitled thereto, and the old certificate cancelled and the transaction recorded upon the books of the Corporation.

The board of directors may make other and further rules and regulations concerning the transfer and registration of certificates for stock and may

appoint a transfer agent or registrar or both and may require all certificates of stock to bear the signature of either or both.

FIXING RECORD DATE

Section 5. For the purpose of determining shareholders entitled to notice of or to vote at any meeting of shareholders or any adjournment thereof, or to express consent to or dissent from any proposal without a meeting, or for the purpose of determining shareholders entitled to receive payment of any dividend or the allotment of any rights, or for the purpose of any other action, the board of directors may fix, in advance, a date as the record date for any such determination of shareholders. Such date shall not be more than fifty nor less than ten days before the date of any meeting nor more than fifty days prior to any other action. When a determination of shareholders of record entitled to notice of or to vote at any meeting of shareholders has been made as provided in this section, such determination shall apply to any adjournment thereof, unless the board fixes a new record date for the adjourned meeting.

REGISTERED SHAREHOLDERS

Section 6. The Corporation shall be entitled to recognize the exclusive right of a person registered on its books as the owner of shares to receive dividends, and to vote as such owner, and to hold liable for calls and assessments a person registered on its books as the owner of shares, and shall not be bound to recognize any equitable or other claim to or interest in such share or shares on the part of any other person, whether or not it shall have express or other notice thereof, except as otherwise provided by the laws of the State of New York.

LIST OF SHAREHOLDERS

Section 7. A list of shareholders as of the record date, certified by the corporate officer responsible for its preparation or by a transfer agent, shall be produced at any meeting upon the request thereat or prior thereto of any shareholder. If the right to vote at any meeting is challenged, the inspectors of election, or person presiding thereat, shall require such list of shareholders to be produced as evidence of the right of the persons challenged to vote at such meeting and all persons who appear from such list to be shareholders entitled to vote thereat may vote at such meeting.

ARTICLE Xl

GENERAL PROVISIONS DIVIDENDS

Section 1. Subject to the provisions of the certificate of incorporation relating thereto, if any, and to the laws of the State of New York, dividends may be declared by the board of directors at any regular or special meeting. Dividends may be paid in cash, in shares of the capital stock or in the Corporation's bonds or its property, including the shares or bonds of other corporations, subject to the laws of the State of New York and to the provisions of the certificate of incorporation.

Section 2. Before payment of any dividend, there may be set aside out of any funds of the Corporation available for dividends such sum or sums as the directors from time to time, in their absolute discretion, think proper as a reserve fund to meet contingencies, or for equalizing dividends, or for repairing or maintaining any property of the Corporation, or for such other purpose as the directors shall think conducive to the interest of the Corporation, and the directors may modify or abolish any such reserve in the manner in which it was created.

CHECKS

Section 3. All checks or demands for money and notes of the Corporation shall be signed by such officer or officers or such other person or persons as the board of directors may from time to time designate.

FISCAL YEAR

Section 4. The fiscal year of the Corporation shall be fixed by resolution of the board of directors.

ARTICLE XII

AMENDMENTS

Section 1. These by-laws may be amended or repealed or new by-laws may be adopted at any regular or special meeting of shareholders at which a quorum is present or represented, by the vote of the holders of shares entitled to vote in the election of any directors, provided notice of the proposed alter-

ation, amendment or repeal be contained in the notice of such meeting. These by-laws may also be amended or repealed or new by-laws may be adopted by the affirmative vote of a majority of the board of directors at any regular or special meeting of the board. If any by-law regulating an impending election of directors is adopted, amended or repealed by the board, there shall be set forth in the notice of the next meeting of shareholders for the election of directors the by-law so adopted, amended or repealed, together with a precise statement of the changes made. By-laws adopted by the board of directors may be amended or repealed by the shareholder.

FORM 3

MINUTES OF ORGANIZATION
MEETING OF
BOARD OF DIRECTORS
OF
[CORPORATION]

The first meeting of the board of directors of [NAME OF CORPORATION] was called and held at _____ , _____ on the _____ day of_____, 20 _____ at _____ .

PRESENT:

There were present:

[NAMES OF DIRECTORS]

being all the directors.

_____was chosen temporary chairman and _____ was chosen temporary secretary of the meeting.

The secretary presented and read a waiver of notice of the meeting, signed by all the directors, which was ordered filed with the minutes of the meeting.

The minutes of the incorporator were read and approved.

The chairman stated that the first business to come before the meeting was the election of officers.

The following persons were thereupon nominated to the offices set forth opposite their respective names, to serve until the next annual meeting and until their successors are chosen and shall qualify:

President _____

Secretary _____

All the directors present having voted, the chairman announced that the aforesaid persons had been unanimously elected as said officers respectively.

The president and the secretary thereupon entered upon the discharge of the duties of their respective offices.

Upon motion, duly made, seconded and carried, it was

RESOLVED, that the form of stock certificate presented and read be and it is hereby approved and adopted, and the secretary is instructed to insert a specimen thereof in the minute book.

Upon motion, duly made, seconded and carried, it was

RESOLVED, that the seal, an impression of which is hereto affixed, be and it is hereby adopted as the corporate seal of the corporation.

The secretary was authorized and directed to procure the proper corporate books.

Upon motion, duly made, seconded and carried, it was

RESOLVED, that the president be and he hereby is authorized to open a bank account on behalf of this corporation in a bank selected by the president.

RESOLVED, that until otherwise ordered said bank be and it hereby is authorized to make payments from the funds on deposit with it upon and according to the check of this corporation, signed by its president.

Upon motion, duly made, seconded and carried, it was

RESOLVED, that an office of the corporation be established and maintained at _____ , in the City of _____ , in the County of _____ , in the State of _____ , and that meetings of the board of directors from time to time may be held either at such office in the City of or elsewhere, as the board of directors shall from time to time order.

Upon motion, duly made, seconded and carried, it was

RESOLVED, that the president and secretary be and they each are authorized to execute and file, or cause to be filed, with the New York State Tax Commission a certificate pursuant to Section 275-a of the New York Tax Law.

The president stated that the corporation had received a subscription to _____ shares of the common stock of this corporation having a par value of _____ Dollars ($ _____) per share.

The president stated further that the subscriber had tendered to the corporation the sum of _____ Dollars ($ _____) in full payment at par for the common stock subscribed.

Upon motion, duly made, seconded and carried, the president and the secretary were authorized to issue to the said subscriber or its nominee certificates representing fully paid and nonassessable common stock of this corporation to the amount of the subscription.

Upon motion, duly made, seconded and carried, it was

RESOLVED, that for the purpose of authorizing the corporation to do business in any state, territory or dependency of the United States or any foreign country in which it is necessary or expedient for this corporation to transact business, the officers of this corporation are hereby authorized to appoint and substitute all necessary agents or attorneys for service of process, to designate and change the location of all necessary statutory offices and, under the corporate seal, to make and file all necessary certificates, reports, powers of attorney and other instruments as may be required by the laws of such state, territory, dependency or country to authorize the corporation to transact business therein, and whenever it is expedient for the corporation to cease doing business therein and withdraw therefrom, to revoke any appointment of agent or attorney for service of process and to file such certificates, reports, revocation of appointment or surrender of authority as may be necessary to terminate the authority of the corporation to do business in any such state, territory, dependency or country.

Upon motion, duly made, seconded and carried, it was

RESOLVED, that the fiscal year of the corporation shall begin the first day of _____ in each year.

Upon motion, duly made, seconded and carried, it was

RESOLVED, that the treasurer be and he hereby is authorized to pay all fees and expenses incident to and necessary for the organization of the corporation.

Upon motion, duly made, seconded and carried, the meeting thereupon adjourned.

_____

[Name of Secretary elected at meeting]

FORM 4

SHAREHOLDERS AGREEMENT

This SHAREHOLDERS AGREEMENT, dated _____ , 20 _____ , is entered into by and among _____ ("Shareholder A"), _____ ("Shareholder B") and _____ ("Shareholder C") (each individually a "Shareholder" and collectively the "Shareholders"), who are all of the shareholders of _____ , a _____ corporation (the "Corporation"). The Shareholders agree as follows:

1. Share Ownership. Each Shareholder owns _____ shares of the Common Stock, $ _____ par value per share, of the Corporation, representing 33 1/3 percent of the total issued and outstanding shares of the Corporation (the "Shares").

2. Legended Certificates. Each certificate representing Shares currently owned by a Shareholder shall be stamped or otherwise imprinted with a legend in substantially the following form:

THE SHARES OF [CORPORATION] REPRESENTED BY THIS CERTIFICATE ARE SUBJECT TO THE TERMS AND, RESTRICTIONS SET FORTH IN A SHAREHOLDERS AGREEMENT, DATED AS OF _____ , 19 _____ , AMONG [SHAREHOLDER A], [SHAREHOLDER B] AND [SHAREHOLDER C]. THESE SHARES MAY NOT BE SOLD OR OTHERWISE TRANSFERRED EXCEPT AS SET FORTH IN SAID AGREEMENT.

3. Subsidiaries. Except as provided in Section 5, the Corporation owns and will own all of the outstanding stock of two other corporations: _____ , a _____ corporation ("Subsidiary A"), and _____ , a _____ corporation ("Subsidiary B"); (Subsidiary A and Subsidiary B each individually a "Subsidiary" and collectively the "Subsidiaries").

4. Issuance and Sale of Shares of the Corporation. Additional Shares of the Corporation, any other equity security of the Corporation or any security convertible into or exchangeable for any equity security of the Corporation

may be issued only with the unanimous written consent of all three Share-holders. During the period beginning on the date hereof and ending _____ years after the date hereof, no Shareholder may sell, give or otherwise transfer in any way whatsoever any Shares of the Corporation or Subsidiaries without the express written consent of the other Shareholders, which consent may be withheld for any reason. At any time after the expiration of such _____ -year period, any proposed transfer by a Shareholder (the transferring Shareholder") may only be made upon written notice to the other Shareholders of the terms of the proposed transfer, including the number of Shares proposed to be transferred, the consideration for such Shares, the method and timing of the transfer and the identity of the proposed transferee, which notice shall include a written copy of the proposed offer from the prospective transferee. Such notice shall constitute an irrevocable offer by the Transferring Shareholder to sell all, but not less than all, of the Shares specified in the notice to the other Shareholders on a pro rata basis and on the same terms as are contained in such notice. In the event that one of the other Shareholders chooses not to accept the Transferring Shareholder's offer, the remaining Shareholder must elect to purchase all or none of the Shares being offered by the Transferring Shareholder. The other Shareholders shall have sixty (60) days from the date notice is given to accept or reject such offer. The acceptance or rejection by the other Shareholders of such irrevocable offer shall not constitute the exclusive remedy of such other Shareholders in the event that the Transferring Shareholder shall convey Shares contrary to the terms and provisions of this Section 4.

5. Distribution of Equity Ownership in Subsidiaries. Any sale or distribution of equity interests in either Subsidiary shall require the unanimous written consent of the Shareholders.

6. Shareholder Entitlements. The Shareholders shall enjoy equal rights and shall be entitled to equal compensation, including perquisites, under this Agreement. Any interference or attempt to interfere by two Shareholders with the rights of a third Shareholder under this Agreement, including but not limited to failing to elect a Shareholder as director of the Corporation and the Subsidiaries and failing to grant a Shareholder compensation (including salary, benefits and perquisites) equal to that received by the other two Shareholders, shall constitute the firing (the "Firing") of that third Shareholder (the "Fired Shareholder") and shall entitle him to sell his Shares back to the Company in the following manner: the Fired Shareholder shall give notice to the Corporation of his intention to sell

his Shares to the Corporation pursuant to this Section 6, which notice shall specifically set forth the events and/or acts which constitute the Firing. The Corporation shall cause to be conducted an audit of the Corporation within a reasonable time following the date of such notice (the "Notice Date"). Such audit shall determine the Fired Shareholder's Net Income (as defined in Section 7 hereof) as of the Notice Date. Within two weeks of completion of the audit the Fired Shareholder shall sell to the Corporation, and the Corporation shall buy, the Fired Shareholder's Shares for a purchase price equal to [_____] times the Fired Shareholder's Net Income. The purchase price shall be paid in the following manner: _____ percent of the purchase price shall be paid on the date the Fired Shareholder tenders his Shares (the "Tender Date") and _____ percent of the purchase price shall be paid on each succeeding one-year anniversary of the Tender Date until the purchase price is fully paid. In the event that, as of the Notice Date, the Corporation's assets include real property or any interest in real property, and so long as the Corporation, in its sole discretion, shall continue to hold such real property or such interest in real property, the Fired Shareholder shall be entitled to (a) one-third of the net income, if any, generated by such real property or interest in real property; and (b) upon sale, if any, of any such real property or interest in real property, one-third of the net income, if any, from such sale.

7. Shareholder Net Income. Under this Agreement, a Shareholder's Net Income shall equal an amount, the numerator of which shall be the aggregate average yearly income of the Subsidiaries based upon the eight fiscal quarters preceding a Notice Date (as that term is defined in Sections 6 and 16) or, in the case of the death of a Shareholder, the date of the death, less all expenses of the Subsidiaries other than salaries, benefits and perquisites of the Shareholders, and the denominator of which shall be three. Any calculation of Shareholder Net Income pursuant to this Agreement shall be according to generally accepted accounting principles.

8. Voluntary Departure of a Shareholder. Any Shareholder who wishes to terminate his employment with the Corporation shall give the Corporation notice of his intention to sell his Shares, and the Corporation shall purchase such Shareholder's Shares in accordance with the provisions of Section 16 hereof.

9. Death or Disability of a Shareholder.

(a) Death: Within a reasonable time after the death of a Shareholder, the Corporation shall cause to be conducted an audit of the Corporation, which

audit shall determine the deceased Shareholder's Net Income. Within two weeks of completion of such audit, the deceased Shareholder's estate shall sell, and the Corporation shall purchase, the deceased Shareholder's Shares. The purchase price shall be _____ times the Shareholder's Net Income as determined by the audit, and shall be paid to the Shareholder's estate in the following manner: the Corporation shall pay to the estate at the time of such purchase one-third of the deceased Shareholder's Net Income. Of the remaining amount, one-half shall be paid to the estate one calendar year after the completion of the audit and the other one-half shall be paid to the estate two calendar years after the completion of the audit. In the event that, as of the date of the Shareholder's death, the Corporation's assets include real property or any interest in real property, and so long as the Corporation, in its sole discretion, shall continue to hold such real property or such interest in real property, the deceased Shareholder's estate shall be entitled to (a) one-third of the net income, if any, generated by such real property or interest in real property; and (b) upon sale, if any, of any such real property or interest in real property, one-third of the net income, if any, from such sale.

(b) Disablement: Upon the permanent disablement of a Shareholder such that his ability to contribute significantly to the Corporation and/or Subsidiaries is substantially impaired, or if a Shareholder is temporarily disabled and it is expected that he will remain disabled as described above for more than _____ years, he shall resign from the Corporation, and he shall sell to the Corporation, and the Corporation shall purchase, his Shares in the manner provided in Section 16. If a Shareholder is temporarily disabled and it is expected that he will remain disabled as described above for more than _____ months, but less than _____ years, for the period of his disablement his salary shall be reduced to one-half of that received by the other Shareholders but his benefits and perquisites shall not be reduced in relation to those received by the other Shareholders. Upon a Shareholder's death, permanent disablement or temporary disablement which is expected to continue for more than three years, in addition to the above, said Shareholder or his estate shall receive a sum of $ _____ per annum from the Corporation for each of _____ consecutive years immediately following his disablement or death. Payments will be made in equal bimonthly installments.

10. Key Man Insurance. Within fifteen (15) days after the execution of this Agreement, the Corporation shall obtain a life and disability insurance policy on each of Shareholder A, Shareholder B and Shareholder C, each in the

face amount of $ _____ , and shall maintain the same until such time as Shareholder A, Shareholder B or Shareholder C, as the case may be, shall have ceased to own any Shares of the Corporation. The Shareholders may, from time to time, cause the amounts of such policies to be increased in equal amounts. Upon the death or disability of any Shareholder, the proceeds from his life and disability insurance policy shall be the property of the Corporation and shall not be included as an asset of the Corporation for purposes of the audit described in Sections 6, 9 and 16.

11. Board of Directors of the Corporation. The Corporation shall be governed by a Board of Directors, which shall consist of Shareholder A, Shareholder B and Shareholder C, as long as each continues to be a Shareholder. In the event that a director ceases to be a Shareholder, the Board of Directors shall consist of the remaining Shareholders.

12. Control of Subsidiaries. Each Subsidiary will be controlled by a Board of Directors comprised of all three Shareholders and any other persons whom the Shareholders shall unanimously elect. The Board of Directors of each Subsidiary will select a chief executive officer or officers for that Subsidiary who will be responsible to the Board of Directors of that Subsidiary for its operations. The corporate objectives, policies and strategies of each Subsidiary will be determined by its Board of Directors and be carried out by its chief executive officer.

13. Other Activities. No Shareholder may undertake or otherwise engage in any of the business activities in which the Corporation or Subsidiaries are normally involved or plan to be involved in any manner that is separate and apart from the activities of the Corporation and Subsidiaries without the express permission of all the other Shareholders. However, business undertaken prior to the signing of this Agreement may be completed by any Shareholder so involved in a manner separate and apart from the Corporation and Subsidiaries' activities.

14. Allocation of Time to the Corporation and Subsidiaries. Every Shareholder shall devote his full time, attention and energies to the business of the Corporation and Subsidiaries and shall not, so long as he remains a Shareholder, be engaged in any other business activity, whether or not such business activity is pursued for gain, profit or other pecuniary advantage, except as otherwise permitted in Sections 13 and 15. Any Shareholder who vio-

lates this provision and continues to so act after written notice from the other Shareholders may have his salary withheld and, in the event of such withholding, shall forfeit said salary from the time of such written notice until he ceases to so act. If such behavior continues for more than _____ months from said written notice, the other Shareholders by unanimous decision may require him to sell his Shares to the Corporation in the manner provided in Section 16, less $ _____ , which sum he shall forfeit.

15. Other Permitted Activities. In the application of the provisions contained in Section 14 hereof, activities which will strengthen the credentials of the Shareholder, and thereby the Corporation and Subsidiaries, will be treated more liberally. However, even in such circumstances, at least a majority of the Shareholder's business time must be devoted to the business of the Corporation and Subsidiaries. The type of activities to be treated more liberally would include, but are not limited to, a membership on a Board of Trustees or Board of Directors or a comparable position with a charitable, corporate, governmental, religious or similar entity.

16. Purchase of a Shareholder's Shares by the Corporation. If the Corporation purchases the Shares of any Shareholder pursuant to Section 8, 9(b) or 14 hereof or for any reason except the death or Firing of a Shareholder, payment for such Shares shall be made in the following manner: the Corporation shall give written notice to a Shareholder (the "Selling Shareholder") of its intention to purchase such Shareholder's Shares pursuant to this Agreement. The Corporation shall cause to be conducted an audit of the Corporation within a reasonable time following the date of such notice (the "Notice Date"). Such audit shall determine the Selling Shareholder's Net Income as of the Notice Date. The Selling Shareholder shall sell to the Corporation, and the Corporation shall buy, his Shares within two weeks after completion of the audit.

In the case of a permanently or temporarily disabled Shareholder, the purchase price shall be _____ times the Shareholder's Net Income, one-third of which shall be paid on the date the Selling Shareholder tenders his Shares to the Corporation pursuant to this Section 16 (the "Tender Date"), one-third of which shall be paid to the Shareholder one calendar year after the Tender Date and the final one-third of which shall be paid to the Selling Shareholder two calendar years after the Tender Date.

In all other cases the purchase price shall be the Shareholder's Net Income, one-fifth of which shall be paid on the Tender Date and one-fifth of which shall be paid on each succeeding anniversary of the Tender Date, until the purchase price is fully paid.

In the event that, as of the Notice Date, the Corporation's assets include real property or any interest in real property, and so long as the Corporation, in its sole discretion, shall continue to hold such real property or such interest in real property, the Selling Shareholder shall be entitled to (a) one-third of the net income, if any, generated by such real property or interest in real property; and (b) upon sale, if any, of such real property or interest in real property, one-third of the net income, if any, from such sale.

17. Solicitation Not Permitted. So long as a Shareholder continues to own Shares, he shall not (a) offer employment to any person who is an employee or prospective employee of the Corporation or Subsidiaries (other than on behalf of the Corporation or a Subsidiary); or (b) solicit any securities brokerage or investment advisory business (other than for the Corporation or a Subsidiary) from any client or customer of the Corporation or Subsidiaries. In the event that any Shareholder (the "Departing Shareholder") ceases to be a Shareholder, then the Departing Shareholder agrees that, for a period of _____ months from the date he sells his Shares, he will not, directly or indirectly, as a sole proprietor, member of a partnership or stockholder, investor, officer or director of a corporation or as an employee, agent, associate or consultant of any person, firm or corporation other than the Corporation or its Subsidiaries, (y) offer employment to any person who is an employee or prospective employee of the Corporation or Subsidiaries upon the date of the sale of his Shares or who was an employee at any time during the one-year period preceding such event; or (z) solicit business of the type engaged in by the Corporation or the Subsidiaries (other than for the Corporation or Subsidiaries) from any person who is a client or prospective client of the Corporation or Subsidiaries upon the date of the sale of his Shares or who has been a client of the Corporation or Subsidiaries at any time during the one-year period preceding such sale.

18. Liquidated Damages and Injunctive Relief. Inasmuch as any damages arising from the breach of Section 17 hereof would be difficult to determine, any Shareholder or Departing Shareholder who violates Section 17 agrees to be liable in the following manner:

(a) Any Shareholder or Departing Shareholder who violates Section 17(a) or 17(y), as the case may be, shall be liable in an amount equal to _____ times the yearly salary or salaries of the employee or employees who were subject to the solicitation which resulted in the violation of Section 17(a) or 17(y). In the event that an employee is a prospective employee, the amount of damages shall be _____ times the yearly salary for the position for which the prospective employee was being considered.

(b) Any Shareholder or Departing Shareholder who violates Section 17(b) or 17(z), as the case may be, shall be liable in an amount equal to _____ times the average fees paid or due and owing to the Corporation or the Subsidiaries by the customer annually over the two years preceding the violation of Section 17(b) or 17(z). In the event that a solicited customer has been a customer for less than two years, damages shall be in an amount equal to _____ times the total amount of fees the solicited customer would have paid had he remained a customer for two years, based upon the average size of the customer's advisory account (if the customer was an investment advisory client) during the period he was a customer and/or based upon the customer's average monthly brokerage fees (if the customer was a brokerage client) during the period he was a customer. In the event that the solicitation is of a prospective customer, damages shall be in an amount equal to $ _____ .

19. Attorneys' Fees. In the event of any breach by any Shareholder or Departing Shareholder of the provisions of Section 17 hereof which leads to a settlement or an injunction, an award of damages or other judgment against the Shareholder or Departing Shareholder, the Shareholder or Departing Shareholder hereby agrees to pay all costs and expenses of every kind, including reasonable attorneys' fees, incurred by the remaining Shareholders and the Corporation or Subsidiaries in connection with obtaining such settlement or injunction, award of damages or other judgment.

20. Arbitration. Any and all disputes, controversies and claims arising out of or relating to this Agreement, or with respect to the construction of this Agreement, or concerning the respective rights or obligations hereunder of the parties hereto and their respective permitted successors and assigns shall be determined by arbitration in _____ , State of _____ , in accordance with and pursuant to the then existing rules of the American Arbitration Association. The arbitration award shall be final and binding upon the parties and judgment thereon may be entered in any court of the State of _____

and federal courts in said state, the jurisdiction of which courts is hereby consented to by the parties for such purposes. The service of any notice, process, motion or other document in connection with an arbitration award hereunder may be effectuated either by personal service upon a party or by certified or registered mail.

21. Survival of Agreement. Any Shareholder who, for any reason, ceases to own Shares shall thereafter have no voting or other rights regarding the operation and control of the Corporation and the Subsidiaries or regarding decisions to be made by the Shareholders pursuant to this Agreement, but shall otherwise continue to be bound by the terms of this Agreement.

22. Entire Agreement. This document sets forth the entire Agreement between the parties. There are no verbal or other written agreements that are part of this Agreement.

23. Termination. This Agreement may be terminated by the unanimous written consent of all the Shareholders owning Shares on the date of termination. This Agreement may be terminated by the written consent of two Shareholders but in such event, for a period of _____ months following the termination, the two Shareholders who consented to the termination (the "Consenting Shareholders") shall not, together, as members of the same partnership, as stockholders, investors, officers or directors of the same corporation or as employees, agents, associates or consultants of or to the same person or company, engage in business of the type engaged in by the Corporation or the Subsidiaries.

24. Successors and Assigns. This Agreement shall be binding on any and all successors and assigns of the Shareholders.

25. Retention of Attorney. Each of the parties signing below certifies that he has thoroughly read and fully understands all the provisions herein and that he has shown this contract to an attorney who has represented him and acted as his advisor in the signing of this Agreement.

26. Governing Law. This Agreement shall be governed by and construed in accordance with the laws of the State of _____ .

We, the undersigned, hereby agree to all the provisions of this Agreement this _____ day of _____ , 20 _____ .

_____
[Shareholder A]

_____
[Shareholder B]

_____
[Shareholder C]

FORM 5

FORM OF VOTING AGREEMENT

AGREEMENT entered into as of this _____ day of _____ , 20 _____, by and among _____ ("Shareholder A") and _____ ("Shareholder B") (individually referred to as the "Shareholder" and collectively as the "Shareholders").

Each Shareholder owns the number of shares of issued and outstanding voting common stock of _____ , a _____ corporation (the "Corporation").

The Shareholders desire to maintain the continuity and stability of the policy and management of the Corporation; and believe it to be in their best interests and the best interests of the Corporation that the shares of the Shareholders now owned or hereafter acquired (the "Shares") be voted in accordance with the terms and conditions.

The Shareholders hereby agreed as follows:

A. Voting

1. The Shareholders hereby agree to pool the voting of their Shares, and to vote or consent with respect to all of their Shares as a block or unit in all votes, in person or by proxy at any and all meetings of the shareholders.

(a) *Vote for Directors.*

(i) *Election.* So long as the board of directors of the Corporation shall consist of _____ directors, the Shares shall be voted for _____ persons nominated by Shareholder A and _____ persons nominated by Shareholder B. Votes for the remaining director position shall be cast for such nominee as the Shareholders are able to agree upon from time to time. If the Shareholders fail to agree upon a nominee, then the nominee shall be _____ or _____ .

(ii) *Replacement.* If any director so elected should die, resign, be removed or become incapacitated or otherwise refuse to act in his or her capacity as

director, the Shareholder who nominated such director shall be entitled to nominate a person as a replacement director.

(b) *Vote on Other Issues.* In the event of a vote of the shareholders involving authorization of any amendment to the Corporation's Certificate of Incorporation or Bylaws; merger, consolidation or binding share exchange; sale or other disposition of all or substantially all of the assets of the Corporation; bankruptcy; dissolution; or any other matter submitted to a vote of the shareholders, the Shareholders agree to pool their Shares and to vote them as a block or unit.

B. Arbitration. If the Shareholders are unable to agree on any matter subject to a vote of the Shareholders, the dispute and the manner of voting the Shares shall be submitted to an independent third party arbitrator in accordance with the rules of the American Arbitration Association.

C. Proxy. In order to facilitate the resolution of any dispute referred to in Section B of this Agreement the Shareholders may grant to such other person as may be designated by the arbitrator chosen by the methods set forth in Section B of this Agreement, an irrevocable proxy to vote the Shares in his or her sole discretion. This irrevocable proxy shall take effect only upon the occurrence of a dispute regarding the manner of voting the Shares.

D. Provisions to Survive Death or Incapacity of any Shareholder. In the event of the death, incapacity or incompetency of any Shareholder, the provisions of this Agreement will be binding on the estate, committee or personal representative of such Shareholder and such estate.

E. Transfer of Shares. Shares may be transferred only in accordance with the terms and conditions of the Shareholders Agreement.

F. Termination of Shareholder Status. A Shareholder shall no longer be treated as a Shareholder hereunder when he ceases to own any Shares.

G. Endorsement of Share Certificates. Certificates for Shares of the Corporation subject to this Agreement shall be endorsed in accordance with the terms stipulated on the back of each certificate.

H. Termination. This Agreement shall terminate upon the happening of the earliest of any of the following events:

1. Reduction in the number of Shareholders to one;

2. The written agreement of all of the Shareholders;

3. The expiration of the term of this Agreement or the failure of some or all of the remaining Shareholders to agree to renew this Agreement;

4. The merger or consolidation of the Corporation with another entity or a binding share exchange between the Corporation and another entity, if the Corporation is not the surviving corporation.

I. Term. This Agreement shall become effective upon the date of this Agreement and shall continue in effect for a period of_____ years from this date.

J. Renewal. This Agreement may be renewed for successive yearly periods. Written consent to such renewal must be given prior to the expiration of this Agreement.

K. Amendment. This Agreement may be amended only by the written agreement of all of the parties to this Agreement, or their lawful heirs and legal representatives or successors.

L. Benefit. This Agreement shall be for the benefit of and binding on the parties to this Agreement, or their lawful heirs and legal representatives or successors.

M. Governing Law. This Agreement shall be governed and construed in accordance with the laws of the State of _____ .

IN WITNESS WHEREOF, the Shareholders have executed this Agreement as of the date and year first written above.

Number of Shares   *Shareholders*

_____   _____

_____   _____

Stock Certificates

This appendix contains stock certificates that have been left blank and can be removed for your use.

For Value Received, _____ *hereby sell, assign and transfer*

PLEASE INSERT SOCIAL SECURITY OR OTHER
IDENTIFYING NUMBER OF ASSIGNEE

unto _____

_____ *Shares*

represented by the within Certificate, and do hereby irrevocably constitute and appoint

_____ *Attorney to*

transfer the said Shares on the books of the within named Corporation with full power of substitution in the premises.

Dated _____ *20* _____

In the presence of

_____   _____

For Value Received, _____ *hereby sell, assign and transfer*

PLEASE INSERT SOCIAL SECURITY OR OTHER
IDENTIFYING NUMBER OF ASSIGNEE

unto _____

_____ *Shares*

represented by the within Certificate, and do hereby irrevocably constitute and appoint

_____ *Attorney to transfer the said Shares on the books of the within named Corporation with full power of substitution in the premises.*

Dated _____ *20* _____

In the presence of

_____   _____

SHARES

NUMBER
1

INCORPORATED UNDER THE LAWS OF THE STATE OF NEW YORK

The Corporation is authorized to issue 100 Common Shares without par value, of one class

This Certifies that

is the owner of

fully paid and

non-assessable Shares of the above Corporation transferable only on the books of the Corporation by the holder hereof in person or by duly authorized Attorney upon surrender of this Certificate properly endorsed.

In Witness Whereof, the said Corporation has caused this Certificate to be signed by its duly authorized officers and to be sealed with the Seal of the Corporation.

Dated

SECRETARY

PRESIDENT

For Value Received, _____ *hereby sell, assign and transfer*

PLEASE INSERT SOCIAL SECURITY OR OTHER
IDENTIFYING NUMBER OF ASSIGNEE

unto _____

_____ *Shares*

represented by the within Certificate, and do hereby irrevocably constitute and appoint

_____ *Attorney to transfer the said Shares on the books of the within named Corporation with full power of substitution in the premises.*

Dated _____ *20* _____

In the presence of

_____   _____

NOTICE. THE SIGNATURE OF THIS ASSIGNMENT MUST CORRESPOND WITH THE NAME AS WRITTEN UPON THE FACE OF THE CERTIFICATE, IN EVERY PARTICULAR, WITHOUT ALTERATION OR ENLARGEMENT OR ANY CHANGE WHATEVER.

For Value Received, ____________ *hereby sell, assign and transfer*

PLEASE INSERT SOCIAL SECURITY OR OTHER IDENTIFYING NUMBER OF ASSIGNEE

unto ____

____ *Shares*

represented by the within Certificate, and do hereby irrevocably constitute and appoint

____ *Attorney to transfer the said Shares on the books of the within named Corporation with full power of substitution in the premises.*

Dated ________________ *20* _____

In the presence of

__________________________ __________________________________

SHARES

NUMBER 1

INCORPORATED UNDER THE LAWS OF THE STATE OF NEW YORK

The Corporation is authorized to issue 100 Common Shares without par value, of one class

This Certifies that

is the owner of

fully paid and

non-assessable Shares of the above Corporation transferable only on the books of the Corporation by the holder hereof in person or by duly authorized Attorney upon surrender of this Certificate properly endorsed.

In Witness Whereof, the said Corporation has caused this Certificate to be signed by its duly authorized officers and to be sealed with the Seal of the Corporation.

Dated

PRESIDENT

SECRETARY

For Value Received, _____ *hereby sell, assign and transfer*

PLEASE INSERT SOCIAL SECURITY OR OTHER
IDENTIFYING NUMBER OF ASSIGNEE

unto _____

_____ *Shares*

represented by the within Certificate, and do hereby irrevocably constitute and appoint

_____ *Attorney to transfer the said Shares on the books of the within named Corporation with full power of substitution in the premises.*

Dated _____ *20* _____

In the presence of

_____   _____

SHARES

NUMBER 1

INCORPORATED UNDER THE LAWS OF THE STATE OF NEW YORK

The Corporation is authorized to issue 100 Common Shares without par value, of one class

This Certifies that

is the owner of

fully paid and

non-assessable Shares of the above Corporation transferable only on the books of the Corporation by the holder hereof in person or by duly authorized Attorney upon surrender of this Certificate properly endorsed.

In Witness Whereof, the said Corporation has caused this Certificate to be signed by its duly authorized officers and to be sealed with the Seal of the Corporation.

Dated

For Value Received, _____ *hereby sell, assign and transfer*

PLEASE INSERT SOCIAL SECURITY OR OTHER
IDENTIFYING NUMBER OF ASSIGNEE

unto _____

_____ *Shares*

represented by the within Certificate, and do hereby irrevocably constitute and appoint

_____ *Attorney to*

transfer the said Shares on the books of the within named Corporation with full power of substitution in the premises.

Dated _____ *20* _____

In the presence of

_____   _____

For Value Received, _____ *hereby sell, assign and transfer*

PLEASE INSERT SOCIAL SECURITY OR OTHER
IDENTIFYING NUMBER OF ASSIGNEE

unto _____

_____ *Shares*

represented by the within Certificate, and do hereby irrevocably

constitute and appoint

_____ *Attorney to*

transfer the said Shares on the books of the within named Corporation

with full power of substitution in the premises.

Dated _____ *20* _____

In the presence of

_____   _____

BARRON'S BUSINESS KEYS

Each "key" explains approximately 50 concepts and provides a glossary and index. Each book: Paperback, approx. 160 pp., 4³⁄₁₆" x 7", $5.95, & $7.95 Can. $8.50, $9.95, & $11.50.

Keys to Buying Foreclosᵒed and Bargain Homes, 2nd Edition*(1294-5)

Keys to Incorporating, 3rd Edition *(1300-3)

Keys to Investing in Common Stocks, 3rd Edition *(1301-1)

Keys to Investing in Mutual Funds, 3rd Edition (9644-4)

Keys to Investing in Options and Futures, 3rd Edition *(1303-8)

Keys to Investing in Real Estate, 3rd Edition *(1295-3)

Keys to Investing in Your 401(K), 2nd Edition *(1298-8)

Keys to Mortgage Financing and Refinancing, 3rd Edition *(1296-1)

Keys to Personal Financial Planning, 3rd Edition *(2099-9)

Keys to Purchasing a Condo or a Co-op, 2nd Edition *(1305-4)

Keys to Reading an Annual Report, 3rd Edition *(1306-2)

Keys to Risks and Rewards of Penny Stocks (4300-6)

Keys to Starting a Small Business (4487-8)

Keys to Understanding the Financial News, 3rd Edition *(1308-9)

Available at bookstores, or by mail from Barron's. Enclose check or money order for full amount plus sales tax where applicable and 18% for postage & handling (minimum charge $5.95). Prices subject to change without notice. $= U.S. dollars • Can. $= Canadian dollars • Barron's ISBN Prefix 0-8120, *indicates 0-7641

Barron's Educational Series, Inc.
250 Wireless Boulevard • Hauppauge, NY 11788
In Canada: Georgetown Book Warehouse
34 Armstrong Avenue, Georgetown, Ont. L7G 4R9
www.barronseduc.com

(#10) R 7/03

More selected BARRON'S titles: